THE NEW COMPLETE IRISH SETTER

Ch. Verbu Maureen, CD.

The NEW
COMPLETE
IRISH SETTER

by E. IRVING ELDREDGE
and CONNIE VANACORE

FIRST EDITION
First Printing — 1983

HOWELL BOOK HOUSE Inc.
230 Park Avenue, New York, N.Y. 10169

Library of Congress Cataloging in Publication Data

Eldredge, E. Irving.
  The new complete Irish setter.

  Bibliography: p.
  1. Irish setters. I. Vanacore, Connie. II. Title.
SF429.17E38   1983   636.7'52   83-18386
ISBN 0-87605-166-2

To
the memory of

WILLIAM C. THOMPSON

whose painstaking research into
the background of the breed
endures today.

Harry Hartnett with Ch. Milson O'Boy.

Contents

AUTHORS' NOTE: Portions of the Irish Setter history in Chapters 5, 6, and 7, and of The Irish Setter in the Field in Chapter 9, are from THE NEW IRISH SETTER by William C. Thompson (published by Howell Book House Inc., but no longer in print), and are included here with permission of the copyright owners.

The Authors

E. IRVING ("Ted") ELDREDGE has enjoyed two lifelong enthusiasms — farming and dogs.

For many years he operated Tirvelda Farms in Virginia — one of the finest dairy farms in the nation. And since 1934 he has been a strong force in the advancement of the Irish Setter.

The Tirvelda prefix, originated by Ted when he was only 12 years old, was derived for the kennels and the dogs he bred, but it has been applied equally well to prize Holstein cattle, chickens, sheep and hogs.

Tirvelda has bred over 100 champion Irish Setters, including many Best in Show winners and top producers. (For more on these dogs, see Pages 158 to 164.) In the judgment of Lee Schoen, a dean among Irish Setter breeders, "Tirvelda has outstripped all others in producing continually improving, sustained quality." Much of this Mr. Schoen attributes to Ted's "extremely keen eye in weighing virtue and fault." This keen eye has also made Ted one of the most popular of AKC Sporting Group judges.

Mr. Eldredge is the Irish Setter Club of America's delegate to the American Kennel Club. He is a member of the Board of Directors of the AKC, and is Chairman of its committee on Canine Health Research and Education.

CONNIE (Mrs. Fredrick) VANACORE is one of America's premier dog journalists, winner of 11 consecutive annual awards from the Dog Writers Association of America. A newspaper columnist, she is a contributing editor of the AKC's official magazine, *Pure-Bred Dogs—AKC Gazette,* and a regular contributor to *Kennel Review* magazine.

Together with her husband, Connie owns the Ballycroy Kennels in Mendham, New Jersey (see P. 254). Dogs they have bred include the Best in Show winner, Ch. Ballycroy's Northern Sunset, who in turn is the sire of two Best in Show winners.

Connie has held offices in the Irish Setter Club of America and in the Eastern Irish Setter Association.

NOTE: A photo of Mr. Eldredge handling Ch. Tirvelda Temptress is on page 165, and one of Mrs. Vanacore handling Ch. Ballycroy Northern Sunset is on page 255.

9

Ch. Tirvelda Final Ruling and Ch. Tirvelda Skylark.

Four-week-old puppies by Ch. Meadowlark's Masterpiece ex Beaverbrook Prelude.

1

Identifying
the Irish Setter

As we look at the Irish Setter today, we see a dog that has evolved from his native shores as a somewhat larger, flashier, more heavily coated dog than his ancestors. It is a dog, however, who has retained the qualities of joy, exhuberance, birdiness and biddability which have won admirers for him on both sides of the Atlantic.

The Irish Setter is a sporting dog, bred to find upland birds, to hunt with stamina and initiative, to point, to retrieve if called upon to do so—and to address each task with confidence and enthusiasm. Not all Irish Setters are trained to hunt, but the innate ability should be there. It is evident when one sees a four-month-old puppy stealthily stalking a butterfly across a lawn, or freezing on point in front of a robin pecking at a worm.

The basic personality of the Irish Setter, plus his dazzling red coat, sets him apart from any other breed. There is no mistaking him, either at home, in the show ring, or in the field.

He is an Irishman—loving, boisterous, carefree, demanding, loyal and gentle. Because he is what he is, with no pretenses, the Irish Setter is not the dog for every family. But for those who cherish his qualities, no other breed will do.

The qualities that make up the Irish Setter are quite clearly defined in the standard for the breed. All breeds registered with the American Kennel Club have a standard of perfection, drawn up by the club which is the custodian of the breed, and approved by AKC. In the case of the Irish Setter, the custodian is the Irish Setter Club of America. Dedicated breeders try to produce dogs which conform as closely as possible to the standard. All those interested in the breed should know and understand it. Written standards are guidelines, road maps, word pictures of the living dog—but of course nothing can take the place of seeing and studying the breed first hand.

All standards, the Irish Setter standard included, are open to interpretation and clarification, since it is impossible to include every nuance of correct conformation. A standard is a little like the Constitution of the United States—it establishes guidelines, but leaves latitude in definition.

The AKC standard for the Irish Setter is quite complete. It has changed little throughout the years, and has remained the same since its last revision in 1960. That it has endured is an indication of its excellence, and of the dedication of Irish Setter fanciers to perpetuate the breed according to its design.

Am. & Can. Ch. Kelly Shannon O'Deke.

Official American Kennel Club Standard
for the Irish Setter

Adopted by the Irish Setter Club of America, Inc., and
approved by the American Kennel Club, June 14, 1960.

GENERAL APPEARANCE: The Irish Setter is an active, aristocratic bird-dog, rich red in color, substantial yet elegant in build. Standing over two feet tall at the shoulder, the dog has a straight, fine, glossy coat, longer on ears, chest, tail and back of legs. Afield he is a swift-moving hunter; at home, a sweet-natured, trainable companion. His is a rollicking personality.

HEAD: Long and lean, its length at least double the width between the ears. The brow is raised, showing a distinct stop midway between the tip of nose and the well-defined occiput (rear point of skull). Thus the nearly level line from occiput to brow is set a little above, and parallel to, the straight and equal line from eye to nose. The skull is oval when viewed from above or front; very slightly domed when viewed in profile. Beauty of head is emphasized by delicate chiseling along the muzzle, around and below the eyes, and along the cheeks. Muzzle moderately deep, nostrils wide, jaws of nearly equal length. Upper lips fairly square but not pendulous, the underline of the jaws being almost parallel with the top line of the muzzle. The teeth meet in a scissors bite in which the upper incisors fit closely over the lower, or they may meet evenly. **Nose:** Black or chocolate. **Eyes:** Somewhat almond-shaped, of medium size, placed rather well apart; neither deep-set nor bulging. Color, dark to medium brown. Expression soft yet alert. **Ears:** Set well back and low, not above level of eye. Leather thin, hanging in a neat fold close to the head, and nearly long enough to reach the nose.

NECK: Moderately long, strong but not thick, and slightly arched; free from throatiness, and fitting smoothly into the shoulders.

BODY: Sufficiently long to permit a straight and free stride. Shoulder blades long, wide, sloping well back, fairly close together at the top, and joined in front to long upper arms angled to bring the elbows slightly rearward along the brisket. Chest deep, reaching approximately to the elbows; rather narrow in front. Ribs well sprung. Loins of moderate length, muscular and slightly arched. Top line of body from withers to tail slopes slightly downward without sharp drop at the croup. Hindquarters should be wide and powerful with broad, well-developed thighs. **Legs** and **Feet:** All legs sturdy, with plenty of bone, and strong, nearly straight pasterns. Feet rather small, very firm, toes arched and close. Forelegs straight and sinewy, the elbows moving freely. Hind legs long and muscular from hip to hock, short and nearly perpendicular from hock to ground; well angulated at stifle and hock joints, which, like the elbows, incline neither in nor out. **Tail:** Strong at root, tapering to a fine point, about long enough to reach the hock. Carriage straight or curving slightly upward, nearly level with the back.

COAT: Short and fine on head, forelegs and tips of ears; on all other parts, of moderate length and flat. Feathering long and silky on ears; on back of forelegs and thighs long and fine, with a pleasing fringe of hair on belly and brisket extending onto the chest. Feet well feathered between the toes. Fringe on tail moderately long and tapering. All coat and feathering as straight and free as possible from curl or wave.

COLOR: Mahogany or rich chestnut red, with no trace of black. A small amount of white on chest, throat, or toes, or a narrow, centered streak on skull, is not to be penalized.

SIZE: There is no disqualification as to size. The make and fit of all parts and their over-all **balance** in the animal are rated more important. Twenty-seven inches at the withers with a show weight of about seventy pounds is considered ideal for a dog; the bitch twenty-five inches, sixty pounds. Variance beyond an inch up or down to be discouraged.

GAIT: At the trot the gait is big, very lively, graceful and efficient. The head is held high. The hindquarters drive smoothly and with great power. The forelegs reach well ahead as if to pull in the ground, without giving the appearance of a hackney gait. The dog runs as he stands: straight. Seen from the front or rear, the forelegs, as well as the hind legs below the hock joint, move perpendicularly to the ground, with some tendency towards a single track as speed increases. But a crossing or weaving of the legs, front or back, is objectionable.

BALANCE: At his best the lines of the Irish Setter so satisfy in overall balance that artists have termed him the most beautiful of all dogs. The correct specimen always exhibits balance whether standing or in motion. Each part of the dog flows and fits smoothly into its neighboring parts without calling attention to itself.

2

An In-Depth Look at
The Irish Setter Standard

THE Irish Setter is one of the handsomest of all breeds; with his glorious coat, extroverted personality and elegant bearing, it is little wonder that he draws admiring glances wherever he goes.

Looking at the complete dog, one should be immediately struck by several important things. First, he should look like an Irish Setter. He should possess those qualities of head, expression, stature, coat and gait that stamp him at once as possessing true Irish Setter type.

He should be in balance, Whether moving or standing still, all parts should fit together to form a graceful whole. No part of the dog's anatomy, whether head, neck, length of back, or height should stand out in jarring fashion from the rest. The temptation to exaggerate one aspect of a dog under the impression that more is better has caused serious problems in many breeds. Nature tries to preserve basic balance, despite the mischief that breeders sometimes do. For instance, one cannot get a short neck and a long body without throwing the whole dog out of balance.

The head of the Irish Setter is distinctive. The expression should be intelligent and kind, with eyes that are dark and soulful. The skull should have length, and be equal from occiput to stop and from top to tip of nose. It should not be broad and short. The ears are long and low set, lying close to the head. The combination of equal and level planes, and expression, make the Irish Setter one of the most appealing of all breeds.

The burnished coat may vary in individual dogs from chestnut red to dark mahogany, and should be flat with sufficient feathering in the chest, body, legs, feet, tail and tips of ears. A healthy coat shines and feels silky to the touch. It should not be coarse, harsh or dry.

15

The Irish Setter's neck blends into smooth, well-angulated shoulders. The back is of moderate length and has well-sprung, but not barrel-shaped ribs. The back slopes gently from withers to tail. The set of the tail should be almost level with the back, and carried straight out or with a gentle upward curve.

The feet should be small, the hind legs well bent at the stifle. Angulation in the rear should correspond to angulation in front. You do not want overangulation in one area and straightness in the other. A dog in perfect balance should meet the eye of the beholder.

One should almost "see" the temperament of the correct Irish Setter. He should give the impression of friendliness and intelligence. He should never be cringing, never wild or vicious, never wary or aloof. His outgoing personality should be evident to anyone who meets him.

All of this together makes for a true overall picture of the ideal Irish Setter.

Now let's take a look at the individual parts.

The Head

"The head should be long and lean, its length at least double the width between the ears. The brow is raised, showing a distinct stop." The key words in this sentence are *"at least."* The proportions of the head are what makes it distinctive, and certainly set it apart from the English or Gordon Setter.

Many Setter heads appear "Cockery." That means they have shortened foreface, and are square in proportions overall. Broad backskulls with narrow, short muzzles, or heads that are too lean with no real stop at the brow are incorrect. Eyes that are slightly slanted, giving a Borzoi appearance are not desirable. Both the coarse, broad look or the too-refined sleek look prevent the *"beauty of head emphasized by delicate chiseling along the muzzle, around and below the eyes and along the cheeks."* Think of two bricks in a straight line, one atop the other. Pull the top brick halfway back over the lower one, and you get a good idea of the correct shape of the head. When looking down on the head, the muzzle should be the same width as the skull. It should not narrow to a point. The backskull should be level and not dropped off in the rear. The foreface also should be level and not downfaced.

"Eyes somewhat almond shaped, medium size, placed well apart, neither deep set or bulging. Dark to medium brown. Expression soft, yet alert." The last four words are most important. The Irish Setter's expression is seen through its eyes. They should be soulful and kindly, soft and intelligent. In order to achieve that look they must not be round, protruding or hard, nor yellow and baleful. An Irish Setter can be mischievous, loving, courageous, friendly. All these expressions of mood and personality should be reflected in the eyes. One does not want to see timidity, fear, or hostility.

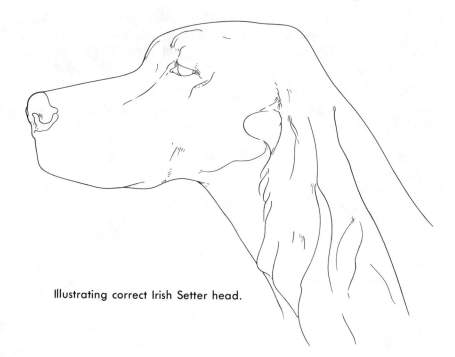

Illustrating correct Irish Setter head.

Faulty — snipey muzzle.

Faulty — dropped off in back skull.

Faulty — downfaced.

Drawings by Larry Stein.

"Ears set well back and low, not above level of eye. Leather thin, hanging in a neat fold close to the head and nearly long enough to reach the nose." High set ears close to the top of the skull spoil that all-important expression. Thick-skinned ears, or those which are too wide, giving the impression of "elephant ears", are far from correct.

A word about the teeth. The standard calls for a *"scissors bite in which the upper incisors fit closely over the lower, or they may meet evenly."* Geneticists much prefer the scissors bite. An even bite, although acceptable in the show ring, is asking for trouble in the whelping box. Too many generations of even bites will lead to either undershot (lower teeth protruding beyond the upper teeth) or overshot (upper teeth way over the lower). Most Irish have good scissor bites. We can be thankful for a minimum of poor bites in our breed, but it is a fault which can easily be introduced. Breeders should also beware of a slightly twisted jaw called a "wry mouth", which is seldom seen, but is very wrong.

The Irish Setter nose should be of ample size with open nostrils which the dog uses to scent game. The standard calls for black or chocolate, and deviations from these colors are rare. The seasons of the year sometimes cause a change in the color. Dryness of the house, or climate, can lighten the nose. In Northern regions, a "snow nose" is common in which the color changes from black to light brown. It almost always returns to its dark color in the spring or summer. Illness or even ordinary sleeping can change the color temporarily, but an active, healthy Irish almost always has the right nose color.

The Body

The body should be *"sufficiently long to permit a straight and free stride."* Notice that in describing the body, "stride" or action, is mentioned first. Since I was not alive when the standard was first written, I don't know whether this was by design or accident, but I agree that stride is all-important. A back that is too short doesn't permit that long, reaching, graceful stride so desirable in correct movement. Also, a dog whose back is too short, can't cope with his hind legs properly and must move with a sidewinding, crab-like gait, so that his rear legs avoid hitting his forelegs. A back that is too long, however, makes the overall dog appear unbalanced. The "locomotive look" is probably worse than a back that is too short.

Mother Nature in her infinite wisdom will design a body so that it comfortably houses all the vital organs. Both lengths in the extreme are wrong. One must train the eye to recognize balance in all things. I must say that gauging balance is the hardest thing for a judge of dogs to master.

The standard does not mention sway back or roach back. Both are wrong.

The standard calls for *"shoulder blades long, wide, sloping well back, fairly close together at the top, and joined in front to long upper arms angled to bring the elbows slightly rearward along the brisket."* This is quite

Illustrating correct Irish Setter topline.
—*Larry Stein.*

a mouthful, a lot to confuse the reader and subject to misinterpretation. To my way of thinking, this is the most difficult part of the standard to understand. You have to see good shoulders to really understand what it all means. Unfortunately, really good shoulders are in the minority in this breed, and others as well. When the shoulders are not angled properly, the result is a dog with straight shoulder bones and straight upper and lower arms. This makes for a short, choppy, up-and-down front action. A reaching stride is not possible because the angle at the point of the shoulders will not permit it. Many dogs with poor shoulder conformation appear to have the shoulders set on too high up on the neck, giving the dog a front-heavy appearance. Think of the modern van whose engine is housed inside, without the front hood that most cars have. If an Irish Setter looks like a van, his shoulders don't slope properly.

The chest should be *"deep, reaching approximately to the elbows, rather narrow in front."* To determine the depth of chest you must use your hands on all but young puppies, who have no feathering. Brush aside the feathers and feel the bottom of the chest. It should come down to a rounded point on a line with the elbows. Don't worry if your puppy's chest is shallow. Generally it will deepen at maturity. The front of the chest is called the "brisket." When you pass your hand across the front of the forelegs just about at the level of the elbows, the brisket should protrude slightly just above the elbow joint.

"Rather narrow in front" is necessary for a driving gait. If the legs are set too wide apart, when the dog gallops the rear legs will interfere with the front legs. At a trot, a deep, relatively narrow chest permits the front legs to reach out straight in front without the rolling or waddling required by a barrel chest.

The ribs are *"well sprung."* Ribs should not be in the shape of a barrel; nor do you want them slab-sided—flat and without spring, like a slab of beef. The ribs should be moderately rounded so that the Setter has plenty of lung room for stamina.

"Loins of moderate length." Some feel that "moderate" is an indefinite word, but the key behind its use is "balance." The distance from the end of the rib cage to the point of the hip bone should be sufficient to keep the dog in balance. A loin that is too long causes a dog to have a soft back or a roach back. A loin that is too short causes a dog to compensate while moving, by overreaching, crabbing or sidewinding.

"The topline of the body from withers to tail slopes slightly downward without sharp drop at the croup." If you watch some handlers in the show ring you'll see them set up their dogs on an angle that would do a ski slope proud. This is wrong. The standard does not call for this at all. Why do they do it? Because it is supposed to look dramatic. Some dogs naturally have an overaccentuated topline because the length of leg from the hip to the hock joint is so long that to set the dog up properly, with the hocks perpendicular to the ground, causes the legs to extend far beyond the body in the rear. This is incorrect, causing an extreme slope.

"Without sharp drop at the croup" means that you don't want your dog to look as if he'd been hit in the rear end with a shovel. Instead, the tail should come off slightly below the level of the back, and the croup should be slightly lower than the shoulders.

Seen in motion from the side, a correctly proportioned dog will maintain that slightly sloping topline. A dog that is too straight in stifle will appear high in the rear. A dog that is overangulated will drop off too far in the rear, and sometimes appear to have a sway back.

"Hindquarters should be wide and powerful with broad, well-developed thighs." Very often we see rear ends on our dogs that are too narrow, connoting weakness. The muscle mass of the thigh is something that seems to be inherited, and even dogs who are exercised regularly will not develop the broad smooth muscle that a *"well-developed thigh"* indicates. Occasionally we find a rear that is too broad, giving a coarse, inelegant appearance. Seeing a dog built correctly in the rear is really the only way to appreciate it.

Faulty topline — high in rear.

Faulty topline — too steep from withers to croup.

Drawings by Larry Stein.

Legs and Feet

The standard calls for *"all legs sturdy with plenty of bone and strong, nearly straight pasterns."* You don't want a weedy, delicate-looking Irish Setter, nor do you want overly heavy bone giving the appearance of clumsiness. The pasterns should be *"nearly straight."* This does not mean absolutely straight, like a Terrier, or angled as much as a German Shepherd Dog. The pastern is the flexible joint above the foot, which absorbs the shock when the foot hits the ground. A slight angle cushions the leg and is necessary in any dog that does a lot of running.

"Feet rather small, very firm, toes arched and close." Hare feet, splay feet, flat feet are all incorrect, as are pads that are thin and unable to withstand running through rough cover.

"Forelegs straight and sinewy, the elbows moving freely with no inclination to turn out or in." This is plainly put and easy to understand, but sometimes difficult to see in a fast-trotting dog. You must train your eye to spot loose elbows and winging feet.

"Hindlegs long and muscular from hip to hock, short and nearly perpendicular from hock to ground. Well angulated at stifle and hock joints." The angulation of the shoulder assembly and the hip to hock assembly should be approximately the same. Often one sees a straight shoulder, combined with extreme angulation in the rear. This gives a flashy appearance standing still, but is incorrect. In moving, the dog's gait will be inefficient. In all likelihood it will hackney in front and overreach in the rear. A dog who is overangulated in the rear tends to have wobbly hocks, and may flail the hind legs trying to get them under its body. At the other extreme is a dog whose stifles are too straight, making for constricted gait with no thrust or drive.

Gait

The gait, or the way an Irish Setter moves, is a very important part of the dog's appearance and its function. The standard mentions the way the dog should move in several places. In the opening paragraph he is described as a *"swift-moving hunter."* The section on body specifies a *"straight and free stride."* The section on gait amplifies this: *"At the trot the gait is big, very lively, graceful and efficient."* The Setter must be happy when he moves, light on his feet and free from a cramped or lumbering gait. The next words are important: *"The head is held high."* Many people lose sight of this when they show their dogs on a loose lead; they allow the head to droop, or let the lead be improperly positioned, causing the dog to strain against it. A loose lead is ideal if your dog moves naturally with his head up; but if that isn't possible, a little tension on the collar just behind the ears may achieve the desired result. Be careful, though, not to string the dog up so tightly that he cannot move out with a free stride. Remember that the faster the dog trots, the more he will have to extend his neck to balance himself and achieve the proper drive.

IRISH SETTER GAIT IN PICTURES

The gait of the Irish Setter is *"big, very lively, graceful and efficient."* These drawings illustrate correct gait, and some common faults found when observing Irish Setters in motion. One must train the eye to notice faults of movement and be able to recognize a good moving dog — whether from the side, the front, or the rear.

Note, too, that the handler — through his use of the lead and his own coordination (or lack of it) — can make an enormous difference in the gait of the dog. He can throw a good moving dog off balance by jerking on the lead, holding the dog in too tightly, or by weaving or changing pace.

The authors are grateful to RACHEL PAGE ELLIOTT, renowned authority on canine gait, for providing the illustrations for this presentation.

Good side movement. This dog shows balance, co-ordination and good foot-timing. The Irish Setter moves with his head held high, but the faster the trot, the more extension he will show through the head and neck.

Left: Good movement going away. As the dog increases speed there will be a tendency to single track, wherein the front legs and the rear legs move under the dog creating a central line of balance.

Right: Good movement seen from the front. The legs from shoulder to foot provide a single, straight column of support.

Some faults of rear movement:

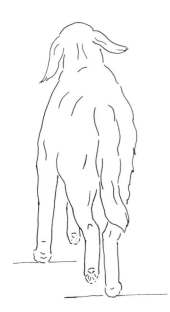

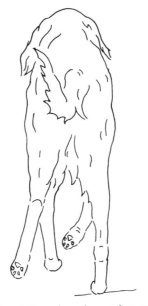

Moving too close, with the hocks nearly touching.

Spraddling, where the rear legs are too far apart and do not converge as the dog gathers speed.

Spread hocks, where the hocks a perpendicular to the ground, tu out.

Some faults of front movement:

Cowhocks, not to be confused with moving close. Cowhocks occur when the hocks turn inward.

Crossing in front. The front legs are not in a straight line from shoulder to ground.

Winging, where the dog flips h terns to the side.

Some faults of front movement (continued):

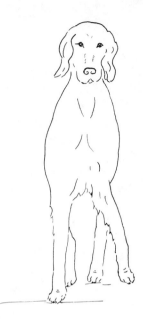

ing out. The dog throws his
to the side. This is often a result
se shoulders.

Paddling, with the elbows tied in and
constricted.

Toeing in. The foot turns inward at the
pastern.

Some faults combining front and rear movement:

Weak pasterns, toeing out in front, moving
close in the rear.

Crossing in the rear, paddling and winging
out in the front.

Crabbing in the rear, twisting elbows in front. Crabbing is the result of a dog who has too much rear leg, or is too short in back, and must compensate by moving to the side in order to avoid hitting his front feet.

Some faults in movement which can be seen from the side:

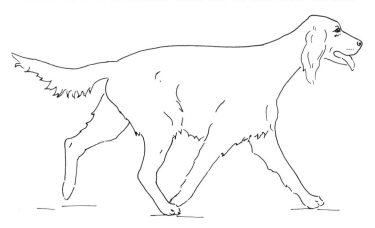

Sickle hocks. These are stiff hocks, with no back swing or extension to the lower leg.

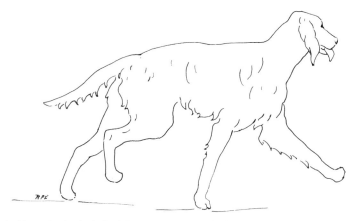

Padding. This dog lacks flexibility in the shoulder, so he hits the ground with a hard and jerky movement.

Overreaching. This is caused by a back that is too short, or rear legs too long or over-angulated. From the front or rear, this appears as crabbing.

Pacing. Legs on the same side moving together.

Hackneying. Although it may appear flashy and attractive, a hackney gait — in which the front legs are raised up with little extension — is very faulty.

"The hindquarters drive smoothly and with great power. The forelegs reach well ahead as if to pull in the ground without giving the appearance of a hackney gait." No up-and-down movement is desirable. It might be flashy to look at, but one should feel that if a glass of water is placed on your dog's back, it won't spill. Pitter-patting along is to be avoided at all costs. A dog that is constructed properly will move properly.

"The dog runs as he stands: straight. Seen from the front or rear, the forelegs, as well as the hindlegs below the hock joint, move perpendicularly to the ground." In other words, cowhocks (hocks turned inwards as your Setter moves) are wrong. Sidewinding or crabbing are both wrong, and flailing or weaving in front is also incorrect. *"With some tendency towards a single track as speed increases."* This phrase gives many "experts" an excuse to pass narrow rear movement as acceptable. That is not what the standard calls for. Correct rear movement starts with a wide, powerful thrust of the rear legs, which is impossible if the legs are set too close together. As the dog moves, the rear legs converge. At a slow gait, in a show ring, for instance, the legs must be fairly wide apart. Very few show rings are large enough, nor does a judge require the exhibits to move at such a fast speed, that one can excuse narrow rear movement. Remember the standard calls for a *"tendency towards a single track."* All dogs, except barrel-chested breeds such as the Bulldog, will tend to bring their front and rear legs under them as they trot. This is because the legs converge towards the center of gravity which is most comfortable for the dog to keep its balance.

Tail

The old saying is that the "tail wags the dog." With the Irish Setter, the tail is a very important part of the anatomy. It should be in balance with the rest of the body, *"strong at root, tapering to a fine point, about long enough to reach the hock. Carriage straight or curving slightly upward, nearly level with the back."* Nothing spoils the look of a magnificent dog more than a tail collapsed and carried down, or carried in a scimitar-like curve up over the back, or a straight tail held at 12 o'clock. A tail coming off the croup too low gives an unpleasant, rounded look to the rear. At a trot, the tail should be held level with or slightly above the back. A wagging tail is a good indicator of the happy Irish temperament.

Size

The standard makes no disqualification as to size, wisely deeming that the *"make and fit of all parts and their overall balance"* are more important. 27 inches for dogs and 25 inches for bitches is considered ideal. Today we see dogs and bitches larger, and only occasionally smaller, but to preserve our gene pool, we must allow for the variations in size, so long as the dog fits together in all its parts.

Coat

The Irish Setter's coat should be *"short and fine on head, forelegs and tips of ears; on all other parts of moderate length and flat. Feathering long and silky on ears, on back of forelegs and thighs long and fine, with a pleasing fringe of hair on belly and brisket extending onto the chest . . . Fringe on tail moderately long and tapering. All coat and feathering as straight and free as possible from curl or wave."*

The coat with its glorious shades on different dogs ranging from deep mahogany to chestnut red is so distinctive and beautiful that it makes the viewer exclaim with delight, whether he is a dog lover or not.

The standard's description of the coat could be improved by some sentence reconstruction, but nevertheless, it conveys the ideal picture. The appearance called for in the opening sentence, however, can only be obtained by a proper show trim. Left alone, the hair on the head of the average Setter is rather long and wavy. Also, today the hair on the tips of the ears is generally left as long as it will grow. The English, on the other hand, keep the hair on the tips of the ears short by trimming.

In the 1920s, '30s and '40s, most Setters had moderately long feathering. Then along came Ch. Sally O'Bryan of Crosshaven and her nephew, Ch. Kleiglight of Aragon. Their feathering was much longer than had been seen previously, and they started the fashion for today's huge coats. Some Sporting people object to the extreme length found on some of our present-day top winners. If one wants a more easily managed coat, though, just turn the Setter out in a field of brambles and burrs. Within hours the coat will be reduced to almost nothing!

The sleek, flat coated look of the show Irish is often the result of careful grooming, trimming and conditioning. In another section of this book you will learn how to care for your dog's coat properly.

So there you have the Irish Setter: *"an active, aristocratic bird dog, rich red in color, substantial yet elegant in build . . . At his best the lines of the Irish Setter so satisfy in over-all balance that artists have termed him the most beautiful of all dogs."* These words need no interpretation or clarification. They express completely what every Irish Setter owner believes and what every dedicated breeder strives to achieve.

Irish Setter puppies, 4-months old.

At left, 17-months old; at right, 16 weeks old.

3

Care and Management

ALL puppies, like all children, need care and management. Some people feel that a puppy can be compared to the average two-year-old child, full of energy and curiosity, ready to soak up all the information it can about the world around it.

A good book on dog care will give the essentials of proper management. The breeder from whom you purchase your puppy should be able to provide you with advice and suggestions.

Each breed has its own characteristics, and raising an Irish Setter presents challenges and subtle differences that should be explored.

First, it must be stated that an Irish Setter is not for everyone. That cute little puppy with its beguiling manner will certainly win the heart of an enthusiastic buyer. The picture of the adult dog maturing into a lovely, sedate Irishman will not happen, however, unless certain management techniques are employed.

The Irish Setter is a slow developer. He remains a puppy both mentally and physically until he is at least two years old. He is an energetic dog, full of intelligence and love for his owner. He is not generally wild and hardheaded, though at some point in his growth, he will challenge authority. He is no different from any other dog, nor indeed any child who tests its parents.

Exercise is critical for the Irish Setter, as a puppy, and all through its life. A fenced yard is a must! It is the only way to maintain the Irishman for house training and exercise. Never tie him onto a pulley or chain. Don't take a chance of him running free. A tie-out stake provides no exercise and a maximum of frustration for the dog restrained in this manner. If left to its own devices to run free, the Irish Setter will follow its nose, and most probably will meet with an accident. The myth that a dog needs to be at liberty to run all day and night should be dispelled. It is simply an excuse

31

A healthy dam insures healthy puppies. Here Ch. Terra Furman's Bit O'Red Coat nurses her litter by Am. & Can. Ch. O'Leprechaun Bushmills, Am. & Can. CD.

Four-month-old puppies by Ch. McCamon Marquis ex Ch. Tirvelda Evensong.

for the owner who does not want to take the responsibility of caring for his dog properly. A fenced yard of adequate size for the dog to stretch his legs and run around, and high enough to discourage jumping over, will simplify your life in managing your Irish Setter. At the same time it will provide him a safe environment in which to grow.

Some people feel that the best way to exercise their dog is to roadwork it. Roadworking an Irish Setter behind a bicycle or the tailgate of a car is dangerous, and can be cruel for an immature dog. Controlled road exercise can be useful to harden up a show or field dog, but one should never force a growing puppy or young dog to exercise in this manner. Growing bones, joints and tendons could be permanently damaged by overexertion through roadworking; your Irish Setter should be allowed to exercise himself until he is at least two years old. Even then, roadwork should never be undertaken on hard surfaces, such as concrete or asphalt.

As in all aspects of training, showing or conditioning, knowing what to do and how to do it, will help avoid costly mistakes. Exercise for your puppy and growing dog is of paramount importance, but it must be the right kind. It is best to let your puppy play as hard as he wants for as long as he wants and then let him sleep. Self-limiting exercise will go a long way towards making an unruly puppy into an easily manageable pet and a joy to have around.

I've stressed exercise, because after 50 years of owning Irish Setters, I believe it is a paramount key to avoiding troubles with this breed. More dogs are given away or end up in pounds because they are unmanageable than for any other reason. Usually the owners admit the dog has been confined for long periods of time without exercise. A family that cannot provide daily exercise for their dog should not own an Irish Setter.

Irish Setters are intelligent and inquisitive. Consequently they get bored easily. They are companion dogs who like to share time and space with their masters. For this reason, basic obedience is useful for the boisterous redhead to channel his energy. You can train your dog yourself with the help of a good Obedience book, or join an Obedience class in your area. If there is a local Irish Setter Club near you, members will help you get started.

Despite exercise and training, there are times when the dog must be left alone, either at home or in a car. If it is to be a show dog, it will spend considerable time traveling and confined. The best way to manage under these circumstances is with a crate.

A crate, either wire, fiberglass, or wood, is the most useful piece of equipment you can purchase for your dog. It can be his home while you are out, his home while traveling with you in the car, his home away from home. It is a help in housetraining, in giving the dog a sense of security and safety, and in preventing furniture from being destroyed by a puppy left to its own devices.

The crate should be large enough for the full-grown dog to stand in, turn around in and lie down comfortably. You should introduce your dog

Irish Setter puppies change dramatically in the course of one year.
Here are puppies from 4 weeks to 12 months of age.

4 weeks.

4 weeks.

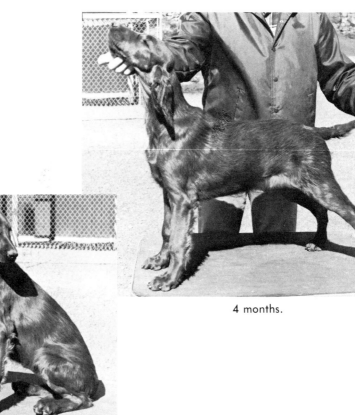
4 months.

4 months.

10 months.

1 year.

to its crate by making it a pleasant experience. Your puppy can be fed in its crate, creating a favorable impression for it. You can put the crate in your bedroom at night, so that the puppy gets accustomed to it, and yet is near you. Accustom the puppy to ride in it when you go for short distances.

A word about car training is in order here. Take your new puppy out frequently for short trips to acclimate him to the car. Most dogs love to ride once they have gotten used to it, but the initial experience should be a happy one. If the only time you take your Irish in the car is to go to the veterinarian, you'll find you'll soon have an unhappy passenger. This can be a disaster for a potential show dog, and a disappointment for those who would like to take their Irish Setter riding for fun.

Health Care

It hardly seems necessary to advise anyone to keep a clean dog, yet many pet owners actually never attend to their Irish Setter's ears, nails, skin or internal environment. It is important to keep the ears clean and dry. Because of the long ears folded close to the head, the Irish Setter is liable to develop ear infections, or pick up parasites, such as ear mites. Regular attention to the ears will prevent problems from starting. Ears should be wiped out with a piece of sterile cotton soaked in a cleansing agent, such as alcohol. The saturated cotton can be wrapped around a finger, or a large cotton swab with a soft stick, and inserted gently into the ear as far as possible without forcing it. This should be done at least every two weeks. If the ears exude a dark or smelly substance, infection should be suspected and veterinary help sought.

Keeping the nails short is essential for both the appearance and comfort of the Irish Setter. Long nails can cause splayed feet and broken-down pasterns. If you start when your puppy is small, and maintain a regular schedule of cutting nails—every fortnight, or at least every month—your dog will become accustomed to this routine. The nails can be cut or filed, but you must take care not to cut into the quick. A little advice from a knowledgeable person can help you to avoid lots of problems with this necessary chore.

Some Irish Setters are sensitive to fleas. One flea can set up all kinds of chronic skin problems in a susceptible dog. Prevention is the key to avoiding misery for the dog and expense for the owner. Simple but rigid and consistent care of the coat and skin, and keeping the environment clean, can prevent your dog from ever having fleas. That it is entirely possible to avoid fleas I can only demonstrate with my own kennel. With some 25 to 30 Irish of all ages in our kennel, located in a very hot, humid, flea and tick area, we have actually not seen one flea, nor have we had any skin problems in at least fifteen years in this location. The secret is simple. A bath every two weeks with an excellent flea soap, immediately followed by sponging on a highly effective flea and tick dip. This will last, even if made wet by heavy rains. We never use a flea collar, as they are not 100%

Ch. Russet Hill Bootlegger (Ch. Tirvelda Michaelson ex Ch. Glendee's Russet Hill My Molly) pictured above as a 10 weeks old puppy, and below as a Best of Breed winning adult.

effective and some dogs are allergic to them. In some areas, spraying the environment with a pesticide is an additional step needed to prevent fleas from hatching.

Another trick which some swear by, but I have not determined its effectiveness, is to give your dog Brewers yeast (one ten milligram tablet per ten pounds of body weight, or the equivalent in granular form.) Effective or not, the yeast has high food value and is useful as an additive to the diet. Some also put a tablespoon of apple cider vinegar into the food each day, claiming this will ward off fleas.

The diet of your growing puppy, as well as of the adult Irish Setter, is very important in maintaining optimum health. A good, balanced commercial diet is the best for your dog. Some Irish Setters go through a skinny, gangly stage in which they appear to be all bones and yet eat practically nothing, or so it seems. Once you have determined that your puppy is in good health, free from internal parasites, giving him a high calorie, high protein diet will assure that he is getting adequate nutrition with less amounts of food. Some people give vitamin supplements to growing pups. Others feel they are unnecessary. One thing that researchers have found is that the addition of calcium to the diet is wrong for fast growing, big dogs. Your puppy will get all the calcium he needs from a good quality food, so stay away from calcium supplements. If it makes you feel better, a little cottage cheese in the diet will provide some additional calcium, but not enough to harm those soft, fast growing bones.

Internal parasites are a concern to dog owners in most parts of the country. Roundworms are particularly prevalent in puppies. Hookworms and whipworms are two other debilitating and sometimes fatal intestinal parasites which are commonly found. Your Irish Setter should be checked periodically for worms—annually without fail, but preferably every six months, especially if the dog has been out of its home territory. Two stool samples should be taken to your veterinarian for examination under a microscope. Worm eggs do not appear in every fecal sample, so you have a better chance of getting an accurate diagnosis with two. If worms are found, the dog should be given medication according to the veterinarian's prescription. Generally two wormings are needed at two or three week intervals to be sure all are cleared from the intestinal tract. Do not use over-the-counter worming pills, and only worm for the specific parasite which has infested your dog.

In addition to intestinal parasites, your puppy, as well as adult dogs, should be tested for the presence of heartworms. This is done by a blood test, usually in early Spring. Heartworm is a devastating disease, transmitted by mosquitos, but easily prevented by the administration of a tablet given daily during mosquito season. In southern climates, many dogs are on the medication all year round, for their entire lives.

In all medical matters, your best ally in raising a healthy dog is your veterinarian.

Obedience training is fun for the Irish, and helps them develop into responsible pets. Here Tirvelda Taralee, CDX (Ch. Tirvelda Nor'Wester ex Ch. Tirvelda Best Regards) takes the high jump.

The dignity of old age shows in the faces of Ch. Wolfscroft My Wild Irish Rose (l) and her son Ch. Wolfscroft Vanguard, UD.

Inherited Disorders

Owners of Irish Setters should be aware that there are certain genetic defects which afflict the breed, and some diseases to which Irish Setters seem prone. Although no one likes to admit that their breed is anything but perfect, responsible breeders realize that only by breeding dogs without inheritable defects will the problems be eliminated.

PRA (*Progressive Retinal Atrophy*) is an eye disease, carried recessively, which causes dogs to become blind. Because it is a recessive gene, and does not always appear in the parents, the only way to detect carriers of this trait is by test mating. Many breeders today are testing their breeding stock to try to eliminate PRA. Irish Setters who are afflicted with PRA begin to show signs at a relatively early age, and puppies four months of age and older can be examined by a veterinary ophthalmologist.

Hip Dysplasia, a malformation of the hip joints, is found in Irish Setters, as well as most other breeds. Although the mode of inheritance is unclear and many factors are involved in this crippling disease, breeding dogs with normal hip conformation will give greater assurance that the offspring will be free of the disease. The Orthopedic Foundation for Animals (OFA) at Columbia, Missouri, is a registry body which will certify hips by reading radiographs sent to them from veterinarians. Many breeders rely on OFA certification, or on the diagnosis by veterinary orthopedic specialists, to determine breeding potential of their dogs.

Some breeders will give total or limited guarantees concerning these two inherited diseases.

Epilepsy is another disease found in Irish Setters. In some cases the carriers are known, in other instances they are obscure. There has been very little genetic research done on this disease in our breed, but it does exist, and breeders with epileptic dogs generally do not use them in their breeding programs.

Hyperosteodystrophy (HOD) is an illness which affects the joints of growing puppies. There seems to be a genetic predisposition to this disease in some lines, though it may be caused by other factors, as well. Some puppies recover normally. Others are permanently affected by it.

Allergies: Some Irish Setters are prone to skin disorders, flea allergies, or allergies caused by other things. Some of these seem to be inherited, or at least there is a predisposition towards inheritance. In rare instances, the skin afflictions are so severe and of such multiple irritants that the dogs must be destroyed. In most allergic cases, however, isolating the cause and treating the animal results in total or partial cure. One should be aware, however, of the genetic predisposition towards allergies.

Hypothyroidism is another condition which affects Irish Setters, and there seems to be evidence that there is a genetic predisposition towards it. The symptoms can vary from mild to severe, causing changes in hair, skin, reproduction, and personality. It is generally detectable and treatable.

Temperament: Although temperament is not a disease, it is inherited to some degree. Environment plays a large role in how a puppy develops, but basic traits are transmitted from parents to offspring. Shyness, excessive timidity, fear, are traits which can be inherited, and are uncharacteristic of the Irish Setter. Aggressiveness is another inheritable and undesirable trait in the Irish Setter. Hyperactivity, extreme nervousness, flightiness are other traits which can have medical origins, but may also be genetic. Only by eliminating animals that display these traits from breeding programs can they be bred out. It is absolutely essential to preserve the good nature of the Irish Setter by using only dogs and bitches with good, sound temperaments for breeding.

Environment plays a large role in how a puppy develops, but basic traits are transmitted from parents to offspring. Shyness, excessive timidity, fear, are traits which can be inherited, and are uncharacteristic of the Irish Setter. Aggressiveness is another inheritable and undesirable trait in the Irish Setter. Hyperactivity, extreme nervousness, flightiness are other traits which can have medical origins, but may also be genetic. Only by eliminating animals that display these traits from breeding programs can they be bred out. It is absolutely essential to preserve the good nature of the Irish Setter by using only dogs and bitches with good, sound temperaments for breeding.

Fortunately for our breed, these afflictions are in the minority, but everyone dedicated to the Irish Setter should be on guard against them.

Vivid proof of the teaching. George G. Alston, co-author of this chapter on grooming, is pictured showing Am. & Can. Ch. McCamon Marquis to one of his many Specialty wins.

4

Grooming the Irish Setter

by Judy Graef with George G. Alston
Photos by Connie Vanacore

AN Irish Setter that is properly cared for is a handsome dog to own. Whether you keep your Setter as a pet or show dog should make little difference in your devotion to its good care. Show dogs require more careful attention to trimming and brushing than a pet, but beyond these considerations, the conditioning which includes exercising, bathing, and veterinary care is the same.

Any animal that is kept in optimum condition, and trimmed to conform to breed type, provides visual pleasure. No matter what grooming products or practices are employed, the goal remains the same. The dog should look as natural as possible without a shaved appearance. The ultimate compliment is having someone remark, "Isn't it nice you don't have to trim that dog!"

Grooming your dog for show requires knowledge of the Irish Setter standard and correct use of various pieces of equipment, shampoos, and rinses. Many techniques are employed to get the best results. Each piece of equipment must be individually selected to perform a given task. No matter how much better the equipment is, it does no good if you don't know how to use it.

When the novice watches the practiced groomer he might walk away with the idea that using the equipment is an easy task. He must remember that the professional has had years of practice; knows what tools to use on various parts of the dog and is experienced in working on a variety of coat textures and coat problems. Through evaluation, the proper tools and techniques are used to get the job done.

A beginner usually finds the equipment difficult to use and frequently

43

either over-grooms or under-grooms his dog. Remember that any method employed to turn out a dog in final show trim is acceptable, just so the dog appears natural and neat in appearance when the job is done.

Some pieces of equipment work beautifully on one type of coat, but are found to be completely useless on another type. Experimentation is the key to eventual success. The results are directly related to the time and effort put into knowing which grooming tools to use, and having the patience necessary to become proficient in their use.

There are advocates of various grooming styles and variations may be found from one area of the country to another. Judges, too, sometimes prefer certain styles. At one show it was known that the assigned judge liked Setters with an "ungroomed" look. On that day handlers known for their polished grooming techniques showed dogs without much stripping or thinning. At the show the following day each of the dogs had been returned to routine trim.

The novice should be observant, ask, weigh the advice of others and use a good measure of common sense to evaluate what he has learned. A professionally groomed dog never looks freshly trimmed and is exhibited clean, well brushed, and with every hair in place. When the competition is close, the best "turned out" dog has the obvious advantage. Good grooming can never turn an average specimen into an outstanding one, but many an average dog in optimum condition can and does defeat a superior animal that is shown in poor condition.

One of the most difficult aspects of grooming is evaluating the various strengths and weaknesses in each animal. Trimming can enhance the strengths and minimize the weaknesses. Grooming cannot be expected to visually hide all faults, but various techniques can camouflage them.

A necessary first step is to honestly evalute the dog's structure and movement. The owner-handler must develop an objective eye through reading the breed standard and through observation. Book knowledge is best coupled with experience to accurately assess the dog. Many professional handlers will evaluate for a fee if asked; schedule a time convenient for both parties and agree on the fee in advance.

Grooming is a slow process *which must be practiced* in order to get the desired results. A last minute two hour session will never produce the finished results of trimming done in slow stages over a period of several weeks.

No amount of proper grooming and bathing will pay off if your dog is not kept in good health, proper weight, and parasite-free. Ninety percent of coat growth problems are related to parasites, unbalanced diet, and poor routine care.

EQUIPMENT

High quality tools are a must when engaging in any trade. Purchasing grooming equipment for your dog is no exception. Buy the most important pieces of equipment first. Then add a few pieces at a time until there is a wide selection of combs, thinners, brushes, and strippers available. *See Photograph No. 1.* It is not necessary to use all tools on any given dog, and all cannot be used with the same effectiveness on any given coat since coats vary in texture and thickness.

Most of the tools can be purchased in pet shops, from concessions found at dog shows, or (often at discounts) from mail order houses through catalogues sent to the dog fancy.

CLIPPERS: Oster produces a professional small animal clipper model A2 or A5. It usually comes equipped with the standard number 10 blade although other blades are available. The A2 model has a removable head. The A5 model has removable blades. The number ten blade is essential since it is used to trim ears, neck, face, and to remove the hair which grows between the pads of the feet. Never use clippers on top of your dog's head. If you do, the light undercoat becomes pronounced. It is more effective to groom this area using thinners, stripping knife, and stone.

Clippers are cared for according to manufacturer's instructions. After each use blades are cleaned with a small brush and lubricated with oil or sprays to keep them sharp.

SCISSORS: Purchase high quality scissors recommended by someone who has had grooming experience. A lot of money can be wasted before finding a good pair that cuts cleanly and maintains a sharp edge. Scissors will last longer if they are kept dry, are never dropped and are stored in their plastic case.

Straight Blade: Used for cutting whiskers, outlining the pad, and shaping the hair between the toes of the foot.

Blunt End: Adds safety for cutting whiskers at the brow or muzzle when a dog is most likely to move.

Thinning: These shears are available with both single and double blade thinning edges. The greater the number of teeth, the more hair can be removed in a single cut. Thinners are used for blending the neck, head, shoulders, hocks, feet, tail, and for removing excess coat that may grow down the outer side of the back leg. These scissors cut most evenly when they are slightly dull.

STRIPPING COMBS: Available in a wide variety of types and price range. This tool's effectiveness varies with individual dogs. Best used where there is a dense undercoat without a lot of protective, heavier top coat or guard hair, it is for removing dead coat and undercoat from the head, body, and flank, and for · blending the hair on the neck. The groomer must experiment with the use of the tool on his dog to find which does the best job. Effectiveness can also vary during the seasons as dogs go through the shedding process or are growing new hair. When new, stripping combs can leave sharp cut marks across the dog's coat giving a scissored appearance. The goal is to dull the blade and then to drag it through the coat to pull out the dead hair.

MAGNETIZED STRIPPING COMB: Similar to a stripping comb but with finer teeth. This tool is best used for removal of dead coat from the body, neck, and top of the head.

DUPLEX DRESSER AND WECK HAIR SHAPER: These two tools are equipped with removable blades. They should only be used for evening long straggly hairs usually found when the Irish changes coat. If any change in color is evident, discontinue. Since this tool is meant to cut hair the blade must be kept sharp and therefore frequently changed.

STONE: Has rough edges and is shaped like a brick cut lengthwise. Drag over the top coat, top of head and neck. Can also be broken into smaller pieces and used with tension between the stone, hair, and thumb for removal of hair.

BRUSHES: It is best to select a natural bristle brush because it will not tear the coat like synthetic materials. Keep the brush clean. The wooden handled brush helps absorb the natural oil which is deposited on the bristles. Select one that has a broad enough face to smooth the top coat.

PIN BRUSH: Named for the one-inch wire pins inserted in the wood backed rubber cushion. This brush is best used to separate hairs in the long furnishings. Never pull this or any other brush through the feathers when you meet resistance, for you will tear coat which takes a long time to grow. Section the hair and work in small areas. Brush from the roots to the end of the hair shaft. The long furnishings will then hang free. If the pins get bent, remove them with pliers so they will not snag and damage the coat. *Caution:* Never leave the brush with the pin side up on the grooming table—the dog may step on it and injure a foot.

THE SLICKER BRUSH: Also separates the coat, and can cause damage by tearing if not used carefully. The wires on this brush are much finer and more dense than on the pin brush. Slide this brush lightly over the top coat and long feathering to align the hair before toweling.

HOUND GLOVE: Removes loose hair and gives a gloss to the top coat. Used shortly before the dog appears in the ring to give a smooth well-groomed look.

STEEL COMB: Select one with graduated teeth; a wide tooth comb separates the hair. After fully combing the feathering, repeat with the narrow tooth comb. A furriers comb has the shortest and finest set of teeth and can be used to align the hair in the top coat. Avoid continuous use of the steel comb on the feathering since it breaks the coat. Many handlers use a comb in the ring when it would be difficult to carry a pin brush. The pin brush is the best piece of equipment to use on the feathering.

NAIL CUTTERS: The **guillotine type** is a favorite of many. This cutter has an oval opening for insertion of the nail. The blade which slices across the opening for cutting may be replaced when it becomes dull. Any amount of nail can be removed so care must be taken to avoid cutting through the quick. The plier type has a guard which can be set to avoid cutting too deeply into the nail. This one squeezes the nail from both sides as it cuts.

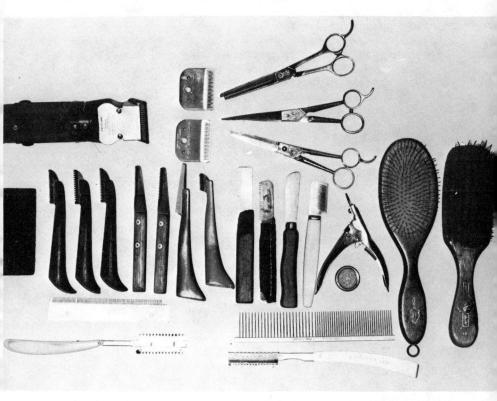

1. Tools used for trimming an Irish Setter: Oster clipper with No. 10 blade, fine 48 tooth thinning shears, straight edge shears, regular 30 tooth thinning shears, stone, variety of stripping knives, Resco nail clipper, grinding attachment for Oster A2 clipper, pin brush, flat natural bristle brush, furriers comb, Duplex Dresser, steel comb, Weck hair shaper.

GRINDING: The Oster A-2 clipper is made with a removable head which exposes a drive shaft to which a plastic grinder can be attached. Sandpaper discs are inserted in the grinder head for polishing the nail after it has been cut. You must be careful to avoid catching the leg feathering in the drive shaft when grinding. Do not grind a dirty nail. The grinder will force the dirt into the nail bed and can cause infection.

A high powered hand tool with a stone attachment is used by some. It is dangerous because of its high speed and quick action. Goggles must be worn to protect your eyes from flying pieces of nail. Many professionals will not allow this particular tool in their kennels. They prefer the Oster A-2 clipper attachment since it is slower acting and gives better control.

Filing is a slow process achieved with a variety of metal hand files. You can smooth rough nail edges after cutting without the danger of suddenly producing a bleeding quick.

KWICK-STOP: This commercial product is sold in powdered form for stopping nails from bleeding when they are cut, ground, or filed too short. Use according to manufacturer's instructions.

TOOTH SCALER: There are many types of scalers available for the removal of tartar build up. One with a flat quarter-inch blade is adequate and does the job. The amateur must be careful not to damage the flesh of the gum. Dogs generally do not enjoy having their teeth scaled, so you might find yourself working on a moving target. Begin slightly under the gumline and pull with pressure against the tooth to the end. Tartar left under the gumline can cause irritation and infection. Brushing with a toothbrush and paste of baking soda and water will help keep the teeth clean. Feeding commercial hard-baked dog bones deters tartar build-up. For chronic cases a veterinarian puts the dog under anesthesia and removes the tartar with an ultra sonic device. Tartar accumulation is one cause of bad breath.

GROOMING TABLE: Excellent for training the dog for show and to gain the necessary control while grooming. The rubber mat prevents the dog from slipping and the arm and loop hold the dog in position for trimming. It is much easier to work on a dog which is elevated above the ground. The table is worth the investment as a back-saving device for the owner as well.

GROOMING TECHNIQUES

Brushing and Combing

Keep your dog free of knots and tangles. This is best accomplished using proper brushing and combing techniques. Dogs which are consistently shown are bathed once a week and thoroughly brushed out twice a week. Correct brushing technique does not tear out the coat. Never brush a dog when the coat is thoroughly dry. Use either plain water, or a mixture of one quarter balsam or creme rinse to three quarters parts of warm water in a plastic spray bottle. Shake well to mix the rinse with the water, then mist the dog with the spray. In cold weather it might be necessary to increase the proportion of water in the creme rinse mix if your dog is prone to flaky skin. Do not spray the top coat directly; spray the brush. If the spray is applied directly to the top it will get to the undercoat and cause lifting. You *can* spray the feathers directly.

Brush the back of the dog with a natural bristle brush in the direction the hair grows. The longer feathering on the ears, ruff, legs, belly, and tail are first combed with the wide tooth comb to free the hair of tangles, and then combed with one with finer teeth. The pin brush is used next to separate the hair so that it hangs freely.

A good brushing is worth "a good feed." Yanking and pulling tears the coat and destroys the growth that you are trying to promote. If the comb or pin brush meets resistance as you work, stop and untangle the coat by hand.

Be sure to lift and part the heavy feathering as you work. Brush the dog in sections. Be particularly careful in areas that mat because of friction between the body parts, such as behind the elbows and in the groin.

Trimming

Anyone who doubts the necessity for trimming a Setter need only look at the before and after photographs (*Photos 2 and 3*) to see how proper trimming enhances the dog's natural beauty.

The most difficult problem created when trimming an Irish Setter is the color change resulting from exposing the undercoat. The degree of change is directly related to the type of coat the dog carries. Color changes most rapidly on the animal that carries a heavy undercoat and very little top coat. This type of coat is the most difficult to trim, has a tendency to curl, and appears moth-eaten unless correct grooming techniques are used.

The easiest coat to groom has a characteristically long, more heavily textured topcoat and little undercoat. Because the topcoat is more profuse than the softer, lighter colored undercoat, the hair lacks curl, grows close to the body over the topline, and the furnishings hang straight.

The animal with almost no undercoat has the least amount of color change when groomed, but also lacks the fullness in feathering associated with mature coat growth.

2. Before trimming.

3. After trimming.

When trimming any type of coat, remember to quit when the color change begins to become apparent. Color change is distracting to the eye, especially when it occurs in places that are trimmed other than under the neck.

The best time to trim is three to four days after the dog's bath, when the hair has regained some of its natural oil and is still clean enough not to dull clipper blades, scissors, and a sharp razor edge. The hair seems to stay against the body naturally without the fluff associated with a new bath. Plan to begin to trim about three or more weeks before the show.

Begin by cutting the nails. Since the nails and feet are extremely sensitive, it is important to separate the time spent on nail cutting and trimming the foot. Cut the nail back at an angle (*Photo 4*) to remove as much of the top of the nail as possible. With light-colored nails the quick is easily seen, but with dark brown nails it is not as easy to determine where to stop. Cut close, but not through the quick of the nail. Cutting through the quick is not only painful to the dog but can make him foot shy.

If the nail does begin to bleed, use Kwik-Stop to halt the flow of blood. Nails must be cut at least once a week to keep the dog walking on the pads of the foot. Nails allowed to grow too long click on the kitchen floor and also can be heard as the dog gaits in an indoor ring. Nails cut their proper length do not touch the floor as the dog stands. A file or grinder can be used afterwards to shape the cut nails. If the quick is left slightly exposed, it will recede by itself if the process is repeated often enough.

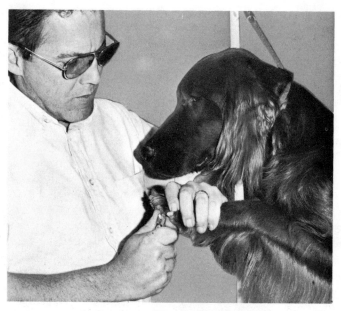

4. Cut the nail back at an angle.

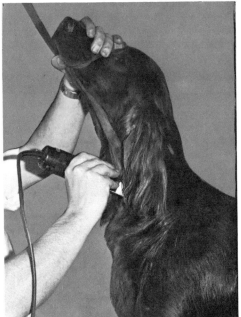

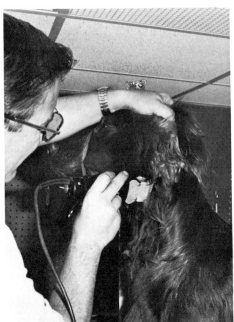

5. Begin by trimming under the neck.

6. Trimming under the ear to the side of the neck.

As you work keep the dog in a standing position. Begin by trimming under the neck (*Photo 5*). Hold the electric clippers like a pencil. The free hand positions the dog's muzzle up to expose the neck to the clipper blades. Start at the chin and cut down the middle of the underside of the neck to about two fingers width above the breast bone. Give time for the clippers to do the job. Do not rush.

Trim with the grain of the hair to an imaginary line drawn parallel to the lower edge of the jaw, under the ear to the side of the neck (*Photo 6*). Hold the ear away from the neck and continue trimming. Stop where the hair changes direction under the ear to where the neck joins the shoulder. The long hair that remains (*Photo 7*) will be removed with thinners, stripping combs, and the stone. It is important to view the neck from the front and side while trimming to gain the best possible effect.

If the dog has been trained to the grooming table and is not frightened of the clipper, it is possible to slip the grooming loop over the muzzle and to tighten it. This allows the groomer access to the entire neck. When the neck is more carefully groomed, tighten the loop on the neck once again. Most dogs will not be terribly cooperative during any phase of the grooming process if they are not exposed to the equipment in easy stages.

EAR: Begin where the ear cartilage meets the skull and trim about one third the length of the ear (*Photo 8*). It is best to hold the ear leather near the bottom and trim with the hair. Never trim the hair that covers the fold at

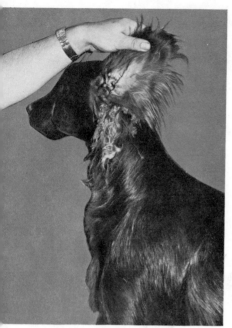

7. Hair under ear before trimming.

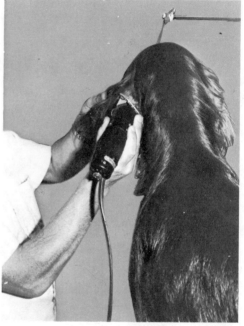

8. Trimming the ear.

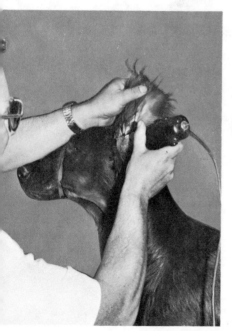

9. Trimming the ear burr.

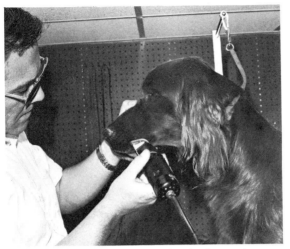

10. Shaping the hair on the dog's muzzle.

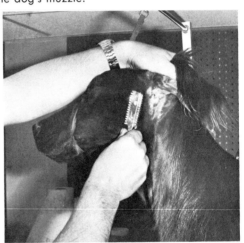

11. Touch up on the cheek.

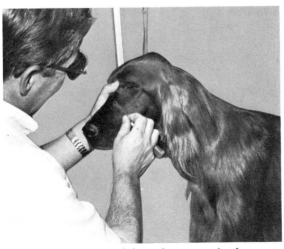

12. Using the Weck hair shaper on the face.

the front of the ear. Leaving the hair along the fold softens the appearance of the ear and helps to enhance the much-desired mild expression which is characteristic of the Irish Setter. Trimming gives the appearance of lowering the ears which acts as a frame for the eyes.

Turn the ear over and clean out the hair from the inner surface close to the ear canal. This allows air to circulate in the canal and helps keep the ear free of infection. Next, raise the ear and trim the ear burr (*Photo 9*). Be careful not to nick the sensitive, small split area on the underside. The ear hangs closer to the face once the hair is removed. You may trim against the grain of the hair under the ear and on the ear burr. Make sure that when the ear hangs naturally, the long hair under the ear is cut down as far as the hair that has been trimmed on top of the ear.

FACE and HEAD: Shape the hair on the dog's muzzle by holding the clipper on the flattest part of the face sideways to the grain (*Photo 10*). As you work remove the whiskers. Check the muzzle from several angles as whiskers are often missed with even the most careful attempt to remove them.

Touch-up the cheek using the Duplex Dresser or Weck Hair Shaper (*Photo 11*). Remember that each contains a razor blade and will cut the hair. Heavy growth left here will add apparent width to the cheek of the dog and coarsen the head. As you work with the razor, comb it with the growth of the hair. The Weck Hair Shaper can also be used to remove the whisker nubs by pulling it sideways to the whisker grain (*Photo 12*).

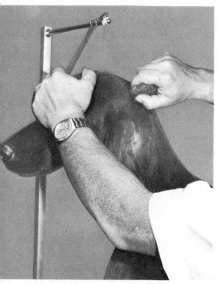 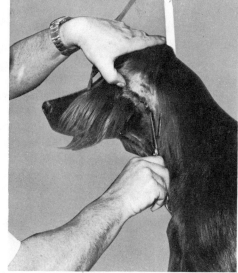

Drag the stone on the top of the head.   14. Blending the hair on the side of the neck.

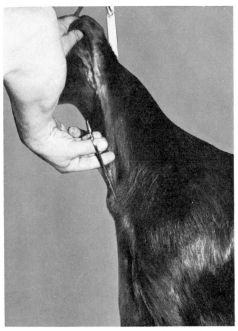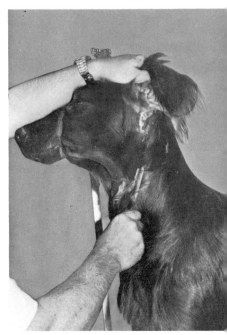

15 and 16. Use the thinning shears along the neck, blending against the grain into the h

Blend the ear to the head with thinning scissors held under the coat against, but not across, the grain of the coat. As you cut, brush the coat to remove the results of each scissoring. Do not cut several times in one spot without brushing and inspecting the results or you will make a hole in the coat, or the hair will appear as if it were cut in steps.

Next, use the stone on top of the head to take off the fuzzies (*Photo 13*). Drag it. Do not pull against the hair. Keep the stone clean as you work. When you have made the head appear as smooth as possible, take the thinning scissors and begin to blend the short clippered hair at the midpoint under the ear into the long hair on the side of the neck (*Photo 14*). Once again, cut against the grain into the coat and brush after each cut. Do not leave steps by cutting across the grain.

To establish a clean neck line between the clippered hair and the longer neck hair use the thinners straight along the neck edge to form a line between ear and shoulder (*Photos 15 and 16*). Make this area appear as natural as possible without a sharp line of demarcation.

Never use thinners by cutting across the grain of the coat. Blend against the grain into the hair. After each cut brush the hair away. Try to layer the hair evenly and gradually so that there is a smooth transition from the longer two-inch hair on the side of the neck to the short-clippered hair on the front of the neck. The change in hair length from longest to shortest is gradual and when properly done is almost imperceptible.

A stripping knife will remove the dead undercoat and help smooth the neckline (*Photos 17 and 18*). Drag the stripper against the coat and with the grain of the hair.

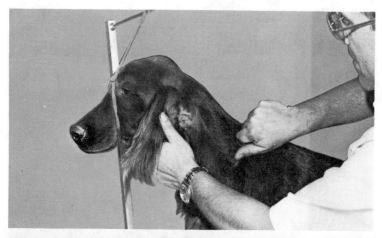

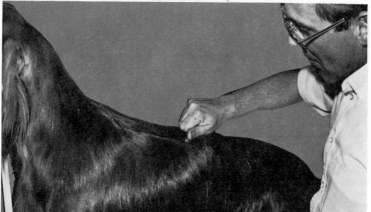

17. and 18. Use a stripping knife to remove dead undercoat. Drag the stripper with the grain of the hair.

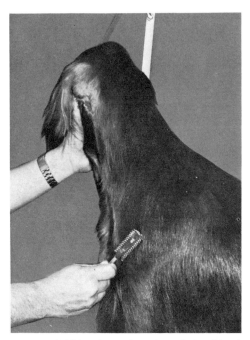

19. Careful blending of neck and shoulder is important.

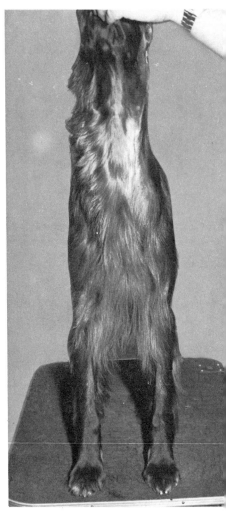

20. The contrast between trimmed and untrimmed sides is obvious.

The careful trimming of the blend from neck to shoulder is very important (*Photo 19*). Too much hair on the shoulder adds bulk where there should be refinement. It is difficult enough to breed a dog with good clean shoulders without allowing a heavy coat to accentuate one that is already loaded. Since there are so many Irish Setters with wide set shoulder blades and straight fronts it is best to concentrate on deemphasizing heaviness through proper grooming. The overall picture of head, neck, and shoulders should be balanced, clean, and pleasing to the eye (*Photo 20*).

FEET: Trimming feet is a time consuming job. It is best to undertrim them at first. You can always take some more hair off but you cannot put it back in time for the show. The most common error here is making holes in the hair between the toes. The goal is to shape the foot to give a clean, compact look.

Cut off the extra hair from the bottom of the pads using the Oster Clippers with a number ten blade (*Photos 21 and 22*). The foot must be clean or you will dull expensive blades as you work. Avoid cutting hair from between the bottom of the pads. Keeping the hair short allows the pads (instead of the wads of hair) to touch the ground and makes the dog use his toes in walking as he should. It also prevents the dog from bringing extra dirt into the house and minimizes the chances of fungus infection. Be careful not to cut the pads or the toes.

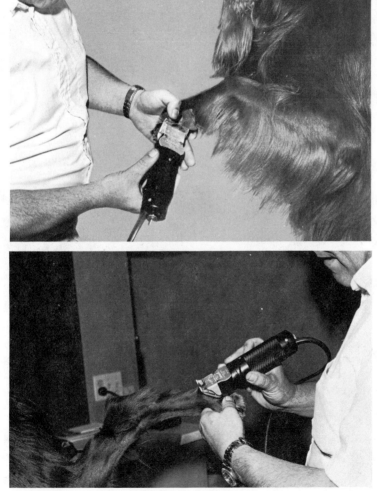

21. and 22. Clip extra hair from bottom of pads, front and rear feet.

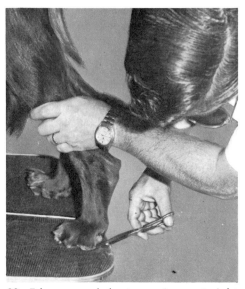

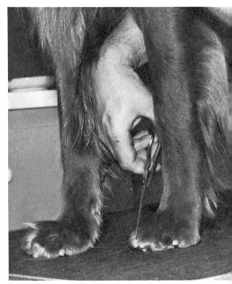

23. Edge around the toes using a straight scissors.

24. Shape the long feathering which grow between the toes.

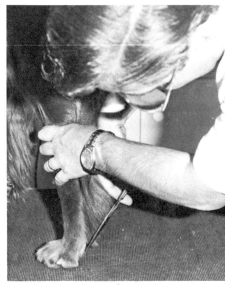

25. Blend the feathering with thinning shears.

26. Shape the fetlock with a straight scisso

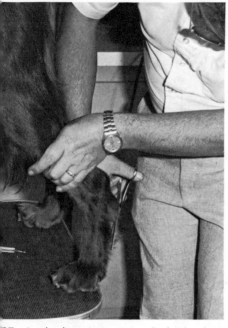

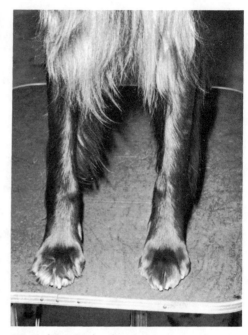

27. Angle the scissors towards the heel.

28. Before and after appearance of the front feet.

Next, edge around the toes with a sharp pair of straight scissors exposing the pads (*Photo 23*). You will use both the points and the blades to achieve a clean, neat appearance.

Shape the long feathering which grows between the toes. From the top, angle the straight scissors from the arch of the toe to the nail (*Photo 24*). Continue to blend by using the thinners with the tips pointed toward the toes (*Photo 25*).

If you discover mats between the toes separate them with your fingers or comb them out with a fine tooth comb. If the mats are allowed to develop the hair retains moisture which helps promote infections.

Shape the fetlock with a straight scissor cutting at an angle (*Photo 26*). The hair here must not touch the floor and should be cut short enough to show off the foot. Never shave the fetlock with the clippers.

The feathering which grows on the hock is also shaped. First brush the hair up. Do not clipper the hair here or the dog's bone will appear slight and the total look unbalanced. Angle the scissors toward the dog's heel and thin at a slight distance from the bone (*Photo 27*). How much hair you leave will depend on the amount of bone the dog has. Brush the hair up again. Trim the ragged ends with the straight scissor.

Notice the difference in the Before and After appearance of the front foot (*Photo 28*). One foot seems to be compact and neatly manicured and

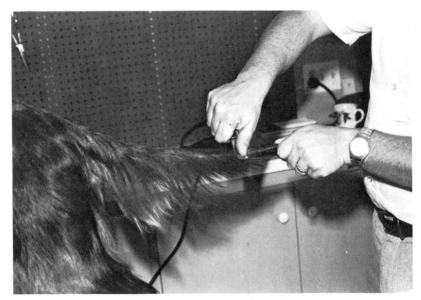

29. Stripping excess hair from the tail.

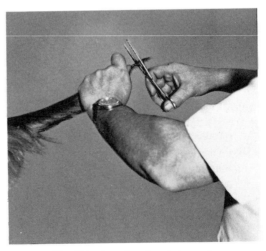

30. Thinning the tip of the tail.

strong in pastern. The untrimmed foot looks flat in comparison because of the illusion created by the length of the hair. The benefit of grooming is obvious.

RUMP and TAIL: Some Irish Setters when left untrimmed will develop a profusion of coat over the rump, base of tail and rear legs. This mass of hair can be made more managable with a stripper. Always work in the direction the hair grows. Patience is necessary, since working with this tool is a slow process if you expect to get the proper results. Always keep in mind that trimming is creative work and your artistic point of view plays an important role in the look of the finished dog.

The Irish that grows too much hair on the outer leg gives the impression of wearing pants. Use the stone to strip this hair from the outer thighs exposing the clean lines of each leg.

Raise the tail and trim away the long hair that grows at the root of the tail. Use the fine tooth thinners. Remove the hair from one to one and one half inches. Do not use clippers here. The hair removal not only promotes cleanliness, but also gives the tail an attractive carriage and defines the body line.

In a well coated dog the hair usually grows too thick along the top of the tail (*Photo 29*). Proceed with the stripper and brush until the tail gracefully tapers from root to tip. Pull all the tail feathering over the last vertabrae and cover the tip with your thumb and forefinger (*Photo 30*). Leave about one half to three quarters of an inch of hair to protect the end of the tail. All the remaining hair is thinned across the end. Next, use the stripping knife to taper the end and eliminate a clean cut appearance. The finished tail has roughly the shape of a triangle.

As you trim, inspect how the dog looks from a distance, Have someone hold the dog in show position to see the results of your effort. Judges often "buy" a standing picture of the dog. This means that the profile of the animal at rest can become more important than the moving picture. Be sure to know how your dog looks in motion, too. Hair may begin to fly in areas where it should remain flat. Touch-up grooming is almost always necessary. Also view your dog at a distance. How will he compare in profile with the other dogs as he stands in line? Trim a dog for what he will look like at twenty feet.

The stone is used to remove hair and smooth the top coat. If you need to remove more hair than dragging the stone through the coat will accomplish, grip the hair between the stone and finger. Then, do not yank, but pull gently.

Complete shaping the long feathering which grows over the rib cage by blending the coat so it will remain flat against the body of the dog over the greatest rib spring. A stripping knife will do a good job here. If the dog is slab-sided it would be necessary to give the look of apparent spring by leaving the fullness of coat here.

A good time to clean the ears and check them for infection is prior to the dog's bath. Put your nose close to the dog's ear canal. Any unusual odor is a sign of wax accumulation or infection. Another sign is a dog that holds his head to one side or frequently shakes his head or scratches his ears and groans. Routinely clean the ears with a cotton ball dipped in mineral oil or hydrogen peroxide. A veterinarian will recommend an antibiotic ointment in case of infection.

BATHING

A necessary first step is to purchase a quality shampoo and rinse. Since different types of coats require different combinations of shampoo and creme rinse it is important to experiment to find the best combination for your dog. Be sure to ask what others use. A shampoo for black dogs is favored by many since it works effectively to give a deeper, rich mahogany color to the coat. A commercial dandruff-free shampoo can help control dry flaking skin, but must never be used close to the animal's genitals since severe skin irritation can result. A good medicated shampoo can also help to minimize skin problems.

You might find that as the seasons change, so does the quantity and quality of your dog's coat. What works beautifully at one time of the year might have to be changed to gain the desired results at another time. Certain high suds shampoos can cause matting of the furnishings and produce hot spots on the skin in warm weather.

Try buying small bottles of any shampoo until the contents prove their usefulness on your dog. However, small bottles are expensive for continuous use since the shampoo is already diluted; the gallon size is most economical since the shampoo is full strength. Save the empty small plastic bottles to mix the shampoo for the bath. Squeeze bottles are both easy to use and safe to handle with your dog in the tub.

It is usually only necessary to suds and rinse your dog once. When the hair becomes brittle or appears lifeless, conditioning involves putting the dog down in oil. *Pro-Grow* is a conditioner which can be rubbed into the dog's skin and coat, or diluted and sprayed from a plastic spray bottle. The dog must be bathed to remove the conditioner once a week. It is then important to shampoo twice and rinse with warm water. When the dog is dry, brush thoroughly and respray with the conditioner. Never show a dog that is put down in conditioning cream or oil without bathing first.

Begin the bath by thoroughly wetting the coat. A hose fitted with a shower head makes the bath an easy task. Protect the dog's eyes by putting a drop of mineral oil in each. Apply the shampoo on the head and then generously apply more to the body, legs, and feathering. Work it into a lather. Be sure to pick up each foot and work the lather in between the toes.

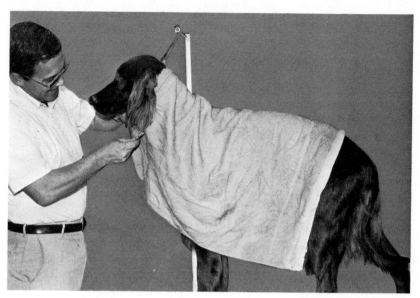

31. Pin towel under the neck with a horse blanket pin.

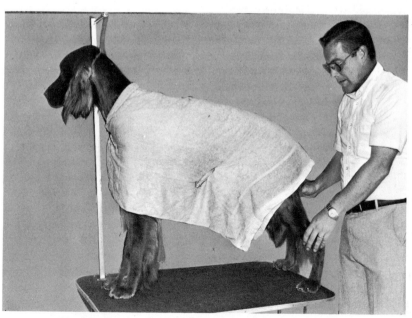

32. Pin the towel in place between chest and loin.

Care must be taken to rinse all the soap out of the coat. When you are finished, the rinse water must be totally clear. Check for soap under the elbows and other difficult-to-rinse spots. When you are finished, squeeze out the excess water. Mix a half dollar size glob of creme rinse at the botton of a bowl with two quarts of warm water. Pour the rinse over the dog just on the top coat. Do not rub the rinse into the undercoat because it causes lifting of the coat when dry. Balsam rinses can cause flaking of the skin in the dry winter months.

While the dog is wet, brush lightly with the slicker brush. Select a bath towel that is large enough to cover the dog from high on the neck to halfway down the tail. It must be wide enough to reach around the dog. Pin the towel under the neck with a horse blanket pin (*Photo 31*). Without disturbing the coat on the dog's back, snap the towel back, pulling tightly. Without easing up on the towel, pin it in place between the chest and loin (*Photo 32*). Toweling keeps the coat flat and is left on the dog until shortly before show time. It also keeps dust and dirt away from the coat. If the dog is to be shown again the next day, towel it again. Remember that the bathing, toweling routine is as important to the final appearance of the dog as proper trimming.

Some people prefer to brush their dogs until dry. Others use a hand-held dryer while brushing. Although it is convenient, avoid continuous blow drying since it tends to break the coat and causes split ends.

Grooming is never completed. After the initial roughing out, frequent touch-ups will prevent the necessity of continuous hours of work which are tedious for both the owner and the dog. Also keep in mind that each dog is different in coat quality and conformation. Continue to experiment until you find the right combination of grooming techniques to produce the best possible finished look for *your* dog. Learning is a continuous process and grooming your dog is no exception.

5

Irish Setter Beginnings in the British Isles

THE origin of the Irish Setter is not known. It is reasonable, however, to suppose that he was evolved for a certain purpose from older breeds by natural or by artificial selection. Records show that the breed was definitely established as early as 1800; but its history prior to that time relies mainly upon tradition, scattered writings and old sporting prints.

While most investigators believe that the foundation stock of the Irish Setter was the setting spaniel, there is a difference of opinion as to what crosses were used. The Bloodhound, Pointer, Irish Water Spaniel, Gordon Setter, English Setter and/or their progenitors have been variously named as possible ancestors. As the early-day sportsmen generally kenneled several breeds, it would seem not unusual for them to interbreed their dogs occasionally in order to improve utility.

Whatever the crosses may have been, the transition from spaniel to setter was apparently very gradual. Sporting illustrations of the period depict setters which resemble spaniels, as in W. Ward's engraving (1806) of G. Morland's painting. A close connection between the breeds is further indicated by the existence in Ireland about 1770, of a variety of setters called red spaniels (in Gaelic, *Modder Rhu*).

W. J. Rasbridge, the breed's most renowned historian, expressed his views of the breed's origin in the March 18, 1982 issue of the English *Our Dogs* magazine:

As I see it, the Irish Setter is one variety of the larger land spaniel which like the lesser land spaniel originated in Spain, whence its name. It happened to be a variety that the Irish took to themselves and made their own, probably in the

67

Setters in 1800—from a painting by G. Morland.

A Red Setter—from a painting by H. B. Chalon, 1816.

18th Century, so that by the mid-19th Century (the breed) was there to be found at its highest level for work and looks . . . Ireland became the center from which the breed was disseminated over the rest of the world. Before that happened, local conditions as regards climate, terrain and game supply had led to this particular breed of Setter exceeding other setting dogs in stamina, toughness when faced with inclement weather, and above all, the will to keep going and not to lose heart and interest if effort proved unrewarding because of scarcity of game. These I regard as the essential characteristics of the Irish Setter, towards the preservation of which all breeding should be directed. A physically or mentally "soft" Irish Setter is, to my mind, a contradiction in terms.

Family strains were established in the early 1700s by English gentry who came to Ireland to acquire land and brought their setting dogs with them. The mixture of the native Irish dogs and the English strains formed the foundation stock for the show and field trial dogs that appeared in the 1860s, according to Mr. Rasbridge. All Irish Setters listed in the first stud book in England came direct, or at one or two removes from Ireland. That makes it an Irish breed, but not an indigenous one, he wrote.

By 1800, setter type had become so well established that one has no difficulty in recognizing the Irish Setter in artwork of that era. Take, for example, the plate, "Setters in 1805" by Sydenham Edwards, showing the three varieties of setters; or the painting, "A Red Setter" (1816) by H. B. Chalon.

During the period from 1780 to 1850, the Irish families took special pride in the purity of their own strains of setters and upon the number of years they had possessed them. A word in passing about some of the noteworthy strains might be of interest.

One of the first Irish sportsmen to rent shooting moors in Scotland (1779) was Maurice Nugent O'Connor, whose red setters had a trace of white on them, but no black. At his death in 1818, Robert LaTouche acquired the dogs, described as being large, dark red, light boned, well furnished and producing white-marked progeny. The French Park strain was owned in succession by three generations of the Lord de Freyne family (1793-1879). Then there were the strains of the Marquis of Waterford, Mr. Mahon, Lord Clancarty, Lord Anglesey, Lord Lismore, Lord Dillon, Lord Rossmore, Lord Forbes, Lord Howth, Sir Frances H. Loftus, Sir George Gore, Earl of Enniskillen, Yelverton O'Keefe, the Misses Lidwell and many others. John G. King was known as the "Father of the Breed" and Harry Blake Knox was the first to speak of the breed as the "Irish Red Setter."

An interesting description of early setters is given by Henry William Herbert, better known under the nom de plume of Frank Forester, who hunted in Yorkshire in 1825 over "Cynthia and Phebe, a pair of orange and white, silky Irish Setters with large, soft eyes and coal-black muzzles, feathered six inches deep on the legs and stern."

The distinguishing mark of the Irish Setter through the years has been

Setters in 1805—from a color plate by Sydenham Edwards.

Setters—an engraving by Martin T. Ward, 1829.

his color, which is likened to that of a freshly opened horse chestnut burr. It has been variously described as red, mahogany, chestnut, blood red and indeed almost every shade between yellow and brown. According to Mrs. M. Ingle Bepler (whose Rheola Kennels in England were established in the early 1900s), three distinct color strains were known in early Ireland—the solid red predominating in the north, the parti-colored red and white in the south and west, and an attractive "shower of hail" variety along the northwest coast. The last-named setters were typical of the breed in points and color, but were sprinkled with uniform, quarter-inch, white spots about an inch apart.

Color was long a bone of contention among breeders, some claiming red as the proper color and others insisting upon red and white, although both strains probably originated from much the same parent stock. The opinion has been expressed that the red-and-whites had superior noses, were more tractable, faster and more enduring in the field, easier to see while hunting, less interbred with other breeds and possessed of longer sterns. They were characterized as having black noses and good feathering. White predominated in their coats and the red was preferably entirely surrounded by white. The red "islands," which could be large or small, were in about equal proportion to the white. Even the so-called red dogs probably carried a little white.

At Mount Loftus, County Kilkenny, Ireland, there was an oil painting of three red-and-white setters, painted in the early half of the nineteenth century. The Dublin bench shows of 1874 and 1875 had separate classes for red setters and for red-and-white setters. Both varieties were described by Anna Redlich in *The Dogs of Ireland* (1949). Even as late as 1964 in Ireland, the red-and-white blood was occasionally infused with that of the solid reds to improve style and head carriage.

To this day color is confused by some. As late as 1977 in a litter of supposed Irish Setters, there were six blacks and seven reds. The unfortunate owner was told by several "expert" sources that black is extremely rare and exceedingly valuable. This is not true. It can only mean another breed succeeded in getting to an Irish Setter bitch in heat.

The first dog show was held in the Town Hall at Newcastle-on-Tyne, England, in conjunction with a poultry show on June 28 and 29, 1859. It was for pointers and setters only, there being sixty entries. Next came the Birmingham, Leeds, Manchester and London shows, which included other breeds as well as gun dogs. Prizes were frequently withheld for lack of merit or for lack of competition. There seemed to be considerable uncertainty as to what constituted true type in Irish Setters, each owner claiming that he alone possessed the ideal dog. Apparently from the description of the entries, the setters were far from uniform in appearance.

Major Hutchinson's Bob, whelped in 1859 and shown four years later, was said in one reference to be "a wide-fronted, thick-shouldered Suffolk cart horse" and in another reference to be "good all over, formed in exact proportion, and with substance as well as symmetry." Be that as it may, it is known that the breeders of that day sought the bloodlines of this dog.

In 1860, there was a famous bench dog called Carlo, said by Idstone to be "pug-headed." Carlo was a red setter with black ear tips, indicative of a Gordon cross. About the same time Captain Allaway's Shot and Dr. Stone's Dash were exhibited. The latter was from stock twenty years in the doctor's kennels. It was said that Dash had white on the head and feet and a white "snake around the neck," but was of good contour.

The celebrated Irish Setter field trial winner, Plunket, whelped in 1868, combined the La Touche and the Hutchinson strains. He was sired by Plunket's Beauty out of Macdona's Grouse, she by Hutchinson's Bob. Although Plunket was small and bitch-like, he possessed speed, endurance and exceptional style on point. He had field trial wins at Shrewsbury, Vaynol and Southampton. Macdona sold Plunket for 150 guineas to R. Purcell Llewellin, who exported him to America, where he was used to improve native stock.

The 1870s bring us to Ch. Palmerston—the dog most influential in establishing the type of Irish Setter from which the modern show dog has been evolved.

The *Kennel Club Stud Book* (1876) gives Palmerston's pedigree as: "By Old Shot out of Cochrane's Kate; Shot by Mr. Evans of Dungannon's Grouse out of June, late the property of Mr. Hammington."

(*Author's Note:* Again we are indebted to Mr. Rasbridge. The following information on Palmerston is—with little change of words—from an excellent series by Mr. Rasbridge which appeared in the English publication *Our Dogs* in 1957. I would like to have been able to reprint the articles in full, but space limits me to these salient bits.)

Even in his lifetime the facts regarding Palmerston were hard to come by, so that today a great deal of uncertainty attaches to everything about him. In particular, it is impossible to make positive statements about his

Palmerston 5138 KCSB.

Head study of Palmerston.

breeding and breeder, his age, or the exact circumstances under which he came into the possession of J. M. Hilliard around the end of 1874.

How he came to Mr. Hilliard is interesting. He had been owned by Cecil Moore, a solicitor in Omagh, who was one of the founders of the Irish Setter Club in Dublin, and who had more to do with the drafting of the standard for that Club than anyone else.

According to Rawdon Lee (writing in 1893): "Mr. Moore, finding Palmerston a rather delicate dog for field work, though most persevering and with an excellent nose, ordered his man to drown him. He did not want anyone to use him for shooting purposes, as he'd passed his prime. Mr. Hilliard met the poor old dog on the way to what was expected to be his watery grave and begged Mr. Moore to give him the dog. Mr. Moore relented, on condition that Mr. Hilliard would keep him for show purposes only."

In an article in *Our Dogs* in 1939, Mrs. Ingle Bepler (who was twelve years old when Palmerston was transferred) offered this version of it: "Palmerston was being led away with a rope around his neck to be drowned and was bought for half a crown by a rescuer."

Mr. Foster (of Deleware Kennel fame) gave Mr. Rasbridge a third version, based on information he had obtained from a Mr. Bond, a friend of Mr. Hilliard's. It stated: "Cecil Moore had used him solely as a gun dog. Like most dogs of the time, he was seldom kenneled, and strolled about at will. Like most old dogs, he was continually getting in the way. One day Moore tripped over him in the office, and became so annoyed that he told the office boy to 'take him to Hell and drown him!' The boy met Hilliard, who bought him for half a crown."

Whether the change of ownership was just an ordinary affair (as still another author, Mr. Millner, believes), or one of the three above versions, is left to the imagination.

Mr. Hilliard commenced showing Palmerston in 1875. He obviously didn't think very highly of him and catalogued him for sale at five pounds. Palmerston won his class and what followed is recounted by Mr. Foster:

> The judge gave Hilliard an idea of Palmerston's value and the latter was on pin pricks lest he should be claimed. Two Englishmen were looking at the dog and Hilliard nervously sent his pal, Mr. Bond, to hear their decision. Mr. Bond reported: "I went up to hear what was going on. One said he was worth the money, the other thought he was shaken in front and too old. They decided not to have him. I shouted to Hilliard: 'Come along and have a drink—they are not taking him!'"

On June 24, 1875, Palmerston won the championship at Belfast. He was next shown at Cork and won under a Mr. Sandell. Mr. Sandell and Hilliard then joined in an arrangement under which the judge was to have Palmerston at his house in London, and they were to split the stud fees. In Sandell's hands, the dog began to be used extensively at stud.

The arrangement with Sandell apparently came to an abrupt end because of differences over money. For an aged dog to earn 200 pounds (at five pounds a visit) in, at the most, five months is not bad going. The suspicion is that in both men's hands the dog did not serve all the bitches he was supposed to have served.

Rawdon Lee describes Palmerston as "an immense dog, 64 pounds and with an abnormally long and narrow head." A writer in the Rural Almanac for 1880 makes the following comparison between Palmerston and another well-known dog, Macdona's Rover. "I know both Rover and Palmerston. Their difference is striking. Palmerston was heavier built, but lacked the finish of Rover. His coat was of that deep, dark blood red." The writer Dalziel gives Palmerston's measurements as 23½″ at the shoulder.

On the subject of Palmerston's head markings, Millner twice notes that the dog "had a slight snip of white on the nose." Another writer, Schilbred, states: "He had a small white blaze on his forehead." Cecil Moore wrote: "The Palmerston strain frequently had what the late Mr. Lort called the 'Palmerston snip', a thin thread of white running down the foreface and in some of his descendants, this amounted to a pretty broad 'blaze' on the forehead."

After his death in 1880, Palmerston's head was mounted and hung in the entrance of the Waldorf Astoria in New York, of which Hilliard's son was manager. It was taken down in 1918, when it passed into the hands of the Irish Setter Club of America. It survived another six years, and then was thrown away by the individual in whose custody it had been placed.

William C. Thompson (author of the original editions of this book) passed on to Mr. Rasbridge a letter he had from Harry Hartnett, the famous handler of Ch. Milson O'Boy. Hartnett had seen the head before it was destroyed, and wrote of its markings: "there was a white blaze between the eyes from about the middle of the skull."

Palmerston's monumental contribution to breed type—an influence that has persisted to the present day—also provides a sharp example of how judges, by their awards, can be a factor in molding type.

It has already been pointed out that neither Cecil Moore or Hilliard could have had a very high opinion of Palmerston. But their opinion of him grew with his show successes. At his first show, the judge who put him up was a Mr. Lort. Lort was the most frequently used judge of his day, but it is by no means certain that he was a good judge. When he came to the United States on a judging tour in 1879, he was bitterly attacked in the canine press here for incompetence. He appears to have been weak and hesitant in his judging, and inconsistent in his placings—except whenever Palmerston was shown under him.

Only a few of Palmerston's sons and daughters came to America. One of the best known of them was Rose, imported by Dr. William Jarvis in 1877. It was Dr. Jarvis who discovered the nick between the Palmerston and the Elcho strains that had a pronounced effect upon Irish Setter history in America, a story we shall take up in the next chapter.

Macdona's Rover 6193 KCSB (Beauty-Grouse).

Ch. Elcho 579 (Oppenheimer's Charley-Oppenheimer's Nell).

Ch. Elcho Jr. 3881 (Ch. Elcho-Noreen).

6

The Irish Setter
Comes to America

IN order to obtain a true picture of the early history of the Irish Setter in America, one should consult the first volume of *The National American Kennel Club Stud Book* (1878).* Only sporting dogs were registered therein, an English Setter called Adonis being number 1 and Admiral 534 being listed first among the Irish. Although the pedigrees of most registrants were recorded for two generations, frequently the data was incomplete. Of considerable interest to Irish Setter fanciers were the phrases used to describe some of the dogs, as red with white feet, red with white frill, and red with white blaze on the face—all of which testify to the common occurrence of white in the Irish breed. Furthermore, colors other than red were listed for a few so-called Irish Setters, indicating crosses in the not-too-distant past. Tom (660) was lemon, Van Clark (663) black and Speed (650) black and white.

Only imported Irish Setters or their progeny could be registered as Irish Setters, the American strains being referred to as Native Setters, which were classified in a separate section entitled "Cross-bred and Other Setters," explained as follows: "Owing to the indefinite character of some pedigrees it was impossible to decide to what breed certain dogs belonged. They were included in the present class to save discarding them altogether." The practice of mating different breeds together was not unusual, as evidenced by the registrations of Irish-Gordon and Irish-English cross-bred setters.

*A copy of this stud book is in the library of the American Kennel Club at 51 Madison Ave., New York City. When the AKC was established in 1884, the National American Kennel Club Stud Books became the beginning stud register.

On January 26, 1876, a bench show was held at the Exposition building in Chicago with classes for imported red or for red-and-white Irish Setters or their progeny; and there were similar classes for native red or red-and-white setters called Irish. The latter dogs were judged according to the standard of the Irish Setter, which was that of Stonehenge published in 1867. Early day shows usually had three classes for Irish Setters: puppy, open and champion.

What gala occasions these early dog shows must have been, even if they were few and far apart! Just imagine crating your dogs, transporting them to the railroad station in horse-drawn vehicles, traveling many miles on slow, non-air-conditioned trains and exhibiting almost a week, following which came the long trek homeward. Perhaps there were recompenses for this in the good fellowship at the shows and in the pride of ownership of great dogs.

It was under these conditions in the decade following 1870, that the Irish Setter gained a foothold in America. Many dogs that made history were then imported from Ireland and England. As they were evidently superior to our native setters in type and certainly in purity of blood, they more or less set the standard of the era.

One of the first importations was Plunket, famous as a field and bench dog in England. Although he sired more than a score of litters from bitches in this country, only a few of the resulting offspring made names for themselves, perhaps because of the paucity of bench and field events at that time. It is noted that many of his puppies carried considerable white, either as a frill or on the feet.

The common practice of crossing breeds is exemplified by the Plunket-Carrie (Irish-English) and the Plunket-Nell (Irish-Gordon) matings. Apparently, Plunket sired good puppies, because a number of repeat matings were made. On three occasions, Kitty (Plunket-Knight of Kerry's Kate) was bred back to her sire. Other well-known setters mated to Plunket were: Diffenderffer's Bess, Devlin's Moya, Jarvis' Kathleen and Hudson's Stella.

No less than nine Irish Setters were imported between 1873 and 1876 from J. M. Niall of Ireland that were sired by Going's Bob (Hutchinson's Bob - Hutchinson's Lilly) out of Niall's Fan (Lord Waterford's Ponto - Miss Warburton's Venus). Included in this group were: Bess, Dash, Derg, Eileen, Fan II, Grouse, Guy, Kathleen and Red Hugh. These dogs must have possessed quality or so many of the same breeding would not have been imported over a three-year period. Probably the American breeders were attempting to secure the blood of Hutchinson's Bob.

Elcho

In the fall of 1875, Charles H. Turner, guiding spirit of the St. Louis Kennel Club, imported Sullivan's Rose, Erin, Frisk and Elcho. Erin won the Greenwood Plate Trophy for Irish Setters at the Memphis field trial of

1876. Although he was an excellent dog afield, he had a bad temper and once attacked his trainer, C. B. Whitford, who in self defense had to knock the dog down with a fence rail. Erin sired Bob, represented as "the best snipe dog that ever lived," and Duck, noted for her outstanding show record—she was defeated only once.

Unquestionably, the greatest bench-winning bitch of her time was imported Lou II, who won first at three Westminster shows and was widely exhibited with her famous son Berkley. Her pedigree traces back to the early days in Ireland when some of the setters were unnamed, being designated as "Lord Lismore's dog" or "Delaney's bitch."

During the 1870s in America it was customary for kennel clubs to own and campaign dogs. Elcho, Erin, Lou II, Thorstein, Sting II and Berkley were owned by the St. Louis Kennel Club; Ben and Fannie Fern by Chicago; Colleen by Westminster; Derg by Baltimore; Doll by Toledo, and Irish Kork by Emporia Kennel Clubs.

Mr. Turner imported Elcho from J. C. Cooper, Limerick, Ireland. The following letter to Mr. Cooper from his trainer relates Elcho's background:

November 6, 1875

Dear Sir:

I give you particulars of my red Irish Setter Elcho. He is by Charlie out of Nell, both of which were especially purchased for their good pedigree and sent out to Russia for breeding purposes. They are the property of Mr. Oppenheimer of St. Petersburg. Charlie was by Pat out of Juno, by Grouse out of Ina, by Derg out of Rhue. Nell was by Heather out of Nance, by Dane out of Loo; Loo by Bone out of Quail. The dog and the bitch both came directly from the strain of Lord Waterford and Marquis of Ormond, and were originally owned by Captain Irwin; you can get no better blood in Ireland. Elcho was pupped May 1, 1874. I trained him myself and he is the best first season dog I ever had. . . . In case you should send him to America it will probably be of interest to whomever may get him across the Atlantic to learn that he is called after the Elcho Challenge Shield, which came to Ireland by the last shot which was fired by me at Wimbleton this year. By this victory the American Rifle Team is supposed to have thrashed creation, having beaten Ireland, Ireland then beating England and Scotland.

(Signed) Robert S. Greenhill

Ch. Elcho, the first Irish Setter to become a bench champion in America, won prizes in shows at Chicago, St. Louis, New York and Boston. To him belongs the honor of being the best Irish Setter of his period in America, not only because of his own awards, but also because of the success of his progeny on the bench and in the field. He was regarded as a great producer and was often referred to as "The Prince of Stud Dogs." Although some thought Elcho's own field qualifications were disappointing, he sired seven field-trial winners: Joe Jr., Berkley, Raleigh, Leigh Doane, Jessie, Yoube and Bruce.

More than 50 bitches had litters sired by Elcho, litters which included

30 bench show winners. He imparted quality, symmetry and refinement to his puppies, which characteristics predominated for several generations.

Although Elcho improved the breed in America as Palmerston did in England, he did not compare as an individual with that superlative specimen, being too low on his legs and much less impressive in head qualities. Elcho was said to have possessed a very dark red coat, a clean-cut 11-inch head, well-placed ears, lean neck, good shoulders, deep chest and properly curved quarters. He measured 24 inches at the shoulder and weighed 56 pounds.

In the spring of 1877, Dr. William Jarvis, Claremont, New Hampshire, acquired Ch. Elcho and kept him for many years as his own private shooting dog. He imported Rose (Palmerston - Flora) and Noreen (Garryowen - Cora) from Ireland. The matings of these two Palmerston bitches to Elcho gave America the finest Irish Setter foundation stock. The Elcho-Rose mating was repeated nine times and the Elcho-Noreen mating five times.

Perhaps one should say a few words concerning Dr. Jarvis, who, in addition to being a successful breeder and importer of Irish Setters, was a sportswriter of high merit. After being graduated from Boston Dental College in 1876, he practised his profession in Claremont and later became president of the New Hampshire Dental Society. He kept his Irish Setters and other blooded livestock on his farm three miles from town. Dr. Jarvis was eminent for his activities as a breeder and judge for more than a quarter of a century and for his steadfast support of the Irish Setter.

Matings among the imported dogs were common and frequently repeated in the decade prior to 1880. From these came the first pure-blooded, American-bred Irish Setters. During the next decade, importations were few; and to satisfy the increasing demand for top quality dogs created by the then flourishing dog shows, many trial matings were made among the American-breds, very few of which were repeated. For studs, the breeders fluctuated from winner to winner, usually without regard for bloodlines or for systematic breeding. In spite of the variation in type and the decided lack of uniformity in the puppies, some good dogs were produced, the most consistent winners of the era being descendants of the famous Ch. Elcho.

Perhaps the ten best known of Ch. Elcho's 197 puppies from 51 different dams were: Ch. Elcho Jr., Ch. Glencho, Bruce, Leigh Doane, Ch. Berkley, Ch. Yoube, Ch. Hazel, Raleigh, Lady Clare, and Norwood.

By far the greatest of them was Ch. Elcho Jr. The early American writers seem to be of one accord in acclaiming him the foremost individual of his breed in the United States, a statement confirmed by his show record. He was exhibited at more than forty shows, ranging from the puppy class at Boston in 1882 to Irish Setter Specials at Chicago in 1891, without a single defeat.

From writers' accounts, it would seem that Ch. Elcho Jr. was an upstanding, rangy dog of harmonious proportions, in which the "extreme limit of refinement" had been attained. He produced five bench champions: Duke Elcho, Edna H, Kildare, Seminole, and Kildare Glenmore. Even though he was not a field trial winner, he was a good shooting dog; and his owner did most of his winter shooting over him in the Carolinas where birds were plentiful. Dr. Jarvis was induced to part with Ch. Elcho Jr. at nearly ten years of age for $1,000 to head the Killarney Kennels of George H. Covert, Chicago. The new owner died within a year of the transfer and the dog's death occurred shortly afterward on November 8, 1891.

B. F. Seitner ranked the most successful Irish Setter sires as follows: Ch. Elcho, Plunket, Rufus, Ch. Glencho, Berkley, Erin, Ch. Elcho Jr., Biz, Norwood, Ch. Chief, Rory O'More, and Stoddard's Bob. Certainly Ch. Glencho, a litter brother to Ch. Elcho Jr., was entitled to high rank, having been the sire of litters from 55 bitches. Although he was considered to be somewhat too big according to the standard of his day, nevertheless he had much quality. Widely shown by his owner, W. H. Pierce, he won seven champion classes.

The decade following 1880 saw a rapid rise of the Irish Setter toward popularity, both on the bench and afield, chiefly due to the Elcho-Palmerston bloodlines.

Big winners among the Irish Setters at the turn of the century did not show the quality of those in the previous Elcho era, perhaps due to a lack of unity among the breeders.

The fact that each considered his own strain as the "standard of perfection" led to a wide divergence in type, the effect of which was evident for a long time. There were many "in and outers" in the dog game; certain individuals, after a few years of activity in Irish Setter affairs, lost interest completely. Were it not for some of the older breeders carrying on at that time, the breed would have suffered greatly.

Another factor that helped to maintain the breed was the importation of dogs from the British Isles. Ch. Winnie II and Desmond II were imported by Charles T. Thompson (Chestnut Hill Kennels), Philadelphia, from Reverend Robert O'Callaghan, England. They were the same breeding as the English champions Aveline and Shandon II. Their sire was Frisco, a grandson of Ch. Elcho, and their dam was Grouse II, a Ch. Palmerston daughter. Here again was the Palmerston - Elcho combination of bloodlines that had contributed so much to the early American strains.

Ch. Aveline "the beautiful," mated to her brother Fingal III, produced Coleraine, a field-trial bitch imported by E. B. Bishop, Hutchinson, Kansas.

A litter brother of Coleraine, Ch. Finglas, was imported in 1891, by S. L. Boggs of Pittsburgh. Apparently, this brother and sister mating was successful, for Ch. Finglas was a bench champion and field trial winner; and also the sire of three bench champions and seven field trial winners. His name occurs in the pedigree of almost every American-bred Irish Setter. His champion daughters were: Bessie Finmore, Red Bess II, and Red Bud

Finglas. Ch. Finglas was the Absolute Winner, All-Age Stake, American Field Trial Club, Columbus, Indiana, 1892.

The imported Irish Setters were well distributed in this country. F. H. Perry, Des Moines, Iowa, imported from Ireland a half-brother of Ch. Aveline, called Claremont Patsy (Frisco - Nellie IX). Nellie was a grand-daughter of Ch. Palmerston. Patsy was best known as being the sire of Chief Red Cloud, one of the forefathers of the Law strain.

A well-known breeder of Irish Setters in the Nineties was J. Gibbons Hawkes, Kenmore, Ireland, who was said to have had 26 field trial winners in his kennel at one time. Among them were the famous Muskerry and nine of his field trial winning get. Muskerry himself was not a field trial winner for the simple reason he never ran in a field trial. Hawkes passed him on to W. Hill Cooper who used him as his regular shooting dog, and he became the basis for his field trial strain. Three of the Muskerrys were imported to America: Blue Rock, Signal and Tearaway. Although Blue Rock was widely advertised at stud by Dr. William Jarvis, his record in America is not impressive.

On the other hand, Signal figured in the pedigrees of many Irish Setters, especially since his bloodlines seemed to nick well with those of the Finglas bitches; and the word "Signal" appeared in dogs' names over a ten-year period.

The importation of these sons of Muskerry to America had the effect of contributing ruggedness and field ability to the Palmerston - Elcho strain. Although Palmerston was in the fourth and the fifth generations of Muskerry's pedigree, the preponderance of other blood served as an outcross for the American stock.

The Gay Nineties in America brought forth many new breeders of Irish Setters. Kennel prefixes like Lismore of the Wall Brothers and Shamrock of the Carmichaels became famous around Chicago. L. L. Campbell and A. B. Truman upheld the Irish standard in California and Samuel Coulson did likewise in Montreal, Canada. A jumbling of the letters in the name of F. M. Thomas made a distinctive prefix for the "Thasmo" dogs. Then there were the Finmores—Bessie, Blanche, Cora, and Ruby—a quartet of bitches exhibited by W. H. Eakins, Columbus, Ohio. About this time kennels were established by F. H. Perry, G. O. Smith, Dr. J. S. Laycock, A. W. Pearsall, F. P. Kirby, George Kunkel, Michael Flynn, Joseph Lewis, and others.

The Law Strain

It has been stated that the Law suffix originated with old Shan Law in Ireland, a point which has not been substantiated. Nevertheless, in America the fountainhead of the Law strain was Ch. Ben Law (Chief Red Cloud - Nancy Finglas), whelped August 22, 1896, and owned by Charles A. Gale, Rutland, Vermont. Although Ben's three-year bench show career was not a straight string of victories, he had sufficient merit to win at

Westminster in 1901, thereby defeating among others, imported Prince Victor and Ch. Rockwood Jr. Mated to a dozen bitches, he sired 60 dogs, including the following seven champions: Conn Law, Hibernian Ben, Gael Law, Shan Law, Pat Law, Shandon Ben, and St. Cloud's Lorna. These six sons of Ch. Ben Law and their offspring played a prominent role in the development of the Irish Setter in America over a forty-year period. Of these brothers, Ch. Pat Law was the most prolific producer, siring 160 sons and daughters. He was owned by Walter McRoberts of Peoria, Illinois.

The Law setters were great shooting dogs. They were the choice of the market hunters in the early part of the century when prairie chickens were shot by the thousands on the Minnesota prairies and shipped in barrels to Chicago. In those days, hotels and railroad dining cars served upland game and wild fowl regularly on their menus. Law dogs were preferred for market hunting because they were bold, rugged "good-doers," sturdy and tireless, and possessed of sure bird finding ability.

Otto Pohl, a druggist and sportsman, owned an aggregation of Irish Setters that established an enviable reputation in field trials and bench shows around the Midwest. In 1909, Pohl bought Ch. Drug Law and Ch. Pat-A-Belle from Walter McRoberts and trained both dogs thoroughly for prairie chicken and quail shooting. Two years later, he became interested in bench shows and exhibited them throughout the Midwest. At that time they were much publicized in the dog literature by a lovely brace picture.

Pohl's first importation was Morty Oge (pronounced Augh), representing English field trial blood. Although this son of Dunboy and Alizon died about a year after his arrival in this country, he was used at stud with 15 bitches; consequently, he figures in the pedigrees of many American-breds of that period. He was a large, coarse, dark mahogany dog with a wide head. His best known son was Donegal's Morty Oge, out of Ch. Pat-A-Belle. This dog was not very successful in the show ring, chiefly because of his mediocre head. However, as he was superb in the field, Pohl did most of his shooting over him. The 17 bitches mated to him during his nine years flooded the Midwest with Morty Oge breeding, which accounted for many good bird dogs.

The second import was Mrs. M. Ingle-Bepler's young dog, Ch. Rheola Clanderrick (Ch. Clancarty Rhu - Rheola Ronda), who came over from England in 1914. Shortly after his arrival in this country, he won his championship easily and was widely used at stud. He was a very popular sire and the name of Clanderrick was carried along for more than forty years.

Two more Rheola dogs were imported in 1915, the dark, profusely coated Rheola Pedro (Galahad - Leverton Lass) and the small Rheola Judy (Rheola Bo'sun - Sh. Ch. Ypsilanti), both tracing back to Ch. Clancarty Rhu. Pedro, an excellent field dog, seemed to pass along to his offspring this field ability as well as his magnificent dark mahogany coat.

Although Rheola Judy was not a show dog because of her lack of size and desirable head character, her chief claim to fame was that she was the

Ch. Drug Law (Ch. Pat Law-Hurrah).

Ch. Drug Law (front) and Ch. Pat-A-Belle.

dam of the noted field trial winner, Donegal's Alizon, and the bench winner, Ch. Donegal's Judy Law, litter sisters sired by Ch. Drug Law.

Contemporary with McRoberts and Pohl were the bachelor brothers, Joseph and Thomas Wall, of Montreal, Chicago, and later Brooklyn. Their prefix which was derived from their ancestral home at Lismore, County Waterford, Ireland, was prominent in Irish Setter circles for forty years. Joseph was an officer in the Irish Setter Club of America and also a dog show judge. Well-known dogs in their kennels included Ch. Lord Lismore, Lord Lismore Jr., Ch. Lismore Colleen, Ch. Lismore Deirdre, Ch. Lismore Macree, Ch. Lismore Brendan, and Ch. Lismore Freedom. The consensus of opinion was that Colleen was the best setter the Walls ever owned. Of the two litter sisters, Deirdre and Macree, the former had the better show record. Ch. Lismore Freedom (Ch. Conn Law - Ch. Lismore Colleen) has been described as large, masculine, of good color, somewhat rough in shoulders, light eyed and a poor mover. In spite of his faults, he won his share of ribbons at bench shows from 1916 to 1921, and was a popular stud. He sired six champions and that wonderful bitch, Craigie Lea Mona, the dam of Ch. Higgins' Red Coat and Ch. Higgins' Red Pat.

Ch. Lismore Freedom and Ch. Midwood Red Jacket, a brother of Ch. Lismore Colleen, were close competitors in the show ring. These two dogs were of different stamp. Freedom was rugged and very masculine, whereas Red Jacket was smooth and refined. Both dogs won twice at Westminster.

The history of the Irish Setter in this country would not be complete without mention of the brothers, Louis and S. A. Contoit, St. Cloud Kennels, in the New York area. From 1889, when Louis registered St. Cloud (Ch. Elcho - Noreen), until his death about 1930, this man (to use his own words) "owned at least 5,000 Irish Setters," many of which carried the St. Cloud prefix. His forty-year career involved numerous champions, a multitude of acquaintances and a profound knowledge of Irish Setters. He preferred type and refinement in his setters and often expressed his opinion about "red Newfoundlands" and "red Dalmatians" in most uncomplimentary terms.

The Contoits were among the first to establish a modern strain of Irish Setters by line breeding. One of their favorite systems of breeding was to mate several sisters to the same sire and then to cross the offspring. They usually retained the bitches and sold the males in the litters. Most of the St. Cloud dogs trace back to Elcho - Noreen or to Elcho - Rose matings. Outstanding among their early sires were Ch. St. Cloud III and Ch. St. Cloud's Fermanagh, both beautiful type setters. The former was Winners Dog 35 times in 39 shows and the latter 10 times with no defeat. Other St. Cloud dogs to win the purple ribbon consistently were St. Cloud's Lorna, Kathleen, Laddie, Lurline, Rosamonde, Ruby, Shanmore, Star and Vida. The Contoits also used the Law dogs and the St. Lamberts in their breeding programs.

Ch. St. Cloud's Blarney (Elcho Ranger - Ch. Red Rose III) was the mainstay of the kennel of working setters owned by Clemer Bell and John

H. Chappell, Oakland City, Indiana. Blarney ran in three field trials, was shown 15 times and sired litters until he was 13 years old. Ch. Virginia Belle and Rob Rollo, both field trial winners, were among his 160 get.

F. A. Johnson, Detroit, owned Ch. St. Cloud's Kenmore (Ch. Heir - at - Law - Daisy Law), said to be a good field dog and popular stud. Cushbawn Desmond was imported from England by F. A. Walsh, Winnipeg. In Oakland, California, Peter N. Hanrahan had several champions named with the suffix "H," as Ch. Pat H, Ch. Jim H and Ch. Margaret H, which traced back to the Glenmore setters of L. L. Campbell. Other Irish Setter fanciers of the period included Stacey B. Waters, Michael Flynn, Fred Kirby, George Thomas and Ben Lewis.

After the turn of the century an increasing number of women became interested in the red setter. There were Mrs. Walter Simmons with Ch. Midwood Red Jacket, Miss E. L. Clarkson with Ch. Lansdowne Red Rose, Mrs. R. W. Creuzbauer with Ch. Lady Dakin II, Miss Elise Ladew with Ch. Carntyne Clodagh, Mrs. E. B. Chase with Ch. Bob White Red Storm, Mrs. E. Alban Sturdee with Ch. Richwoods Roy, Miss Marie Louise Welch with Ch. Barney O'Flynn and Mrs. Helen M. Talbot with Ch. Muskerry Fen. Miss Welch wrote a little book, *Your Friend and Mine* (1934), about the beauty, courage, affection and intelligence of the Irish Setter.

The 1920s

In the decade following World War I, there was an unprecedented increase in the number and popularity of Irish Setters. At least 200 of them were imported then from Canada and the British Isles. Interbreeding the many unrelated strains led to wide variations in breed size and type—as far apart as Spaniels, Whippets, Pointers, and St. Bernards, except in color. Even among the champions there was a decided lack of uniformity. Before the decade passed, however, there emerged from this "melting pot" a new, stylish, streamlined Irish Setter destined to set the type of the modern dogs. The old Law strain was on the decline, while the Boyne family originated by J. A. Carbery, Drogheda, Ireland, was ascending.

One characteristic of the era was the valiant attempt of Irish Setter owners to reinstate their breed in field trials. In the old days the red dogs had competed on even terms with other gun dogs. They had always been considered to be reliable shooting or "meat" dogs, but for one cause or another they lost caste in the trials. Various reasons were advanced for this, including breeding solely for the bench, slow maturing of puppies, lack of style and staunchness on point, the color handicap and loss of interest among owners.

Although the red setter seemed hopelessly outnumbered in field trials, there were some staunch backers of the breed as a field dog. One of them was G. O. Smith, Wheeling, West Virginia, who had imported the field trial winner, Young Signal, back in 1893. Thirty years later he was still interested to the extent that he imported several well-known stud dogs, including Tipperary Eamon, Billy Palmerston, Bran of Boyne and Raneagown.

The Irish Setters of Dr. John D. DeRonde (Palmerston Kennels), New York City, were in the forefront for about ten years. This enthusiastic breeder, judge and president of the Irish Setter Club of America kept approximately sixty dogs in his country kennels, from which he sold setters to almost every state in the Union, even as far west as California. Mary Pickford, the famous movie star, owned one of his breeding.

DeRonde's first big circuit winner was imported Tyrone Larry (Tyrone Terry - Sonora Norma), whelped in 1917 and purchased at three years of age from E. C. Howard, Montreal. This dark red, typey, 56-pound dog soon became a Canadian and American champion. His head was rather plain and his chief fault was quite straight stifles. In spite of this he built an enviable reputation during his long life. Widely advertised at stud, he was the sire of more than 140 registered offspring, many of which were exhibited at shows or run in field trials.

Ch. Palmerston Connemara Grand, Ch. Palmerston Jerry and Ch. Palmerston Red Mike also were owned by DeRonde. It is said that he refused a $10,000 offer for the last two-named dogs. Undoubtedly his best setter was Connemara Grand, imported from New Brunswick and the winner of 76 championship points and Best of Breed twice at Westminster.

One of the outstanding competitors of the Palmerston setters was Ch. Londonderry's Legion (Judge Law - Glencho Sally Oge), purchased for $1,000 from John Noroney, Toronto, to head the Londonderry Kennels of Charles H. Jackson, Forked River, New Jersey. This beautiful, dark red, 65-pound dog was a great favorite with the majority of judges.

Among the get of Ch. Londonderry's Legion was Ch. Londonderry's Legion II. Legion II established a breed record by completing his championship at the early age of nine months and 27 days. He rated high as a sire with such prominent get as Ch. Peggy Belle, Ch. Rascal Red Pat, Ch. Sheila Tullyval and Orchid Lady, the granddam of Ch. Milson O'Boy II and Ch. Milson Top-Notcher.

One of his sons from Ch. Lady Betty was Lewis H. Starkey's Redwood Ranger, first registered as Sunny Jim Redjacket. This changing of names, not unusual in the Twenties when transferring ownership of a dog, was most confusing. Ranger, an excellent specimen and one of the pillars of Redwood breeding, was the sire of Ch. Redwood Rita. When he had been shown only a few times, he injured a vertebra, which disfigured him, and his show career ended.

A contemporary of Legion was Ch. Celtic Admiration, later named Admiration quite appropriately because he was greatly admired for his beautiful head. He was owned by Dr. T. Joseph O'Connell, the 1924 New York State Trap Shooting Champion. This dog was the sire of Ch. Elcova's Admiration and the grandsire of the renowned Jordan Farm Abe.

About 1909, the kennel prefix St. Val appeared in the names of some excellent Irish Setters which carried the early Lismore and St. Cloud bloodlines. The profile of one of them adorned (in bas relief) the bronze medal of the Irish Setter Club of America. St. Val was the kennel name of Warren Delano, Jr. At his death, the kennel was dispersed.

In 1923, his daughter, Miss Laura F. Delano, Rhinebeck, New York, decided to continue the strain as a memorial to her father. After considerable search she acquired some of the same strain in Kerry Boy of Knocknagree (Ch. St. Joe Kenmore's Boy of Kelt - Glencho). Starting with this dog she bred setters of quality under the Knocknagree prefix. Among them were Ch. Duna Girl, Ch. My Duna Girl, Ch. Patricia Girl, Ch. Redleen Girl, Can. Am. Ch. Clondeen Girl, Can. Am. Ch. Cragie Girl, Can. Am. Ch. Lea Girl and Can. Am. Ch. Colley Boy (all of Knocknagree); and there was a whole dynasty of Kerry Boys, continuing at least to Kerry Boy of Knocknagree VIII.

On several occasions, the Knocknagree Irish Setters won the Best Team in Show award at Westminster and at the International.

Miss Delano was a judge as well as a breeder. In an address to the Irish Setter Club of America in 1952 she said, "Perfection is one goal for the Irish Setter, be it yours or your neighbor's. For me the tears of joy that have come to my eyes each time the great dogs have come under my sight and hands cannot be exceeded by any other joy. We must never let the attainment of this perfection discourage us and it will not, if we stick to what is top."

The Milson prefix, which played such an important role in Irish Setter history, was used by Sidney H. Sonn, Harrison, New York, from 1923 to 1930. Sonn started with three-months-old Milson Peggy (Ch. Lismore Freedom - Ch. Swifty Holden). Although this medium-sized, well-balanced setter became a popular favorite at shows and won her championship readily, she was probably best known as being the dam of Ch. Milson Sonny, Ch. Sheila IV and Ch. Fetridge's Pat, all sired by Ch. Higgins' Red Pat.

A kennelmate of Peggy, the lovely Milson Colleen (Kennard - Lismore Norna), died young; but in her one and only litter were Ch. Terence of the Cloisters, Ch. Patsy VI and Ch. Milson Tess. The bloodlines of both Peggy and Colleen were represented in Ch. Milson June Blossom.

Sonn's breeding program involved eight homebred bitches, including three that were not champions: Milson Pat's Girlie, Milson Goldie and Orchid Lady. Later generations proved the wisdom of his choice of brood matrons. Not an advocate of line breeding, he used various stud dogs from outside his own strain. For instance, Ch. Patsy VI produced litters from seven different sires.

About 1930, the Milson bloodlines were transferred to Harry Hartnett, then later to the Caldene Kennels of Dr. Jay W. Calhoon and again to the Knockross Kennels of Welrose L. Newhall.

Edwin M. Berolzheimer, president of the Eagle Pencil Company,

Ch. Rheola Clanderrick (Clancarty Rhu-Rheola Ronda).

Ch. Tyrone Larry (Tyrone Terry-Sonora Norma).

chose "of the Cloisters" as his kennel suffix, a term quite appropriately applied to his beautiful estate high above the Hudson River at Tarrytown. The architecture of his home with its high vaulted ceilings, enormous fireplaces and walls decorated with coats of mail, contributed to the theme of baronial or cloistered halls.

One of the top show dogs in the kennels was Ch. Terence of the Cloisters (Ch. Elcova's Terence McSwiney-Milson Colleen), noted especially for his beautiful front and exceptionally good feet. At the Cloisters all the dogs were trained to the gun. Berolzheimer became interested in field trials; and until his death in 1949, he energetically championed the cause of the Irish Setter in this competition.

At one time in his kennels there were four generations of field trial Irishers, headed by the first American Kennel Club Irish Setter field champion, Elcova McType (Ch. Elcova's Terence McSwiney-Modoc Bedelia). Mac, from field trial winning parents, won the All-Age Stake thrice at Irish Setter Club of America trials; but due to heartworm he ran in only a few trials. Among his noted descendants were: F. Ch. Clodagh McTybe, F. Ch. Shaun McTybe, Tyron McTybe, Brian McTybe and Rufus McTybe (all of the Cloisters).

Mac was bred and trained by one of America's foremost dog trainers, Elias C. Vail, who devoted most of his life in one way or another to the progress of field trials and dog research. His methods of training were aptly described by Ella B. Moffit in *Elias Vail Trains Bird Dogs* (1937). Vail was prominently identified with Irish Setters for many years. Although his Elcova dogs won frequently at shows, their chief renown was in the field. Ch. Elcova's Terence McSwiney, Ch. Elcova's Admiration, F. Ch. Elcova's McTybe, Elcova's Kinkie and Modoc Bedelia were best known. Vail ran his setters fearlessly in the trials at a time when other breeds were represented in overwhelming numbers and it was an uphill task for an Irish Setter to win.

Just as Colonel Bradley's Kentucky thoroughbreds had names beginning with "B," so the Kenridge dogs were registered with "K." C. C. Stillman, who popularized the Morgan horse in America, built the elaborate Kenridge Kennels in 1922 for his son, Elliot. Located on his spacious estate at Storm King Mountain, Cornwall, New York, they were complete to the last detail, including office, kitchen, hospital, grooming room and indoor exercise rings. Redwood walls, electric stove, no-draft windows, food chutes to the kitchen, a setter skeleton, microscope, life-size paintings and statuettes of the dogs were but a few of the special features. Percy Stoddard, who designed the kennels, was placed in charge of the establishment with its Irish Setters, Cocker Spaniels and Pointers.

Initially six Irish Setters were purchased from Dr. DeRonde, including Palmerston Molly Bawn; and from Canada came the foundation brood matron, Ch. Kenridge My Dear, Best Sporting Dog at Framingham in 1924.

Heading the Kenridge Kennels was Ch. Bergniel Red Helmet (Lord

Ch. Terence of the Cloisters, left; F. Ch. Elcova McTybe.

Ch. St. Cloud's Fermanagh III (Ch. St. Cloud VII-St. Cloud's Colleen).

Lismore II - Bergniel Guri), a most attractive dog with pleasing type and flowing gait—a consistent winner on the bench from 1923 to 1928. His most important win was Best in Show over 500 dogs at Paterson, New Jersey in September 1925. Incidentally, Best in Show and Group judging became an official procedure at American shows in 1925. The first Irish Setter to be crowned Best in Show was Ch. Modoc Morty Oge (also called Kildare's Morty Oge) at Des Moines on April 3, 1925. The second Irish Setter to win the award was imported Ch. Tadg at San Francisco and Oakland in May 1925.

Red Helmet was the sire of seven champions, among which were Emily Schweitzer's Ch. Verbu Red Mollie and William R. Lubben's Ch. Rex's Red Don. Ch. Kenridge My Dear had four litters by him. He died in 1928, on the same day that his master, young Elliot Stillman, was killed in an automobile accident in Arizona. Soon afterward the Kenridge Kennels were dispersed. At the time they housed four champion stud dogs, Ch. Terence O'Brien Law, Ch. Kenridge Kinsman, Ch. Kenridge Kelvin and Ch. Kenridge Klondyke. Although the period in which the Kenridge dogs were before the public was relatively short, they established a reputation because of the marvelous condition in which they were shown. They had a notable influence on the breed.

Interested in Irish Setters about this time were two parties of the same name but spelled differently, Mrs. Carl F. (Olga B.) Nielsen (Bergniel Kennels), Laurel Hill, New York, and C. Frederick Neilson (Rosecroft Kennels), Shrewsbury, New Jersey. The former, raising quality stock until 1926, mated her imported Molly of Laurel Hill to Ch. Lismore Freedom to obtain Ch. Bergniel Prince Charming and Bergniel Guri, the dam of Ch. Bergniel Red Helmet. The latter registered his Rosecroft prefix as early as 1905 and it was still current forty years later.

Another long time breeder and judge of Irish Setters, Mrs. E. Alban Sturdee, Albany (later Toronto), obtained her first dogs from Walter McRoberts in 1912. Probably the best known stud dogs in the kennel were Ch. Glencho Lanty and Glencho Morty O'Callaghan.

A noted favorite of the era was Ch. St. Cloud's Fermanagh III, preferred because of his refined type, general balance, grand head, perfect shoulders and deep chest. He was one of the first setters to possess the stylish, streamlined body and the elegant, upright carriage of neck and head so apparent in his pictures. This dog came honestly by these good points, being line-bred from Ch. St. Cloud III and the illustrious old Ch. St. Cloud's Fermanagh. As he had the ability to pass quality to his offspring for several generations, his influence on the breed was noted throughout the country in such kennels as Milson, Knocknagree, Hedgewood, Hollywood Hills, Rosecroft, Ruxton, Wamsutta and others.

Ch. St. Cloud's Fermanagh III was shown under the colors of Mrs. Cheever Porter of New York City, and was an ancestor of her famous Ch. Milson O'Boy and Ch. Rosecroft Premier.

A son of Fermanagh III, called Ruxton's Stop Light, headed the kennels of Ernest D. Levering, Ruxton, Maryland, for several years. These kennels contained several imported Irish Setters, including Ch. Queen of Barrymore, Ch. Sensation Dempsey, Letchworth Daisy, Niall of Aileach, Achler and Sally of Ballybay. Both Niall and Ruxton's Condonderry placed five times in shooting dog stakes at Eastern trials. At the time of his death in 1938, Levering had assembled a fine kennel of working setters. Perhaps his most important contribution to the Irish Setter in America was a litter by Ch. Higgins' Red Coat ex Ruxton's Tadg, in which there were four champions: Ch. Ruxton's Mollie O'Day, Ch. Maggie the Irish Lady, Ch. Ruxton's Wanda and Ch. Ruxton's Sean of Gruagach. He supplied foundation stock for the breeding programs of Jack Spear, Ward Gardner and Warren K. Read, Jr.

One of the most unique personalities in Irish Setter affairs and a man who contributed a large share of his life to the breed was William Cary Duncan. He owned gun dogs as a boy, even against his father's wishes. He loved setters—all three varieties—and for a time maintained the Thistlerock Kennels with R. B. Adams. Much of his interest lay in field trials until heart weakness interfered; but dogs proved to be a great relaxation from his intensive profession of writing musical comedies for Broadway. His best known setter was Ch. Elcova's Admiration, who was acquired from Elias Vail.

But it was not as a breeder that Duncan was eminent; he was the Irish Setter Club of America delegate to the American Kennel Club and breed correspondent for at least twenty years prior to his death in 1945. One has only to read his columns touched with Duncan humor and human interest to appreciate his real forte. Then, too, one never tires of reading his *Golden Hoofs,* a story about the famous trotter Goldsmith Maid; and *Dog Training Made Easy.* The sportsmen knew him as dog editor of *Outdoor Life.*

The Twenties will be remembered for their imported Irish Setters. No less than 30 Boyne dogs came from the kennels of J. A. Carbery, Drogheda, Ireland; about a dozen setters sired by Eng. Ch. Gruagach transferred from England; and others representing Gadeland, Glenariff, Ravenhill, Rheola, Sulhamstead and Wizbang strains arrived in America.

The Eng. Ch. Terry of Boyne (Eng. Ch. Brian of Boyne - Young Norah of Boyne) was imported in 1923 at the then record price of $2,600, to head the Woodbine Kennels of F. R. Wingerter, Hurdland, Missouri. Terry was not a big dog as he weighed only 59 pounds, but he was well balanced, deep chested and beautifully coated. Afield he was an excellent shooting dog, stylish and staunch on point. He died of pneumonia about two years after he came to America; however, in this short time he sired 259 progeny from 55 dams in 71 litters. Apparently he was not entered in bench shows and field trials in this country. Eight of his sons and daughters were imported from Ireland: Flora, Paddy, Kevin, Lanark, Mattie, Murty, MacQueen and Sean (all of Boyne).

Another importer of Irish Setters was Fred J. Lefferdink, Hickman,

Nebraska, whose Modoc kennel name graced the pages of sporting journals for more than three decades. Being actively engaged in field sports, he always required that his adult dogs be trained to the gun. Toward that end he acquired and bred utility stock.

On the West Coast about 1914, Mrs. Nancy Lee Fletcher Nannetti obtained Peggy O'Shagstone (St. Lambert's Larry - Noreen), who traced back to the older California strains. With Peggy as a start, Mrs. Nannetti developed her Shagstone Kennels of homebred champions famous through the years. In the 1920s, there were Ch. Joan, Ch. Irish Elegance, Ch. Copper Nob, Ch. The Duchess, Ch. Chancery Joan, Ch. Fine Feathers and Ch. The Bronze Baron (all O'Shagstone). The last three named dogs won Best in Show awards. At that time bench shows in the West were few and far apart, so several years were usually required to finish a champion.

Between 1926 and 1931, John M. Colbert of San Francisco, had eight imported Irish Setter bitches in his Shanagolden Kennels, including: Achler, Aryan, Ajmer, Bell O' Erin, Gertrude of Gramsceugh and Mairgread Dileas. He also owned the two imported brothers, Eng. Sh. Ch. & Am. Ch. Tadg and Ch. Liam (Eng. Ch. Gruagach - Oona of Derrynane). Tadg acquired an American championship in short order, winning 2 Bests in Show, 8 Sporting Groups and 10 Bests of Breed. His most popular win was to top 500 dogs at the 1925 Golden Gate Bench Show by the blind ballot of five judges. His best known get were Ch. Maura of Shanagolden and Ruxton's Tadg. Liam, not as good a bench specimen as Tadg, was said to be short in head and neck, and wide in skull.

Colbert purchased from the East the famous old campaigner, Ch. Bob White Pat Storm (Ch. St. Cloud's Fermanagh - Ch. Bob White Red Storm) and used him with some of his imported bitches to get Ch. Paddy of Shanagolden, Ch. Emma of Shanagolden and Ch. Duffy of Shanagolden. Paddy was a good sire, producing Ch. Baggage of Shanagolden, Ch. Barrymore of Shanagolden, Ch. Sheik of Shanagolden, Ch. Jordan Farm John and Ch. Wamsutta Cleopatra. In 1931, Colbert sold Emma for $1,500 and Paddy for $2,500 to Warren K. Read, New Bedford, Massachusetts; Sheik for $1,000 to Victor Eisner, Atherton, California; and Ch. Maura of Shanagolden to Robert W. Gerdel (Killbuck Kennels), Wooster, Ohio. These dogs played most important roles in the breeding programs of many kennels. It is significant that the strain represented by Ch. Bob White Pat Storm returned to the East.

7

The Middle Years

IN 1923, William W. Higgins, Charleston, West Virginia, imported from J. A. Carbery, Drogheda, Ireland, a small dark mahogany, profuse-coated Irish Setter named Higgins' Paddy of Boyne (Eng. Ch. Terry of Boyne - Dora of Boyne). Although Paddy did not compete in bench shows or field trials, he became famous as a sire and exerted a great influence on the breed in America. It was not that his offspring from fifteen of the sixteen bitches bred to him were outstanding, but that his matings with Craigie Lea Mona resulted in a most successful nick.

Craigie Lea Mona (Ch. Lismore Freedom - Clare II), bred by Maurice Brill of Mount Kisco and owned by Higgins, came from good old American stock carrying the blood of Ch. Conn Law, Ch. Lismore Colleen, Ch. St. Cloud's Fermanagh and Ch. Bob White Red Storm. She was a relatively large, solid red bitch; and not timid as some rumors would have it. She was professionally trained afield by O. S. Redman. Although never in the show ring, she was of excellent conformation.

The Big Six

Paddy sired four litters from Mona, all bred by Higgins. From this combination came six champions of great renown and importance to the breed:

Ch. Higgins' Red Pat, whelped 4-26-24
Ch. Higgins' Red Coat, whelped 9-30-27
Ch. Sister A. C. F., whelped 9-30-27
Ch. Barney of Boyne, whelped 5-30-28
Ch. Rose of Sharon II, whelped 5-30-28
Ch. Patricia of Boyne, whelped 2-1-29

Ch. Higgins' Red Pat (Higgins' Paddy of Boyne-Craigie Lea Mona).

Ch. Higgins' Red Coat (Higgins' Paddy of Boyne-Craigie Lea Mona).

Paddy was the sire of one other champion, bred by Maurice L. Baker and owned by Jack Spear, called Ch. Tyronne Farm Jerry, out of Ch. Hedgewood Judy. Mona produced only six champions.

It is of interest that Ralph and Irene Hallam of Chicago, at one time owned all six champions together with their sire and their dam—probably the greatest aggregation of Irish Setters ever assembled in one kennel. He is said to have paid $5,000 for Red Pat, $1,250 for Sister and $7,000 for the others. Many believe that Red Pat was the best Irish Setter that ever lived; Red Coat, of course, was the noted sire of 30 champions; Sister had but one litter; Rose of Sharon II never whelped any puppies; while Barney and Patricia were bred together in a brother and sister mating. The progeny of Paddy and Mona almost usurped bench show honors in America for a quarter of a century. Afterward, it became increasingly difficult to preserve a fair percentage of this blood, but nearly every American-bred Irish Setter had some of it in his pedigree.

The strain possessed certain outstanding qualities such as clean, arched necks flowing into beautiful shoulders, extreme depth of chest with accompanying short forearms, and lovely eye and ear placement. When the dog reclined on the bench with body in upright position, the shoulder blades were nearly horizontal, which served to emphasize their length and layback. Refinement even to a fault, breed type exemplified by thin lips and ear leather, blood vessels showing in the muzzle and well domed occiputs— all imparted distinctive Irish Setter quality. The strain has been criticised at times for light eyes, for heads small in proportion to the bodies and for gay tails. It is observed that both long and short coats were found on Red Coat progeny and occasionally some white markings. In spite of these faults which appeared infrequently, the strain was far above average. The dogs were slow in developing, usually requiring more than eighteen months to mature; but they did not grow coarse with age—they were "lasters."

Isn't it true that the popularity of a breed more or less parallels the sensational show wins of some prominent representative of the breed? Red Pat's unusual American Kennel Club record of 24 Bests in Show, 43 Bests in Group and 74 Bests of Breed awards did much to bring the Irish Setter to public favor. A wonderful showman and campaigner, Pat traveled thousands of miles in his career on the bench from the time he was first exhibited in the Novice Class at Westminster in 1926, until his farewell appearance at Madison Square Garden six years later. In his first seven shows, his class wins were not impressive, but thereafter his record was a seldom broken string of victories at the largest shows. He became an American and Canadian champion.

One of the highlights of his career was the 1926 Sesquicentennial show in Philadelphia, where he was the choice of the "Squire of Inglehurst," Charles T. Inglee, for Best of Breed over the superbly conditioned and perfectly ring mannered Ch. Londonderry's Ambition.

It was an award of historical importance when Red Pat won Best in Show at the first Morris and Essex event, a spectacular one day show with

Ch. Barney of Boyne (Higgins' Paddy of Boyne-Craigie Lea Mona).

Ch. Rose of Sharon II and Ch. Sister A.C.F.

504 entries held May 28, 1927, on the polo field of the famous Giralda estate of Marcellus Hartley Dodge, Madison, New Jersey. By this splendid win the ringside favorite acquired a leg on the Percy A. Rockefeller Silver Trophy.

Pat was awarded first in the Sporting Group at the second Morris and Essex Show by A. F. Hochwalt; and it was at this occasion that the contest in Irish Setters was between the two past masters of the handling profession, Ben Lewis with Pat and Percy Roberts with Ch. Bergniel Red Helmet.

The Dr. Davis Memorial Cup for Best Irish Setter was won by Pat in 1926, 1927, 1928 and 1930. He also won the Cornwall specialty show in 1930 and Best of Breed at Westminster on three occasions. He placed Best in Group at Worcester County show, September 1, 1930, in an entry of 72 Irish Setters, including 17 champions. It was at this show that the Parade of Champions was introduced. Harry Hartnett handled Pat on the Eastern Circuit and Colonel R. L. Davis guided him in the Midwest. In his career on the bench he defeated even his own brothers and sisters. About the only top-ranking contemporary that he did not defeat was Ch. Delaware Kate; and it seems that these two never met in the show ring.

As a young dog Pat was field trained by O. S. Redman. He and his sister, Ernst Nancy Langhorne, were entered in the Derby Stake (29 starters), West Virginia Field Trial Association, October 1925; but neither dog placed.

Twenty bitches were bred to Red Pat, resulting in 65 registered offspring and including six champions: Ch. Ardmore Ringleader, Ch. Duke of Red Pat, Ch. Cloudburst Red, Ch. Fetridge's Pat, Ch. Milson Sonny and Ch. Sheila IV.

Red Pat died of cancer in the veterinary hospital at the University of Pennsylvania on July 9, 1932.

In 1930, when Hallam purchased the Higgins' dogs, Red Pat was a champion and all the others except Sister had not been shown. Dr. A. C. Foster got Sister A. C. F. (note the doctor's initials) as a puppy from his friend Bill Higgins and easily put eleven championship points on her at big Eastern shows. Hallam speedily finished her championship requirements with a five-point Best of Breed at Greenwich. Thereafter, she was shown infrequently because she was the household pet of Irene Hallam. Sister might well rank as one of the great Irish Setter bitches of America and certainly she was far ahead of her time in type. Her extreme length of neck and well proportioned body combined to produce an unusually stylish appearance. It is unfortunate that the mold in which Sister was cast has been lost. She had only one litter, that sired by the beautifully headed Ch. St. Cloud's Fermanagh III; and in this litter there was only one dog, Sigvale's Captain Costigan.

The literature is scant concerning the first three years in the life of Sister's litter brother, Ch. Higgins' Red Coat. He was first shown under the Hallam colors at Cedar Rapids and at the Western Specialty show in 1930.

His next show was Westminster, which stands out as of particular interest in Irish Setter history, because Hallam showed the "Big Six" full brothers and sisters. Mrs. E. A. Sturdee placed Ch. Rose of Sharon II as Best of Breed and Red Coat as Winners Dog. This was really the start of his career under Harry Hartnett's guidance, which eventually totaled to one Best in Show and 36 Best of Breed awards. Although his bench record may not be as good as that of Red Pat, he placed in the Sporting Group twice at Westminster and three times at Morris and Essex. In 1931, he was transferred to C. Frederick Neilson of Rosecroft fame, who owned him until his death in July 1939. The last eight years of his life were spent in Hartnett's Milson Kennels at Harrison, New York, where he lived the life of Riley.

Red Coat's claim to fame is as the sire of 30 bench champions. He is credited with 220 registered get from 39 bitches, representing 45 litters. The largest litter, whelped September 13, 1934, from Red Pal Mag and bearing the Oakdene suffix of Dr. Gilman S. Currier, contained 14 puppies.

Probably Red Coat's most famous litter was that containing four champions, whelped September 4, 1932, from Ruxton's Tadg (Ch. Tadg - Ch. Mairgread Dileas). Then there were three other litters, each containing three champions from Colleen Girl of Knocknagree, Ch. Queen Maive and Ch. Redwood Rita.

In August 1930, Hallam started Rose of Sharon II and her litter brother, Barney of Boyne, on the Midwestern Circuit where the former consistently won Best of Breed and the latter Winners Dog. Handled by R. L. Davis on the Southern Circuit, Rose continued to win; however, at Kansas City she lost to Ch. Delaware Kate. The following year Red Pat, Barney and Patricia were frequently shown in the vicinity of Chicago and in the South, where they usually accounted for top breed honors. The relative ranking of the Hallam dogs varied somewhat under different judges. A summary of their bench records as tabulated from *American Kennel Gazette* follows:

	Best in Show	Best in Group	Best of Breed
Ch. Higgins' Red Pat	24	43	74
Ch. Higgins' Red Coat	1	13	36
Ch. Sister A. C. F.	0	3	10
Ch. Rose of Sharon II	4	19	27
Ch. Barney of Boyne	0	1	9
Ch. Patricia of Boyne	5	9	14

At eight years of age Ch. Rose of Sharon II, handled by Hollis Wilson, won two Best in Show and ten Best of Breed awards at Midwestern shows in 1935. She was one of the finest moving Irish Setters of all time; she would literally "float" around the show ring. Rose never had any puppies.

Ch. Barney of Boyne was a strongly built dog of pleasing proportions, but his skull was wide, a fault he passed along to many of his progeny. In brother and sister matings of Barney and Patricia, two litters were whelped, the first of which contained Patricia of Boyne II and Rosemary of Hallamshire.

Ralph Hallam died of pneumonia in November 1935, after which his famous kennel of Irish Setters was widely dispersed. Old Paddy of Boyne died shortly before his owner.

There is an interesting story concerning J. A. Carbery of the Boyne Kennels. Since this famous Irish kennel had such an impact on our American dogs, it is well worth the telling. It was originally told to W. J. Rasbridge by Percy Bishop, a member of the Bishop family, famous in Pointer and Setter trial history for three generations over fifty years ago. The same story was again repeated to Mr. Rasbridge some twenty years later by Earnest Scott of the famous Herewithem Pointers, whose reputation for getting the facts has never been doubted, and who would not have passed on the story if he had questioned its accuracy.

At one time Carbery and Percy Bishop were in some sort of partnership. The two men had a falling out, and Bishop was chucked out. While Carbery was in England judging, Percy Bishop claimed he went back to the kennels (to which he had retained the key) and opened all the kennel doors, so that any bitch was accessible to any dog, including the powerful yard Bloodhound and a Flat-coat.

There is no question that the Boynes of the early '20s showed Bloodhound-Flat-coat traits. A notable example of the former was the bitch Maga who showed haw and was very throaty. Many Carbery pedigrees of this era peter out into Setters not registered and of odd breeding, but that some were retained and influence the breed today can be left to the reader's imagination. Certainly this could account for the loose eyelids, and Mr. Rasbridge and others attribute bloat found in the breed today to the Bloodhound cross, however it was introduced—deliberately or accidentally!

The Descendants of Red Coat

It was during the early Thirties that Dr. Arthur A. Mitten of Philadelphia, acquired the Smoot collection of Setters for his Happy Valley Kennels. Included were four English Setter champions and the famous imported Irish Setter, Ch. Delaware Kate (Ravenhill Phil - Delaware Mill Lass). Kate, a champion in England, Ireland and the United States, was never defeated by an Irish Setter in America—Kate and Red Pat did not meet in competition. She won 8 Bests in Show and 21 Best in Group awards. In the show ring she had personality plus—a big, upstanding, magnificent bitch that no judge could overlook. Some ranked her as the top Irish bitch of all time. Her death in 1932 from complications while whelping a litter sired by Ch. Cloudburst Red, brought great sadness to her owner and serious loss to the breed.

After Ch. Higgins' Red Pat and Ch. Higgins' Red Coat came their sons and daughters to hold the center of the stage. Red Pat's blood was not especially influential, but Red Coat's effect on the breed was tremendous. As the years passed, there was scarcely an American-bred Irish Setter without some of his blood.

The history of the 1930's is one devoted largely to the Ch. Higgins' Red Coat family. Many of the best bitches of the day were sent to Red Coat or to his well known sons. Among these matings certain litters stood out as superlative.

Some branches of the family became especially prominent—those lines from his three sons: Ch. Milson O'Boy, Ch. Kinvarra Son of Red Coat and Ch. Redwood Russet of Harvale.

Ch. Milson O'Boy (Ch. Higgins' Red Coat - Milson Miss Sonny), owned by Mrs. Cheever Porter of New York City, was one of the greatest show dogs of all time. If ever a dog had public appeal it was he, and those who saw him will never forget him. There are many interesting stories about O'Boy, some of which were recorded in a book by Dr. Jay W. Calhoon, published as a memorial to O'Boy.

In a five-year period, Ch. Milson O'Boy accumulated 11 Bests in Show, 46 Bests in Group and 103 Best of Breed awards. He won Best in Show at Morris and Essex in 1935, over an entry of 3175 dogs of 73 breeds, including 120 Irish Setters. After his retirement at the height of his career in 1938, he led an easy life as a pet devoted to his mistress. On June 29, 1945, he died in his sleep at 13 years of age and was laid to rest in the peaceful quiet of Hartsdale Cemetery.

As time passed, it became apparent that O'Boy was a key producing sire. According to the records, he sired 163 puppies in 41 litters. Outstanding among his sons were Ch. Milson Top-Notcher and Ch. Milson O'Boy II. Top-Notcher was owned at various times by Milson Kennels, Rosecroft Kennels, Caldene Kennels and the Honorable Mrs. Katherine St. George, U.S. Congresswoman from New York. Mrs. St. George and Mrs. Allan A. Ryan, her daughter, were co-owners of several noted Irish Setters, including imported Ch. Beorcham Blameless, imported Ch. Red Sails of Salmagundi, Ch. Jordan Farm Lady and Ch. Headliner the Flaming Beauty.

Top-Notcher was awarded Best of Winners at the 1935 New England specialty the first time shown. During the next five years he acquired 5 Bests in Show, 29 Bests in Group and 115 Best of Breed awards. He was an excellent show dog and seldom failed to place in the Sporting Group. He was a smaller dog than O'Boy and unlike his sire, was inclined towards timidity.

Ch. Milson O'Boy II is identified with one of the greatest kennels of the breed—Knightscroft, owned by Joseph P. and Henrietta M. Knight. Shortly before his death in 1980, Joseph Knight wrote of Knightscroft's beginnings:

"Along about 1932, Mrs. Knight and I received a present of an Irish Setter dog from Fred Nielson of Rosecroft Kennels, which we registered as Louden Knight's Terry. This started us on Irish Setters. Terry was no show

Ch. Milson O'Boy (Ch. Higgins Red Coat ex Milson Miss Sonny).

Ch. Milson Top-Notcher (Ch. Milson O'Boy-Milson Squire's Janice).

Ch. Rosecroft Premier (Ch. Milson O'Boy II ex Rosecroft Fern).

Ch. Caldene Mickey Mischief, owned by Virginia Backstrom
(Milson O'Boy II ex Jordan Farm Molly).

dog, but became a fine quail dog.

"Not too long after, Fred Nielson began to disperse his kennel and gave us several of his fine bitches. We studied the breed, attended some shows and did some breeding, but soon found we were not producing really good Irish Setters.

"We decided to get a real good stud and bought from Harry Hartnett a dog named Milson O'Boy II, who we later finished to championship. We bred him to several Milson bitches, notably Rosecroft Fern, Rosecroft Mona and Rosecroft Kitty Kelly, with good results. Then we began to click.

"One day, we put several pups in the station wagon and went down to Fred Nielson's in New Jersey to get his opinion. He fell in love with one called "Billy" and wanted to buy him. We told him that because of all he had done for us, we couldn't sell him anything, but the pup was his to keep. This fellow, the first champion of our breeding, was Rosecroft Premier—a many time Best in Show winner.

"During the course of our Irish Setter career, we actually bred 37 champions, many of which I handled for the kennel and for clients." The 37 included such famous names as Ch. Knightscroft Danny O'Boy, Ch. K. Dollymount Dan, Ch. K. Fermanagh, Ch. K. Patty Boyne, Ch. K. Squire Muldoon and Ch. K. Symphony. Knightscroft was dissolved following Mrs. Knight's death in 1963.

Ch. Rosecroft Premier (Ch. Milson O'Boy II ex Rosecroft Fern, 4-9-38) was acquired by Mrs. Cheever Porter. Of bold and fiery disposition, Premier cut quite a figure in the show ring where he amassed a record of: 12 Bests in Show, 53 Bests in Group, and 124 Bests of Breed. He won ten specialty shows. Outstanding among his progeny were Ch. Seekonk Patty O'Byrne, Ch. Milson Christopher Robin, Ch. Caldene Jamaica, Ch. End O'Maine Luckalone and End O'Maine Sarah Jane.

Ch. Milson O'Boy II was also an ancestor of three Shawnlea champions, bred by May H. Hanley, Rehoboth, Massachusetts. Ch. Shawnlea's Purcell O'Gorman was one of the top ten Irish Setters of 1950. Ch. Shawnlea's Fanfare, a stylish, well balanced Irishman, had a fine bench record, including three Best in Show wins. Miss Hanley bought her first Irish Setter in 1933, a son of Ch. Wild Irish Ringleader. She owned dogs of Knightscroft, Wamsutta, Charles River and other bloodlines.

The Milson Kennels of Sidney H. Sonn were managed by Harry Hartnett from 1923 to 1930. Then on the death of Mr. Sonn, Harry purchased the kennels and bred and exhibited many fine Setters. He handled the four brilliant stars to Best in Show wins: Red Coat, O'Boy, Top-Notcher and Premier. In 1944, when he retired in poor health, the Milson breeding stock was transferred to Dr. Jay W. Calhoon, Uhrichsville, Ohio.

The doctor first became interested in Irish Setters in 1936, when he purchased Judy Legore Colquohoun as a puppy from Dr. Clyde Leeper. She later became an American and Canadian champion. He also acquired

Knockross O'Boy, owned by W. L. Newhall, (Ch. Caldene Mick O'Boy ex. Ch. Sharoc Coquette).

Ch. Knightscroft Symphony, owned by Helen Naylor
(Ch. Knightscroft Erin Elan ex Ch. Knightscroft Aileen Adair).

Ch. Baggage of Shanagolden, Jordan Farm Patsy, Jordan Farm Molly and the Milson dogs. Next he bred his matrons to the following sires: Ch. The Baron Gore, Ch. Killbuck Red Duke, Ch. Milson O'Boy, Ch. Milson O'Boy II, Ch. Harvale Hero, Ch. Rosecroft Premier, Ch. Seekonk Patty O'Byrne and others. The fusion of Milson and Jordan Farm bloodlines produced excellent results that have had a lasting effect on breed type in America. Among the 20 or more champions of Caldene prefix were: Ch. Caldene Judson, Ch. C. Jamaica, Ch. C. Picardy and Ch. C. M'Boy. Ch. Caldene Patrice and Ch. Caldene Pixie were considered great brood matrons. At times there were 60 dogs in the kennels and puppies were sold to all parts of the United States. Ch. Caldene Mickey Mischief represented the strain in the West. When the Caldene Kennels was dispersed in 1952, most of the stock, including Picardy, Polly and Rita, went to the Knockross Kennels of Welrose L. Newhall, Coraopolis, Pennsylvania.

The successful breeding program of Dr. Calhoon and the preservation of the Milson bloodlines was carried on by "Slim" Newhall. For a time Ch. Caldene Mick O'Boy (sire of 9 champions) was his foremost stud dog; but in 1960, Mick's son Knockross' O'Boy took over—he became sire of 36 champions. Although Knockross' O'Boy obtained 14 points toward a championship, he did not acquire the title because he accidentally became blind in one eye. His progeny included the Wheatleys' Ch. Caldene Ailene, Mrs. Charles Crawford's Ch. Knockross' Ruby, Mrs. C. E. Holvenstot's Ch. Knockross' Sally, Walter McCoy's Ch. McCoy's Squire of Verbu, Emily Schweitzer's Ch. Verbu Erin and Ch. Verbu Maureen, Dr. H. F. Kinnamon's Ch. Knockross' Red Patti and others. Ruby was bred to Ch. Draherin Irish Regardless four times and produced 21 champions from these matings. Among them were Ch. Shannon's Shawn of Erin, Ch. Shannon's Erin, Ch. Major O'Shannon, and Ch. Shannon's Laird Shane.

Other Ch. Milson O'Boy progeny of note included the Oakdene litter from Red Pal Mag, the Milhaven one from Princess Dido, O'Waccabuc from Loughdune O'Waccabuc, O'Flynn from Ch. Cloudburst O'Flynn of Lastery, Kinvarra from Ch. Kinvarra Zoe and Hedgewood from Hedgewood Lea Mona.

Although Mag never became a champion, she produced six champions in three litters. One of her litters by Ch. Higgins' Red Coat contained 14 puppies. Rather exceptional was the fact that all eight placements in the Junior Puppy Classes at the 1935 Morris and Essex Show were awarded to dogs from this litter. Dr. Gilman S. Currier bred several Oakdene champions, including Ch. Judge Red Pal of Oakdene, Ch. Rosie O'Grady O'Oakdene and Ch. Oakdene's Barbarossa.

In the Princess Dido litter, Serena should be mentioned as the important producing dam of five West Coast champions. The O'Flynn litter contained Ch. Pat McCauley O'Flynn, bred by Marie Louise Welch and owned by Harry A. McCauley of Baltimore. The Independence Day litter from Ch. Kinvarra Zoe will be remembered for Ch. Kinvarra Ensign and Ch. Maggie the Irish Lady II.

Ch. Caldene Ailene, owned by Frank and Katherine Wheatley (Knockross O'Boy ex Ch. Katy-Did of Maple Ridge).

Ch. End O'Maine Luckalone, owned by Hollis and Jo Wilson (Ch. Rosecroft Premier ex Ch. End O'Maine Best Wishes).

Ch. End O'Maine McCabe, owned by Orrin Evans (Ch. End O'Maine Luckalone ex Kendare Nano Nagle).

The Hedgewood Lea Mona litter, owned by Maurice L. and Beryl Baker, Minneapolis, Minnesota, could well typify what O'Boy did for the breed. There were ten puppies, as alike as ten peas. Domed top-skulls, low-set ears, lovely heads, gorgeous shoulders and great depth of chest were apparent at an early age.

It was the Bakers' custom to name their Setters after famous horses. Starting with the Law strain in 1925, they linebred for 16 or more generations to the Paddy of Boyne - Craigie Lea Mona strain with occasional outcrosses, the practice being to select the best bitch in each litter to propagate the strain. They bred forward using young blood and did not repeat matings. Outstanding among the Hedgewood champions as excellent examples of refined breed type were Ch. Hedgewood Rhea Rita, Goldsmith Maid of Hedgewood, Ch. Hedgewood Plainsman, Ch. Hedgewood Regret and Kendare Color Bearer. Maurice's keen observation of desirable qualities in dogs has been a valuable asset in breeding and showing; and it led to his competence as an all-breed judge.

The End O'Maine Setters of Hollis and Jo Wilson, Amherst, Wisconsin, were known from coast to coast. Hollis hunted over Setters as a boy and later owned Irish Setters in partnership with a fellow townsman, J. W. Delaney. About 1924, he established the End O'Maine Kennels. His first Irish Setter champion was Ch. Raggen of Lanark. Next he bought Ch. Belle's Anniversary, bred her to Ch. Golden Dawn of Gadeland and thereby obtained End O'Maine Autumn Leaf. From then on there was an unbroken succession of End O'Maine bloodlines.

The Wilsons were advocates of breeding to noted sires. They raised brood matrons of traditional End O'Maine quality, such as the following champions: End O'Maine Beg Pardon, Kathleen, Burnie Burn, Encore, Refrain and Pigeon. Undoubtedly their favorite female was Ch. End O'Maine Best Wishes. It is of special note that the Ch. Carrvale's Terry Terhune - End O'Maine Claret litter, whelped 3-14-57, set a breed record at the time in that it contained seven champions.

End O'Maine dogs served as foundation stock in many kennels. For instance, Joyce Holzman Nilsen's Ch. Kinvarra Portia, the dam of a dozen champions, made a tremendous contribution to the breed, as did Ch. End O'Maine McCabe, owned by Professor Orrin Evans of the University of Southern California Law School. The Wilsons retired from showing dogs and raising Setters in the summer of 1962, when Hollis became a dog show judge.

Another who contributed many years of his life to the progress of the Irish Setter was Jack A. Spear, Tyronne Farm Kennels, Tipton, Iowa. The kennel name was derived from County Tyrone, Ireland, the ancestral home of the Spears.

In 1934, Jack purchased Jordan Farm Nancy and Ch. Tyronne Farm Joan from Jordan Farm Kennels and Ch. Tyronne Farm Jerry from Maurice Baker. Early in the following year he bought the famous producing dam and lovely show bitch, Ch. Ruxton's Mollie O'Day from E.

Ch. Tyronne Farm Clancy
(Ch. Tyronne Farm Tipperary-Ch. Tyronne Farm Kay).

D. Levering, showed frequently and widely, and soon his Setters were well known. In the course of time he obtained Ch. End O'Maine Kathleen from Jo Wilson. The two Red Coat daughters were mated to Ch. Kinvarra Kermit in what seemed to be two perfect nicks. The Kermit-Mollie litter of 2-13-39 contained six champions; and the Kermit-Kathleen litter of 8-27-39 had four. Mollie, first bred at seven years of age, had only five litters and 35 puppies in her lifetime; but she produced 14 champions. Her daughter, Ch. Tyronne Farm Debutante, a large well proportioned Setter, was a universal favorite.

O'Flare and Collette were best known as field trial winners. One cannot hope to name all the prominent Tyronne Farm field dogs, but some of them stand out, as Merriwynne, Countess, Kay, Frolic, DeEtte and others.

Ch. Tyronne Farm Malone
(Ch. Kinvarra Kermit-Ch. Ruxton's Mollie O'Day).

Over the years most of the Spears' Setters were homebreds, some of the champion sires being: Tyronne Farm O'Brien, Tipperary, Malone and Shanahan. O'Brien was a rugged individual, Tipperary was more refined, the grand-headed Malone stamped his get with size and style, and Shanahan threw puppies of nice breed type.

The Tyronne Farm dogs had their own individuality, difficult to describe, yet easily observed. In the show ring they were prominent for thirty years, winning fifty or more championship titles and at least fifty Best in Show awards. Ch. Tyronne Farm Clancy, the top winning Irish Setter for 1949, was awarded 19 Best-in-Show ribbons. His most thrilling win was Best in Show at Morris & Essex in 1950. Ch. Tyronne Farm Shanahan after completing his title was never defeated in the breed, always placed in the Group and won five Best in Show awards.

Some of Jack's dogs were transferred to various sections of the United States where they served as foundation stock for other kennels. Ch. Tyronne Farm Malone II, owned by Kinvarra Kennels, has had an impressive effect on the breed, even extending for several generations. On the West Coast, Ch. Tyronne Farm Malone through Ch. Seaforth's Dark Rex and Ch. Innisfail Color Scheme has made a great contribution— approximately 75 per cent of the California Irish Setter show dogs have his bloodlines. The Webline, Enilen, County Clare, Lismoro, Glendee, Wildwood, Shamrock, Yorkhill and other kennels had Tyronne Farm stock.

Ch. Tyronne Farm Shanahan
(Ch. Tyronne Farm Malone-Ch. Tyronne Farm Merriwynne).

Lee M. Schoen, Master of the Kinvarra Kennels in Darien, Connecticut, prominent judge, breed historian, successful author of animal stories, prominent in the New York City wholesale fur business and a past president of the Irish Setter Club of America, is in the author's opinion, one of the foremost authorities on the breed in the world.

Kinvarra, a township in County Galway, was selected from a list of 500 name possibilities (scientifically, by vote, as though the owner sensed some future significance). The name (said to mean "Community of Kin") was registered in 1932, several years after Lee began to rear Irish Setters, and three years after the first of a flow of importations that continued (except during World War II) virtually uninterrupted for nearly half a century.

In the early years Kinvarra was partnered by Mrs. H. D. Werden. This kind lady, always so helpful to all who asked her for advice, was a conditioner-groomer supreme. Lee likes to point out how lucky he was to have been associated with her.

The most important of his early importations was the bitch, Borrowdale Yseult of Kinvarra. Lee describes her as being not much over 23 inches in height, dark, lustrous and very beautiful to watch in the field. Mated to the successful show dog, Ch. Kinvarra Son of Red Coat, she produced the small but elegant, Ch. Kinvarra Craig. And from these three dogs came a line of champion descendants that carry on today in most of the breed's more prominent kennels.

A steady stream of champions came from this kennel in the 1930s, '40s and '50s. The last included Ch. Kinvarra Bootsie, not only an excellent brood matron but a successful field trialer as well, trained and handled by her owners. Ch. Kinvarra Mary Eileen, queen-pinned a big day for Kinvarra when she came from the Novice Class to go Best of Breed at Morris and Essex in 1957, while her litter brother, Ch. Kinvarra Lord Raglan, also from Novice, took Winners Dog, Reserve (from first Open) fell to Ch. Kinvarra Kimson—all at the same show! The next year, Kimson was first in the Group at Westminster!

In 1936 Lee imported the bitch, Ch. Kinvarra Mollie of Gadeland, for the author. She became the foundation bitch at Tirvelda. How she did is best described in Schoen's own words:

"Ted wrote me in London asking which of three particular bitches was the best in Britain and most suitable for American competition. I dutifully jotted down which I preferred, then debated with myself: was it fair *not* to tell the boy—then fourteen—that I had myself bought for Kinvarra a younger bitch I rated best of all?"

Lee lost that debate: ten-month-old Mollie crossed the Atlantic with him for delivery to Eldredge—fortunately, in that before Eldredge's inquiring letter arrived (by air on the Hindenburg, no less), Mrs. Baker, mistress of Gadeland, had already booked her for export to Kinvarra. Under the agreement, however, her first litter's sire, and best puppy in it, would be chosen by Kinvarra.

Ch. Kinvarra Kermit
(Ch. Kinvarra Craig-Ch. Kinvarra Mollie of Gadeland).

Subsequently, for that first litter, Mollie was bred to Craig. The result became breed history. In a litter of fourteen, later to do much winning, Schoen, with the tribe just over two months, narrowed his choice down to two males. After much looking and posing, Lee was at a loss as to which he should take. Finally, closing his eyes, he reached for the dog destined to be one of the all time Irish Setter greats—Ch. Kinvarra Kermit; the other, Tirvelda Barrymore, became the only one in that outstanding litter who did not amount to much! Such is Lady Luck. A good example also of the questionable results in picking future top winners at that age. Many claim to have done it, and have the proof in a champion selected at that age or at birth. But if successful, much of it is luck; one rarely hears about the mistakes made!

Kermit, beautifully proportioned and well-coordinated like a champion athlete, with an extremely gay and friendly disposition, won several Bests in Show, but it is as a sire that he made his greatest impact. Bred to bitches that Schoen astutely thought would make a contribution to the breed, Kermit sired 29 champions, an incredible figure since a major portion of his progeny reached showable ages during the sharply shrunken activity years of World War II. That this clever breeder chose bloodlines carefully can be seen today. There is not a prominent kennel that does not have Kermit behind it.

Kinvarra has inflexibly followed one rule all through its history: no animal has ever been housed there which did not have regular field work

Ch. Kinvarra Portia, owned by Joyce and Athos Nilsen (Ch. Kinvarra Kermit ex Beg Pardon Rury Limerick).

and, almost invariably, a crack at the trials—with a decent degree of recognition and acclaim. Schoen also was not laggard in understanding the value of Obedience training. One of the first Obedience classes in this country, set up by Mrs. Whitehouse Walker in 1936, contained a single Irish Setter—from Kinvarra.

There is so much more that could be written about the man and Kinvarra but this book has its limits. It should be mentioned, as perhaps his most important contribution, that many today owe their success to the advice Lee has so freely given all these many years. I, for one, owe my start entirely to him; he firmly planted ideas and type in my mind in those early years that carry me forward today. Many others have been schooled at his knee. This modest man is a wealth of experience and knowledge that can be profitably tapped for years to come by the newcomer to the breed and oldtimer as well.

Kinvarra formed the basis of Kelly Fox's Kilkara Kennel. Kelly, now of Prospect, Kentucky owned Ch. Kinvarra Lord Raglan, C.D., Ch. Kinvarra Flicker, Ch. Kilkara Redwing and others.

In the Forties, Dr. Milton O. Hager, Eggertsville, New York, owned the Honors Even Kennels, which housed Ch. End O'Maine Patridge (a son of Kermit), Ch. Red Ranger Pat (a son of Jordan Farm Abe), Ch. Kinvarra Portia (a daughter of Kermit) and a number of Honors Even champions from these dogs.

The Thenderin Kennels of Joyce and Athos Nilsen have had wide experience with Irish Setters of various bloodlines. Their story is told in detail in our next chapter.

Undoubtedly one of the most famous and also the most traveled Setter with the Thenderin prefix was Ch. Thenderin Brian Tristan (Ch. End O'Maine Luckalone - Ch. Kinvarra Portia), whelped in California on St. Patrick's Day 1948. He was purchased as a puppy by James R. and Mary Fraser, who lived in 17 different places in 23 years. When Brian came to them at the airport in Cleveland, he burst out of the dog crate with all his dynamic energy. As a young dog he was most unmanageable and willful— he even fought a horse—but as he matured he became obedient, responsive, dependable and dignified. He was an intelligent companion, a marvelous personality and a strong, sound Setter.

In the period from 1950 to 1954, Brian won 10 Bests in Show, 23 Sporting Groups and 61 Bests of Breed. He topped the Group at both Westminster and the International in 1953, an exceptional achievement.

Although he was a great showman, his most important contribution to the breed was as the prepotent sire of 30 champions. The extraordinarily high quality of Irish Setters in America, particularly in the Michigan-Ohio area, can well be attributed in no small part to Ch. Thenderin Brian Tristan. American and Canadian champions Cherry Point Brask, Esquire of Maple Ridge, Headliner The Flaming Beauty and Michael Bryan Duke of Sussex are good illustrations of this quality.

Ch. Thenderin Brian Tristan
(Ch. End O'Maine Luckalone-Ch. Kinvarra Portia).

Ch. Redwood Russet of Harvale, owned by Lewis Starkey and then by Ted Eldredge, with some of his champion get (Ch. Higgins Red Coat ex Ch. Redwood Rita).

The Frasers have owned Irish Setters since 1928. Cu-Machree is the Frasers' kennel name, which is Gaelic for "Dog of My Heart." Although no longer a breeder, Jim has now obtained his judge's license.

A third important branch of the Red Coat family was headed by Ch. Redwood Russet of Harvale (Ch. Higgins' Red Coat - Ch. Redwood Rita). Redwood was the prefix of the late Lewis H. Starkey who lived in New York and later moved to Pasadena. From the half brother and sister mating of Redwood Ranger and Redwood Ruby, Starkey obtained Ch. Redwood Rita, a somewhat masculine, showy bitch. She produced five champions in two litters by Ch. Higgins' Red Coat: Ch. Redwood Regent, Ch. Springbrook Marchioness, Ch. Springbrook Margot, Ch. Harvale Hero and Ch. Redwood Russet of Harvale. Regent completed his championship in five straight shows and was never defeated in breed competition. Unfortunately he died as a three-year-old. The two Springbrook sisters were owned and shown by Harold Correll. Later Marchioness returned to Redwood and in 1939 Lewis Starkey gave her to Ted Eldredge. Hero was a marvelous Setter—everyone liked him. He spent several years at Dr. A. C. Foster's kennels and many of the Manorvue dogs trace back to him.

Starkey also owned Am. & Can. Ch. Redwood Rhoda, a Best in Show bitch and the dam of Redwood Rocket. This fine son of Ch. Higgins' Red Coat sired 14 champions, six of them in one litter. Rhoda was known for her charming personality and it was said that she would shake hands with a judge when he gave her a prize ribbon. After her death Rhoda was prepared by the Peabody Museum at Yale as an exhibit of an outstanding specimen of the breed.

To return to Russet, he was shown on the West Coast from 1936 to 1939, was seldom defeated in the breed and usually placed in the Group. At the 1946 Specialty Show of the Irish Setter Club of Southern California, fifty of his sons and daughters appeared in the ring with the old dog as a "living pedigree" exhibition.

The 16 champions sired by Russet represented Crosshaven, End O'Maine, Kendare, Waterford, Hollywood Hills, Philacre, and other kennels. His Crosshaven progeny were especially well-known, including Ch. Copper Coat of Crosshaven in the North Pacific region, Ch. Faig-a-Baile of Crosshaven in California, Ch. Cul De Sac of Crosshaven in Salt Lake City and Ch. Kleiglight of Aragon in the Midwest. Russet was also given to Ted Eldredge by Lew Starkey, and spent the last seven years of his life at Tirvelda.

Ward Gardner, Walla Walla, Washington, started his Crosshaven Kennels in the early 1930s with two well bred bitches, Ch. Lady Mac of Shanagolden and Ch. Ruxton's Shannon of Boyne. In 1937, the latter whelped a litter of 11 puppies by Redwood Rocket that included six champions. One of them, Ch. Sally O'Bryan of Crosshaven was said to be the first of the heavily coated Irish Setters. Sally was the top winning bitch in America in 1939, and the runner-up was her litter sister, Ch. Stardust of

Crosshaven. When they were campaigned that year at 26 shows in the West and Midwest, they won almost all the honors. Later both of them were mated to Ch. Redwood Russet of Harvale, which represented a famed double cross to Ch. Higgins' Red Coat. Sally produced Ch. Faig-a-Baile of Crosshaven, later owned by Ted Eldredge, while Stardust was the dam of Ch. Kleiglight of Aragon and Ch. Molly of Crosshaven.

Ch. Kleiglight of Aragon (1939-1952), one of the truly great Irish Setters of America, was owned by "The Old Maestro" H. Jack Cooper, Franklin Park, Illinois, who bred and showed dogs for over forty years. Although he had many breeds, he always kept English or Irish Setters. Among the early Irish dogs at the Aragon Kennels were Can. Ch. Automatic Red, Ch. Quinn of Aragon and Leona Automatic Betty. Then there were the numerous imports: Conn of Sonora, Patsy O'Flynn, Delaware Phil, Rheola Benjudy, Shemus Og of Boyne and the most famous of all, Ch. Golden Dawn of Gadeland O'Aragon (Eng. Sh. Ch. Rheola Bryn-Lassie O'Murrell). Dawn had probably the longest registered Irish Setter name.

Fresh from his many laurels in the big English shows at Crufts, Crystal Palace and Birmingham, Dawn raced to his American championship in eight weeks (under seven different judges) in 1932 and then went along to win 4 Best in Show and 15 Best in Group awards.

He was the prepotent sire of 253 registered offspring in 73 litters. There were many repeat matings. Leona Automatic Betty and Patricia of Aragon each had four litters sired by him. He was the grandsire of Ch. Kinvarra Mollie of Gadeland, the foundation bitch of Tirvelda.

On Fathers' Day, June 19, 1938, 37 of Dawn's sons and daughters, young and old, gathered at Aragon Kennels to pay their respects to him. Five of his eight American champion get acted as hosts. They were Lady, Joan, Norna, Babs and Terry of Aragon. More than 300 persons dropped by during the afternoon to witness an informal bench show of his non-champion progeny. The closing scene of the day was long to be remembered as the sunset glow played upon the burnished coats of Golden Dawn and his children.

Another one of Cooper's Setters to achieve wide recognition was Ch. Kleiglight of Aragon, who finished his championship at 13 months of age, and in seven years' time accumulated 21 Bests in Show, 55 Bests in Sporting Group and 104 Bests of Breed. He won the breed at Westminster three years in succession.

Kleiglight, or "Pete" as he was called, was the prolific sire of 595 registered offspring in 131 litters from 94 bitches. Ch. Mahogany Sue O'Aragon had five litters by him and Ch. Charles River All Afire had six. The 30 champions that he sired carried the names of Beauty, Knocknagree and others. His bloodlines have had a pronounced effect on Midwestern Irish Setter strains. Pete died of a stroke in 1952; and when Jack Cooper died the following year, the Aragon Kennels were continued by Mrs. Ethel Cooper.

Ch. Golden Dawn of Gadeland O'Aragon
(Ch. Rheola Bryn-Lassie O'Murrell).

Ch. Kleiglight of Aragon
(Ch. Redwood Russet of Harvale-Ch. Stardust of Crosshaven).

Dick Cooper has followed the family tradition by handling many Irish Setters, among them the top winning dog in history, Ch. Starheir Aaron Ardee.

Harold Correll of Bernardsville, New Jersey was a foremost authority on dogs, having been a handler for 35 years, holding AKC license number 1. He was twice Dogdom's Man of the Year and a recipient of the Fido Award. He died of a heart attack on August 8, 1965 at the age of 65. He will be especially remembered by Irish Setter fanciers for his long and loyal support of the red dogs. Among the early Tercor dogs were Patricia, whelped in 1924, and Red Mike. The Corrells at one time owned the famous Ch. Knightscroft Patty Boyne, the two Springbrook sisters, Margot and Marchioness, and Ch. Faig-a-Baile of Crosshaven. From these and others came numerous Tercor setters, many of which were not shown extensively as Harold showed dogs for others. It is said that in his long career he handled 500 dogs to their championships, among them Ch. Charles River Color Sergeant, Ch. Knightscroft Patty Boyne, Ch. Knightscroft Symphony, Ch. Phantom Brooks Burgundy, and Ch. Dix-Mac Mignola. He handled many dogs for Mary McCune and Ida Capers (Dix-Mac).

Frank and Dorothy Cory (Devon Irish Setters) of Arlington Heights, Illinois owned Wamsutta Dream Girl and Knightscroft Golden Glow, both of which had litters by Ch. Kleiglight of Aragon. They acquired Ch. Charles River Color Sergeant from John Downs. Frank died while at a show in November, 1947 and Dorothy continued to campaign Sarge with Dick Cooper piloting the dog. He won Best in Show at the 1949 Chicago International. Twelve years later his great, great grandson, Ch. Conifer's Lance repeated the win, also with Cooper at the end of the lead. Color Sergeant sired 250 offspring including 17 champions. Because his progeny were widely distributed from coast to coast, his influence in the breed has been very pronounced. He was a strong, bold, intelligent dog with a marvelous disposition.

Ch. Red Sails of Salmagundi (Beorcham Blazes-Beorcham Radiant) was brought to America by Percy Roberts for Justin Griess. He was later transferred to John Downs of Sudbury, Mass. and then to Mrs. Alan A. Ryan. As his bloodlines differed from the American strains, they served as a distinct outcross. He contributed great quality to his progeny, especially sound rears, impressive style and exceptional spirit. Particularly good was the Red Sails-Wamsutta Susie Q combination that produced the Charles River champions: Color Sergeant, Blazing Beauty and All Afire. Downs continued his strain in the East represented by Ch. Charles River Streamliner.

Charles and Shirley Ford (Blayneywood) of Belleville, Michigan owned Pats' Irish Folly, CD. His dam, Peggy Primrose, mated to Ch. Tyronne Farm Malone II, produced Ch. Kinvarra Malone and Ch. Kinvarra Shiela. Shiela bred to Ch. Draherin Irish Chieftain, also sired by Malone II, produced Ch. Blayneywood Country Squire. Both Squire and

Ch. Charles River Color Sergeant, owned by Frank and Dorothy Cory (Ch. Red Sails of Salamagundi ex Wamsutta Susie Q).

. Charles River Streamliner, ned by John Downs (Ch. rgeant Red Sails of Devon ex arles River Dream Girl).

Ch. Red Arrow Show Girl, CDX, owned by Lawrence and Eleanor Heist (Ch. Hollywood Hills O'Shaughnessy ex Marted Annie Rooney).

Ch. Blayneywood Country Squire, owned by Marion Darling (Ch. Draherin Irish Chieftain ex Ch. Kinvarra Shiela).

Ch. Kinvarra Malone were well-balanced, beautiful Irish Setters with excellent show records.

James and Evelyn Hale (Haleridge) of Malibu, California were primarily known for providing the Irish Setters that were featured in the Walt Disney movie "Big Red." However, the Hales also bred these champions: Rhu Shane, Joy, and Sean of Haleridge. They were also active in Obedience.

The Red Arrow Kennels of Lawrence and Eleanor Heist of Fontana, California are best represented by Am. and Mex. Ch. Red Aye Scraps, Am. and Mex. UD and the star of "Big Red." Scraps' stand-in was Ch. Red Arrow Smooth Sailing. The most titled of the Heists' dogs was Dual Champion Red Arrow Show Girl, UDT and Mex. PC. She was the dam of 8 Red Arrow champion progeny, 6 of them sired by Am. and Can. Ch. Esquire of Maple Ridge.

Hayden and Lois Martin who bred Sunny Acre Irish Setters in Gary, Indiana, were well known for two dozen champions descended from Aragon and Denhaven lines. Gaye of Sunny Acre was perhaps the favorite because of her outstanding conformation and intelligence. Red Dawn of Sunny Acre had 4 Best in Show awards. Sunny Acre dogs were important in the breeding programs of Mid-Oak, Hotze, End O'Lane, and others. In 1961, "Doc" Martin retired from professional handling to become a judge.

Eldon McCormack (Eldomac) of Yakima, Washington owned Ch. Cherry Point Brask II, Ch. Eldomac Senarc Rhu and others.

William B. (Barry) and Marion Neville owned one of the largest Irish Setter kennels in the United States. Their Red Barn Kennel in Blauvelt, New York was established in the 1940s on foundation stock from Knightscroft, Boxley and others. Ch. Knightscroft Primrose, a double cross to Ch. Milson O'Boy II, produced Ch. Red Barn Rosabelle, UDT. In 1952 the Nevilles obtained Ch. Kendare Red Dawn who became the sire of 13 Boxley, Maple Ridge, and Red Barn champions. One of these was Ch. Boxley Holly Anne who was the dam of a litter of 5 champions in 1953 including Am. and Can. Ch. Red Star of Hollywood Hills, CDX, Red Barn Red Stardust, Royal Charm, Royal Holly, Royal Talisman, and Redstar

Talent Scout. Talisman sired 7 champions, including Ch. Red Barn Tallyrand, Ch. Phantom Brooks Brian Boru and others. Barry died in 1979.

Mrs. Cheever Porter of New York City was a longtime enthusiast of the Irish Setter. In addition to her famous early dogs, Ch. Milson O'Boy, Ch. Rosecroft Premier, and Ch. St. Cloud's Fermanagh III—of whom we have already written—she also owned such notable winners as Ch. Shawnlea's Fanfare, Ch. Kinvarra Malone, Ch. Wautoma, Ch. Tyronne Farm Rex, Ch. Cherry Point Brask, Ch. Webline Rio Hondo, Ch. Courtwood Spring Son, Ch. Powderhorn Yankee Rifleman, and Ch. Meadowlark's Anticipation. From the '50s on, her dogs were handled by Jane Forsyth. Mrs. Porter always owned an Irish Setter, and her interest in the breed did much to keep it in the limelight. She was a member of many local Irish Setter clubs as well as the Irish Setter Club of America. She died in 1980 at the age of 92.

Doris Swain (Laurel Ridge) of Canton, Massachusetts bred a litter from Ch. Honors Even Rakish Jane which contained Am. and Can. Ch. Laurel Ridge Star Rocket, Bombshell and Firecracker, named in honor of their birthdate—Independence Day 1951. Star Rocket and another Laurel Ridge champion, Paddy O'Shea, had impressive show records. Doris is now a judge of Irish Setters.

Leslie and Helen Walsh of Monrovia, California bred a dozen or more Waterford champions after 1930, including Bronze Monarch, Comet, Red Pat, Margaret, Ruth, Sally, Coolan and others. Helen Walsh has held a judging license for many years.

In 1944 Leone Wixson, Copper Country Kennels of Tucson, Arizona, bought a three-month-old puppy from Waterford Kennels, who became Ch. Waterford Sally and was a noted producer. Her daughter, Ch. Copper Country Trilby, bred to Ch. Seaforth Dark Rex, produced three champions.

In 1962 Mrs. Wixson and James Jordan purchased Thenderin Endorsement, a very sound, stylish, medium sized Setter. Finishing his championship at Westminster, he went on to win the Southern California Specialty in 1963. Mrs. Wixson's latest champion, co-owned with Mrs. William B. Allen, is Ch. Thenderin Loyal O'Mulholland.

Dr. Robert Way of Levittown, Pennsylvania was a veterinarian and an artist who created anatomical drawings for veterinary journals and also for the ISCA illustrated standard. He raised Irish Setters under the Windsor prefix, among which were Windsor Brilliant Challenge, Windsor Michael Son O'Kelly, and Dariabar Adonia. Dr. Way died suddenly in 1980.

Dr. James and Phyllis Wilson of Milltown, Wisconsin bred Cherry Point Setters. Jim was raised with sporting dogs as his father, a veterinarian, kept field dogs including Irish Setters. Jim was also a veterinarian. He raised litters from Milson, Red Barn, Hedgewood, Tyronne Farm and other strains. The Wilsons bred their Ch. End O'Maine

Ch. Verbu Maureen, CD. (Knockross O'Boy ex Ch. Caldene Maura), left, and Ch. Cherry Point Brask (Ch. Thenderin Brian Tristan ex Ch. End Main Encore).

Ch. Carrvale's Terry Terhune
(Ch. Carrvale's Sergeant Terrence-Tyronne Farm Sherry).

Encore to Ch. Thenderin Brian Tristan, producing the famous Am. and Can. Ch. Cherry Point Brask, Chukar and Hun. The Wilsons owned Ch. End O'Maine Morning Bird, one of seven champions in a litter by Ch. Carrvale's Terry Terhune ex End O'Maine Claret. Jim also had field trial winners that are descended from field Ch. Ike Jack Kendrick.

Dr. Herman Carr, who died in 1962, and his wife Martha, raised Irish Setters from about 1938. His first dogs were from the Denhaven and Devon Kennels. Ch. Carrvale's Sergeant Terrance, a son of Ch. Charles River Color Sergeant, completed his championship at 12 months and 9 days. There were 10 Carrvale champions, among them Terry Terhune, Lad O'Lark and Billy Boy.

Jane Gavin of Gavingarth Kennels owned Ch. Gavingarth's Bonnie Heather, sired by Tarawil's Sequoia, a member of the famous litter of seven champions by Ch. Carrvale's Terry Terhune ex End O'Maine Claret.

Ernest and Virginia Lewis of Pacific Palisades, California owned the great Ch. Innisfail Color Scheme, CD, the prepotent sire of 25 champions, who had a tremendous influence on the breed in California. (See also Field Trial section.)

John and Harriet Pelissier were professional handlers and bred several Garden State champions, including Ch. Garden State's Reno's Blaze, owned by Helen Olivo.

Others active in the '60s were George Glassford who bred dogs under the Tuxedo prefix. Among the prominent Tuxedo dogs were Ch. Tuxedo's Sugar and Spice, dam of the noted show dog, Ch. Tuxedo's Duffy of Mos'n Acre, owned by Frances Phillips. He also owned and bred Ch. Tuxedo's Royal Trooper, who was Best of Breed at Westminster in 1960. Tom Glassford, George's son, is currently a professional handler.

William and Lauretta Golden of Pacific Palisades owned Ch. Webline Mi-Golden Flame, CD (Ch. Innisfail Color Scheme ex Ch. Knightscroft Erin McCuhl). In 1963 Flame whelped the "Golden" litter with the musical names, sired by Ch. Thenderin Chaparal Cayenne. They were: Symphony, Crescendo, Lyric and Jubilee. The latter, Ch. Webline Golden Jubilee, CD, became one of the top Sporting dogs during his career.

Ann and Peer Buck owned the Muckamoor Kennels in Plover, Wisconsin, with a combination of Knightscroft and Kinvarra breeding. Although they did not engage in an extensive breeding program, their quality was such that half of every litter finished their championships. After Peer died, Ann continued the pattern. Her most successful litter probably was the litter sired by Muckamoor Michael McGuire out of Ch. Weblyn Masterpiece (leased from Lee Prescott). From this litter came Ch. Muckamoor Marty McCuhl who finished with five majors. He sired only six litters before he died suddenly at age four, but there were 15 champions in those. One she kept was Ch. Muckamoor Candia Audie. Ann was a professional handler for years. She served on the Board of ISCA and judged the Sweepstakes at the first National Specialty.

Nial and Marie Koonts, who are now both judges, owned many Irish

Ch. Wolfscroft Amaranthus
(Ch. Brynmount Maydorwill Brandyson-Ch. Knightscroft Dixie Belle).

Ch. Innisfail Color Scheme
(Ch. Seaforth's Dark Rex-Thenderin Champagne).

Setter champions, among which were: Ch. General Beauregard, Ch. Aragon's Rustic Rover, Ch. Argo Lane's Countess of Cork, Ch. Mid-Oak Rose of Sharon, Ch. Rusthill's Irish Serenade, Ch. Rusthill's Irish Duke, CD. Ch. General Beauregard (Ch. Tyronne Farm Malone II ex Knockross Fern) was a consistent winner at shows, and sired 8 champions.

Jack Funk has had a lifelong interest in Irish Setters, starting when he was 11 years old. A longtime professional handler he has finished several hundred champions to title. Since 1939, when he acquired Ginger The Flaming Beauty, there have been many Flaming Beauty champions, including Patrick, Sally, Duchess and Michael. The most famous was Am. & Can. Ch. Headliner The Flaming Beauty (Ch. Thenderin Brian Tristan ex Ch. Larrie of Tidewater), who topped all Sporting dogs in 1962 show wins. He was retired from the ring in 1963 with 9 Best in Show, 56 Best in Group and 103 Best of Breed awards. Several of his progeny have become champions. Jack also bred Am. & Can. Ch. Tamara of Last Chance, who figures in the pedigrees of Ch. Patrick of Tidewater, Am. & Can. Ch. Conine's King of the Reds and three Muckamoor champions.

The Banshee Kennels of Ivan and Leonore Klapper, established in 1947, have Knightscroft and Red Barn lines. The beautifully-headed Ch. Knightscroft Lady Vogue, CD, was their foundation bitch. She was the dam of Ch. Banshee Sharpshooter, Ch. Banshee Rebel Brigadier, CD, and Ch. Banshee Vogue of Antrim, and was the granddam of Ch. Banshee Bushwhacker. Ivan was President of the Irish Setter Club of America for 12 years, and although no longer breeding, the Klappers maintain their interest in Irish Setters.

Dr. Wolfgang A. Casper started in Irish Setters in 1946 after returning from military service in World War II. His first dog was a Knightscroft bitch, Knightscroft Dixie Belle. An outcross mating to an English import, Ch. Brynmount Maydorwill Brandison, produced a litter to bear the chosen kennel name Wolfscroft—in line with Rosecroft and Knightscroft. Out of this litter came Ch. Wolfscroft Amaranthus, CDX. Amaranthus came home one day with his left foot dangling; the tendons completely severed from a bad accident. Veterinarians gave up on him, but Dr. Casper convinced an orthopedic surgeon from the same hospital where he was an attending physician to repair the leg. Miraculously, Amaranthus went on to earn his Obedience degree and his championship title.

In 1948 Dr. Casper reorganized the Eastern Irish Setter Association, which after the war was down to five members. He became its president for five years, and later was named an honorary member. In 1949 Dr. Casper was a founder of the Staten Island Companion Dog Training Club and trained all his champions to Obedience titles. There were sometimes as many as 17 dogs in his house.

Dr. Casper was a board member of the Staten Island Kennel Club and its AKC delegate, and a board member of the Irish Setter Club of America, and of the English Setter Association of America. He founded the Combined Setter Clubs of America, Inc. in 1960 and for over 15 years was show chairman for the show, which is held the day before Westminster. He was also an associate member and board member of the Association of Obedience Clubs and Judges, and was an AKC-approved judge of all Sporting breeds and the Group. He died, at the age of 80, in March, 1982.

Webline Kennels, owned by Dick and Madeline Webb, was originally formed in 1953 as a partnership between Dick and Avril Roslyn and named Weblyn. To avoid confusion, Weblyn and Webline is a continuous breeding line.

Four dogs—Ch. Knightscroft Erin McCuhl, Ch. Innisfail Color Scheme, CD, Ch. Thenderin Margevan Minstrel, and Margevan's Dawn— were the first owned by Weblyn. "Color Scheme" sired a total of 12 litters and produced 29 champions. Erin McCuhl whelped one litter of 4 with 4 champions resulting. Dawn whelped two litters with 4 champions.

An early highlight in their breeding program was the mating of Color Scheme and Erin McCuhl that produced Ch. Weblyn Mystic Mark, Ch. Weblyn Madrigal, Ch. Weblyn Mi-Golden Flame, and Ch. Weblyn Masterpiece. These, in turn, produced about 40 champions, including several #1 Irish in the country and Best in Show winners. Included were— Ch. Webline Rio Hondo (Madrigal), Ch. Webline Wizard of Macapa (Mark), and Ch. Webline Golden Jubilee (Flame).

Webline never owned more than four adult Irish Setters at one time and their breeding program was limited to no more than two litters in any one year. In spite of, or perhaps because of, this rather limited activity, they have been honored by winning many awards from the Irish Setter Club of America's annual list, including Sire of the Year, and Dam of the Year. Webline was also the recipient of two of the most important awards: "Litter Breeder of the Year" six consecutive years and "Breeder of the Year" for ten years in a row.

Some of their Best in Show and Specialty Show winners were: Ch. Innisfail Color Scheme, CD; Ch. Weblyn Limelite, CD; Ch. Webline Zingaro; Ch. Webline Wizard of Macapa; Ch. Webline Golden Jubilee, CD; Ch. Webline Mystic Mark; Ch. Webline Rio Hondo; Ch. Webline Fame 'n Fortune; Ch. Webline Free 'n Easy; and their latest, Ch. Royal Oaks Fortune's Fella.

Dick was a well-known handler, and now both the Webbs are popular judges.

The Westwind Irish Setters were established in 1942, when Luz and Clyde Holvenstot bought a bitch puppy, Knightscroft Magic, from Joe and Henrietta Knight. As a high school student Luz had visited the Knightscroft Kennels, and had begun to attend dog shows, so it was logical that (during her years of study of veterinary science and her eventual graduation with a B.S. degree in Animal Husbandry) the acquisition of her first breeding bitch would be from the kennel she knew.

Magic was by Ch. Milson O'Boy II ex Ch. Rosecroft Kitty Kelly. This puppy was trained for her CD title on the Holvenstots' 120-acre farm. Bred to Ch. Knightscroft Fermanagh, a son of Ch. Milson O'Boy II and Ch. Knightscroft Erin Elan, Magic produced their foundation which, along

Ch. Webline Golden Jubilee, owned by William and Loretta Golden (Ch. Thenderin Chaparal Cayenne ex Ch. Webline Mi-Golden Flame, CD).

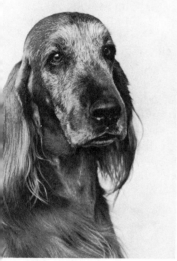

Ch. Weblyn Mystic Mark, owned by Dick and Madeline Webb (Ch. Innisfail Color Scheme ex Ch. Knightscroft Erin McCuhl).

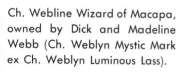

Ch. Webline Wizard of Macapa, owned by Dick and Madeline Webb (Ch. Weblyn Mystic Mark ex Ch. Weblyn Luminous Lass).

with other Knightscroft bred bitches, established the kennel.

During the thirty five years a valuable cross was made by breeding to "Slim" Newhall's Ch. Caldene Mick O'Boy and Knockcross O'Boy, to the Jo and Audrey Jennings' Ch. Titian Intrepid, a grandson of Ch. Knightscroft Fermanagh, and to Ch. Red Star of Hollywood Hills, CDX. Acquired later was Ch. Knockross' Sally, who was shown to her championship by Luz.

In recent years, Luz has ceased breeding and showing, but has acquired her judge's license for all Setters.

Mr. and Mrs. J. Brooks Emory owned the Phantom Brook Kennels in the early 1940s. They started with a bitch from the Bullet Hole Kennels, which were nearby. Dodie heard that the owner, because he was only interested in the field, put to sleep all the bitches as soon as they were whelped and only kept the males. She prevailed upon that gentleman to give her a bitch puppy. That turned out to be her first champion, Bullet Hole Clare, in 1949, and she became the foundation of Phantom Brook.

The most famous of the Phantom Brooks became Ch. Phantom Brook's Burgundy. His was a Cinderella story. On one of Dodie's trips over to her handler, Annie Rogers (Clark), who was living in New City, one of the bitches fell out of the station wagon and was lost for a week. The young couple who had found her realized she was something special, and finally, through an ad in the paper, returned her to Phantom Brook, for which Dodie gave them a reward of $25. A couple of years later this couple came to her, and said they were moving to Maine to try their luck at farming, and would love to have a puppy to take with them. She told them to go to the yard where many dogs were exercising, and to pick out a puppy. They did and Dodie charged them only $25.

Another year or so passed, and the couple phoned her from New Jersey. They were living in a four story walk-up, a baby was on the way, money was short, and although they loved the dog, they just couldn't keep him.

So Harold Correll was phoned and was asked to go and see the dog, to see if it was worth taking him back. A few weeks passed, and when nothing was heard from Harold she phoned him again, and he simply said, "You'll see the dog at the Philadelphia show." At that show Burgundy, looking beautiful, went Best of Breed from the classes. The next day at Camden, Burgundy went Best of Breed again and Group I. Harold had sold him to Mrs. McCune for somewhere in the four figures. She loved the dog, and he was successfully campaigned to his championship and to win of the Golden Leash award.

Another great dog from Phantom Brook, Am. and Ber. Ch. Phantom Brooks' Brian Boru had his picture used to illustrate the standard in an ISCA Club pamphlet. It is still being used to this day, some twenty years after it was taken. This is food for thought for those who think the breed has changed in type — Brian could enter the show ring today and go right to the top.

Ch. Webline Fame 'N Fortune, owned by Mr. and Mrs. William Klussman (Ch. Webline Wizard of Macapa ex Ch. Webline Zamara).

Am. & Can. Ch. Webline Rio Hondo, owned by Mrs. Cheever Porter, Bea Kelleher & Webline Kennels (Ch. Draherin Auburn Artistry ex Ch. Weblyn Madrigal).

Ch. Westwind Scarlet Cascade, owned by Luz Holvenstot (Ch. Westwind Scarlet Tempest ex Ch. Westwind Scarlet Starkist).

After Brooks died, Dodie reduced the kennel and now no longer breeds. She is a licensed judge.

The Fred Pools have been breeding Irish Setters since 1946. Their first brood bitch, Princess Beautiful Sun d'Or, gave them a start with 14 puppies in her first litter! Since that time they have finished a number of champions, among whom are: Flann's Sir Boss, Flann's Crimson Glory, Flann's Crimson Mollie, Wharfwood's Valentine, and Flann's Earl of Whitehall.

AKC and Bermuda Champion Flann's Sir Boss was a good producer. As a Special, he was shown 32 times, and placed 29 times in the Group, 13 of them Firsts. He also had one Best in Show. His last breeding produced the illustrious young Ch. Flann's Sir Andrew Jackson, a BIS Specialty winner. His performance still ranks first for a Texas-bred Irish Setter.

Fred organized the Irish Setter Club of Texas eighteen years ago, and was president of it for nine years. He was re-elected president in 1975. The Pools spearheaded the breed in Texas. They exhibited in dozens of shows where they had the only Irish Setter entry, and their first champion had 27 points before she ever encountered a major. When she did, on two consecutive days she took them both and finished with 33 points and 21 BOBs.

Brenwood Kennel was established by Fran and Baird Wallis in 1958 with the purchase of Ch. Hotze's Red Rose. Rose proved to be a great brood matron producing 12 champions. She attained her championship undefeated in the classes, twice going on to BOB. There was an aura of beauty and vitality about her that commanded attention. Rose was awarded the Irish Setter Club of America Best Matron Trophy and earned for the kennel the Breeders Trophy in 1962. Also that year her progeny captured the Breeder Exhibitor, Winners and Best of Winners awards and was runner-up for the Golden Leash award.

By the time Rose was four years old, three of her progeny by Ch. Gaye Michael of Sunny Acre had also obtained their bench titles: Ch. Hotze's Red Ruby; Ch. Sir Jeffrey of Sunny Acre; and Ch. Lady Beth of Sunny Acre. A fourth from that litter, Hotze's Red Debra, was subsequently shown to title.

Four champions again were produced in her litter sired by Ch. Kingpin of Jilda (owned by the Wallises): B. Kingpin; B. Rhythm; B. Red Knight; and B. Starfire.

Other champion children of Rose were B. Vagabond, B. Roseapenna, B. Wine of the Liffey, and Sunny Acre's Top of the Mark. Ch. B. Brandy (by Ch. B. Red Knight ex Ch. Hotze's Red Debra) later became one of the foundation matrons of Herb Nichols (Twinacres) breeding program.

Both Rose and her daughter, Debra, had been Hotze's gun dogs and many of Rose's offspring became proficient hunters. Ch. B. Kingpin and Ch. B. Rhythm were outstanding field dogs. Many times they worked tirelessly at the Chicago area gun club getting the day's limit of pheasant for more than one party of hunters.

The natural ability and intelligence of these beauties was proven over

. Taradell's Bright Future (Ch.
y Michael of Sunny Acre-Ch.
ra's Theme).

Ch. Seaforth's Red Velvet, owned
by George and Barbara Brodie
(Charles River Red Don ex
Charles River Juanita).

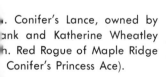

. Conifer's Lance, owned by
ank and Katherine Wheatley
h. Red Rogue of Maple Ridge
Conifer's Princess Ace).

and again as the three Wallis children participated in Obedience training as part of the upbringing of the young ones, prior to their entry in bench shows. Now in Denver, it is hoped activities at Brenwood will commence once again.

Buck and Laverne Stines were owners of one of the breed's three most highly titled Irish Setters, Dual Ch. County Cork's Red Knight, UD—the others being Dual Ch. Red Arrow Show Girl, UDT, and Dual Ch. Tyrone Mahogany Mike, CDX.

Red Knight died in 1974 but his accomplishments should be recounted. He finished his championship in 1963 with a five point major at the Golden Gate show. Shown only six times as a Special, he was BOB in three. He finished his CD in three straight shows; in fact, in his first event, the ISCPSC 1960 Specialty, he was highest scoring dog in the trial. He received his CDX also in three straight shows in consecutive weekends, and went to his UD title in five shows. He had four scores of 199!

Red finished his field championship in 1964. He was never run in a Puppy Stake or Derby Stake. He compiled a record of 19 wins and 46 placements, all in Senior Stakes. Between 1961 and 1967 he won nine consecutive Irish and All Setter Amateur Gun Dog Stakes! He won his last trial at ten years of age.

The Stines also own Field Ch. County Cork's Bold Knight, CD, and hopefully he will also win the triple crown. Another of their dogs is Ch. County Cork Candy, CD, who has the distinction of having all three of the much-titled dogs mentioned above in her pedigree. Candy finished her show championship with three California majors. She also had four field points. Unfortunately she had to be retired early due to illness in the Stine family.

Joseph and Marilyn Slick decided in 1962 that they wanted to show and breed Irish Setters, after having owned a series of pets. They purchased Shannon's Shawn of Erin from Betty Crawford when he was 16 months of age. Shawn finished his championship in three months and had a Best in Show by the age of three. In 1965 he became a Canadian and Bermuda champion with another Best in Show to his credit and was in the top ten Irish in the United States.

1965 saw the addition of "Shamie," Shawn's sister. She had been in three homes before the Slicks acquired her; was skinny, coatless and scared to death, but they worked hard with her and started to show her, and Shawn, as a Special. For two years they traveled the country over on weekends. After "Shamie" finished, she was bred to Ch. Blayneywood Country Squire. This mating produced five famous champions and won for the Slicks the Breeder of the Year award from the Irish Setter Club of America. From this litter the Slicks kept Ch. Incendiary Belle and Ch. Bronze Blaze of Tamarisk. The latter was in the top ten Irish in the country for two years in a row, owner-handled all the way.

Marilyn was a professional handler and a member of the Board of Directors of ISCA for many years, where she admirably performed the

Ch. Seaforth Dark Rex, owned by Joyce and Athos Nilsen (Ch. Tyronne Farm Malone ex Ch. Seaforth Red Velvet).

herculean job of Trophy Chairman.

Roy and Nedra Jerome own Innisfail, a name which to many Irish Setter breeders refers to the famous litter of three champions by Ch. Seaforth Dark Rex ex Thenderin Champagne: Ch. Innisfail Color Scheme, Ch. Innisfail Encore and Ch. Innisfail Mona Lisa. References to Color Scheme appear elsewhere in this book.

Although having had Irish Setters since 1946, the Jeromes have not bred extensively. They have owned Thenderin Champagne, Ch. Thenderin Checkmate, Ch. Margevan Madcap of Innisfail, Ch. Glen Erin's Pride of Innisfail and Ch. Rad's Rondelet of Innisfail. Most of the well-known kennels are represented in their pedigrees—Kinvarra, Charles River, End O'Maine, Tyronne Farm and Thenderin. The combination of dogs they have owned culminated in the pedigree of Ch. Innisfail Flashback's Design, an eight times Best in Show winner, owned by Dr. Selma Stoll.

Nedra, an artist of note, has contributed portraits each year of ISCA award winning Irish Setters. Roy has served as a Board member of the ISCA, and is an approved judge.

George and Barbara Brodie established their Seaforth Kennels in the 1940s with the acquisition of their great bitch, Ch. Seaforth's Red Velvet from John L. Downs of the Charles River Kennels. Red Velvet was bred to Ch. Tyronne Farm Malone and from that breeding came Chs. Seaforth Dark Rex and Seaforth Poetry of Motion. Due to George's career the breeding operation was limited but numerous fine champions were produced.

Deserving of special mention was Dark Rex. Sold to Thenderin as a youngster, he was not only a great show dog but a real type-setting sire. The sire of many champions, his most famous offspring was Ch. Innisfail Color Scheme, a famous sire in his own right.

Dark Rex interestingly enough was a monorchid. Had the AKC rule disqualifying such dogs been in effect then, Dark Rex would never have been shown and probably seldom used at stud. What a tragedy this would have been for the breed.

I remember judging the Southern California Specialty years ago and giving this magnificent dog BOB at the age of ten, after which he was permanently retired. I was aware of Rex's condition, and in the event I had Rex offspring under me I very carefully examined every male to see whether he had passed on this characteristic. Later in checking the catalogue, I found I had close to one hundred of his children and grandchildren under me. Not one male in the entire show was abnormal nor have future generations shown that Rex passed on this trait. He was the principal dog responsible for the early great success of Thenderin, Webline and Innisfail, to mention just a few famous kennels.

Although the Brodies discontinued breeding in the '60s, their interest in the breed is just as keen. Every prominent Specialty in the East will see them in attendance and both the Brodies have been honored by being asked to judge at the National Specialties of the Irish Setter Club of America— Mr. Brodie at the second and Mrs. Brodie at the third.

When Bob Bridell was 12 years of age he obtained his first Irish Setter, Peggy of Aragon II, a daughter of Ch. Kleiglight of Aragon. He showed Peggy in Puppy and Children's Handling Classes; and later on he bred her to a son of Ch. Charles River Color Sergeant. This mating resulted in Ch. Tara's Theme, the foundation brood matron of the Taradell Kennels. She produced 5 bench champions, including the Best in Show winner Ch. Taradell's Bright Future and Virginia Hardin's well-known Ch. Runwild Fiona. Theme placed in 5 stakes at field trials.

An informal shot of Ch. Seaforth Dark Rex.

8

The Irish Setters of Today

AS ONE LOOKS at the previous chapter, one is struck by the interweaving of bloodlines, and the overlapping of generations. The lives of the great breeders span decades, some of them still active, others still influencing the breed by the stock which they have produced.

The Kinvarras, Knightscrofts, Thenderins, Tirveldas, come down through the pedigrees of most of today's Irish, and it will be for historians in the future to trace their influence as years progress.

In this chapter we will look at those actively involved in the breed during the 1970s and 1980s. Here the reader will find familiar names and new fanciers, insuring a continuing broad base of breeding stock to perpetuate the Irish Setter in the United States and Canada.

Airheart, Elizabeth — *Padre Island* — Corpus Christi, TX
Miss Airheart acquired her first Irish in 1965, and her first show quality Setter—Cherry Point Padre Isle Mist—shortly thereafter. Misty had accumulated 11 points, including her majors, when it was necessary to put her down. She had only two litters. From the first came Ch. Padre Island South Wind, and from the second Ch. Padre Island Sea Storm, CD. Sea Storm produced a growing list of champions that include Ch. Limerick Lane Merry Maker and Can. Ch. Limerick Lane Tom Bombodil. Miss Airheart is an AKC-approved judge of the breed.

Allen, Bill and Dilly — *Whiskey Hill* — Tucson, AZ
Bill and Dilly Allen purchased their first show puppy, Ch. Thenderin Trailblazer, in 1963 and acquired their foundation bitch, Ch. Thenderin Jacynth, a few months later. When bred to Leone Wixson's Ch. Webline Very Coppercountry, Jacynth produced the outstanding Thenderin "E" litter which included Ch.

Thenderin Expectation and Ch. Thenderin Etching. Bred to Trailblazer, Jacynth produced Ch. Whiskey Hill's Drummer Boy. Additionally, the Allens have owned Ch. Innisfail Gaelic Glory; her pointed daughter, Whiskey Hill Irish Miss; Ch. Thenderin Guarantee, Winners Bitch at the 1975 ISCA National Specialty Show; Ch. Thenderin Loyal O' Mulholland and the pointed Loyal-Expectation granddaughter, Coppercountry Charm, which Dilly co-owns with Leone Wixson. Bill is an approved judge and the Allens have been active in Irish Setter club activities for many years, including founding the Irish Setter Club of Greater Tucson, Inc.

Alston, Mary Ann — *Fieldstone* — Pasadena, MD

Known primarily as a professional handler, Mary Ann has bred (or co-bred) five litters of note. Two were from Ch. Gala Glen's Cherries Jubilee, who she co-owned with Mrs. Carolyn Warner—the first was sired by Ch. Tirvelda Distant Drummer, the second by Ch. McCamon Marquis. She then leased Glen Cree Merriment (Ch. Tapnar Barnstormer ex Glen Cree Maggie Malone) from Rose Marie Ross and bred her to Ch. McCamon Marquis. Of this litter two champions are finished—Ch. Fieldstone Torchbearer, co-owned by Frank and Patricia Villano, and a bitch, Ch. Fieldstone Trace of Burgundy, co-owned with Connie Vanacore. Ch. Meadowlark's Chances Are (Ch. McCamon Marquis ex Ch. Meadowlark's Interlude), co-owned with Rose Marie Ross, was bred twice. The first breeding was to Ch. Meadowlark's Argosy and the second to Rockerin Royal Ragen. Mary Ann is also breeder (with Laura Cunningham) of a litter out of Beaverbrook Prelude by Ch. Meadowlark Masterpiece.

Anderson, Dr. Judson T. and Evelyn H. — *Autumnwoods* — Colorado Springs, CO

Autumnwoods had its beginning in 1967 with Bangor Flame O'Flicker, CD (Ch. Kinvarra Flicker ex Bangor Bonanza). Their second Irish, Ch. Bangor Javelin (Ch. Taradell's Synbad ex Ch. Bangor Bric-a-Brac, CD) became well-known in the Rocky Mountain region, handled by Sally Terroux.

From Slim Newhall, they acquired the breed-winning Ch. Knockross Cris O'Malley and her half-sister, Knockross Polly O'Malley. The breeding of these bitches to Javelin produced the Knockross "H" and "J" litters. (The Andersons have adopted the Knockross prefix from Slim Newhall, since their foundation stock all stems from that line.) One of the "J" litter, now Ch. Knockross Jama's Song, was winner of the Open class and Reserve at the 1979 National Specialty.

Anderson, Thomas E. and Kathy — *Kachina* — Tempe, AZ

Ch. Dunholm Kachina Doll (Ch. Tirvelda Michaelson ex Ch. Dunholm Katrina), co-owned by the Andersons and Dennis J. and Cynthia Sporre, was Best in Sweepstakes at the Second National Specialty. She finished with all majors, co-owner handled, won the ISCA 1975 Winners Bitch Award, and was runner-up for the Golden Leash Award. The Andersons and Sporres also co-own Dunholm Blueprint Cannonade (Ch. Candia Indeed ex Dunholm Lancashire Lass).

Andrews, Claire — *Kimberlin* — Providence, RI

Claire Andrews acquired her first purebred dog, an Irish Setter bitch, in 1947. Since that time, she has been consistently active in both conformation and Obedience with her dogs, and in limited breeding, has consistently produced winning stock.

Her foundation bitch, Ch. Shawnlea's Gayla, was purchased from Miss May Hanley. This bitch proved herself by winning the Irish Setter Club of America's

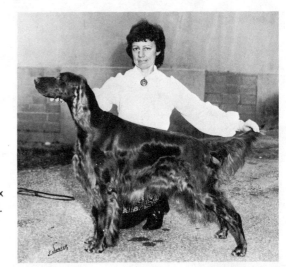

Ch. Kimberlin Cara (Ch. Celou's Lex McCrory ex Ch. Shawnlea's Gayla).

Am. & Bda. Ch. Kimberlin Kyrie (Ch. Tirvelda Sportin' Life ex Ch. Kimberlin Cara).

Am. & Can. Ch. Draherin Marietta (Ch. Draherin King's Ransom ex Ch. Draherin Annie Laurie).

coveted "Golden Leash" award in 1961. She was the dam of Am. & Can. Ch. Kimberlin Encore, who in 1964 began his illustrious career by going Best of Breed and third in the Group at Westminster, winning from the Open class. Encore also won the "Golden Leash" for 1964.

In 1971, Ch. Kimberlin Cara was listed as Top Producing dam. Bred to Ch. Tirvelda Sportin' Life, Cara produced Am. & Can. & Bda. Ch. Kimberlin Kyrie, who was the No. 1 Irish Setter bitch for 1973. Bred to Ch. Danalee Bright Legend, Cara produced Ch. Kimberlin Keela, who also won the "Golden Leash." During her career Cara was entirely breeder-owner handled, and was the winner of several Sporting Groups.

In 1981-82, a dog by Ch. Thenderin William Muldoon ex Kyrie (Ch. Kimberlin Killea O'Topo, owned by J. and B. Topliss), was a top contender on the West Coast.

Arland, Mrs. Thomas C. — *Charlton* — Colorado Springs, CO

Am. & Can. Ch. Charlton's Tory of Tipperary was Winnie Arland's first champion. Purchased from Draherin, he finished his championship by going first in a Group and was the sire of five champions. Other prominent dogs at Charlton were: Ch. Draherin Ivy Leaguer, Best in Show winner; Ch. Shannon's Empress, dam of several Charlton champions; Ch. Candia Fatima; and the lovely Ch. Draherin Marietta, a Canadian Best in Show winner with many Specialty and Group wins in the United States.

One dog, however, has stood out above all others in the kennel. Ch. Candia Indeed at this writing is the sire of 52 champions, which tops the record of Ch. Tirvelda Michaelson as the breed's leading sire. Indeed has had a phenomenal career as a stud. So good were his litters that many breeders bred the same bitches back to him two or three times—in one case, four times—for repeat litters of champions. It is interesting that this son of Ch. Bayberry Kincaide ex Ch. Candia Fatima was a grandson of Michaelson's litter sister, yet the two sires produced totally different types.

"Long John", as Indeed was known, came in a trade for an English Cocker puppy. He finished at two years of age, winning his points at three Specialties. By the age of three, he had already sired six champions. By the end of 1975, he had pointed offspring out of twelve different bitches.

It is a tragedy for the breed that Indeed died from bloat at the age of eight. Had he lived, or had the AKC permitted frozen semen at the time of his death, I do believe he would easily have reached the century mark in number of champions produced.

Bairrington, Col. (Dr.) Jerrold D. and Jane E. — *O'Cairn* — Devine, TX

O'Cairn Farms derives its name from Ch. Jo-Ett's Rolling Rock, the sire of the Bairringtons' first Irish Setter bitch, Rolling Rocks Lady O'Cairn. O'Cairn is Gaelic for "of the rock."

The O'Cairn kennel program includes field, Obedience and conformation. Until 1974, the interest was principally in field and Obedience. When Ch. Kerrizan's Meg O' Limerick Lane, a daughter of Ch. Willowdale Crimson Count, was obtained from Joe and Irish Smith (Limerick Lane), she was bred to Ch. Tirvelda Telstar, and a litter was whelped in October, 1977.

Sara's Lord Sean O'Cairn, CD, has several field trial wins, and a placement of 4th at the National Field Trial. His get, O'Cairn's Kathleen Devine, won every Sweepstakes entered as a puppy, and has finished out of the money only one time in fifteen shows.

Ch. Candia Indeed
(Ch. Bayberry Kinkaide ex Ch. Candia Fatima).

Ch. Shawnlea's Gayla (Ch. Shawnlea's Fanfare ex Shawnlea's Duchess of Argyle), left, and Ch. Shawnlea's Fanfare (Ch. Charles River Lance O'Lane ex Shawnlea's Jane Barlow).

Baron, Bernard and Wilma — *Gentree* — Valley Stream, NY

The favorite dog at Gentree was Ch. Westwind Scarlet Gay Blade (Ch. Taradell's Bright Future ex Ch. Knockross Polly). Gay Blade sired 8 champions, including Ch. Dariabar Wilma Baron, named for the real Wilma Baron. Another favorite was Gentree Aphrodite, a bitch with both bench and field points. The Barons also bred Gentree Ballyshannon Kara (co-owned with the Miloves) to Ch. Ballycroy's Northern Sunset (Ch. Tirvelda Nor'Wester ex Ballycroy's Rua Catlin) producing Gentree Merry-Go-Boy. "Chuck" was pointed, but was injured and retired from the ring. He was bred to Gentree's Autumn Jade to produce Ch. Gentree Bonanza.

The Barons were editors of the ISCA 1975 National Pictorial, and Bernie for several years was Secretary of the National Specialty. He was one of the founders and is a former president of the Irish Setter Club of Long Island, where Wilma also held office. Both are active in Eastern Irish Setter Association and in the Westbury Kennel Club. In 1982, Bernie became president of the Irish Setter Club of America. He is an approved judge of many Sporting breeds, including Irish Setters.

Bayless, Helen A. and Madeline — *Enilen* — Woodland Hills, CA

James W. Bayless, a prominent member of the Irish Setter Club of America, died in November 1964. Mrs. Bayless and her daughter have continued the outstanding Obedience activities of the Enilen Kennels.

They have owned 5 UDT champions: Van Ayl Dennis Jerold, Tyronne Farm McCorkney, Red Barn Rosabelle, Enilen Ginger Snap and Enilen Michael Terrence. Jerold's Obedience record has never been equalled. McCorkney, a Best in Show Setter, has participated in more tracking tests than any other Irishman. Rosabelle was the dam of 3 champions. Ginger is an American and Mexican champion. Terrence has a Mexican PC (Perro Companero or Companion Dog) and a PR (Perro Rastreador or Tracking Dog) in addition to his American UDT degree.

Madeline's Corkney's Garmhac is a CDXT and PC.

Behne, Noel and Fran — *Tapnar* — Correales, NM

Tapnar's foundation bitch, Ch. Draherin Merry Kerry, acquired from Lucy Jane Myers, produced five champions. From the Ch. Shannon's Erin litter came multi-BIS winner, Ch. Draherin King's Ransom, sire of 29 champions, and his sisters Ch. Tapnar Avant-garde and Ch. Tapnar Angelica. Angelica was the dam of Ch. Tapnar Joanna, who in turn, bred only once, produced two champion sons. Angelica, bred to Ch. Candia Indeed, produced finished offspring in the United States, Canada, and Mexico. Another sister, Tapnar Adventuress, CD, bred to Ch. Tirvelda Distant Drummer, was the dam of four champions in the Tapnar "E" litter. Then, Merry Kerry bred to Ch. Bayberry Tobago resulted in two Group winners, Am. & Can. Ch. Tapnar Barnstormer and Ch. Tapnar Banshee Brogue. Another son of this combination, Tapnar Ballaghaderreen, has the distinction of being the only unpointed Irish Setter to win BOB at a major Specialty from the Veteran's Class—at almost nine years of age.

Bergren, Renette — *Cairncross* — Libertyville, IL

Now a very successful young professional handler, Renette received her early training under the guidance of Larry Downey. She has finished a growing number of champions, and presently owns Ch. Tuxedo's Formal Occasion (a Ch. Blayneywood Country Squire son), Ch. Kilgary Ballyvaughan (a grandson of the full brothers, Ch. Shannon's Erin and Ch. Major O'Shannon), and Ch. Kilgary Aman (a double Erin grandson).

Berman, William H. and Ruth B. — *Wenvarra, Reg.* — Potomac, MD

The Bermans' first Irish Setter, purchased in 1963, was Ruth's Wenvarra of Kinsale, CDX, a Ch. Kinvarra Redstone daughter out of a Wendover import. Bred to Ch. Kinvarra Malone in 1966, she produced Group and Specialty winner, Ch. Wenvarra's Malone O'Redstone, CD, and Specialty winner, Ch. Wenvarra's Misty Malone, CD, the brother-sister foundation of the elegant Wenvarra type. Misty was bred to Ch. Kinvarra Flicker in 1970, and from the litter they kept Ch. Wenvarra Ondine who was Best of Winners at the Eastern Irish Setter Association outdoor specialty in 1972 and continued her ring career successfully as a Special. Ondine and Malone produced Ch. Wenvarra Malone. The Bermans made their first outside acquisition with the purchase of Ch. Spiretop Sorceress, who finished in five successive weekends of showing in 1975.

They have continued a program of line breeding with litters by Am. Bda. & Can. Ch. Redwhiskey's Royal Jester, Ch. Tirvelda Telstar and Ch. Tirvelda Distant Drummer. From the latter litter, two dogs have finished, Ch. Wenvarra Warlock and Ch. Wenvarra Waterwitch.

As time permits, the Bermans also pursue degrees in Obedience work.

Bresnahan, Donald and Valerie — *Donoval* — Westlake, OH

The Donoval Kennel began with a pet bitch, Jody's Irish Brandy. Brandy's pedigree contained both show and field lines. The Bresnahans liked the combination, but when it came time to breed, they preferred to breed to a show line. A breeding of Brandy to Ch. Starheir Aaron Ardee produced their foundation bitch, Donoval's Merry Megan.

Megan, bred to Tristans Crimson Bishop (a son of Ch. Tirvelda Earl of Harewood and Starheir Quintessence), produced Donoval's first homebred champion, Am. & Can. Ch. Donoval's Crimson Crown, who completed his Canadian title at 19 months of age, and his American title at 26 months, going Winners Dog at one of the largest ISCA National Specialties. Crimson Crown ("Mac") was among the top winning Irish in the country in 1980 with numerous Breed and Group wins to his credit.

Brooks, William and Patsy — *Bayberry* — Decatur, GA

In response to my invitation, Bill and Patsy Brooks write:

"In one way or another, the dogs and bitches that figured prominently in the "building' of Bayberry were there because they were essential to the theme of combining so many of the great ones of the past—Champions Kinvarra Kermit and Portia, Tyronne Farm Malone I and II, Seaforth Red Velvet, Thenderin Brian Tristan, Michael Bryan Duke of Sussex, Hartsbourne Sallyann of Tirvelda (and the legacy of Hartsbourne behind her) and Tirvelda Nutbrown Sherry.

"Without the generous encouragement and help of Ted Eldrege our efforts would not have been so rewarding. The two foundation bitches of Bayberry—Ch. Tirvelda Cathy O'Rinn (Ch. Michael Bryan Duke of Sussex ex Ch. Tirvelda Nutbrown Sherry) and Ch. Tirvelda Bayberry Sundown (Ch. Blayneywood Country Squire ex Ch. Tirvelda Divine Sarah) had behind them most of the prepotent greats of the past. Both bitches gained fame in the show ring. Cathy won the ISCA Best Bitch and Best Opposite Sex Awards in 1965, and Sundown won her

Ch. Tirvelda Cathy O'Rinn (Ch. Michael Bryan Duke of Sussex ex Ch. Tirvelda Nutbrown Sherry).

Ch. Westwind Scarlet Bay Blade (Ch. Taradell's Bright Future ex Ch. Knockross Polly).

Ch. Bayberry Sommerset
(Ch. Kinvarra Malone ex Ch. Tirvelda Cathy O'Rinn).

championship points at four straight Specialties, earning for her owner the ISCA's Amateur Handler Award.

"From these two bitches came bench champions, Companion Dog degree winners, Specialty winners, Group winners, all-breed Best in Show winners, ISCA Award winners and a Westminster winner. Mainly, these honors came either through Cathy's two sons—Ch. Bayberry Sommerset and Ch. Bayberry Kincaide, or through the breeding of Sundown to Sommerset.

"Bred to Ch. Kinvarra Malone, Cathy produced Ch. Bayberry Cherokee Red Arrow and Ch. Bayberry Sommerset. Bred to Ch. Kinvarra Flicker, Cathy produced Ch. Bayberry Kincaide, Ch. Bayberry Bristol Cream, Ch. Bayberry Sparkling Burgundy, Ch. Bayberry Russet of Kinvarra, Ch. Bayberry Raffles, and Ch. Bayberry Bronson of Palomar. Of these, two are Group winners, and three are Specialty winners. A broken tail left a seventh Flicker - Cathy son one point short of his championship.

"From Sommerset and Sundown came Group and five times Best in Specialty winner, Ch. Bayberry Sonnet. Sonnet was also ISCA's Best Bitch and Best Opposite Sex Awards winner in 1972. Another from this breeding, Ch. Bayberry Happy Time, CD, was a breed winning and Group-placing bitch, with Specialty wins to her credit. In only six months showing in 1971, Happy rose to #5 Irish Setter Bitch in the nation. Though Sonnet was only able to produce one litter, both she and Happy have produced notable champions for Bayberry.

"Sommerset, in his too brief span of life, produced 11 champions that distinguished themselves with Specialty wins. Sommerset progeny, Chs. Tirvelda Distant Drummer, Bayberry Sonnet and Palomar's Rollingbay Molly are all multi-Best in Specialty winners. Himself a Group and Specialty winner (owner-handled), Sommerset was sire of all-breed Best in Show winners, Ch. Tirvelda Distant Drummer and Ch. Squire's Sean of Essex. A Sommerset-Sundown son in South Africa is also a multi-Best in Show winner.

"Among the notable get of Am. & Can. Ch. Bayberry Kincaide are the famed Ch. Bayberry Tobago and Ch. Candia Indeed. Both, like their sire, were Specialty winners. Tobago, after a successful show career, proved himself a sire of excellence, and Indeed—winner of the ISCA Top Sire Award two years in succession at an early age—became possibly the most popular sire of his time."

"These facts testify to the quality of these and the prepotency of those behind them. They all provided as near to human companionship as one could ask, magnificent temperament, stable, sweet, buoyant spirit, dignity, intelligent, courageous, loving, sensitive to how we felt, self-assured, never aggressive, never timid either, and delightful personalities. They are all still missed, but what a gift to have been blessed by any one of them, but to have them all . . ."

Patsy and Bill Brooks have served on many breed club rosters. Patsy was Corresponding Secretary for ISCA and both assisted in the formation of the Potomac Irish Setter Club and the Irish Setter Club of Georgia. Bill is now an approved judge of Setters and has judged at many Specialty shows.

Brown, W. Douglas and Carol L. — *Redwhiskey* — Wallingford, CT

The Browns' first show quality Irish, Glen Cree Bridey Murphy, was purchased in 1968. Shortly after, they purchased an 11-month-old bitch who was to become their first champion, Ch. Victory's Royal Sensation, CD. In 1970, Kelmora Sabre Dance and Ch. Smoke Dream of Tamarisk were acquired, and later—with the Dunns (Ronita Irish Setters)—Ch. Tirvelda Court Jester. With limited breeding, Redwhiskey has produced more than 15 champions. Most have been Specialty winners.

In 1968, Ch. Victory's Royal Sensation, CD, was bred to Ch. Tirvelda Nor'Wester. This breeding produced three champions; Am. & Can. Ch. Redwhiskey's Brandysniffer, Ch. Redwhiskey's Baroness, and Am. & Can. Ch. Redwhiskey's Trace of Victory.

In 1971, Sensation was bred to Kelmora Sabre Dance, producing Am. & Can. Ch. Redwhiskey's Sabre Dance who won several Best of Breeds and Group placements, and Ch. Redwhiskey's Royal Victory, who, in 1974 won the ISCA Best Bitch award.

The most noted Redwhiskey litter was the breeding of Ch. Tirvelda Court Jester to Glen Cree Bridey Murphy in 1972. This breeding produced Ch. Redwhiskey's Merlyn, Ch. Redwhiskey's Harbor Master, Ch. Redwhiskey's Holiday Velvet, Ch. Redwhiskey's Happiness Is, Am. & Can. Ch. Redwhiskey's Happy Talk, and Redwhiskey's Humoresque (pointed). Of the five that finished, all but Harbor Master was a Specialty winner. He completed his title in less than ten weeks with several Best of Breed and Group placements, including a Group 1. Am. & Can. Ch. Redwhiskey's Happy Talk completed her championship entirely from the Bred-by-Exhibitor class with four majors.

Buehler, Dr. George M. and Valerie — *Brynmount* — Jeffersonville, IN

Mrs. Buehler has been associated with Irish Setters all her life, the Brynmount prefix being adopted from her aunt, Mrs. Jean Clarke, who owned the Brynmount Kennel in England. Their foundation bitch is Ch. Tirvelda Evenson, whose first litter of thirteen pups was sired by Am. & Can. Ch. McCamon Marquis.

Burgasser, Carol Anne — *Shalimar* — Baldwin Park, CA

Carol Burgasser got her start in Irish Setters in 1968, when she bought Kamron Connemara from Ron and Renee Taylor. "Casey" earned her CD in three countries, and was Carol's foundation bitch. She was first bred to her sire, Ch. Legend of Varagon, UDT, a breeding that produced three Canadian champions, including Kamron Avante Garde, winner of the *Kennel Review* Best Puppy award for 1970.

Her next purchase from the Taylors was Kamron Dominique, who also became a *Kennel Review* Best Puppy award winner (with 27 wins) and went on to become Am., Mex., Can., Bda. & Intl. Ch. Kamron Dominique, the most titled bitch in Irish Setter history. She scored many breed wins in the States, and a BIS from the classes in Mexico.

Carol acquired Julerin Kamron Joy, a Legend daughter, whom she bred to Ch. Danalee Bright Flash, a Legend son. This mating produced the top Irish Setter bitch in the country in 1975, Ch. Shalimar Kai of Callaway.

A breeding of Dominique to Ch. Thenderin Yeoman J.G. produced Ch. Shalimar Windsong, who finished in just two months. Carol's future breeding plans include the combining of her two winning Dominique/Joy lines.

Burkhart, Harriet T. and Bogie, Dale — *Dariabar* — Vincentown, NJ

I asked this successful mother-daughter team to write their own kennel history, which follows:

"We have often been asked the meaning of the name Dariabar. It represents for us a beautiful, romantic, but mythical place . . . a lost Treasure Island, spoken of by Sinbad, who found this place to be reality with riches untold.

. Bayberry Kinkaide (Ch. Kin-
rra Flicker ex Ch. Tirvelda Cathy
Rinn).

. Donoval's Crimson Crown
istan's Crimson Bishop ex
noval Merry Megan).

. Tirvelda Court Jester (Ch.
velda Rustic Duke ex Ch. Tir-
da Maidavale).

The determining factor in the beginning foundation (1946) was Belfield Jeffrey Dail, a gift from Miss Helen Naylor of Belfield Kennels, owner of the greatest all time winning Best in Show bitch, Ch. Knightscroft Symphony. Jeff was pure Knightscroft. He produced our first Dariabar animal, Dariabar Copper Clad. Copper Clad was the pick of the litter and was given away to friends, only to be returned to the kennel at age three. He was shown, pointed and died suddenly at an early age. Before he died, I acquired a sturdy bitch, Irish Rose IV. She and Copper Clad produced the first Dariabar-bred champion, Baron O'Dariabar of Windsor, who was given to Dr. Robert F. Way. "Baron" then produced two champions for us, Dariabar Range Finder and Dariabar Copper Ranger, and also Dariabar Flame Came Home. These last two came from Sadrina of Quaker Point, our English import (Wendover, Maydorwill and Hartsbourne). Flame, incidentally, was returned to the kennel at age 6½ after three homes—hence his name, Flame Came Home. He was shown and pointed and died while in the South, about to be finished by Michele Leathers. Flame was sire of two champions, Dariabar Ringmaster and Dariabar Roland O'Toole, out of a breeding with Dariabar Emerald O'Flynn.

In the mid-'50s we leased Erinhaven Laurie Muldoon (Knightscroft-Milson family) and bred her to Copper Clad. This produced Dariabar Discovery, who when bred to Irish Rose, gave us Dariabar True Love, mother of Ch. Dariabar Range Finder, and Ch. Windsor Michael Son O'Kelly. Next, we acquired Sunburst Squaw of Redfeather, a Laurie Muldoon daughter, sired by a pure Knightscroft linebred champion.

In 1965, Padraic O'Flynn of Fair-Green joined our stud force at age 4½. He was a large son of Knockross O'Boy and a closely linebred bitch of the Knockalong and O'Flynn family. He was destined to fit into a pattern of being combined with the Squaw and also the get of Range Finder and vice versa. Unfortunately, the pattern was interrupted by his death, but not before he produced Ch. Dariabar Ambrette and her sister Emerald from Squaw, and Ch. Padraic O'Flynn of Greenwich from a daughter of Squaw and Range Finder. Padraic was shown very limitedly. He was BOW at the Eastern Irish Setter Assn. Spring Specialty in 1966 under William Thompson, who had the courage to give him the 5-point win in spite of his graying face, but, with 14 points, he died of bloat right after the show. In all, Padraic produced 6 champions and a Utility degree winner. Bred to a daughter of Ch. Titian Inteprid and Ch. Tirvelda Witch, he produced Ch. Little Chap's Shaman O'Sheen, Ch. Dariabar Ola Hinob O'Flynn, and Hinob Crimson Dawn, CD, CDX, UD.

Following his get into the next generation, Ch. Dariabar Ambrette when bred to Ch. Westwind Scarlet Gay Blade produced Ch. Dariabar Gay Baron and Ch. Dariabar Wilma Baron; Emerald, bred to Flame Came Home produced Ch. Dariabar Ringmaster and Ch. Dariabar Roland O'Toole; and Bradford produced Ch. Karen's Kelly Green Victory ex a Ch. Gay Blade daughter. Dariabar Dawn Mist, a Padraic daughter, produced Ch. Dariabar Peyton, sired by Range Finder. Ch. Dariabar Ola Hinob O'Flynn, bred to Ch. Sunny Acre Top O' The Mark, produced the top winning Field Ch. Dariabar Jotunn O'Flynn, CD.

In the 1970s we acquired Ch. Tirvelda Beau James (sire of six champions) as an older dog, and he won many Veteran classes at Eastern Specialties. He died at age 13—one of the dearest Irish Setters who ever lived with us. We also imported two littermates from Wendover Kennel in England—Wendover Rugbee of Dariabar and Wendover Crickett of Dariabar, sired by Ch. Wendover Gentleman. Our most recent champion is Dariabar Brady O'Baron, a son of Ch. Dariabar Gay Baron ex a Ch. Ringmaster daughter."

Harriet has been active in several Irish Setter clubs. She was a professional handler from 1949 to 1970, when she resigned her license.

Bussey, Dirk T. and Betty P. — *Shamrok* — Clinton, NY

A young kennel, the Busseys have Tirvelda Sunset Celebration and Tirvelda Spring Song, co-owned with Tirvelda. Betty is co-founder of the Irish Setter Club of Central New York.

Camp, Diane M. — *Woodland Brook* — Atlanta, GA

Diane's foundation bitch, Camp's Penelope of Pace (Rogue's Barry ex Lady Glow of Von Arnell) was purchased in 1967 from Mrs. Anne Steiner. She was never shown, but at age seven was trained for field trialing. In her short two year career she won 7 points and placed fourth in Amateur Gun Dog at the First National Field Trial of the ISCA.

In 1971, Penelope was bred to Ch. Harmony Lane's Red Oak. Diane kept a bitch from this breeding and she became Dual Champion and Amateur Field Ch. Cynthia of Woodland Brook. Cindy was Best Puppy at the Georgia National Specialty in 1972. In 1973, she obtained her bench title in three months with three majors, always being shown by Anne Smith of Harmony Lane. At the time she was being shown, Diane worked her continuously in the field. Because there are so few field trials in the South, a co-ownership with Anthony Baron was established. Then, in four consecutive trials, Cindy became the breed's tenth Dual Champion, and in just three more trials she became the breed's first to have the title, Dual Ch. *and* Amateur Field Champion.

Out of the same litter was Woodland Brook's Shannon Lane, CDX, the first Irish in Georgia to obtain a CDX. Combined scores were 194½.

In 1974, Cynthia was bred to Ch. Thenderin William Muldoon. From this breeding, Diane kept another bitch, Ch. Woodland Brook Mist of Autumn. Misty completed her title at age two, with three majors.

Christie, Dr. L. Glenn and Constance — *Killagay* — Crozier, VA

Noted for field, Obedience and bench activities, this former California kennel, now in Virginia, was started by Janet and Mark Kelsey, and Mark's sister, Connie. The Kelseys are no longer active and it remains for the Christies to carry on the Killagay prefix.

Connie is determined to keep the breed multi-purpose. She fully believes that Irish Setters can both be beautiful and hunt well. Among the Field Trial champions produced are Field Trial Ch. Killagay's Brandy Appetizer; FTC Killagay's Bit O'Dellarobia—who, at under two years became the youngest Irish Setter in AKC history to finish in the field; FTC Killagay Duke of Rust O'Fur, CDX, and FTC Killagay's Gidget of Ireland.

Brandy Appetizer and Bit O'Dellarobia belong to Bob and Jean Oram of Los Altos, California (Bob was chairman of the 1974 ISCA National Field Trial). Duke of Rust O'Fur is owned by Don and Patty Harris of Chico, California. And Gidget is owned by Jake Huizenga, the grand old man of field trainers.

In Connie's own words: "Our field dogs all carry lovely to outstanding coats, and range in size from 30 to 25 inches. Most are sired by bench champions and are bred to meet the standard. No twisting of interpretation. None are little Red Setters."

That this is a dual strain is borne out by the bench champions: Ch. Killagay's Kelsey, CD; Ch. Killagay's Carrie, CD; Ch. Killagay Aaraon's Party Boy, CD; Ch.

Padraic O'Flynn of Fair-Gree
(Knockross O'Boy ex Roxan
O'Flynn of Fair-Green).

Ch. Onesquethaw Kate O'Finn (Red
Barn Talleyrand ex Onesquethaw
Kathy O'Shea).

Dual Ch. & Can. Ch. Killagay's
age of Tara, Am. & Can. CD,
(Robalee Endeavor ex Fld. C
Killagay Bit O'Dellarobia).

Killagay's Sea Charis, CD; Ch. Killagay's Cinnamon Charlin, CD (owned by Karen and Gary Wilson, also transplanted from California to Virginia). Latest to finish (in the Fall of 1979 as an eight year old) is Dual Ch. Killagay's Image of Tara. This remarkable bitch is also a Canadian champion and a Can. and Am. CD, and as if this were not enough, she is the first to win the V.C. degree title of the Irish Setter Club of America.

Clemons, Mrs. Arthur and Kurtik, Eileen — *Onesquethaw* — Selkirk, NY

Onesquethaw, meaning "good harvest," was the name of an Indian tribe from which came the kennel name for the Clemons' Irish Setters in 1949. Since that time, more than 12 Obedience title winners have been trained by the Clemons. Riley's Ramsey MacDonald was the first Irish Setter in New York state to gain the UDT suffix. Other proud moments for the kennel include Ch. Onesquethaw Star Dancer going Winners Bitch at Westminster in 1963; Ch. Onesquethaw Kate O'Finn, Best Puppy at the Combined Specialty in New York, 1966, Best in Sweepstakes at New England Specialty 1966, Winners Bitch at the first Potomac Irish Setter Specialty, and finishing in Maine in 1967.

Orpha continues to carry on a very limited breeding program that has produced 10 champions. With the support of her partner, Eileen Kurtik, she remains dedicated to the fancy. One of her breeding, Ch. Onesquethaw Mourna Fleming (Ch. Smoke Dream of Tamarisk ex Onesquethaw Cara Dooley), owned by Bonnie Jo Hall, was one of the top brood bitches of the year for 1981.

Conlon, Laurie and Tom — *Palomar* — Winston, GA

Palomar's first Irish Setter, Buck Acres' Ember of Brask (Tipperary Point Brask ex Ch. Baker's Buck-Ette) was obtained in 1967, and became their first champion in 1968. Their foundation bitch came in 1968—Bayberry Tiffany of Tirvelda, CD (Ch. Bayberry Sommerset ex Ch. Bayberry Sundown). With 5 points, including a major, she broke her tail in 1973, which ended her chances of championship. Ember and Tiffany basically started the Palomar family.

Ch. Palomar's Rollingbay Molly, sired by Ch. Bayberry Sommerset and out of Palomar's Peggy O'Neill (an Ember/Tiffany daughter), finished owner-handled with three majors, including a BOB at the ISC of Georgia Specialty. At her death, three days after a repeat win of BOB at the Georgia Specialty in 1975, she left Palomar with several promising youngsters, sired by Ch. Candia Indeed.

Ch. Bayberry Bronson of Palomar (Ch. Kinvarra Flicker ex Ch. Tirvelda Cathy O'Rinn) was purchased from Bayberry Kennel as a puppy in 1970. He finished his championship owner-handled, a Group winner, and is the sire of Ch. Palomar's Gaelan Gypsy, Ch. Palomar's Gijet Cajun Classic and Ch. Palomar's Bayberry Canon.

Ch. Palomar's Southern Star, a son of Gaelan Gypsy and Bayberry Southerner (younger full brother of Ch. Candia Indeed), finished in six weeks with four majors, two at Specialties, and is already making a name for himself as a sire. His daughter, Palomar's Morning Star, was undefeated in 22 point show puppy classes including the National and Georgia Specialties. And her two brothers, Capricorn and Squire Copperfield, took the points each time they were first shown from Novice. Ch. Palomar Skyrocket Corcaigh, another Southern Star son, was Winners Dog at the 1981 National Specialty on the way to his title.

But just when the future looked so bright, tragedy struck and the Irish Setter world lost one of the most outstanding ladies to ever grace our breed. Laurie, much loved, passed away in 1980. However, the kennel is continuing under the guidance of Laurie's daughter-in-law, Andrea.

Conner, Dr. William Curtis, Jr. and Nancy — *Tainaron* — Montague, MA
The Tainaron Kennel came into existence in 1969 when Nancy received an Irish Setter bitch from Curt as a wedding present. This bitch became Ch. Tainaron Saffron Replica, CD. She was a Ch. Tirvelda Nor'wester daughter and was acquired from Bob Reese. Nancy and Curt have shown several other dogs, including Ch. Tainaron Charisma (Saffron's daughter by Ch. Tirvelda Earl of Harewood), Am. & Can. Ch. Meadowlark Drury Lane, Am. & Can. & Bda. CD, who was the winner of several ISCA and local club awards, and Meadowlark's Nuance who was Reserve Winners Bitch from the puppy bitch class at the 1976 National Specialty. They are breeders of Ch. Tainaron Mr. Minstrel by Ch. Rendition Erin of Sunny Hills, and co-breeders with Nancy Marino of Tainaron Breath of Spring and Tainaron Promises to Keep, pointed get sired by Ch. Shawnee Sundance.

The Conners Obedience-train all their dogs. In a 15-month period Nancy finished three CDs including Tirvelda Cormac, CD, and Tainaron Escapade, CD. Curt has added further dimensions to their hobby through his skill in photography, and his work portraying the Irish Setter here and in Russia has been published in the AKC *Gazette* and in Setter magazines.

Crawford, Betty — *Shannon's Kennels* — North Jackson, OH
Betty acquired her first Irish Setter bitch, Shamrock of Erin, from George Glassford (Tom's father) in 1953), and her first male, Knockross Nero, from W. L. Newhall in 1954. Nero bred to Shamrock produced Ch. Shamrock's Shawn of Erin, Ch. Shamrock's Red Rogue, CD, and Shamrock's Penny Royal, CDX.

Betty writes: "It wasn't until 1960, when I purchased Knockross Ruby, that I found a bitch suitable to my standard, and she was almost two at the time of purchase. I showed her along with Draherin Irish Regardless, owned by Lee and Betty Miller. They finished a week apart."

In 1962, Ruby and Regardless were bred, and a new and important chapter in Irish Setter history began. These two were bred together four times.

The 1962 litter produced: Am. Ber. & Can. Ch. Shannon's Shawn of Erin, who went to the Joseph Slicks; Am. & Can. Ch. Shannon's Sharon (Crosby); Ch. Shamie, also owned by the Slicks; Am. & Can. Ch. Shannon's Laird Shane and Ch. Shannon's Miss Sassy, retained by Betty Crawford. Shawn won Bests in Show in the States and Bermuda, Shane was a Best in Show winner in Canada, and Sharon was a multi Specialty and Group winner.

The 1964 litter produced: Am. Ber. & Can. Ch. Shannon's Erin, owned by Lucy Jane Myers (much more is written of this famous Best in Show winner and leading sire in the section on Draherin Kennels); Am. & Can. Ch. Major O'Shannon, owned by Albert Greenfield, Jr.; Ch. Shannon's Gayla O'Rugh (Rugh); Am. & Can. Ch. Shannon's Susie Starlet, CD (Weick); Am. & Can. Ch. Bet-Lee's Gaye Blade (Berardinelli); Ch. Shawn Shannon (Brennan); Ch. Canyon Copper O'Boy (Reynolds) and Betty Crawford's Ch. Shannon's Empress.

Erin and Major were both multi Best in Show winners. Erin for years held the position of top sire in the breed, and Major (so ably handled by Tom Glassford) was top Setter in 1968, 1969, and 1970. Major won two Quaker Oats awards, and both brothers twice won the breed and placed in the Group at Westminster. Susie Starlet and Gayla were top winning bitches for the year in the time they were campaigned.

Major O'Shannon (Ch. Draherin Regardless ex Ch. Knockross).

Am. & Bda. Ch. Villa-Dan Stacey Shine Bright (Valhalla Georgie of Villa-Dan ex Riverview's Sparkling Sherri).

. Palomar's Southern Star ayberry Southerner ex Ch. lomar's Gaelan Gypsy).

Most of Ruby's produce have several champion sons and daughters, some having Best in Show wins. Most prominent was Susie Starlet's Ch. Starheir's Aaron Ardee, bred and shown to his championship by Paul and Lorraine Weick. Later, under the ownership of Mr. and Mrs. Hugh Rumbaugh, he became the top winning Irish Setter of all time.

Betty is a well-known and highly regarded professional handler. She has been very active in many kennel clubs, serving as President and Chairman of Field Trials and Specialties, and has served on the Board of Directors of the Irish Setter Club of America.

Cunningham, David and Laura — *Beaverbrook* — Knoxville, TN

Laura and David train and show American Saddlebred horses professionally at Beaverbrook Stables, and both are licensed horse show judges. Laura's interest in Irish Setters began in 1966 when a customer of the stable gave her an unregistered male puppy, christened "Red". Obedience classes led to Obedience trials (with an I.L.P. number) and a CD, and then the desire to have a show dog.

In 1971, Wilson Farm Dove of Kincora—one year old, elegant and heavy coated bitch, by Ch. Tirvelda Earl of Harewood ex Ch. Wilson Farm Mourning Dove—became the foundation bitch for Beaverbrook Irish Setters. The kennel has always been kept small, usually no more than five adult Irish. The Cunninghams also own two champion Rottweilers.

A daughter of Dove's, Beaverbrook Country Claret (by Ch. Blaynewood Country Squire) has produced many of the pointed dogs currently shown under the Beaverbrook prefix. Another Dove daughter, Beaverbrook Prelude, and a Dove half-sister, B. Reverie Gael, are pointed.

In 1977, all breeding stock at Beaverbrook underwent test-matings for P.R.A.—Dove, Claret and Prelude all passed, demonstrating genetic non-carrier status, and the two younger bitches, Lyric and Wilson Farm Beaverbrook Kyri were genetically clear through parents' test-matings.

Beaverbrook dogs that have won Obedience titles for other owners include B. Fen Hollen, CD (Hubbs), B. Red Brandy Dust, CDX (Smith), and B. Fanfare, Can. CD (Engoglia).

Czarnecky, David and Susan — *Kerry-Eire* — Buffalo, NY

The Czarneckys had been in Irish Setters for five years, Dave doing Obedience work and Sue showing in conformation, before breeding their foundation bitch, Ch. Danalee Cover Girl to Ch. Candia Indeed. From this breeding came Am. & Can. Ch. Kerry-Eire Revolutionary, Ch. Kerry-Eire Little Rebel and several other pointed offspring.

Revolutionary, handled by Tom Tobin, was the No. 1 Irish Setter in the nation, and No. 3 Sporting, for the year 1980. At time of this writing, he had won 6 all-breed Bests in Show, 11 Specialties, 25 Groups and 168 BOB awards. Little Rebel, owner-handled, also has nice wins to her credit including BOB at the ISC of Southern California Specialty, 1979.

Daniel, Ervil C. and Ann R. — *Villa-Dan* — Batavia, OH

The Daniels have had Irish since 1957. Ch. Daniel's Misty Dawn, CD, was their first champion. Misty, bred to Am. & Can. Ch. Major O'Shannon, produced Am. & Can. Ch. Tuxedo Comanche Majorette, owned by Dr. R. D. Helferty.

Their Encore's My Sally, needing only a major to finish, was bred and her first litter produced puppies with P.R.A. Several of the dogs were on the brink of their championships when eye problems struck, and the Daniels discontinued breeding activities for a while.

The Daniels' major contribution to the breed has been their effort to eliminate inherited problems. They have had seven P.R.A. test-mated litters, which has covered all the dogs in their kennel.

One of the finest bitches bred at Villa-Dan has been Am. & Bda. Ch. Villa-Dan Stacey Shine Bright. Named Outstanding Producer for the year 1980 by *Kennel Review,* she was #1 Irish Setter Dam and #3 Sporting Group Dam (tied) in the nation. Her offspring scored many unique wins, including BOB, BOS and BOW at the same show. At five shows (two of which were majors) these littermates took both WD and WB. Bred to Am. & Can. Ch. Santera Tamberluck, CD, Stacey produced the successful V-litter of six champions (four finished in 1980, two in 1981): Ch. Villa-Dan Victorian Express, Ch. Villa-Dan Valentina, Ch. Villa-Dan Vindicator, Ch. Villa-Dan Victriss, Ch. Villa-Dan Visual Fantasy and Ch. Villa-Dan Vallejo. The V-litter proved very prepotent, and many of their offspring under the age of two are pointed.

Dash, Susan E. — *McDerry* — Naples, ME

Susan's first Irish Setter was a Ch. Laurel Ridge Star Rocket granddaughter, given to Susan on her tenth birthday in 1965. In 1971, Susan and her mother obtained McDerry's Hengate Blue Skies (a triple descendant of Ch. Charles River Streamliner) from Barbara Antio. Although never shown, Blue, mated with Dual Ch. Donnington Crackerjack, produced: McDerry's Fair Lady, CDX, field pointed and Canadian bench pointed; Am. & Can. Ch. McDerry's Make Ready and Can. Ch. Hide-A-Way Crimson Shawn, a sister-brother team who were often WB and WD at the same New England shows.

Blue's second litter, from Kelmora Sabre Dance, produced their most outstanding brood bitch, Can. Ch. McDerry's Alanna By The Sea, CD. "Amy" placed in a number of Specialties, the comment being "Beautiful bitch, but so big!" With this in mind, they bred to a smaller dog, Ch. Tirvelda Red Baron of Dunholm. This was a most exceptional nick, and was repeated three times. The first litter produced: Ch. McDerry's Even Keel and his pointed sisters, McDerry's Effervescence (co-owned with Sheryl Withington), McDerry's Ebbtide, McDerry's Endorsement, and McDerry's Easy to Love, CD.

Also added to their kennel (bought as young puppies) were Am. & Can. Ch. Redwhiskey's Kiss Me Kate and Ch. Redwhiskey's Invincible, CD. At only two, Invincible already produced Specialty winning puppies and two Obedience title holders.

Dee, Norbert and Nena — *Camelot* — Stone Mountain, GA

The Camelot Kennel was established in 1978 with the breeding of the Dees' Am. and Can. Ch. Major O'Shannon daughter, Shane's Irish Tara Dee, to Ch. Meadowlark's Masterpiece. Masterpiece's bloodline, which includes Ch. Tirvelda Michaelson and Am., Can., & Mex. Ch. Draherin King's Ransom, complemented Tara and produced Chs. Camelot's Cloud Chaser and Camelot's Cover Girl. Both won BOBs from the classes over Specials on the way to their championships. The Camelot breeding program continued with the mating of Tara to Ch. Scarlly's Showboat, which produced Camelot's Gambler and Camelot's I Love Lucy, who as a puppy won two Specialty Best in Sweepstakes. Camelot Setters is also the home of a Showboat littermate, Ch. Scarlly's Sassafras, who finished at the age of two by winning two Georgia Irish Setter Club Specialties.

Dunn, Robert and Anita — *Ronita* — Killingworth, CT

The experts aver that you make your own good luck. The Dunns start in Irish disputes that:

In 1971 they purchased a pet bitch puppy from Doug and Carol Brown for a nominal sum. Six months later they answered an ad in the local paper from someone wanting only a good home for a young adult male.

The bitch puppy turned into Ch. Redwhiskey's Royal Victory. Her first five points were won at the Golden Triangle Specialty in May 1973, where she placed Best of Winners. By August she had 16 points with four BOW majors—all owner-handled by Anita! She won the ISCA Golden Leash award for that year. In 1974 she won at 40 shows, which included 16 BOBs, 2 Group firsts, 5 Group seconds, 2 Group thirds and 2 independent Specialties. She won the ISCA Best Bitch award for that year. Again owner-handled.

The young male became Ch. Tirvelda Court Jester. Carol Brown became a co-owner and finished him in 1972. In his first two litters he sired ten champions!

Pressing their luck still further, the former pet bitch and give-away dog were mated. The result: Am., Bda. & Can. Ch. Redwhiskey's Royal Jester—a Best in Show winner, breeder-owner-handled at Gloucester KC in August 1975; Ch. Redwhiskey's Maidavictory, and Ch. Redwhiskey's Royal Legend.

Royal Victory, dam of 9 champions out of the first 16 puppies she whelped, won the Irish Setter Club of America's Brood Bitch of the Year Award in 1978.

The Dunns acquired Ch. Courtwood Spring Son, co-owned with Cindy Trefrey. Spring Son was finished at Ronita and was specialed extensively. In 1979, Mrs. Cheever Porter leased Spring Son and with Jane Forsyth piloting the six-year-old dog amassed an enviable record.

Long since thoroughly sold on the breed, the Dunns decided on Ronita as their kennel name. The first litter to bear the Ronita prefix was out of Royal Victory by Ch. Candia Indeed. Six of eight from that combination finished their championships.

In 1980, Ronita was disbanded. Anita has retained Royal Victory. Bob is now married to the former Ann Savin, well-known exhibitor of dogs from Thenderin in California, and is now concentrating on and successfully showing dogs of this bloodline.

Earl, Joe and Jett — *Jo-Ett* — Bonner Springs, KS

Jo and Jett Earl fell in love with the Irish Setter as a show dog in the 1950s, when they purchased Shamrock Flamingo from the late Floyd and Ina Mae Crosley. Subsequently they purchased Shamrock Heather. Both dog and bitch finished and were bred together several times, producing, among others, Ch. Jo-Ett's Rudolph O'Bonner, Ch. Jo-Ett's Rollin' Rock and Ch. Jo-Ett's John Francis.

Marvin Oetting of School of the Ozarks bought three, all of whom became champions. Ch. Jo-Ett's Hu She O'Bonner and Ch. Jo-Ett's Tina Maria O'Bonner were bred to Ch. Tirvelda Michaelson. One of those puppies, sold to Jack Mandel of Chicago, became Am. & Can. Ch. Jo-Ett's Marvelda Blazer, finishing by going Group I under Hollis Wilson.

In the 1960s the Earls purchased Jo-Ett's Marflow Esquire (Ch. Marflow Defender ex Tuxedo's Copper Mist). He played an important part in their breeding program.

Ch. Jo-Ett's John Francis was sold to Hugo and Judy Kosmel, and when bred to their bitches produced both field and show champions, including Ch. Redbart Chico, CD, owned by the Earls.

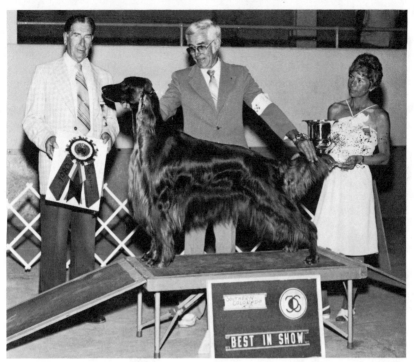

Am. & Can. Ch. Kerry-Eire Revolutionary
(Ch. Candia Indeed ex Ch. Danalee Cover Girl).

Ch. Courtwood Spring Son
(Ch. Candia Indeed ex Ch. Shannon Kelly O'Green).

158

Eitel, Sue — *Huntington* — MD

Sue's foundation bitch was Am. & Can. Ch. Wilson Farm Megan Huntington, a daughter of Ch. Tirvelda Earl of Harewood and Ch. Wilson Farm Country Charm. She was the younger full sister of Ch. Mos'n Acre Wilson Farm Harmony, Best of Breed at the ISCA's first National Specialty.

Bred to Ch. Santera Tamberluck, CD, Megan produced a large litter and five weeks later this outstanding bitch died. Her offspring hopefully will carry on for their outstanding dam.

Sue also owns the Earl son, Can. Ch. Wilson Farm Cash'l Huntington. Cash'l when bred to Can. Ch. Beaverbrook Canadiana (owned by Jack and Gloria Langelier), produced Sardonyx Huntington Heritage, Am. & Can. Ch. Sardonyx Free 'N' Easy, Am. & Can. Ch. Sardonyx Cashelle Huntington and Ch. Sardonyx Sounded Impact.

Eldredge, E. Irving ("Ted") — *Tirvelda* — Middleburg, VA
(Portions of this biography were written by Clyde Smoot)

E. I. (Ted) Eldredge has been breeding Irish Setters since 1934 when he acquired his first show bitch from Lee Schoen of Kinvarra Kennels. She was imported Kinvarra Mollie of Gadeland, a bitch of such prepotent type that one of his bitches 40 years later resembled her almost exactly. She was shown to her championship by Harold Correll, undefeated in the classes.

Ted has owned or bred over 100 champions, including the top producing dam in the breed, Ch. Tirvelda Nutbrown Sherry, and the second leading sire in the breed, Ch. Tirvelda Michaelson, who was a Sherry son.

Ch. Kinvarra Mollie of Gadeland was bred to Ch. Kinvarra Craig. That breeding produced Ch. Kinvarra Kermit and Ch. Tirvelda Malva. Kermit proved to be a highly successful stud for Schoen.

A series of disasters almost wiped out the budding Tirvelda line until 1957 when he imported Hartsbourne Sallyann of Tirvelda from the kennels of Mrs. Eileen Walker in England. Sallyann finished her championship quickly and was bred to Ch. Kinvarra Malone. Malone was the great-great grandson of Mollie of Gadeland, and had inherited the original type that Eldredge strove to perpetuate. The Malone - Sallyann matings produced Ch. Tirvelda Sybil and Ch. Tirvelda Nutbrown Sherry. All dogs of the current Tirvelda breeding stock trace to one or the other of these litter sisters. Ted acquired Malone from his owners, the Fords of Michigan, and he remained at Tirvelda until he died at the age of 15.

Sybil became an excellent show dog with the necessary verve to compete in the ring. Sherry was very relaxed and calm, but it was her sons who made the lasting imprint on the breed. She was bred to Ch. Michael Bryan Duke of Sussex and produced a litter of 12 puppies, 11 of which finished their championships. The remaining male died of heartworm complications. Those who finished were: Ch. T. Michael Bryan, Ch. T. Michele, Ch. T. Cathy O'Rinn, Ch. T. Tiara, Ch. T. Nor' Wester, Ch. T. Michaelson, Ch. T. Rick O'Shea, Ch. T. Earl of Harewood, Ch. T. Kensington Red, and Ch. T. Barabas.

As a footnote to breed history it is worth recounting how the litter brothers Nor'Wester, Earl, Michaelson and their sister Cathy O'Rinn were rescued from complete oblivion by odd twists of fate. Profoundly influencing the breed through their offspring, with the possible exception of Kensington Red, who started too late in his life, all of these dogs almost disappeared into pet homes. Ted tells the story:

"Nor'Wester, sold at four months to Major Leonia Prescott in Oregon just did not

Ch. Dariabar Ringmaster
(Dariabar Flame Came Home ex Dariabar Emerald O'Flynn).

Ch. Tirvelda Beau James
(Ch. Tirvelda Rick O'Shea ex Ch. Dureen O'Tara).

do well in that kennel. Shown a few times on the West Coast as a puppy, he was very small with little coat and was not what Leonia expected. Discouraged with him, and since I sold him as a potential show dog, I bought him back sight unseen. Prior to getting him I debated hard with myself whether to bring him home or let Leonia place him in a home without papers. Had air freight cost as much then as it does today, undoubtedly I would have said "find a good home for him." Instead, I brought him to Virginia. As soon as I saw him I realized that all he needed was maturity. Holding him out until he was three, he went into the ring piloted by Michelle Leathers Billings, and the rest is history. He was only a 26-inch dog, but with such a flat, heavy, dark coat that no one ever noticed his size; he looked much bigger than he was. In a six months period, he won 21 Sporting Groups, and 3 Bests in Show for Tirvelda. He was then retired to a life of luxury with Ed and Helen Treutel and died at 14 in 1976. Bred a limited number of times, he sired 17 champions. Quoting Lee Schoen in an article written in 1978: 'To select from such a galaxy of Tirveldas would take more than my kind of courage, but if narrowed to a single all-around animal, my choice would fall on Ch. Tirvelda Nor'Wester—for spirit, design and manufacture and the ability to reproduce these attributes in litter after litter, directly, then through his numerous progeny.'

"While at the Treutels, Nor'Wester was bred to Ch. Tirvelda Best Regards, a top winning bitch. That breeding produced Ch. Tirvelda Sportin'Life and Ch. Tirvelda Valentine, who was ISCA's Best Bitch.

"Ch. Tirvelda Earl of Harewood was also sold at four months. Returned at 12 months, as his owners could no longer keep him, I was shocked. He was tiny and had no development. We try to check the homes our dogs go into carefully, and in dismay I asked if they had followed my instructions. They said "Yes" on diet, but they had never wormed him. And the only time he was ever off a leash was in their basement! I kept him for three months, got weight on him and freed him of worms. I just could not keep another dog, and having no demand for pets, told the head dairyman on our farm that I'd have to find an excellent home for him. He told me he had a friend in northern Pennsylvania who owned a dairy farm, loved dogs, hunted, and would give this puppy a very good home. Since Earl was so small (not over 24½″), and since I knew my dogs never grew after one year old, I let him go without papers.

"Two years later I started receiving calls from the farmer, who wanted to return Earl. The farmer had had a heart attack and had to disperse his herd, and could not hunt any more. For six months I stalled, telling him I just couldn't take a three-year-old male. After the farmer's second heart attack, I reluctantly agreed to take Earl. When he arrived, my eyes literally fell out! The dog was beautiful. Tremendous dark, flat coat, ideal weight, lovely head and body, and *big!* I couldn't believe it. Obviously his development had been arrested in his first home and then at his age and with the good food he received, nature came to the fore and he grew to 27-27½″.

"His condition was such that I immediately sent him to Michelle Leathers, as with farm life at Tirvelda I knew his magnificent coat would not last long. He finished very quickly. His last championship points and his first win for his new owners, David and Ruth Wilson, was a Best of Breed from the classes at the Potomac Irish Setter Specialty. He became the personal hunting dog of Dave Wilson, and their foundation stud. He was the sire of twenty champions.

"Ch. Tirvelda Michaelson was sold to a man who my sixth sense told me was bad, but he was so convincing I let Mike go. (A week later he would have been sold to John and Anne Savory, who would have given him a marvelous home, but it was too late.) Mike's new owners allowed him to go to a puppy mill, where he was used on bitches of very poor quality.

"A year later, I decided to try to find Mike. The man was in Vietnam and divorced from the wife. The wife's new husband was traced to Korea and knew nothing of his new wife's dogs, but he gave me the address of his mother-in-law in Canada. She vaguely remembered that her daughter occasionally kept her dogs with someone

velda Telstar (Ch. Tirvelda
elson ex Ch. Tirvelda
Mab).

velda Sarabande (Ch. Tir-
Michaelson ex Ch. Tir-
Queen Mab).

velda Queen Mab (Ch. Tir-
Rustic Duke ex Ch. Tirvelda
vale).

named Rose in a town in North Carolina. By now two years had passed, but we were getting closer.

"In a lucky strike I called a telephone operator (I wish I knew her name) and told her the whole story of my search for Mike. She kept trying for days to locate "Rose," and called a week later to say she had a concrete lead. She had located a Rosewood Kennels, who knew all about Mike. Yes, he had had Mike, but the dog had been taken a few months before by a man with seven children and no money to feed them, let alone a dog. He doubted Mike was still alive, but he agreed to try to locate the man, who owed him money, and he needed to use a stud.

"Several more months passed, and I called again. This time the go-between said the dog had been taken to a veterinarian, and that was all he knew. I was dismayed, after all this time, but I called the veterinarian, and once he learned I was no friend of the go-between puppy miller, he told me that some people in a very poor part of town had called to complain of an abandoned Irish Setter that was turning over garbage cans. He went to get the dog and kept it for several weeks, then realizing it would never be claimed he told his attendant either to find a home for it or put it down. He couldn't remember if it was a dog or bitch. He said he would check.

"Several months more went by, when one night a man called to say he had a dog that he thought I might be interested in. He wanted to drive right up, and although I was very excited, I sensed the man thought he had a gold mine, so I didn't want to appear too eager. I said I'd be down on the Tar Heel circuit in two weeks and to wait until that time. The man said he had tried all the Irish names he knew, and when he came to "Mike" the dog responded, and that's why he thought it was mine.

"Finally, the day arrived. Walter Nickerson was with me and when we drove up to the small house, there was an Irish Setter chained to a tiny house. The house was so small Mike could not get his entire body inside. But there was no mistake that it was Mike. He had bushy hair all over his head. His feathers were completely hacked off, his eyes and ears were infected and he was emaciated, but he knew me, and he was all over me with joy.

"Then the negotiations commenced. The man wanted $1,000 and gave us a big story about how Mike was the best of his hunting dogs. We knew that was a lie and proceeded to tell him what terrible shape the dog was in and we'd pay $50 for him, and he should deliver him to the show the next day.

"The next day, the man came and Moss-Bow helpers paged me to come to one of the gates. John Savory went with me then, and as soon as I saw Mike I grabbed the rope and shoved $50 into the man's hand. But he was such a mess I couldn't bring him home to be near the other dogs, so on the Savorys' advice we drove him to the Vine Animal Hospital. Dr. Lou Vine fell in love with him and kept him three months. He only charged me $125 for all the work and time he put into him.

"Finally it was time for Mike to come home. When he stepped out of the car he seemed to grin all over. He knew exactly where he was, and he seemed so pleased that his long ordeal was finally over.

"It took some time to get the AKC paperwork straightened out, so he could be shown. Mike Leathers took him and he finished in two weeks with a Group first from the classes on the Florida circuit. Because he had such a rough life, I decided never to show him again. His hard life never affected his temperament, he was a character and reigned as King of Tirvelda until his death in November, 1976 at the age of 14. He sired 50 champions.

"Ch. Tirvelda Cathy O'Rinn and her sister Penny were sold to the Rinn family. They were unable to keep both and asked me which one to keep. At the same time Bill and Patsy Brooks came to me looking for a bitch. I sent them to the Rinns and they selected Cathy, who turned out to be one of the great bitches, winning her championship at 16 months and producing eight important champion offspring."

Ch. Tirvelda Maidavale (Ch.
Legend of Varagon, UDT, ex Ch.
Tirvelda Sabrina).

Ch. Tirvelda Tudor Minstral, UD (Ch.
Tirvelda Distant Drummer ex Ch. Tirvelda Sarabande).

Ch. Tirvelda Distant Drummer
Ch. Bayberry Sommerset ex Ch.
Tirvelda Red Heather).

Ch. T. Michael Bryan died at an early age, the result of a fire at the kennel of Horace Hollands. He did produce Ch. T. Sabrina when bred to his aunt, Ch. T. Sybil.

Ch. T. Rick O'Shea was owned by the late Walter Nickerson. He was the sire of Ch. T. Beau James, himself a noted sire used heavily by Gala Glen and Dariabar. Sabrina, bred to Ch. Legend of Varagon, UDT, produced Ch. T. Tambourlane and Ch. T. Maidavale. Maidavale bred to Ch. T. Rustic Duke (the younger full brother of Sherry and Sybil) produced Ch. T. Queen Mab, Ch. T. Court Jester, and President Richard Nixon's dog, King Timahoe.

Queen Mab, bred to Michaelson, produced Ch. T. Telstar, Ch. T. Sarabande, Ch. T. Morning Star, Ch. T. Gay Ribbons, T. Mary Poppins, T. Samaria, and T. Red Poppy. Mary Poppins won 10 points before being retired. Samaria was killed in an auto accident before she could be shown, but was the dam of some noted Meadowlark champions.

Telstar is the sire of Am. & Can. McCamon Marquis, twice a National Specialty winner and the top Irish Setter in 1978 and 1979. Marquis retired from American competition with 101 Group firsts, a record for the breed. He became top Irish Setter in Canada in 1981, shown by his breeder Sue Korpan of Saskatoon, Saskatchewan. During his career in the States he was co-owned by Mrs. Korpan and Lillian Gough and handled by George Alston. Telstar, a double grandson of Michaelson, is the sire of a growing list of champions and is one of two males kept at Tirvelda, the other being his grandson, T. Rhodes Scholar, a Marquis son.

Another important dog at Tirvelda was Ch. T. Distant Drummer, (Ch. Bayberry Sommerset ex Ch. T. Red Heather, who was a Ch. Blayneywood Country Squire ex Ch. Divine Sarah daughter.) He had great potential as a show dog and a stud, but ran into numerous problems on both counts. He died of bloat at the age of 7, the only incidence of this disease ever to strike at Tirvelda. Nevertheless, he sired several champions and is the grandsire of many promising youngsters.

Ch. T. Hunter's Moon is another Michaelson son who proved to be an outstanding show dog and sire. He is co-owned with Mrs. Celeste Gavin of Old Lyme, Connecticut.

It can be reliably stated that the Tirvelda influence is felt in every important Irish Setter strain today.

Fahmie, Mike and Arlene — *Corcaigh* — Chester, NJ

Arlene Fahmie first showed Irish in 1972 when she purchased Westwind Scarlet Tipperary (Ch. Shannon's Laird Shane ex Ch. Westwind Arabesque) from Luz Holvenstot of Westwind Kennels. "Tipper" won points as a pup, but was retired needing a major to finish his championship.

Arlene then co-owned a bitch, Westwind Scarlet Escapade with Luz Holvenstot and bred her first litter. From that litter, sired by Ch. Tirvelda Michael Seamus, she kept Westwind Scarlet Matchmaker. Rarely shown as a young dog, he won the Bred By Exhibitor class at the ISCA National Specialty in 1978, but because of a health problem was retired from the ring with 5 points.

To introduce a different line, Mike decided to buy from a breeder outside of his area. The Fahmies went to Laurie Conlon (Palomar) and purchased a bitch puppy, Palomar's Splendor of Corcaigh (Ch. Palomar's Southern Star ex Palomar's Damesele Tirvelda). "Missy" finished her championship at the age of three.

Palomar's Skyrocket of Corcaigh (Ch. Palomar's Southern Star ex Gala Glen's Autumn Nocturn) was the next arrival at Corcaigh. He finished after a short

Ch. Tirvelda Wild Wings (Ch. Meadowlark's Masterpiece ex Ch. Tirvelda Morning Star).

Ch. Tirvelda Nutbrown Maid (Ch. Ash-Ling Celebration ex Ch. Tirvelda Sarabande).

Ch. Tirvelda Temptress (Ch. Kimberlin O'Killea O'Top O ex Ch. Tirvelda Sarabande).

show career at the age of three, going Winners Dog at the 1981 ISCA National Specialty on the way to his title. At about the same time the Fahmies purchased Ch. Meadowlark's Madrigal (Meadowlark's Honor Guard ex Ch. Meadowlark's Ebbtide) from Rose Marie Ross.

"Tiffany" was bred to Charlton's Treasure Trove, producing 2 males and 3 bitches. Both males remained with the Fahmies and in 1981, being shown only at Specialties, consistently won equal numbers of class wins and several Best Puppy and Best in Sweeps awards. "Tiffany" was then bred to Ch. Meadowlark's Argosy.

In 1980 Meadowlark's Aria O'Deargain was acquired from Rose Marie Ross (Charlton's Treasure Trove ex Ch. Meadowlark's Impossible Dream). She finished her championship in four months with three majors. "Amanda" was Arlene's first owner-handled Irish to finish, and she said "What a joy that was!"

Farrington, Dick and Shirley — *Shawnee* — Riverside, CA

In 1969 the Farringtons purchased their first Irish Setter, Can. Ch. Shannon's Red Eagle, as a pet. Interest in showing led to the purchase of Am. & Can. Ch. Rendition's Indian Summer as a 7-week-old puppy in 1971. She was to become the foundation of Shawnee, producing ten champions from three litters sired by Ch. Candia Indeed. From the first litter came Chs. Shawnee Sundance and Sundown; the second produced Chs. Shawnee Indian Sonnet, Indian Breeze, Indian Red Dove, Indian Trailblazer and Indian Meadow. From the third came Chs. Shawnee Prairie Scout, Prairie Wildfire, and Pipedream O'Charlton, twice winner of the National Specialty. Indian Summer was ISCA Best Matron for 1980 and her granddaughter, Shawnee Wind 'N Willow for 1981. Shawnee is also the home of Am. & Can. Ch. Draherin Illumination, dam of Am. & Can. Ch. Shawnee Sierra Storm Cloud, a Canadian Best in Show winner. Storm Cloud, bred to Sundance, has continued the Shawnee breeding program and perpetuated the best of their foundation dams. To date, 14 champions carry the Shawnee prefix and 4 co-bred champions carry the Rusticwoods Kennel name. Shawnee has won numerous breeder awards from the ISC of So. Cal. and the ISC of the Pacific as well as the ISCA.

Field, Robert and Mary — *Bryfield* — Phoenix, AZ

The Fields had their beginning in 1956 when Bob Field bought his wife, Mary, their first Setter, "Brydie". They became enchanted with the breed and carefully selected two outstanding puppies who became their foundation stock, Ch. Candia Fawn and Ch. Candia Eve.

Fawn's fantastic showmanship and indomitable spirit, coupled with her style and soundness, made her a favorite both in and out of the ring. Her love for the show ring was passed to her get, with 6 champions in her "R" litter alone. Eve has consistently stamped her get with heavy dark coats, dark eyes and strong driving hindquarters. She, too, is the dam of numerous champions. Both bitches were proclaimed "Third Generation Top Producers" by *Kennel Review* magazine.

Bob, as an AKC handler, showed the Bryfield dogs throughout the Southwest and California. Some of the outstanding champions: Ch. Bryfield Sun Imp; Ch. B. Rogue Shannon; Ch. B. Ricoshet; Ch. B. Rum Runner; Ch. B. Russet Holly; Ch. B. Radiant Lady; Ch. B. Portrait O'Eve; Ch. B. Peppermint Patty; and Ch. B. Pride 'n Perfection. Bob has retired from handling and is now an AKC judge.

Fleming, Sam and Jackie — *Magadoon* (formerly Hollybrook) — Little Rock, AR

The Flemings' start in Irish began with Ch. Gala Glen Forget Me Not (Ch.

Ch. Michael Bryan Duke of Sussex
(Ch. Thenderin Brian Tristan ex Ch. Merrilynn of Glenfield).

Ch. Tirvelda Michaelson
(Ch. Michael Bryan Duke of Sussex ex Ch. Tirvelda Nutbrown Sherry).

Tirvelda Beau James ex Gala Glen Wood Sprite) and Gala Glen Rocky Rogue (Ch. Glendee Bourbon on the Rocks ex Gala Glen Merry Kerry). They next acquired an older sister of Forget Me Not, Gala Glen Bells A-Ringin'. After finishing, she was bred to Ch. Innisfail Flashback's Design, the first champion bitch sent to him. This breeding produced Ch. Sir Shadrach of Hollybrook and Ch. Hollybrook Serenade. A repeat of this breeding produced Ch. Gala Glen's Hollyberry, who finished with two major Specialty wins, and Can. Ch. Gala Glen's Donner O'Magadoon. There are others pointed from this second litter.

The Flemings also own Ch. Gala Glen Michelob, a son of Ch. Tirvelda Michaelson and Ch. Gala Glen September Dawn, who is in turn sire of Ch. Glenrob's Peter O'Toole.

Fortune, Robert and Phyllis — *Tullamore* — Knoxville, TN

In 1970 the Fortunes purchased their foundation bitch from Joe and Irish Smith; she became Ch. Tullamore Lear O'Limerick, CD. Also in 1970 they purchased a daughter of Ch. Tirvelda Earl of Harewood and Ch. Wilson Farm Partridge who, bred to Ch. Bayberry Sommerset, produced their Ch. Tullamore Kathleen, and their well-known Ch. Tullamore Desperado. From the same litter came Can. Ch. Tullamore Hail Adios, who has won a number of Bests in Show in Canada, and Brazilian Ch. Tullamore Winchester who also has won Bests in Show in his country; Ch. Tullamore Bull Abadden and Tullamore Serenity, both point winners at Specialty Shows—quite a litter!

Foxwell, Mary Ann — *Foxfyre* — Aberdeen, MD

Established in 1967, Mary Ann's foundation bitch was Neerbs Scarlet Tara (4 point major). Bred three times, she produced Ch. Foxfyre's Dublin Shawn, Ch. Mos'n Acre Foxfyre Flair, and the outstanding bitch, Ch. Foxfyre's Scarlet Ember, CD. Ember finished the years 1974-75 as the No. 1 bitch on the East Coast and No. 2 bitch nationally. She was owned by Dale Hood of Towson, Maryland.

Francis, Charles and Sharon — *O'Irish* — Surrey, B.C. Canada

"O'Irish", owned by Charles H. and Sharon P. Francis, bought its first Irish Setter in 1962. Ch. Bayknoll Early Autumn, won 19 Groups and two All-breed Bests in Show in Canada. He was a professionally trained gun dog.

They purchased Cherry Point Kathleen O'Irish and campaigned her to Canadian Championship. She was bred to Early Autumn which resulted in several Group winners and two all-breed Best in Show winners, Can. & Am. Ch. O'Irish Derrybrien, and Can. Ch. O'Irish Dangerman. Dangerman won 25 Groups and a Best in Show in Canada. They obtained Can. Ch. Julerin High Hopes of Kamron, CD (a Legend of Varagon daughter). Bred to Dangerman, High Hopes produced their third consecutive generation of Canadian Best in Show dogs—Can. Ch. O'Irish Jonquil and his litter brother Can. Ch. O'Irish Jet Setter. The latter is their top winning Irishman, with 52 Group 1st, and 9 all-breed Bests in Show in Canada.

Can. Ch. O'Irish Celebrity, the Group winning female, gave them two sons from different sires who went on to Bests in Show. Both were owner-handled to their wins, and make the fifth and sixth Canadian Best in Show winners produced at O'Irish.

Fritkin, George and Judy — *Elvatowne* — CA

The Elvatowne Kennels got under way with the purchase of Tirvelda Bridget in 1967. Bridget was bred to Ch. Tirvelda Middle Brother to produce the Fritkins' first champion, Ch. Elva Sunset Blaze.

Ch. Tirvelda Touch of Fire (Ch. Tirvelda Distant Drummer ex Ch. Tirvelda Sarabande).

h. Tirvelda Drum Chant (Ch. Tirvelda Distant Drummer ex Tirvelda Nutbrown Maid).

h. Tirvelda Rhodes Scholar (Ch. Mcamon Marquis ex Tirvelda Nutbrown Maid).

Their purchases, Tirvelda Fortunata and Draherin Eloquence, both became champions. In 1973, Fortunata bred to Ch. Tirvelda Michaelson produced Am., Can., Mex., Ecuadorian & Ber. Ch. Tirvelda Blarney of Elvatowne, Am., Mex. & Can. Ch. Tirvelda Shamus of Elvatowne, Am. & Colombian Ch. Tirvelda Elvatowne Saga. All three were Best in Show winners. The first two were successfully shown by Dr. John Patrick Jordan and his son, Dennis, in many countries—Blarney is a champion in seven countries.

In 1974, the Fritkins' Ch. Draherin Thunderation produced Ch. Elvatowne Thunderstruck, another very successful Group winner who is owned by Charlotte Kay in Florida.

Frydrych, Joseph B. and Margaret — *Argo Lane* — Warren, MI

Joe Frydrych received his first Irish Setter as a birthday present in 1943. Next came Can. Ch. Jiggs Dandy of Galway (Can. CDX & Am. CD).

In addition to being a former professional handler, Joe is a noted Obedience trainer. At least a dozen Argo Lane setters have obtained Obedience titles. In 1953, the Frydrychs obtained Am. & Can. Ch. Esquire of Maple Ridge (Ch. Thenderin Brian Tristan ex Crosshaven Lea of Maple Ridge), who won 1 Best in Show, 15 Groups and 95 BOB awards. However, it is as the sire of 31 champions that Squire is especially renowned. Among his champions are Ch. Argo Lane Lad of Ulster, Ch. Argo Lane's Rixans Squire, Am. & Can. Ch. Argo Lane's Tippity Wicket, the famous litter of six champions ex Bench and Field Ch. Red Arrow Show Girl, UDT, and others. Much of the high quality of Irish Setters in the Detroit area should be credited to Esquire—strong, sound, short-bodied, beautifully coated dogs with wonderful dispositions.

Fuelling, Jeanette and Tom — *Brynlaw* — Hillsboro, OR

Established in the late 1960s, the Fuellings' first champion was Ch. Thenderin Wishing Star, a litter sister of William Muldoon. Two other of their bitches, Glenavan Magnificent Edition, CD, and Ch. Brynlaw As You Like It are by their sire, Thenderin Filibuster.

Furman, Bob and Edith — *"Terra Ferma"* — Oakdale, LA

The Furmans, formerly of Kansas and now of Louisiana, have owned outstanding field and show dogs since 1953. Their first dogs were hunters but after being bitten by the show-bug in 1968, the dual dog became their goal. Their strain was developed by a selective breeding program on their foundation bitch, Ch. Lady Ann O'Shea, CD (of Jo-Ett's and Shamrock background). She was bred to Ch. Glendee's Bourbon on the Rocks, CD, Ch. Blayneywood Country Squire and Ch. Bayberry Sommerset. The produce was bred to Ch. Shannon's Erin, Ch. Thenderin William Muldoon and Ch. O'Leprechaun Bushmills, CD. The Furmans have finished 10 champions of their breedings, of which Ch. Terra Furman's Moonshine Tech, a multi-Group and Specialty winner was the best known. Their champion bitches are field and Obedience trained.

The Furmans are active club workers. Bob has served as show chairman for all-breed clubs and helped organize the ISC of Greater Kansas City, and both have served on the Board of Directors of the ISCA.

Gallagher, Mrs. Patricia P. — *Gala Glen* — Melbourne, FL

Gala Glen Kennels had its start with three Irish Setters who were of different backgrounds but who were themselves inbred and linebred. First came the bitch Ch. Harmony Lanes Sandpiper, CD, a Ch. Conifer's Lance daughter, who was

Ch. Redwhiskey's Royal Victory (Kel-nora Sabre Dance ex Ch. Victory's Royal Sensation, CD).

Ch. Redbart Chico of Jo-Ett, CD (Ch. Jo-Ett's John Francis ex Fld. Ch. Shamrock Su O'Shannon).

Can. Ch. Wilson Farm Cash'l Huntington (Ch. Tirvelda Earl of Harewood ex Ch. Tirvelda Toma Maid).

(L to R) Am. & Can. Ch. Rendition's Indian Summer (dam), Am. & Can. Ch. Shawnee Sundance, Am. & Can Ch. Shawnee Sundown, Ch. Shawnee Indian Sonnet, Shawnee Indian Meadow, Shawnee Prairie Breeze (Sire in three litters: Ch. Candia Indeed).

tightly bred on Ch. Thenderin Brian Tristan through Ch. Red Rogue of Maple Ridge and Ch. Esquire of Maple Ridge. Ch. Sunny Acre Top O' the Mark came next, a product of a grandmother to grandson breeding. Mark finished his championship in four shows with 19 points. Next came Gala Glen Bedelia, who was closely inbred to Knockross O'Boy.

A breeding of Mark-Sandpiper produced Gala Glen Wood Sprite, CD. Sprite had points but was kicked in the shoulder by a horse before finishing. Sprite when bred to Ch. Tirvelda Beau James produced four champions: Ch. Gala Glen Bells a-Ringing', Ch. Gala Glen Brocade, Ch. Gala Glen Forget Me Not, and Ch. Gala Glen Sparkling Rose.

Bedelia was then bred to Mark and from this litter came Ch. Gala Glen Bittersweet and Ch. Gala Glen September Dawn. Not only was Dawn a top show bitch, finishing her championship in five straight shows and winning Groups as a Special, but she also gave Gala Glen four champions. From a breeding to Ch. Bayberry Russet of Kinvarra came Ch. Antrim Adonis of Gala Glen, who finished in two weekends, and Ch. Antrim Acres Autumn Heather, who finished with four majors. Bred to Ch. Tirvelda Michaelson, Dawn produced Ch. Gala Glen Michelob and Ch. Gala Glen Miss Behavin. Also from this litter was Gala Glen Maggie Me Love, who has proven to be such a good producer.

Mrs. Gallagher acquired Ch. Red Royal A Bit of Barney, whose sire was Dawn's brother. Barney finished quite easily, taking a Group First on the way. When bred to Heather, he produced Ch. Innisfail King's Destiny and Ch. Innisfail Kismet of Gala Glen. When bred to a Dawn daughter, he produced Ch. Gala Glen Cherries Jubilee and several others lacking just a few points to finish. Barney died at the early age of four.

Ch. Gala Glen Bells A-Ringin' was bred to Ch. Innisfail Flashback's Design. From the first litter came the Group and Specialty winner, Ch. Hollybrook Serenade, and her brother, Ch. Sir Shadrach of Hollybrook. From the second litter came Ch. Gala Glen Hollyberry and several others that were pointed.

Pat Gallagher is a former Board member of the Irish Setter Club of America, a licensed judge and the author of *Irish Setters Today* (Tentagel Press).

Gavin, Celeste and John — *Gabhantyr* — Old Lyme, CT

The Gavins obtained Tirvelda Brengwain from Ted Eldredge as their foundation bitch. Later they co-owned Am. & Can. Ch. Tirvelda Hunter's Moon with Tirvelda Farms. Treve's excellent show record made him the No. 1 amateur-handled Irish Setter in 1975. He was the winner of 7 Specialties (including the 1977 Combined Specialty), an all-breed Best in Show and 21 Groups. He has produced three all breed Best in Show winners, one being Ch. Powderhorn Yankee Rifleman, bred by Alan and Barbara Kloss. Treve also produced Ch. Wind-n-Tide Sophistication (McGarry) who was Best of Winners at the 1978 National Specialty and Best Opposite at the 1980 National.

In her second litter, Brengwain, bred to Rockherin Merri Chris, produced Am. & Can. Ch. Tirvelda Sprig of Gabhantyr. Sprig became one of the top winning bitches in the history of the breed, winning three all breed Bests in Show in the United States and one in Canada and 14 Groups. She was shown in 21 Specialty Shows, boing BOB or BOS in 20. In 1978, she won the Irish Setter Club of America National Specialty over the largest entry to that time, and again won at the 1979 Combined Specialty. While being campaigned, Sprig was co-owned with Dr. Robert Helferty.

After Sprig's retirement, the Gavins began campaigning a young dog co-owned with Mrs. Thomas Arland, Ch. Shawnee Pipedream O'Charlton. He became an all breed Best in Show winner and the winner of 10 Specialties, including the Irish Setter Club of America National Specialty in 1980 and 1981.

Gilbert, Irene and Jim — *Dungannon* — North Ft. Myers, FL

Dungannon's first litter was whelped in 1979 (by Ch. Thenderin William Muldoon out of their Thenderin Mystique, CD), producing four outstanding young bitches, two being pointed as puppies, and two others having 5 point major reserves as puppies. Other breeding stock owned by Dungannon are Ch. Thenderin Bounty Hunter, CD, and the multi-Group winning bitch, Am. & Can. Ch. McKendree's Bold Elegance.

Goff, Cecil and Diane — *Briarwood* — Jefferson, OH

Briarwood came into being with the purchase of Holly of Briarwood Farm, a Christmas present, in 1965. Their next acquisition was a daughter of Ch. Marflow's Red Defender, Briarwood's Heather O'Hara, and she was the dam of the first Briarwood litters. But it was not until the arrival of Ch. Starheir Donovan O'Briarwood (Am. & Can. Ch. Bronze Blaze of Tamarisk ex Am. & Can. Ch. Shannon's Susie Starlet) that the kennel began to win.

A gift from the Winegards, Oakhill Rixans Copper Penny—a daughter of the Winegards' Am. & Can. Ch. Argo Lanes Rixans Squire—was bred to Donovan to produce the first Briarwood champion, Briarwood's Flame of Fortune. Another Donovan daughter, Ch. Briarwood's Meadowlark, bred to the Slicks' Am., Can. & Ber. Ch. Shannon's Sharon of Erin produced Ch. Briarwood's Blazing Sunset, Ch. Briarwood's Regina and Ch. Briarwood's Dust Commander. Yet one more Donovan daughter, Ch. Starheir's Briarwood Charisma, has finished as this goes to press.

The Goffs, having surrounded Donovan with his daughters, decided to purchase another male. From George and Ruth White they obtained O'Dorseys Chief Ironsides (by Ch. Wilson Farm Hallmark ex Ch. O'Dorsey's Glow of Tamarisk), who finished his championship quickly with points won at the Ohio and Michigan specialties and two other 5-pt. majors.

Gonsor, Raymond and Valerie — *Varagon* — Mission Hills, CA

The first Varagon litter, producing Ch. Maveric of Varagon, CDX, appeared in 1958.

The Varagon breeding program clearly confirms the respect the Gonsors had for their lovely foundation bitch, Ch. Innisfail Best Regards, CDX. "Banshee," known for her long head and neck, angulated shoulders, deep chest and clean topline, is still reflected in the Varagon dogs of today. One can easily see "Banshee" influence behind Am. Mex. Ch. Crimson Satan of Varagon, CD, and Ch. Varagon Bold Splendor. The Gonsors are strong believers in line breeding, (as demonstrated in the "Banshee"-Color Scheme litter, which produced Champions Enchantment, Legend and Flashback). They feel outcrosses should only be done to bring in stamina or other desired qualities. Their litter by Ch. Maveric of Varagon, CDX, ex Ch. Ballyheigh of Haleridge shows the successful outcome of one such outcross. This litter produced Sundance of Varagon, 14 points, two majors, and Star Fire of Varagon, 14 points, three majors, who never finished due to misfortune. Another example of the few outcrosses they attempted was the breeding of Ch. Enchantment of Varagon to Ch. Michael Bryan Duke of Sussex, producing Ch. Donamar Bold

Ch. O'Irish Jet Setter
(Can. Ch. O'Irish Dangerman ex Can. Ch. Julerin High Hopes of Kamron, CD).

Ch. Elvatowne Thunderstruck
(Ch. Draherin Thunderation ex Draherin Bittersweet).

Echo of Varagon and Bold Beauty. Products of these outcrosses were selectively bred to each other, as noted in the breeding of Bold Beauty to Maveric to bring forth the beautiful Ch. Bold Splendor. Maveric also sired Ch. Varagon Red Baron, when bred to a daughter of Flashback and Bold Beauty.

Focusing on line breeding, crosses of Crimson Satan were successfully made to daughters of Am., Can. & Mex. Ch. Scarlet Flash of Varagon. Satan and Scarlet Flash were both sons of Ch. Flashback of Varagon.

Today, we find both Val and Ray judging.

Hahnen, Susan M. — *Courtwood* — St. Paul, MN

Sue, born into an active hunting family, always wanted a Sporting dog. The Hahnens acquired their first Irish Setter in 1955, shortly after their marriage. Sue credits Mr. and Mrs. James Fraser with beginning help and encouragement.

However, it was in 1971, with the coming of Shannon Kelly O'Green, that Courtwood came into prominence. Since this bitch has played such an important part in Irish Setter history, it is well worth documenting her story and that of her offspring.

Kelly came to Sue quite by chance. She was owned by a young girl who was more interested in horses than in showing dogs. Kelly seemed destined to live in a barn until one day the girl gave her back to her breeder. The breeder, in turn, found an eager buyer in Sue.

Kelly took her first 4-pt. major in her fifth show, and finished at the 1972 Minnesota Specialty by going BOB from the classes. She finished with four majors, owner-handled.

But illustrious as her show career had been, her real fame was to lie in the whelping box. Kelly was the result of an outcross mating, and after a good deal of studying pedigrees, backgrounds and dogs, Sue made the decision to breed her to (future Ch.) Candia Indeed. She first saw Indeed when he was but three months old, and was impressed. He had the pedigree and seemed to be the type she wanted. Seven months later, when Indeed was 10 months old, he was mated to Kelly.

Actually, Kelly and Indeed were mated four times. From the first litter of ten, eight became champions: Am. & Can. Ch. Courtwood Spring Heir (Specialty and Group winner); Am. & Can. Ch. Courtwood Spring Venture (Specialty and Group winner); Am. & Can. Ch. Courtwood Spring Gentry (Group placement winner); Ch. Courtwood Spring Son (Specialty and all-breed Best in Show winner); Am. & Can. Ch. Courtwood Spring Flare (Group placement winner); Am. & Can. Ch. Courtwood Spring Charm; Ch. Courtwood Spring Mist; and Ch. Courtwood Spring Breeze.

The second litter, known as the "Summer" litter, produced: Am. & Can. Ch. Courtwood Summer Forecast, who finished at 12½ months; Ch. Courtwood Summer Magic and Ch. Courtwood Summer Fancy. (Forecast was Best in Sweepstakes at the National in 1975, and is a multiple Best in Show, Specialty Show and Group winner, all breeder-owner-handled.)

The third litter, the "Fall" litter, produced: Ch. Courtwood Fall Moon, CD. The fourth litter, the "Winter" litter, produced Ch. Courtwood Winter Sportsman and Ch. Courtwood Winter Green.

The remarkable fact about this very successful 'nick' is that not only are the sire and dam distantly related, but the sires and dams of both Indeed and Kelly were distantly related. So much for theories expressing the desirability of line breeding.

Sue is now successfully inbreeding various combinations of Kelly's and

Ch. Meadowlark's Madrigal (Meadowlark's Honor Guard ex Ch. Tirvelda Meadowlark's Ebbtide).

Ch. Gala Glen Bells A-Ringin' (Ch. Tirvelda Beau James ex Gala Glen Wood Sprite).

Ch. Terra Furman's Moonshine Tech (Ch. Glendee's Bourbon on the Rocks, CD, ex Ch. Lady Ann O'Shea, CD).

Indeed's offspring. Ch. Courtwood Spring Flare was bred to Ch. Charlton's Moon Lover (Ch. Courtwood Summer Forecast ex Can. Ch. Kinsale's Charlton) and from a litter of nine, five are finished. Out of a breeding of Ch. Courtwood's Summer Magic to Moon Lover, two are finished.

Haigler, Frank, Pat and Kim — *Rendition* — Fullerton, CA

Rendition started in 1967 with the acquisition of its namesake Ch. Tyronne Farm Rendition (Sir Michael Galway of Glendee ex Lady Kerrybrooke). Shortly after, the Haiglers acquired his sister, Am. & Can. Ch. Michael's Patti O'Shea, who became their foundation bitch and first champion. Patti was top winning bitch on the West Coast in 1968 and 1969. Since Patti's background was Tyronne Farm mixed with Draherin and End O'Maine, Pat decided to continue in that direction. From two litters by Ch. Shannon's Erin came Ch. Rendition O'Hara of Sunny Hill, Ch. Rendition Tippi of Sunny Hill, Ch. Rendition Erin of Sunny Hills, Ch. Rendition Renegrade, and Rendition Siobhan (ten points).

From this litter Pat kept Tippi and Erin. After finishing Tippi, it was decided to breed her to her litter brother, Erin, which produced Ch. Rendition Santana. Santana was shown in Open only four times going BW at ISCA Second National, BW Far West Setter Specialty, BW ISC Seattle, BOB ISC Arizona. It was then decided to breed Tippi to Ch. Candia Indeed. That litter produced Ch. Rendition Stoney Mountain, WD at ISC Arizona, and Ch. Rendition Honeybear.

In 1972 Am., Can. & Mex. Ch. Draherin King's Ransom was sent to them from Lucy Jane Myers and was campaigned to three Bests in Show and many Group Firsts and placements.

Honeybear was bred to the Best in Show winner, Ch. Rendition St. Patrick, a Ransom son. When her puppies were ten weeks old, Honeybear jumped the fence and was killed by a car—a great emotional loss to the Haigler family for she was Pat's favorite bitch. Patrick proved himself to be a top stud dog and was runner-up for Best Sire in 1975 and 1976. Sire of 20 champions and many pointed offspring, he died in 1981 at the age of 14.

Erin was sent to Rose Marie Ross, Meadowlark Kennels in Virginia, where he proved to be a top sire, having 7 champions to his credit at the time of his death in 1982.

The Haiglers' next successful litter was breeding Rendition Jennifer (Erin daughter) to Ch. Candia Indeed. This was the litter that produced Am., Can. & Mex. Ch. Rendition Chantilly Lace, Ch. Rendition Bridget Duffy, Rendition Kerri and Rendition American Express. Chantilly Lace was a great show bitch who won her first 5-pt. major from the 6-9 Specialty puppy class. She was Top Bitch in 1976 and 1977 and No. 4 Irish Setter in the country in the latter year. She was bred to Ch. Shawnee Pipe Dream O'Charlton, producing several champions and pointed get.

Hall, Bonnie Jo — *Hallmark* — Delanson, NY

Hallmark is a family operation, and the work is shared by Bonnie, her cousin Gail Tannenhaus, Bonnie's ward—Dori Nasholts, and their close friend, Eileen Miller.

Bonnie's involvement with Irish Setters begain in 1968 with a birthday gift from her fiance. Onesquethaw Shawna Moran won her CD with ease. Bonnie then purchased Onesquethaw Mourna Fleming, who became an American and Canadian champion, and Hallmark's foundation bitch.

Next acquired was a male puppy who became Ch. Thenderin Summer Breeze. Breeding Mourna to Summer Breeze produced four champions in the first litter,

h. Hollybrook Serenade (Ch.
nisfail Flashback's Design ex
h. Gala Glen Bells A'Ringin').

h. Enchantment of Varagon
h. Innisfail Color Scheme ex Ch.
nisfail Best Regards).

m. Can. & Mex. Ch. Scarlet
ash of Varagon (Ch. Flash Back
Varagon ex Fantasy's Scarlet
dy).

and three in the second. Three became Group winners, and one went on to become the top winning Irish in the country.

The noted offspring from this combination include: Ch. Hallmark Jameson, Ch. Hallmark Stargazer (a Group winner), Ch. Hallmark Canaan Star, Ch. Hallmark Nancy Whiskey, Ch. Hallmark MacAlpine Fusilier (Group I for 5-pts. at Long Island KC), and the most famous of all, the bitch Ch. Hallmark Courtin N' Kitchen ("Mindy"). Mindy, owned by Bonnie, Gail Tannenhaus, and Eileen Miller, and handled by Eileen, is a multi Best in Show winner, and in 1982 was the top winning Irish Setter—the only Bitch ever to achieve that distinction.

Hardin, Virginia — *Runwild* — Northbrook, IL

Virginia has had Irish Setters since the '20s. The first came from Miss Coolidge's Innisfree Kennels, followed by Aragon dogs from Jack Cooper and a bitch of Kinvarra breeding. With the purchase of Verbu Christopher Oogh from Emily Schweitzer, Virginia became interested in Obedience training, finishing Chris' UD in 1950.

Runwild Kennels was registered in 1947 with Ch. Runwild Fin McCoul, CD, her first champion and Group winner. Ch. Runwild Alannah, CD, bred to Ch. Charles River Color Sergeant began a long line of Runwild Champions linebred to Ch. Red Sails of Salmagundi.

Because Virginia was a licensed handler from 1950 through 1976, breeding was limited to an average of one litter every three years—just enough to keep her bloodlines going.

Runwild Fiona, a granddaughter of Alannah's, bred by Robert Bridell, finished her championship at 11 months, 20 days and started participation in field trialing. At 11 years, Fiona was still placing in field trials and winning Bests of Breed. She had 20 field trial placements. From her two litters, five finished to championships including Group winners, R. Fitzgerald and R. Finnagain, the latter winner of 6 all-breed Bests in Show and 9 field trial placements. Finn was the sire of champions and field trial winners including Dual Ch. Mollycoddled Misty, CD, and BIS Ch. Mahogany's Socair Buacaill, CD. Fiona's daughter, Ch. R. Finnola the Fay (16 field placements) bred to Ch. Charles River Streamliner produced Ch. R. Connemara (8 field placements), who was bred to Ch. Regal of Rustic Hill—a Finnagain grandson. This breeding produced Group and multiple-Specialty winner, Ch. R. Kilkenny, sire of her present winners, Ch. R. Brian O'Donohoe (out of Ch. Lady Tress O'Donahoe T.C.) and R. Caitriona (out of R. Norna O'Finnagain—a Finnagain granddaughter). Brian was in the Top Ten Irish Setters (all systems) for two years with numerous Group and Specialty wins. He also has field trial placements. Caty has 4 points toward her F.T. championship.

Virginia has done as much for Irish Setters as anyone in the breed. She is one of a select few who has operated in all spheres of the sport—conformation, field and Obedience. The history of her kennel could be much longer but with her usual modesty very little information was sent me.

She has been a hard working and dedicated officer of the Irish Setter Club of America for many years. In 1978 she began judging and her years of experience is much sought after in the ring. In 1979 Virginia was elected President of the Irish Setter Club of America. She was re-elected in 1980 and 1981, and has served with distinction.

Ch. Runwild Fiona (Ch. Sergeant Red Sails of Devon ex Ch. Tara's Theme).

Ch. Runwild Brian O'Donohoe (Ch. Runwild Kilkenny ex Ch. Lady Tress O'Donohoe, TC).

Ch. Rendition Tippi of Sunny Hill (Ch. Shannon's Erin ex Ch. Michael's Patti O'Shea).

Ch. Flash Back of Varagon
(Ch. Innisfail Color Scheme, CD, ex Ch. Innisfail Best Regards).

Ch. Maveric of Varagon, CDX (Ch. Rhu Shane of Haleridge ex Ch. Innisfail Best Regards).

Ch. Starheir Donovan O'Briar-wood (Am. & Can. Ch. Bronze Blaze of Tamarisk ex Am. & Can Ch. Shannon's Susie Starlet, CD)

Harris, Don and Patty — *Rust-of-Fur Kennels* — Oreville, CA

The Harrises purchased their first Irish Setter in 1966, and immediately became interested in Obedience and field trialing. Because of his heavy coat and 29″ height, they were told he could not run in the field, but he became Fld. Ch. Killagay's Duke Rust-Of-Fur, CDX, and was handled by Don and Patty to all of his titles.

Their second dog came from Bill and Loretta Golden (Jubilee Farms), and became their first field champion (finishing six months before Rusty)—Fld. Ch. Jubilee Farms Kismet (4 show pts.).

Their next dog was to come from a breeding of Fld. Ch. Killagay's Duke Rust-Of-Fur, CDX, with Eric's Lady of Innisfail—she became Fld. Ch. Rust-Of-Fur's Maid of Diamonds. Maid has had such feats to her credit as: derby points at 7 mos. of age, puppy points shortly after, and placing in senior stakes before her second birthday. She finished her field championship at 2 years, 8 months of age, and was a winner at retrieving and non-retrieving trials in all parts of the country. This litter also produced Ch. Rust-Of-Fur's Queen of Hearts (O. M. Hanes).

Maid was bred to Ch. Rendition Stoney Mountain to produce their outlaw litter: Rust-Of-Fur's Jessie James, Butch Cassidy, Sundance Kid, Billy the Kid, Yosemite Sam, Doc Holiday, Diamond Jim, Annie Oakley, Diamond 'Lil, and Calamity Jane. These offspring are winning in the show ring and at the field trials today.

The Harrises went to Pat Haigler (Rendition Irish Setters) for their next dog, Rendition Gingerly Spiced. Ginger is a littermate to Ch. Rendition St. Patrick. They bred Ginger to Rust-Of-Fur's Royal Flush (Maid's brother) with the resulting pups: Dual Ch. Rust-Of-Fur's Blue Thyme Babe (O. Johnston); Ch. Blue Magic (Harris) field points; Ch. Hello Dolly (Downey) field placements; and Am. & Can. Ch. Howdy Doody (Harris).

Rendition Gingerly Spiced's second litter was by Butch Cassidy (whelped 6-30-80), with all pups carrying the Rust-Of-Fur I'ma prefix. The ones going forward from this litter are, I'ma Dandee (Simton-Harris), I'ma Impresser (Harris), and I'ma Ole' Smoothie (Harris).

Maid of Diamonds produced her second litter (1 dog and 1 bitch) by Doc Holiday (8-1-81). Both were kept by the Harrises to carry on the dual abilities of their line.

Patty has served on the Board of the Irish Setter Club of America.

Harris, Myra and Thorne D. — *Glendee* — New Orleans, LA

A lovely spring afternoon in 1952, a drive along the bayous of New Orleans, a frolicking "Mahogany Red Dog" on the green grassed levee, and that was it! In July of that same year, Thorne gave Myra her first Irish as a birthday present. Although Tyronne Farm Finnigan II, "Mike," was purchased as a show dog, two young boys prevented the Harris family from extensive showing. Nine years later, shortly after Mike died, another birthday present arrived, Tyronne Farm Midnight Flash. Flash won his first point at 8 months and finished at 20 months with a Group first from the classes.

Glendee Kennels was born with the purchase of Tyronne Farm Midday Flame. Flame finished at two and half years old, also with a Group first from the classes. The name "Glendee" was derived from the combination of the two Harris boys names.

Flash and Flame produced Glendee's first litter in 1962. From this union came the first homebred champions, Ch. Sir Michael Galway of Glendee and Ch. Glendee's Duke of Wicklow. This was the only litter sired by Flash, but Flame lived to produce five more champions: Ch. Glendee's Velvet Moon, Ch. Tyronne Farm Flite O'Morn and Ch. Glendee's Miss Pilot Light, sired by Ch. Tyronne Farm Rex; and Ch. Glendee's Bourbon Banchee and Ch. Glendee's Star O'Sibley, sired by Ch. Glendee's Bourbon on the Rocks, CD.

The next foundation bitch to arrive at Glendee was Ch. Tyronne Farm Gloribee. Glory did not become a member of the kennels until she was three years old, and Myra finished her in five months. Glory produced seven litters for Glendee. Two of these were one puppy litters. She was bred to four different sires and the results were noteworthy—12 champions for Glendee. From Ch. Tyronne Farm Hallelujah came Ch. Glendee's April Love. Glory was then bred to Ch. Webline Golden Jubilee, CD, and from a nine puppy litter, five finished and three were pointed. This litter produced three Multi Best in Show winners, Ch. Glendee's Bourbon on the Rocks, CD, Ch. Glendee's Duke of Sherwood and Ch. Glendee's Drambuie Delight. Two litter sisters also finished, Ch. Glendee's Trouble Step and Ch. Glendee's Copper Penny. A repeat breeding to Jubilee produced only one bitch, Ch. Glendee's Enchantress of Erin. Glory was then sent to Ch. Sir Michael Galway of Glendee and produced Ch. Glendee's Grand Rouge and Am. & Can. Ch. Glendee's Sweet Molly Malone. The last litter Glory gave Glendee was sired by her son, Ch. Glendee's Bourbon on the Rocks, CD. Only one bitch came from that union, Ch. Glendee's Irish Glory, a truly lovely Group winning bitch, who later produced two Group winning daughters, Ch. Glendee's Irish Playgirl and Ch. Glendee's Autumn Flame, CD, three generations of Group winners.

From December 20, 1964 to April 14, 1966, Ch. Tyronne Farm Rex made his home at Glendee. He sired four litters and produced six champion Irish.

Merry's Dell's Evening Star was purchased by Glendee, and although she died at the early age of three years, she gave the kennel two champions when bred to Draherin Jiminy Cricket—Ch. Glendee's Nip O'Brandy and Ch. Glendee's Fly by Night.

The untimely death of Ch. Glendee's Miss Pilot Light, from bloat, was a blow to Myra and Thorne. However, from her two litters sired by Ch. Glendee's Bourbon on the Rocks, CD, came four champions: Ch. Heaven Hill's Mister Terrific, Ch. Glendee's Little Miss Stacy, Ch. Glendee's Jack of Diamonds and Ch. Glendee's Russet Hill by Mollie.

The acquisition of Am. & Can. Ch. Tirvelda Sincerely Yours, a Canadian Best in Show bitch midway through her life produced Can. Ch. Glendee's Intrepid. Bred to Bourbon on the Rocks, she produced Ch. Glendee's Enchantress of Erin, a full sister to Ch. Glendee's Bourbon on the Rocks, CD, whelped one litter and the results were, Ch. Glendee's Red Zeus Shanadoah, CD, and Ch. Glendee's Amor, CD. The sire was Ch. Tirvelda Oberon Bruce.

Ch. Glendee's Bourbon on the Rocks, CD, was one of the most famous Irish bred at Glendee. Handled exclusively by Myra, an amateur at the time, Rocky finished his championship title at 18 months, in six weeks, undefeated in the Open classes. He won his first Best in Show before he was two years old, and was 3rd in the Sporting Group at Westminster before he was three. He was semi-retired at age five with a record of 4 all breed Bests in Show, 1 Best of Breed Specialty, 23 Group Firsts and 35 other placings. Shown sparingly after that he acquired two more Group firsts and two Best of Breeds at Specialties from the Veterans Class. Rocky was also Best Veterans dog at the third National Specialty of the ISCA. He was the

Am. & Mex. Ch. Candy K's Broadway Joe (1), (Am. & Can. Ch. Draherin Ivy Leaguer ex Candy K's Wild Rose) and Am. & Mex. Ch. Candy K's Red Foxx (r) (Ch. Candy K's Broadway Joe ex Candy K's Daisey).

Am. & Can. Ch. Michael's Patti O'Shea, Ch. Rendition O'Hara of Sunny Hill and Ch. Rendition Renegrade.

sire of 12 AKC champions, 5 Canadian champions, and an Australian champion. His children and grandchildren are still winning in the show ring.

At the first Irish Setter Club of America National Specialty, an Irish Setter breeder from Australia, Mr. Graeme Lack, was touring the USA in search of Irish Setters to bring back to his country. After visiting kennels in the North, South, East and West, he decided upon a bitch, Robalee Tara of Saratoga from California, and requested she be bred to Ch. Glendee's Bourbon on the Rocks, CD. He was to take pick of the litter dog and bitch. Later, the Harrises learned that the two puppies from the union, then about three years old, were causing quite a sensation in Australia. The male, Robalee Yank of Brodruggan had to be temporarily pulled from the public stud service as his contracts became too numerous to handle. He was offered at stud at four times the going rate (about $500). Yank, although not shown to his title, is now the sire of a number of Australian champions.

Ch. Glendee's Little Miss Stacy, a Rocky daughter, was sent to Ch. Thenderin William Muldoon and produced Ch. Glendee's Sunset Stripper.

In August 1976, Glendee Kennels acquired a lovely young bitch, a daughter of Ch. Candia Indeed, Rossell Bridie Rose. Bridie finished quite easily and was sent to Ch. McCamon Marquis. The result of that union was Ch. Glendee's Diamond in the 'Ruff, Ch. Glendee's Stone Cutter, Ch. Rossel Rosalee and Ch. Charlton Oriental Jade. Both Jade and Stone Cutter achieved exceptional show records with numerous Bests in Show and Group wins. Stone Cutter was bought by Sr. Mauricio Tuck Schneider and was sent to Brazil following his successful show career in the States in 1982. Jade is owned by Larry Nash and Susan Kilbey, who handled her.

In September 1980, Myra and Thorne celebrated their 18th year of breeding Irish Setters. During that period the kennel has produced 34 American champions, including 3 multi-Best in Show winners and 10 Group winners, 2 Canadian champions, a Brazilian champion and 9 Obedience titleholders.

Heidbreder, William, Loretta and Maxine — *Russet Hill* — Waynesville, MD

The Heidbreders' first Irish Setter, Rusty, obtained in 1967, was a great shooting dog. In 1974, Mrs. Heidbreder braved the long drive from St. Louis to Virginia, by herself, to bring their foundation bitch, Ch. Glendee's Russet Hill My Molly (Ch. Glendee's Bourbon on the Rocks, CD, ex Ch. Glendee's Miss Pilot Light) to Ch. Tirvelda Michaelson. I'll never forget that breeding! Try as we did old Mike could not get the job done. Finally to our vet for an artificial breeding. Only to be told it would be a waste of money, Molly was too far out of heat. I whispered to him "go ahead anyway, it will give her something to hope for on the trip home."

The result was a litter which has one champion, and three others pointed.

The star of the litter was Ch. Russet Hill Bootlegger. At very limited showing and with young Maxine handling, Buddy's career comprised of over 50 Best of Breed wins, 3 Specialties and a Best in Show. He also had many other Group placements. His untimely and unfortunate death cut his career short when he was just 5 years old, but the Heidbreders have continued on with his progeny, already pointed and well on their way.

Hill, Ron and Cindy — San Bernardino, CA

The Hills campaigned Tirvelda Lord Brian Boru to his title in co-ownership with Ann and Rich Boyer. They also put a CDX on their Shane of Dublin.

Hobbs, Dorothy Dell — *Merry-Dell* — Merrillville, IN

The first setter that Dorothy and Von Hobbs acquired was Fleetwood Farms

Am. & Can. Ch. Courtwood Summer Forecast
(Ch. Candia Indeed ex Ch. Shannon Kelly O'Green).

Ch. Runwild Finnagain
(Ch. Carrvale's Terry Terhune ex Ch. Runwild Fiona).

Sedan de Ville, one of a litter whelped in a Cadillac on the way to the veterinarian. Sedan de Ville's litter sister, Am. & Can. Ch. Fleetwood Farm Coupe de Ville is the dam of Am., Can. & Bda. Ch. Merry-Dell's Autumn Glory. She was the top winning Irish Setter bitch of 1963 and 1964. Another Hobbs setter was Ch. Draherin Irish Chieftain, a son of Ch. Tyronne Farm Malone II. Other Merry-Dell champions were Copper Chief, Bronze, and Daring Damsel. After Von Hobbs' death the Merry-Dell kennel was reduced in size, producing an occasional litter. Dorothy is now an AKC-approved judge.

Hobbs, Jack and Mary-Lou — Annandale, VA

Ch. Bayberry Tobago was the result of the Hobbs' only breeding, their Tirvelda Valorinn Patrice to Ch. Bayberry Kincaide. Tobago had an outstanding class record of five majors, became a Specialty Best of Breed winner with many Group wins and placements, and placed in the Top Ten breed lists for 1971 and 1972. He was the sire of seven AKC Champions and five CKC Champions, with many others pointed. He died in 1981.

Hoffman, John and Susan — *Red Hue* — Akron, OH

The Hoffmans' own Ch. Fleetwood Farms Kerry Rose (Ch. Fleetwood Farms Grand Marshall ex Ch. Shannon's Gypsy), a multi-Specialty winner. Their latest champion is Interlude Antrim Heir (Ch. Rendition Erin of Sunny Hills ex Ch. Meadowlark's Katy of Misty Morn) who finished with majors at two Specialties.

Hughes, Dale and Dolores — *Candy* — El Cajon, CA

Candy Kennels was established in 1965 but it was not until 1968 that a five-year-old bitch, Kinvarra Ember, winner of many ribbons, promoted their interest in showing. They then purchased a female and a male of the Varagon-Aragon bloodline. The male became their first champion—Ch. Candy K's Herk Murphy, and the female—Miss Waggs to Riches—won many breeder awards offered by the ISCA for her one and only litter that produced three champions: Ch. Candy K's King of the Road, Ch. Candy K's Donavan and Am. & Mex. Ch. Candy K's Silky Sullivan. Ch. Donavan, in turn, sired the 18-month Best in Show male, Ch. Candy K's Patrick Murphy, and Ch. Silky Sullivan produced the four times Best in Show winner, Am. & Mex. Ch. Candy K's Twice-A-Prince.

After finishing three champion litter brothers, Dale and Dolores decided upon a Ch. Shannon's Erin son as an outcross and purchased Ch. Candia Dandi from Sally Reese. Dandi was small for California competition but managed to win two Irish Setter Specialties in 1972 and produced two champions in his first breeding at Candy K's (Ch. Candy K's Modeen and the lovely Am. & Mex. Ch. Candy K's Katie Dunn).

Since then Candy Kennels has finished many champions, all owner handled by Dale Hughes. In 1980 their beautiful Am. & Mex. Ch. Candy K's Red Foxx helped make breed records in California with 12 Best of Breeds and several Group firsts and seconds. She was bred to Ch. McCamon Marquis and these offspring began to appear in 1981.

Huizenga, Jake D. and Sara L. — *Oxton Kennels* — Salinas, CA

Jake and Sally have been devoted to the dual purpose Irish Setter for the past 40 years. They have trained and handled several bench and obedience trial winners including Ch. Oxton Rex, CDX, and Ch. Oxton's Irish Perfection, CDX (who was also a field trial winner). Jake always hunted over his show dogs, and following the

Ch. Shawnee Pipedream O'Charlton (Ch. Candia Indeed ex Am. Can. Ch. Rendition Indian Summer).

Ch. Tirvelda Sprig of Gabhantyr (Rockerin Flynn ex Tirvelda Brengwain).

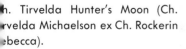

h. Tirvelda Hunter's Moon (Ch. rvelda Michaelson ex Ch. Rockerin ebecca).

Am. & Mex. Ch. Legend of V[...]
gon, UDT, PR, PU, Can. CDX [...]
Innisfail Color Scheme ex Inni[...]
Best Regards).

Am. & Can. Ch. Shannon Kelly
O'Green (St. Patrick of Alpine
Meadows ex Citadel Daybreak of
Tipperary).

Ch. Donamar Bold Echo of Var[...]
gon (Ch. Michael Bryan Duke [...]
Sussex ex Ch. Enchantment [...]
Varagon).

dual concept, he began field training show dogs. He field trained and finished two of the breed's few Dual Champions—Dual Ch. Merry Kerry Quite Contrary (owned by M. & K. Gerdis) and Dual Ch. Duffin Miss Duffy, CD (owned by E. Schweitzer). In the 1950s his Field Ch. Oxton's Shosaph was the first Irish Setter Field Trial Champion in over a decade.

The Huizengas were instrumental in promoting Irish Setters in the field in California, and were among the organizers of the Irish Setter Club of the Pacific (San Francisco) and the Irish Setter Club of Central California, Inc., clubs dedicated to the duality of the Irish Setter.

Now in their 70's, both are still active in promoting the breed. Sally runs Oxton Kennels and Jake helps young people train their Irish Setters for the field and show ring. (See also Field Trial section.)

Iacobucci, Louis — *Celou* — Providence, RI

Louis' first Irish Setter was a Shawnlea bitch which he bred to a Charles River dog to obtain Celou's Sheena MacRory, his foundation bitch. It is from her that 6 Celou MacRory champions descend: Lex, Alvin, Kallyanne, Irish Prince, Tracey and Rory II. His breeding of Ch. Celou's Tracey MacRory to Ch. Michael Bryan Duke of Sussex produced a litter of 10, all of which finished their championships. Louis was President of the Irish Setter Club of America for six years, and is active in the Providence Kennel Club.

Jennings, Peter S. and Cynthia P. — *Hearthstone* — Danbury, CT

Since their first litter in 1960 (including Ch. Hearthstone High Hopes and Ch. Hearthstone Gay Ladybird), the Jennings' have maintained a small kennel, producing from time to time only strictly line-bred Irish Setters. They have handled their own dogs to championships (Ch. H. Glory Bee, Ch. H. Bonfire, Ch. H. Muldoon). Both have been very active in all aspects of the dog fancy and are now licensed judges.

Johnson, Michael P. and Judith A. — *Kilgary* — Cave Creek, AZ

The Kilgary Kennels was established in December 1971 and since that date a number of home-breds have made their championships. The foundation animals included Starheir's Ingin Catlin, a daughter of Ch. Major O'Shannon and Ch. Merry-Dell's Heiress. Unfortunately this lovely bitch died at four, one point short of her championship after having been Winner's Bitch at the Combined Specialties in New York and at the Milwaukee Specialty. Luckily she produced the Best in Show winner, Am. & Can. Ch. Kilgary Bally Vaughan to carry on her sterling qualities.

The Johnsons' next purchase was the youngster who became Am., Can. & Bda. Ch. Dunholm's Finn McCool (Ch. Shannon's Erin ex Ch. Tirvelda Bridget Susie Ann). Finn won a number of Best in Shows and over 100 Groups in Canada. He was the top Sporting dog in Canada in 1974 and 1975.

Another of their foundation Irish was the very beautiful Ch. Charlton's Auburn Tresses. A daughter of Ch. Draherin Auburn Artistry and Ch. Shannon's Empress, she finished her championship with three 5-pt. Specialty wins. Later, bred to Ch. Thenderin William Muldoon, she produced three champions: Ch. Kilgary Dungannon, a Specialty winner; Ch. Kilgary Dunshauglin, a Group winner, and Ch. Kilgary Dunbarry. Dungannon was sold to Thenderin Kennels.

Still another foundation bitch, Ch. Draherin Tamara, produced the well-known Group winner, Ch. Kilgary Aman.

Johnstone, Tom and Barbara — *Kintyre* — **Anoka, MN**

The Johnstones began in 1974 with the purchase of Wilson Farm Kintyre Mist (Ch. Wilson Farm Hallmark ex Ch. Tirvelda Toma Maid). Mist's daughter, Ch. Kintyre Sugar-N'Spice was Best Puppy at the 1977 National Specialty. The Johnstones also purchased Meadowlark's Morning Star (Meadowlark Honor Guard ex Ch. Tirvelda Meadowlark's Ebbtide) and Meadowlark's Aristocrat (Ch. Candia Indeed ex Ch. Tirvelda Meadowlark's Ebbtide).

Tom and Barbara are charter members of the Columbus Irish Setter Club and Tom was its first President.

Jones, Mr. and Mrs. Dale R. — *Dajos* — **Puyallup, WA**

The Jones started in 1967 and their first title holder was Dajo's Danny Boy, CDX, who obtained his degree by 14 months. Their foundation animals included Ch. Argo Lane Fidelity, Am. & Can. Ch. Mid-Oaks Kelly and Halcar Autumn Sherry. Their first homebred champion, Dajo's Sir Guy, finished his championship by taking three 5-pt. majors in one weekend, and went on to many wins of the Group in a fine show career.

Kimmel, William and Karen — *McBoscage* — **Dover, PA**

The Kimmels began their kennel in 1969 and finished their first champion with the aid of Mary Ann Alston. This bitch, Ch. Mosn'n Acre Wilson Farm Harmony, by Ch. Tirvelda Earl of Harewood ex Ch. Wilson Farm Country Charm, had the high distinction of winning Best of Breed under W. J. Rasbridge at the First National Specialty of the Irish Setter Club of America in 1973, owner-handled.

Harmony, or Song as she was known, had a total of 14 puppies out of litters by Ch. Tirvelda Rustic Duke, Ch. Tirvelda Distant Drummer, Ch. Candia Indeed and Ch. Tirvelda Hunter's Moon. Various misfortunes took a severe toll of these promising few puppies, but in 1979 the Kimmels finished a bitch from the Song/Indeed litter, Ch. McBoscage Song's Heiress—this time, breeder-owner-handled.

I asked how their unusual kennel name was evolved, and was told it comes from Gaelic and means "sons of the thicket or woods." The Kimmels are active charter members of the Lower Susquehanna Irish Setter Club and the Irish Setter Genetic Registry.

Kipp, James J. and Sandra — *Londradh* — **Waterloo, IA**

Lonradh, a small midwestern kennel, started in 1972 by acquiring Muckamoor Meath Maginn, and she finished her championship owner-handled. She had three majors and in one, went from the classes over seven Specials. The other two majors were won at Specialties. She was bred only once, to Ch. Tirvelda Telstar, producing a litter of five puppies. All have been shown, with Lonradh Sunset Jubilee having finished. Lonradh Scarlet Knight has a CD title. The Kipps are planning a limited breeding program combining Tirvelda and Muckamoor lines.

Klinck, Edith, David and Mary — *Orchard Farm* — **Windsor, Ontario, CAN**

Orchard Farm Kennel had its beginnings in 1938 when Harold Klinck purchased Tyrone Farm O'Shea from Jack Spear. Over the years Mr. Klinck bred several champions including Can. & Am. Ch. Lucky of Orchard Farm and the multi-Best in Show winning Can. & Am. Ch. Danny of Orchard Farm.

After the death of Mr. Klinck in 1965, most of the stock of the kennel was lost. The kennel was revived by Edith, David and Mary Klinck with the foundation bitch

...mpion Bayberry Tobago (Ch. ...berry Kinkaide ex Tirvelda ...ice).

Am. & Can. Ch. Rendition Chantilly Lace (Ch. Candia Indeed ex Rendition Jennifer).

Foxfyre's Scarlet Ember, CD (Ch. ...n Acre Wilson Farm Harvest ex ...b's Scarlet Tara).

Can. & Am. Ch. Rebecca's Irish Lace (Ch. Tirvelda Michaelson ex Ch. Rockherin Rebecca). Lacey was bred to Ch. Bayberry Tobago and produced Am. & Can. Ch. Orchard Farm Catch the Wind, Am. & Can. Ch. Orchard Farm Shamaranne, Can. Ch. Orchard Farm Sundancer (9 AKC pts.) and Orchard Farm Red Delicious. Shamaranne is the dam of a very promising young dog, Orchard Farm Fanfare, sired by Can. Ch. Tara Hill Orion. She also has a litter sired by Am. & Can. Ch. McCamon Marquis.

Orchard Farm Kennel also includes Can. Ch. Tara Hill Orion (Ch. Tirvelda Telstar ex Ch. Rockherin Rebecca), co-owned with B. Brewbaker, and Rockherin Diana (Ch. Tirvelda Hunters Moon ex Rockherin Jennifer), co-owned with Katherine Wheatley.

Kloss, Alan and Barbara — *Powderhorn* — Newtown, CT
The Klosses started their kennel with the 'Dublin' prefix in 1966. Their foundation bitch, Dublin Mist, bred to Ch. Hearthstones High Hopes, produced Ch. Dublin's Irish Rebel.

In 1970 they purchased Tyerwood Southern Comfort, who finished her championship handily. Bred to Ch. Tirvelda Hunter's Moon, Southern Comfort produced Am. & Can. Ch. Powderhorn's Liberty Belle, who finished exclusively from the Bred by Exhibitor class. As a special she became the first breeder-owner-handled Irish Setter bitch to go Best in Show in 15 years in America, at the Central New York Kennel Club over an entry of 1,000. Her litter brother, Ch. Powderhorn Yankee Rifleman (owner-handled by John Van Der Kruik) captured the Breed over specials at the ISCCC Specialty. He was later purchased by Mrs. Cheever Porter, and ably handled by Jane Forsyth. Rifleman became the first Irish Setter in 12 years to win the Group at Westminster 1978, and was the #2 Sporting dog in 1979.

A second litter, sired by McKendree's Danny Boy of Milyn, produced Ch. Powderhorn's Independence (co-owned with Anita Van Der Kruik) and Ch. Powderhorn Frontiersman.

Both Alan and Barbara have decided to making showing a side career and have applied for their judges' licenses.

Knight, Hank and Judy — *Kamberland* — Howell, MI
Judy obtained her foundation bitch from Joe and Marge Frydrych—Argo Lane Flaming Fantasy (Ch. Esquire of Maple Ridge ex Ch. Argo Lane Tippity Wicket). She was bred to Ch. Argo Lane Star of Dawn, owned by Ken and Shirley Opp, and this breeding produced Ch. Kenshire Killarney Kinsman. Fantasy was then bred to Argo Lane Reddy Teddy. When the pups were 10 days old, Fantasy died of bloat. The eight pups were raised on tube and bottle; and Hank's sister Cheryle took Kamberlands Flaming Fury. Fury went on to finish his Canadian Championship and his CD. When bred to another Kamberland bitch, he produced Ch. Kamberland High Spirits. Fury also led Cheryle on from Junior Showmanship to a career as a professional handler.

The Knights' next addition was Rox-San Danny Boy, a Blayneywood Country Squire son from Rox-San Kennels. Danny was BOW (5 pts.) at Detroit at 20 months, and finished at two years. BOB and Group placements were followed by his lease to Albert Greenfield.

With several pointed young Irish and many plans, disaster struck in the form of P.R.A. Six young Irish were eventually taken to M.S.U. and Hank and Judy eliminated most of their stock. They kept a young bitch out of Danny and Summit Rise Sendai Doll, Kamberland Summit Rise Solo. Solo was bred to Ch. Crimson

Ch. Powderhorn Yankee Rifleman
(Ch. Tirvelda Hunter's Moon ex Ch. Tyerwood Southern Comfort).

Ch. Powderhorn's Liberty Belle
(Ch. Tirvelda Hunter's Moon ex Ch. Tyerwood Southern Comfort).

Am. & Can. Ch. McCamon Marquis
(Ch. Tirvelda Telstar ex Ch. McCamon Royal Burgundy).

Satan of Varagon, CD, and produced Ch. Kamberland Akiba in Command and Ch. Kamberland Asti in Command. Akiba has been test-bred, cleared and placed in field training. Although really too old to compete (6 yrs), Kiba did well with a clean find at his first and only trial. His daughter, Kamberland Dstari, is presently in field training and Kiba is competing in Obedience.

Korpan, James and Sue — *McCamon* — Saskatoon, Saskatchewan, CAN

We asked Sue to write her own kennel history:

"Our kennel originated in 1967 when we acquired two Irish Setters within a year. Although both were pet quality, they were excellent hunting dogs of the old Ardee line. The two "old men" are still with us even though we have shifted our interests to the show ring.

"Our third Irish Setter was a Shannon's Erin daughter, who we showed to her Canadian championship. With "Morgan," Ch. Pacesetter Morgan McCamon, came the realization that a quality show animal must have the breeding behind it on both sides of the pedigree. Thus arose our 4,000 mile trip visiting prominent Irish Setter breeders in the Central and Eastern United States. On this trip, in 1971, we acquired our foundation bitch, multi-Best in Show winner, Am. & Can. Ch. McCamon's Royal Burgundy from Beurmann and Elizabeth Brewbaker.

"Burgundy is by Ch. Tirvelda Michaelson ex Ch. Rockerin Rebecca. Her show record and progeny have proven her undeniable quality. Burgundy was Best of Winners at the second National Irish Setter Club of America Specialty over an entry of 375, her first time shown in the United States. She followed this with another Best of Winners at the Irish Setter Club of Ohio Specialty in 1975. Shown only seven times in Canada in 1975, she was the Number 1 Irish Setter bitch in Canada and the Number 3 Irish Setter, having earned three all-breed Bests in Show to add to her previous show and Sporting Group wins.

"With Burgundy we have tried to combine the best of the Tirvelda and Rockerin lines. Burgundy at 11 years of age is the dam of 23 CKC champions and 7 AKC champions. Six more of her get need only one major in the United States.

"From Burgundy's first litter, sired by Can. Ch. Rockerin Mississauga Chief, came four Canadian champions and our Am. & Can. Ch. Chief O'McCamon, a multi-breed and Group winner in both countries.

"One of our most successful breeding combinations—and one we repeated three times—was the breeding of Burgundy to Ch. Tirvelda Telstar. From the first litter of this combination came two of our most outstanding show dogs and producers: Well known to the dog show world is Am. & Can. Ch. McCamon Marquis. Marquis (or Chance, as he is known to many) achieved a show record that will go down as one of the greatest in breed history. He won 36 all-breed Bests in Show, 25 Specialty Bests of Breed and 157 Sporting Group Firsts in the United States and Canada. While he was in the United States he was co-owned with Mrs. Lillian Gough, a partnership for which we are very grateful. He was the top Irish Setter in the United States in 1977 and 1979, handled by his great friend, George Alston. He then returned to Canada, and owner-handled, was Number 1 Irish, Number 2 Sporting Dog in Canada in 1981. Marquis was the first Irish Setter ever to win two Irish Setter Club of America National Specialties.

"Marquis is now retired from the show ring, but is proving himself to be an extremely prepotent sire. To date he has 26 AKC champions with many more pointed offspring yet to come. Two of his offspring, Ch. Charlton's Oriental Jade and Ch. Glendee's Stone Cutter finished in the top three Irish Setters in the United

States for 1981, both being multi-Best in Show and Specialty winners. Stone Cutter was No. 2 Irish Setter in 1981.

"Of equal quality and now proving her worth as an excellent producer is Marquis' litter sister, Am. & Can. Ch. McCamon Grande Dame. "Tarin," a multi-Best in Show winner in Canada and a Specialty winner in both countries, finished as No. 3 Irish Setter and No. 1 bitch in Canada in 1977. From her first litter she produced Am. & Can. Ch. McCamon Prairie Sage and several Canadian champions. Tarin has also been bred twice to her uncle, Ch. Tirvelda Hunter's Moon. From the first litter, now just over two years of age, has come Can. Ch. McCamon Winter Lace, Can. Ch. McCamon Winter Blush, McCamon Winter Promise and Am. & Can. Ch. McCamon Winter Knight. A repeat litter from this combination is equally promising—a bitch, McCamon Gossamer Moon has 9 Canadian points at 9 months and a brother, Ch. McCamon Moonwalker completed his Canadian championship at 11 months.

"A littermate to Marquis and Grande Dame, McCamon Katrina Doll, is also an American and Canadian champion.

"In the two repeat breedings of Burgundy to Telstar there are four CKC champions and one AKC champion, Am. & Can. Ch. McCamon Somermead Galadriel. Others need only majors to finish.

"Another successful combination was that of Burgundy bred to Int. Ch. Tirvelda Blarney o' Elvatowne. This produced Am. & Can. Ch. McCamon Spellbinder and Am. & Can. Ch. McCamon Anastasia, who was BOS to Marquis at the National Specialty in 1979. Anastasia bred to Marquis produced Ch. Somermead National Acclaim.

"Our next generation, Can. Ch. McCamon Winter Lace bred to Marquis is showing promise.

"For our success we pay tribute to Am. & Can. Ch. McCamon's Royal Burgundy and her outstanding sire and dam, and to the people who bred them. We thank them for helping us to establish our line."

Kosmel, Hugo and Judy — *O'Shannon* — Sycamore, IL

Hugo and Judy have been devoted to the Irish Setter breed for more than 15 years. A pet named Shammy Shelly O'Shannon, out of O'Farrell-Tyronne lines, got them interested in field trials. The Kosmels then purchased Ch. Jo-Ett's John Francis (Ch. Shamrock Flamingo ex Ch. Jo-Ett's Heather) and Shamrock Sue O'Shannon (Dual Ch. Mahogany Titian Jingo ex Red-San of Charles). Sue finished her Field Championship in 1972, making her the top winning field bitch in the country. In 1973 she finished her Amateur Field Championship—the first to obtain this title in the Midwest.

Sue was then mated to Ch. Jo-Ett's John Francis, and from this litter came Ch. Vindicator Blud of O'Shannon, Ch. Red Bart Chico of Jo-Ett's, CD, and Field and Amateur Field Ch. Dame Duchess O'Shannon. Duchess followed in her mother's footsteps by becoming top Field winning Bitch in the country in 1974. Also out of the O'Shannon Kennels came Ch. Heavenly Brandy O'Shannon, Fld. Ch. O'Shannons Pathfinder, and many more pointed field dogs.

Kramer, Mrs. Lynda — *Red Shadow* — Spring, TX

Lynda Kramer's Red Shadow Kennel came into being in the early 1970s with Draherin based stock. Lynda keeps no more than six Irish at one time and breeds only when there is a need for a new puppy (one to two litters a year). Although

Am. & Can. Ch. McCamon Grande Dame (Ch. Tirvelda Telstar ex Ch. McCamon Royal Burgundy).

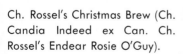

Am. & Can. Ch. McCamon's Royal Burgundy at 10½ years old.

Ch. Rossel's Christmas Brew (Ch. Candia Indeed ex Can. Ch. Rossel's Endear Rosie O'Guy).

proud of her bitches Ch. Draherin Firefly and Group-placing Darajen's Flamming Red Shadow, her favorite is her special Ch. Rossel's Christmas Brew, Best in Show, Group and Specialty winning Son of Ch. Candia Indeed. Lynda is a co-founder and past president of the ISC of Houston.

Kubacz, Randy and Anne Marie — *Ramblin' Red* — Freehold, NJ
Randy and Anne Marie met at a Field Trial. They were married in 1975. At that time they owned Randy's first Irish Setter, a pet shop puppy that became Amateur Field Ch. Galway's Red Disappointment, CD, and Anne's show Irish, Shannon's Kerry of Windsor, UD, and Ramblin' Red Avelle.

Their Double National Champion, Field Ch. and Amateur Field Ch. Ramblin' Red Banshee placed second in ISCA's National Futurity, and the following year won both the ISCA Open Limited Classic and Amateur Classic. After a brilliant performance, Banshee became the first National Champion in 1979 at the ISCA's annual trial at Rend Lake, Illinois, and in 1980 repeated this win in Ardmore, Oklahoma.

The Kubaczes are also active in conformation. Their Ch. Ramblin' Red Avelle, CD, VC, is one of the first to win the ISCA's versatile certificate. Avelle has had two litters, the first by Ch. Draherin King's Ransom, which contains four pointed littermates and Best of Breed winner Ch. Ramblin' Red Guinevere, and the second by Ch. Shawnee Pipedream O'Charlton.

Lafferty, Joan E. — *Jela* — Elmendorf, TX
Jela is a small Texas kennel concentrating on Obedience and breed competition. Miss Lafferty's first champion, a son of Ch. Tirvelda Michaelson and Padre Island Sea Marina, CDX, is Mex. & Am. Ch. Jela's Irish Rebellion, CDX. Also residing at Jela are Jela Mister Mack, CDX, Jela Victory of Olympia, CD, and Redburs Kate. Joan also owned Dariabar Scarlet Penelope, CDX, TD, who earned her tracking degree at almost ten years of age.

LaShot, Dorothy — *Niebline* — Creswell, OR
Dorothy LaShot started her Niebline Kennels in 1966 with a year-old Cherry Point bitch, a half brother/half sister breeding both by Ch. Cherry Point Brask. Ch. Cherry Point Kerry Niebline finished easily and proved to be an excellent producer for her kennels. Of note, her litter sister was the foundation bitch for Padre Island Kennels in Texas.

Kerry's first breeding, to Ch. Cherry Point Shanahan, produced Niebline's first homebred champion, Niebline Bold Venture. Her next breeding, to Ch. Tirvelda Michaelson, produced the multi-group and Best in Show winner, Am. & Can. Ch. Niebline Streamliner. Kerry's last breeding was to Bayberry Flickerson (Ch. Kinvarra Flicker - Ch. Tirvelda Cathy O'Rinn) which produced Ch. Niebline Scarlet Ribbon. Dorothy also acquired Kerry's litter sister, Cherry Point Duchess. She was bred to Ch. Chivas of Varagon which produced the Specialty winner, Ch. Niebline Typhoon.

Introduced to Dorothy's breeding program was Tirvelda Red Poppy, a young bitch by Ch. Tirvelda Michaelson ex Ch. Tirvelda Queen Mab, and she proved a valuable asset by producing Ch. Niebline Spellbinder. Dorothy also acquired the lovely bitch, Tiranog Charleen Marty, who she handled to championship in less than six months.

Currently several young hopefuls sporting the Niebline prefix are being campaigned on the West Coast. The Spellbinder son, Ch. Niebline Locomotion,

m. & Mex. Ch. Candy K's Twice-Prince (Am. Can. Ch. Candy K's ky Sullivan ex Candy K's ypsy).

. Candia Dandi (Am. Can. a. Ch. Shannon's Erin ex Can. . Candia Abigail, CD).

. Hearthstone Muldoon earthstone's Irish Imp ex arthstone's Fortune Teller).

has won a number of Groups and Specialty Bests of Breed under the ownership of Gary and Starla Trivilino of Oak Harbor, Washington.

Lea, Bruce and Caren — *Tarahill* — Van Nuys, CA

The first two bitches and foundation of Tarahill were acquired from Thenderin in 1968: Ch. Thenderin Endeavor, CD, a very successful campaigner in 1970 with wins that included BOS at Westminster, and Ch. Thenderin Hestia of Tarahill, CD. Hestia is the dam of their first males, Ch. Thenderin Future of Tarahill and his litter brother, Ch. Thenderin Foremost, UD. The latter is owned by Mr. and Mrs. Beaugereau in Arizona.

Lemmer, David E. and Sandra J. — *Rox-San* — Olonomowoc, WI

A small kennel, with never more than six adults at home, the Lemmers began in 1961, and average only one litter a year.

The kennel name Rox-San was derived in honor of the dog who sparked the interest in showing and breeding, a Golden Retriever named Lady Roxanne. Their first champion was Ch. Killane Boru of Argo Lane, purchased as a 4-year-old from the Frydrych's Argo Lane Kennels and finished shortly thereafter. The foundation bitch was Rox-San Sweet Dream, purchased as a youngster from the Dorwayne kennels of Wayne and Dorothy Piper. She was a product of Caldene breeding, her sire being Ch. Caldene Patrician, and her dam, Dorwayne's Kristi Shannon, CDX. Sweet Dream earned her CD and her first two points with 10-week-old pups at home, and was killed by a car shortly thereafter. From this, her only litter, came the lovely Ch. Rox-San Auburn Treasure, CD, the future foundation of all Rox-San champions. The first breeding of Boru to Auburn Treasure produced but one pup, who had 9 pts., all majors, handled by his 16-year-old owner, at the time of his death. From their second litter came the fine producer—Rox-San Color Me Red, dam of three champions, all Specialty winners. Then Auburn Treasure was bred to Ch. Blayneywood Country Squire, producing the "D" litter whose notables are: Am. & Can. Ch. Rox-San Danny Boy, Specialty winner, Group and BIS winner; Ch. Rox-San Debutante, CDX, also a Specialty winner; and Rox-San Dream Maker, CDX. Rox-San Color Me Red bred to Ch. Donamar Bold Echo of Varagon produced Ch. Rox-San Elegant Erin, who finished the day before his seventh birthday by winning BOB from the classes at the Spring '75 Western Specialty, his second Specialty win and fourth major. Color Me Red was next bred to her half-brother, Ch. Rox-San Danny Boy, producing the Lemmers' Ch. Rox-San Fame and Ch. Rox-San Flirtation. Fame won his first points at the ISC Milwaukee '73 Specialty and finished there the following year, with his sister Ch. Rox-San Flirtation winning BOS at the same show. The pointed Rox-San Joshua and Can. Ch. Rox-San Statesman are co-owned with Mark and Dianna Bromaghim.

Sandra is a judge of Irish Setters. The Lemmers also own English Cocker Spaniels.

Liggett, Gene and Clare — *Limited* — Freehold, NJ

It was love at first sight between the Liggetts and Ch. Shannon's Erin at Westminster. To them he was the perfect show dog. Soon after they purchased Tirvelda Flame of Erin from Ted Eldredge, and then the Erin son, who became their first Champion, bred by Lucy Jane Myers, Ch. Draherin Conqueror. Conqueror sired the breed and Specialty winner, Ch. Limited County Clare, a bitch owned by the Ed Janeczkos. He also sired Ch. Wynquest Troop Commander, a Group and

Hinsdale Jim Dandy O'Farrell
Sunny Acres Mahogany Caper
Ch. Red Mist O'Finley).

& Mex. Ch. Tirvelda
O'Elvatowne (Ch. Tir-
chaelson ex Ch. Tir-
tunata).

Bda. & Mex. Ch. Tir-
rney O'Elvatowne (Ch.
Michaelson ex Ch. Tir-
tunata).

Specialty winner, co-owned with Major James Golden. The Liggetts also owned the brother-sister duo, Ch. Sportmirth Blazing Legend and Ch. Sportmirth Bright Promise.

Many of the Liggetts' dogs were trained and handled by their daughter, Lynda. Her first time in Junior showmanship Lynda took Best Junior Handler honors with Conqueror. Lynda also owned and bred Silky Terrier champions and is currently showing Whippets in addition to her first love, the Irish Setter.

Long, Jeanette M. — *Merryborne* — Columbia, SC

Jeanette's first show Irish Setter, obtained in 1967, was Ch. Harmony Lane's Risin' O' The Moon, a Ch. Conifer's Lance granddaughter. She was bred only once to a Ch. Cherry Point Brask son and produced only four puppies, two of whom finished, breeder-owner-handled: Ch. Harmony Lane Bourbon of Booze and the Specialty winner, Ch. Harmony Lane's Chief Topic. Bourbon was bred to Jeanette's Specialty-winning Ch. Heather Kate's Molly, and they produced Ch. Merryborne's Movin' On, another Specialty winner. All dogs finished their titles owner-handled. Also, there was Ch. Wyndover's Autumn Ambush, a Group-winning son of Ch. Webline Wizard of Macapa. Presently at Merryborne are a Ch. Thenderin William Muldoon son, Chandar Legend of Merryborne, a triple cross to Ch. Bayberry Kincaide, and a litter by Ch. Shawnee Pipedream O'Charlton.

Lowell, Elizabeth and Donald — *Tamarack* — Westbrook, ME

The Lowells operate as an entire family. The boys, Scott and Larry, are active in all phases of Tamarack which started in 1963.

Their first dog, Bonigal of Brian, UD, was Maine's first utility Irish. Next came Tamarack Kerry Dancer, a male of Seaforth and Charles River breeding, who became their foundation stud. Two of his sons, Lake Line Rust Wind and Lake Line Brandy of Hengate, placed Best of Winners at New England Specialties—1972 and 1973. Brandy went on to become Maine's first Canadian and American champion.

A Kerry daughter, Thenderin G. C. Robin Tamarack became a Canadian and American UD titleholder. Three of her offspring have Canadian championships and Canadian Obedience degrees.

Lyons, Tom and Constance — *Spiretop* — Broad Run, VA

Spiretop was established in 1958 with the purchase from Kinvarra of a puppy bitch by Ch. Sergeant Red Sails of Devon ex Ch. Kinvarra Mary Eileen. Unfortunately this bitch died, but two more bitches were obtained from Kinvarra. One was a daughter of Ch. Draherin Gaye Malone ex Ch. Brianwood Gaelic Girl; the other by Ch. Draherin Irish Chieftain ex Ch. Kinvarra Sheila. The first champion produced by the Lyons they did not retain. He became Ch. Kinvarra Viking.

Then, according to Connie, this ended the first phase of the kennel. Struck by P.R.A., the Lyons waited a period of time before acquiring Tirvelda Wildfire, a daughter of Ch. Blayneywood Country Squire and Ch. Tirvelda Divine Sarah. Bred to Ch. Tirvelda Nor'wester, Wildfire produced the Specialty winner, Ch. Tirvelda Firethorn, who (briefly owned by Mrs. Cheever Porter) won a number of Groups. Wildfire was then bred to Ch. Tirvelda Tambourlane, which produced Spiretop Siobhan, the dam of the lovely bitch, Ch. Spiretop Sorceress, BOW at the Eastern Specialty in 1975. Sorceress was acquired by Bill and Ruth Berman. Another shown to her championship by Connie was the bitch, Tirvelda Burning Bright.

endee's Bourbon on the CD (Ch. Webline Golden ex Ch. Tyronne Farm e).

Ch. Tyronne Farm Gloribee (Ch. Webline Golden Jubilee ex Tyronne Farm Victoria).

Dunholm Finn McCool (Am. Bda. Ch. Shannon's Erin ex irvelda Bridget Susie Ann).

Ch. Candy K's King of the Road, Am. Mex. Ch. Candy K's Silky Sullivan, Ch. Candy K's Donavan.

Ch. McKendree's Bold Venture (Ch. Donamar Bold Conquistador ex McKendree's Misty Moment).

McCrory, Dr. Wallace and Sylvia — *Liafail* — Pound Ridge, NY

Sylvia has had Irish since childhood. Her first used to follow her pony over the Devonshire moors in England. In the fifties, the McCrorys purchased an Irish Setter from Jack Spear, when they were living in Iowa.

In 1969, the McCrorys obtained the English imported bitch Brackenfield Pheasant, CD, (Eng. Ch. Brackenfield Orichale Juniper ex Gaelge Gretar) from Miss Sybil Lennox. This bitch was bred in 1972 to Ch. Smoke Dream of Tamarisk, a son of Ch. Blayneywood Country Squire ex Ch. Shamie, and the mating produced the Specialty winning bitches Ch. Liafail Brackenfield Brigid and Am., Can. & Bda. Ch. Liafail Brackenfield Beauty. Beauty was bred to Ch. Courtwood Spring Son and produced Ch. Liafail Lady Gregory, Ch. Liafail Country Mist, CD, and Ch. Liafail Son of Ballylee. Beauty was next bred to Ch. Rendition Erin of Sunny Hills and produced the Group-winning Ch. Liafail Lovely Light and Am. & Bda. Ch. Liafail Sea Urchin, owned by Karolynne McAteer and Frances Robinson.

McKendree, Mr. and Mrs. H. E. — *McKendree* — Jacksonville, FL

The McKendrees started in 1964 with the puppy bitch, Cindy Jean II. Cindy was pointed, and the cornerstone of their kennel, when—at the age of five—she died from bloat.

In five generations, their breeding produced Ch. McKendree's Sheridan Kelsey, Ch. McKendree's Southern Venture, and Ch. McKendree's Bold Venture. Bold Venture was shown to his championship by the McKendree's young daughter, Jan. Their biggest thrill was "Stanley's" Best in Show at Orlando in December 1974, with Jan handling, followed by Best of Breed at Westminster, 1975. Sold to Mrs. Cheever Porter, Bold Venture went on to become the No. 1 Irish Setter in America for 1975, 1976 and most of 1977, with many Groups and Bests in Show.

More recent McKendree champions include Am. & Can. Ch. McKendree's Bold Elegance, who scored her first Group from the BBE class and, in modest showing, has added another Group and several Group placements. Another fine dog is Ch. McKendree's Thorin Oakenshield (by McKendree's Danny Boy ex McKendree's Sea Breeze), owned by Winifred and Toni Thomas.

Marx, Sid and Susan — *Windscent* — Medford, NJ

Sid and Susie Marx started their Windscent Irish Setters in the early 1960s with the purchase of a pet bitch, Scott's Lady. It was the personality and love of this Irish, more than the few ribbons she won, that "hooked" this family on going further with their Setters. The first few years were involved in a great deal of study and a limited breeding program that produced Ch. Windscent Aquarius and Ch. Windscent Don Quixote.

Recent years have seen Windscent Irish Setters narrow down their breeding program in an attempt to combine some of the strengths found in the Seaforth, Thenderin, Tirvelda, and Bayberry lines. The Marxs' have owned such fine animals as Ch. Seaforth's Echo of Dark Rex and the lovely Ch. Bayberry Sonnet, winner of ISCA's award as Top Bitch of the Year.

Sid Marx has been an AKC licensed handler and is now an approved judge of Irish Setters.

Marver, Daniel A. and Sally — *Marverbrook* — Plymouth, WI

Sally and Dan's Marverbrook Kennels was founded in 1965, but their first two Setters were lost, one due to dysplasia, the other to distemper. They then bought four dogs from Draherin, one of which was Candia Ambrosia. She became their first champion, and bred to Ch. Shannon's Erin produced four puppies, all to finish later: Ch. Marverbrook Camelot, Ch. Marverbrook Citation, Ch. Marverbrook Challenger and the bitch, Ch. Marverbrook Carion. Camelot and Carion have won many Bests of Breed at all-breed and Specialty shows. Dan also professionally handles Irish Setters.

Mehring, William and Lynne — *Shangrila* — Pinckney, MI

The Mehrings began in 1966 with the purchase of a pet male for hunting and companionship. He went on to become Ch. Red Cedar's Prince Michael, UD (Ch. Red Cedar's Dennis ex Ch. Tristan's Lucky Penny) one of the breed's top Irish Setter Obedience dogs. Mike would have qualified for both Obedience Championship and the Versatility certificate had they been in effect before his death. He was a magnificent dog who promoted the Irish Setter every time he walked into the Obedience ring.

Ivor Glen Katherine Coleen is their foundation field bitch. She goes back to Fld. Ch. Sulhamstead Norse D'Or and the breed's first Dual Ch. Tyrone's Mahogany Mike. She is the dam of Field Ch. Shangrila's Maggie O'Casey and five other field-pointed offspring.

Recent bench champions are: Shannon's Scarlet Urchin (Ch. Sharon's O'Boy ex Ch. Bet-Lee's Gaye Robin), Folie's Flann of Shangrila (Wilson Farm Jessie Brian ex Valmar's Lady Love of Mike), and Shangrila Amber Shea O'Kelly (Ch. Tirvelda Distant Drummer ex Milesian's Merry Maura). Scarlet was bred by Betty Crawford and Flann and Amber are homebred.

The present generation includes Shangrila Scarlet O'Hara (multi-Sweepstakes and Specialty class winner) and Majestic Michael of Shangrila, bred and co-owned by Pam Schaar. Scarlet O'Hara is by Tirvelda Eamon of Gabhantyr ex Ch. Shannon's Scarlet Urchin, and Michael is a handsome son of Ch. Santera Tamberluck, CD, ex Gay Star of Erin, CD (a linebred Argo Lane Lad of Ulster granddaughter). A daughter of Scarlet, Ch. Shangrila Moon Shadow finished at the 1982 National Specialty.

Their breeding program relies heavily on the brothers, Tirvelda Michaelson, Earl and Nor'wester. Also prominent in their pedigree are Knockross O'Boy, Ch. Argo Lane Lad of Ulster and Ch. Draherin Irish Regardless.

Mickow, Roy and Bernice — *O'Farrell* — Hinsdale, IL

Roy and Bernice purchased their first Irish Setter from End O'Maine in 1937, but it wasn't until 1966, when they acquired the O'Farrell kennel name with the purchase of Red Rascal O'Farrell, that their kennel blossomed with winners.

Three years prior to Red Rascal their first litter came along—a combination of Sunny Acre and O'Farrell breeding. Since that time, Hinsdale and O'Farrell have been used on all their dogs names; and to add to the accumulation of names, their place is known as Red Dog Ranch. Fourteen champions have been bred by the Mickows along with several CDx. Some of their noted champions are Ch. Red Rascal O'Farrell, Ch. Hinsdale Lollipop O'Farrell, Ch. MacIntosh Jim O'Farrell, Ch. Hinsdale Jim Dandy O'Farrell, Ch. Flaming Bridget O'Farrell. The latter, piloted by Dick Cooper, won the Top Bitch award offered by the Irish Setter Club of America in 1975.

The entire Irish Setter fancy was tremendously saddened when Bernice, very respected and very popular, passed away in 1976—just after judging a Specialty Sweepstakes. Roy carries on, in a more limited fashion, and is now working on a Field Championship.

Ch. Charlton's Oriental Jade (Ch. McCamon Marquis ex Ch. Rossel Birdie Rose).

Ch. Mos'n Acre Wilson Farm Harmony (Ch. Earl of Harewood ex Ch. Wilson Farm Country Charm).

Ch. Wilson Farm Burgundy (Ch. Irvelda Earl of Harewood ex Ch. Wilson Farm Partridge).

Morris, Deirdre A. — *Ash-Ling Farm* — **Hendersonville, NC**

In 1971 Deirdre bought Glenavan Taste O'Honey from Mary Olich as her foundation bitch. "Tammie" was bred to Ch. Webline Rio Hondo, producing Glenavan Stinger of Ash-Ling, CD, a breed winner from the classes. 'Tammie' was then bred to Ch. Draherin King's Ransom which produced the outstanding Ch. Ash-ling Celebration (finished with a BOB and Group 3rd at Santa Barbara, owner/handled). Celebration has been bred to a number of outstanding bitches and his get are winning points from the puppy classes, and finishing to championships from Coast to Coast. His sister, Ch. Lapointe's Lady Kate Ash-Ling, finished her championship in 4 months with 4 majors, and is also proving a top producer. She is the dam of the BIS Ch. Glenavan Harvest Moon and has several other pointed get.

Mowbray, Patricia A. — *Braemoor* — **Lanesboro, MA**

In 1972, Pat obtained a puppy bitch from Claire Andrews, which was to become her first champion, Am. & Can. Ch. Kimberlin Bright Jewel (Ch. Tirvelda Earl of Harewood ex Ch. Kimberlin Cara). She also purchased the puppy, Tirvelda Ever Amber (Ch. Tirvelda Hunter's Moon ex Tirvelda Brengwain). Amber finished with two majors, in one weekend. Bright Jewel and Amber were both shown to their titles by Pat. Two other dogs make up the kennel: Thenderin Splendor of Autumn; and Tirvelda Dunholm Dutchess (co-owned with Tirvelda).

Ever Amber produced Braemoor's first homebred champion, Ch. Twin Lights of Braemoor, owned and handled by Carla Pratt. Another Amber son to make championship is Ch. Baremoor Ever On (by Ch. Wilson Farm Burgundy).

Pat now owns Ch. Wilson Farm Burgundy, the son of Ch. Tirvelda Earl of Harewood and Ch. Wilson Farm Partridge.

Mullet, Frank and Marian — *Dutch Valley* — **Edmeston, NY**

Dutch Valley began operations in 1971 with a foundation bitch from Dariabar Kennels. Bred to Ch. Tirvelda Michaelson this bitch produced Ch. Dutch Valley Red Feather and Ch. Dutch Valley Flaming Arrow who finished with four majors. They also bred Ch. Dutch Valley's Sundance Kid (Ch. Tirvelda Earl of Harewood ex Dutch Valley Dancing Flame) owned by Julianne Waters.

Mumford, Marvin and Joyce — *Auburn* — **Charlestown, IN**

Marvin and Joyce bought their first Irish Setter in 1964, but it was not until 1975 that they became interested in showing. In 1977 they acquired Tirvelda Brynmount Auburn, a son of Ch. McCamon Marquis ex Ch. Tirvelda Evensong, and in 1978 they bought Tirvelda Distant Bell (Ch. Tirvelda Distant Drummer ex Ch. Tirvelda Sarabande). They recently finished Ch. Brownstone's Celebrated Gold (Ch. Ash-ling Celebration ex Ch. Villa-Dan Valentina) and imported, with Val and George Buehler of Brynmount Kennels, Calum of Barnside.

Myers, Gregory A. and Barbe Jo — *Barmyre* — **Shippensburg, PA**

The Myers' foundation includes Tirvelda Easter Bonnet, Tirvelda Dark Mirage and Tirvelda Mystic Morn. A breeding program is being developed around these three bitches.

Myers, Lucy Jane — *Draherin* — **Duluth, MN**

Draherin, one of the truly great kennels of all time, was started by a young girl in her teens in 1948. A six-month-old son of Ch. Pinebrook High Hat and End O'Maine Refrain, obtained from Hollis Wilson of End O'Maine, was the first

Am. Can. & Bda. Ch. Liafail Brackenfield Beauty (Ch. Smoke Dream of Tamarisk ex Brackenfield Pheasant, CD).

Ch. Rox-San Flirtation (Am. & Can. Rox-San Danny Boy ex Rox-San Color Me Red).

Ch. Red Cedar's Prince Michael, UD (Ch. Red Cedar's Dennis ex Ch. Tristan's Lucky Penny).

Irishman to be owned by Lucy Jane. With this acquisition, an illustrious chapter in Irish Setter history commenced.

Almost immediately young Lucy Jane bought a puppy from Jane Ridder, a friend of the Myers and niece of Laura Delano of the Knocknagree Kennels. The dam, Sue of Witchwood, was straight Knocknagree breeding.

Lucy Jane, with what has turned out to be remarkable ability repeated many times throughout the years, selected this youngster at two weeks of age. He became the first dog to bear the Draherin kennel name, Draherin Mahcree O'Rhue, the first Draherin Canadian and American champion, the first Draherin Best in Show winner, the second CDX Draherin titleholder and the 30th champion offspring (at age 8) of his famous sire, Ch. Kleiglight of Aragon.

Incidentally, the translation of this dog's name is "little red brother of my heart." Draherin meaning "little brother" was retained as the kennel name.

Then for bitches, Lucy Jane went to Thenderin. This was the kennel that unknowingly had put the high school girl into Irish Setters. Lucy Jane had seen Hollis Wilson handle Thenderin Brian Tristan in the Open class at the 1948 Minneapolis show. That dog so captivated her that she was "hooked" on Irish forever. From Thenderin she was able to obtain the 13-month-old bitch, Thenderin Elixir. Lucky was her kennel name, and lucky it certainly was, as all the famous greats that have made Draherin what it is today descended from that lucky purchase.

But "Lucky" wasn't so lucky in the beginning. It looked as if she would never reproduce. Bred to Jack Spear's Ch. Tyronne Farm Malone she missed twice. Then with the assistance of Joyce Nilsen, the attempt was made to breed "Lucky" again— this time to Ch. Seaforth Dark Rex. She only produced two puppies, but as often happens once you get a difficult animal pregnant whether it be a horse, cow or dog, once you get the ball rolling you successively get offspring. The two became Ch. Thenderin Ocean Breeze, owned by the Stanley Wrights, and Thenderin Ocean Glow, CD, who came back to Draherin.

Lucky's next litter was by the dog Lucy Jane had admired so much, Brian Tristan—now a famous champion, of whom more is written in another chapter. From this came Ch. Draherin Centurion, CD, a dog whose influence can still be found in the pedigrees of the Irish of the Pacific Northwest. Another became Ch. Draherin Coronado. He was owned by Floyd Crosley of the Shamrock Kennels in Nebraska, and his blood can be found in many dogs from that state.

Two bitches from this litter made lasting contributions to the breed. Draherin Coronation was the granddam of Am. & Can. Ch. Draherin Billy Boy, the sire of Dr. Robert Helferty's many time Best in Show winner, Ch. Kelly Shannon O'Deke. The second bitch from the litter was Draherin Coronet who became the foundation bitch of the Glen Cree Kennels. Coronet through her daughter Glen Cree High Time when the latter was bred to Ch. Draherin County Leitrim, lives on through her grandson, Am. & Can. Ch. Draherin Bachelor Boy. Bachelor Boy, owned and shown by the late Cmdr. Thomas Threlkeld, broke all Canadian records by winning close to 70 Bests in Show.

High Time was also the dam of Glen Cree Bridey Murphy, the foundation for the Browns' Red Whiskey Kennel in Connecticut. More on Bridey Murphy, an outstanding producer, is told in the Red Whiskey kennel history.

In her third turn in the whelping box, Elixer produced, by Ch. Tyronne Farm Malone II, two litter brothers who were designed to go down in Irish Setter history as two of the most influential half dozen sires in Irish Setter history. These two

Am. Can. & Bda. Ch. Shannon's Erin
(Ch. Draherin Irish Regardless ex Ch. Knockross Ruby).

Am. Can. & Mex. Ch. Draherin King's Ransom
(Ch. Shannon's Erin ex Ch. Draherin Merry Kerry).

brothers, Ch. Draherin Irish Regardless and Ch. Draherin Irish Chieftain can be found in the pedigrees of almost every top winner and producer from the early 1960s to the present, to further extend the contribution to the breed of type and temperament of their great granddam, Ch. Kinvarra Mollie of Gadeland, the English import selected by Lee M. Schoen to be the foundation for Tirvelda.

Still another litter out of Elixir by Patrick Red Jacket, a dog purchased by Lucy Jane for $75 and who had 14 points before his untimely death, produced the Best in Show bitch, Ch. Draherin Echo of Elixir, a bitch designed to do great things for Draherin.

Back to the litter brothers Chieftain and Regardless. From the former came, among many other noted animals, the great Best in Show winner and sire, Ch. Blayneywood Country Squire, owned by Marion Darling and later acquired by his handler, Larry Downey. Chieftain also sired the lovely Best in Show bitch, Ch. Merry-Dell's Autumn Glory.

Regardless was bred four times to Betty Crawford's Ch. Knockcross Ruby, and together they produced 19 champions. These included a number of Best in Show winners, the most famous being Am., Can. and Ber. Ch. Shannon's Erin and Ch. Major O'Shannon. Other noted champions produced by Regardless were Ch. Tuxedo's Duffy of Mosn'Acre, a multiple Best in Show winner for Frances Phillips, and Ch. Wilson Farm Country Charm, one of the cornerstones of Wilson Farm.

Echo of Elixir, the half-sister of Regardless and Chieftain, was bred to Ch. Innisfail Color Scheme. During the long whelping period of the resultant litter Lucy Jane unintentionally fell asleep after seeing nine puppies safely delivered. A tenth was born and during its whelping, Elixir laid on and smothered all four bitches in the litter. A tragedy that can never be measured because that that tenth puppy became Lucy Jane's favorite bitch, Ch. Draherin Annie Laurie. One male became the noted sire, Ch. Draherin Auburn Artistry. What might some of the other bitches been?

Annie Laurie was exceptionally prepotent. When bred to Ch. Draherin Field Sergeant, a son of Ch. Red Sails of Devon, she produced Ch. Draherin Jane Eyre, later to become equally famous as a brood bitch. Bred to Irish Regardless she produced Ch. Draherin Party Doll and Ch. Draherin Pandora. Bred to Ch. Shannon's Erin, she produced two outstanding litters which included a number of champions.

Annie Laurie was bred for her last litter to Ch. Draherin King's Ransom (Ch. Shannon's Erin ex Ch. Draherin Merry Kerry). Kerry was a lovely bitch who I remember to this day as she stood out in a great Open class of at least 22 bitches at a Colorado Specialty I judged a few years back. Annie Laurie by Ransom produced the equally beautiful Best in Show bitch belonging to Mrs. Thomas Arland, Ch. Draherin Marietta. Annie Laurie produced 13 champions for Draherin.

Annie's litter brother, Ch. Auburn Artistry, is a dog also hard to forget. I saw him first as I watched the then Jane Kamp handle him in the Open class at Chicago. I had the feeling then, and told Jane as she walked out of the ring, that I had a hunch that dog would be a great sire. My hunch was correct. Too big for most—it wasn't his height, he was 28½", as much as bone—he was overdone in every respect, but at the same time he was beautifully balanced with a glorious head and powerful body and quarters. He had much to offer not only in type but in his breeding as well.

Perhaps the most remembered Artistry litter was that out of Dick Webb's, Ch. Weblyn Madrigal. Six from that combination finished, the most noteworthy being Mrs. Cheever Porter's many time Best in Show winner, Ch. Webline Rio Hondo.

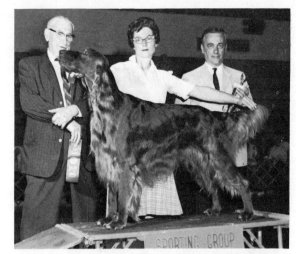

m. & Can. Ch. Draherin Auburn
rtistry (Ch. Tyronne Farm
Malone II ex Ch. Thenderin Elixir).

h. Draherin County Leitrim (Ch.
Draherin Auburn Artistry ex Am.
Can. Ch. Yorkhill's County Kerry
CD).

m. & Can. Ch. Draherin Bach-
lor Boy (Ch. Draherin County Lei-
im ex Glen Cree High Time).

But it was the Artistry son, Ch. Draherin County Leitrim, who was designed to carry forward the Artistry blood. Again as a spectator at a Chicago show I saw Leitrim for the first time. He was very much like his sire, heavy boned, a bit overdone, with a tremendous wooly Minnesota winter coat. A few months later I had him under me in Texas, with a different handler. His coat had smoothed down and because of this I didn't recognize him at all. I gave him five points. Then in Arizona he appeared in the ring once again under me with his new owner, Warren Ellis. This time dark, sleek, almost out of coat. He was tremendously impressive, again totally unrecognizable. I could have sworn he wasn't the same dog I had seen and admired in Chicago. Beautifully balanced, powerful, he didn't look the overdone dog I had seen at that time. I gave him another five points. It was dramatic proof to me how a dog can change in looks, depending on body coat and length of feathering. Many dogs out of coat reveal their faults and don't look well. This dog looked well in whatever coat he was carrying!

County Leitrim sired many champions including the aforementioned Am. & Can. Ch. Draherin Bachelor Boy. He produced six champions in one litter for Bryfield Kennels in Arizona, and four more out of Warren Ellis' Ch. Webline Venus. He produced two famous champions for Mary Olich out of Ch. Mistyglades Miss Magnificent: Ch. Glenavan Sensation and Ch. Glenavan Hallelulia, and their litter sister who, because she lost an eye could not be shown, but whose son, Ch. Ash-ling Celebration, finished by going from the classes to Best of Breed over a huge entry at Santa Barbara in July of 1977. Leitrim also sired Glen Cree Bridey Murphy and was the grandsire of Ch. Victory's Royal Sensation—the two Red Whiskey foundation bitches.

Elixir and Echo of Elixer have come down through other famous present day lines. The Rumbaughs' Ch. Starheir's Aaron Ardee, who won more Bests in Show than any other Irish in this country, and who sired many noted champions, traced back to these bitches.

Two others from this family deserve special mention, Ch. Draherin Echo's Guy and Ch. Draherin Echo's Hope, the foundation animals of Sally Reese's Candia Kennels. Hope produced nine champions by Ch. Muckamoor's Marty McCuhl. Many of these became the foundation of other noted kennels. They include Ch. Candia Ambrosia for the Marver's Marverbrook Kennels, Champions Candia Eve and Fawn for the Fields' Bryfield Kennels. Also Ch. Candia Pride, one of the loveliest bitches I have ever seen, and a great producer. Bred to Ch. Draherin Auburn Artistry before she went to Lucy Jane, Pride lives on through one of her champion offspring, Ch. Candia Camille. Camille in turn produced Ch. Candia Fatima. Fatima has gone down in history as the dam of what can only be described as the breed's most sensational sire, Mrs. Thomas Arland's Ch. Candia Indeed.

I have saved the most famous of the Draherin dogs to bring this history to the present—Ch. Shannon's Erin.

Erin? Shannon? Why did Lucy Jane acquire a dog from another kennel when she had so many good ones herself? In the first place Erin was one half Draherin breeding. He was out of the second litter by Ch. Draherin Irish Regardless, and Lucy Jane had greatly admired the first litter from the same sire and dam. She also felt a male from this combination would strengthen toplines. Those were reasons enough to want a puppy.

Visiting Betty Crawford's kennel to see the litter, Lucy Jane was struck by the independence and spirit of one little fellow. At that age, however, his front didn't look quite right, so he was left behind. One month passed and on a spur of the moment decision Betty was asked to send the dog to Draherin.

The rest is history. 1966 marked the start of a brilliant show career. Erin came out in the Open class at the Milwaukee Specialty. He went through to Best of Winners to garner his first five points. Then, in rapid succession, five more points at the Western Irish Setter Specialty in Chicago, and the same again at the Minnesota Specialty to finish—all wins owner-handled, and the first Irish Setter in history (to the best of Lucy Jane's knowledge) to finish with three 5-pt. Specialty wins.

As a Special, still handled by Lucy Jane, he won the breed at Westminster in 1967, followed by consistent winning of the breed at all the big shows from coast to coast: Beverly Hills, Chicago International, Westchester, Philadelphia and once again at Westminster. But let Lucy Jane describe the Westminster wins in her own words:

"So often I've been asked, 'What was your biggest thrill?' My 'cup runneth over' for I have two to remember! The first was the Garden in 1967 when, in the final moments for Best of Breed, Erin and I stood in a row with Larry Downey and Ch. Blayneywood Country Squire, and watched Jane Forsyth work her magic with Rio Hondo, and Dick Webb work his with Wizard of Macapa. What a magnificent handling exhibition they put on! Judge Joseph Knight finally turned to the table and after an eternity it seemed, marked his book, and turned slowly back to the four of us. He started toward Jane, hesitated, moved toward Dick, then stepped suddenly to Erin and pointed to him! Had not someone pounded me on the back, I am positive I would still be there today—frozen to the ground in disbelief.

"The best was to come that night, when still in a state of shock—and white as a sheet, they told me later—we waited to go into the Group. The steward called for the eligible dogs to come into the ring. No one moved, again he called us—someone pushed me—and out we went, like a shot out of a cannon. It was like diving off a 130-foot platform. Out we went and down that huge green matted floor—all the way to the end, to our marker. It was not until we were almost there that it dawned on me that no one else had started out into the ring until Erin and I were almost down to the end. I know I turned even whiter. And later on, clutching tight that precious fourth place rosette, we floated out of the ring in a dream."

Erin gained another Best of Breed and another Group 4th at Westminster in 1968. After, Erin went to California to be piloted by Dick Webb. In his third appearance on the West Coast he went all the way through to Best in Show at Golden Gate Kennel Club. That year, in very limited showing, Erin won 6 Bests in Show and 20 Group Firsts. During his career, he won many BOBs at Specialties throughout the country, and finally coming out of the Veterans class at the Southern California Specialty he went on to top the breed in a record entry.

But it is as a sire he will be long remembered. For years the top sire in the breed was W. L. Newhall's famous Knockcross O'Boy, but Erin took over and with 43 champions to his credit remained as the top sire in the breed's history for a number of years.

Actually the numbers of champions a sire produces make little difference. It is the quality of the get that counts. Erin has produced many, many great sons and daughters who are designed to write breed history for years to come. They are too numerous to mention, but a few stand out. His first to finish, the Best in Show winner, Ch. Draherin Questionnaire, became a noted sire himself. Ch. Draherin King's Ransom, another Best in Show winner, sire to date of 20 champions, is owned by the Rendition Kennels. There are the famous Marverbrook four, of which Camelot and Carion have won so many Specialties. Then there are Ch.

Draherin Legendary, another Best in Show winner, Ch. Draherin Windjammer, and Ch. Dunholm Finn McCool, the top Sporting dog in Canada for two years in a row, and so many more.

Pages could be written about Draherin. I asked Lucy Jane for a detailed history. It belongs here. Students of the breed would welcome it, but it is a herculean job to chronicle all the dogs over all the years since the Draherin inception. Lucy Jane just did not have the time to do it. I was on my own, and I feel that my effort is inadequate. Someday, perhaps, the story of this great breeder will be told in its entirety. It deserves to be made a permanent part of Irish Setter history.

Lucy Jane exemplifies the outstanding attributes all of us should try to emulate. She is intensely dedicated to the welfare of the breed, she is extremely hard working and has built Draherin with the physical work of her own hands, and the power of her own intelligence. I wonder if the future will produce Irish Setter breeders that will be able to contribute as much? The sticktoitiveness so brilliantly demonstrated by Lucy Jane seems to be lacking today.

Newlon, Terry G. and Sandra L. — *Santera* — Mt. Airy, MD

The Newlons' foundation bitch, Ch. Wilson Farm Scarlet Tirvelda, CD (Ch. Tirvelda Earl of Harewood) was purchased as a puppy from the David Wilsons in the early 1970s. Bred to the Nor'wester son, Ch. Ballycroy's Northern Sunset, she produced the Specialty Best of Breed and Group winner, Am. & Can. Ch. Santera Tristan Troubador, and Ch. Santera Tamberluck, CD, Specialty and all-breed Best in Show winner. Tamberluck also won a Best in Show in Canada in 1978. Tamberluck is the sire of numerous champions and Tristan had also made his mark by producing several champions before his death.

Terry is a past president of the Potomac Irish Setter Club. Sandy, now Mrs. Norbert Novocin, is continuing the Santera line. Tamberluck was test-mated clear of PRA, and all of Sandy's young stock is genetically clear.

Nilsen, Joyce — *Thenderin* — Venice, CA

This account of one of the great kennels in this country was sent to us by Mrs. William B. Allen. Joyce has always been reluctant to recount her own success.

There have been well over 200 champions bearing the Thenderin prefix, many of which have been Specialty, Group and Best in Show winners. The include four National Specialty winners—two Winners' Bitch awards, a Best in Sweepstakes and a Best of Breed (Ch. Thenderin William Muldoon in 1974).

As a young high school girl in Buffalo, New York, Joyce Holzman trained her first Irish Setter, Ranger's Red, CD, in Obedience. Just before she moved with her family to California in 1946, she purchased Ch. Red Ranger Pat (a son of Jordan Farm Abe) and the marvelous Ch. Kinvarra Portia (a daughter of Ch. Kinvarra Kermit and Beg Pardon Rury Limerick). Portia became the foundation of Thenderin Kennels, producing 12 champions. Her descendants throughout the country have had great influence on the breed.

Joyce became a professional handler and married a fellow handler, Athos Nilsen in 1953. Athos died about five years ago.

It is impossible to list all the important Thenderin dogs, but we will give a brief history of those most influential to the breed.

Ch. Kinvarra Portia (Ch. Kinvarra Kermit ex Beg Pardon Rury Limerick) whelped three important litters. The first, by Ch. Red Ranger Pat produced: Thenderin April Anthem, the dam of Thenderin Champagne, who became the foundation bitch for Roy and Nedra Jerome's Innisfail Setters; Ch. Thenderin

Amaranth, who when bred to Imp. Ch. Brynmount Maydorwill Brandyson, produced Ch. Thenderin Benedictine. (Benedictine was the dam of Thenderin Wind Warrior and Thenderin Whistler, whelped in 1956, and Ch. Thenderin Endorsement, whelped in 1958); Ch. Thenderin All Spice, who when bred to Ch. Rheola Shawn of Bail-lo produced Lucy Jane Myers' Ch. Thenderin Elixir and Joyce's Ch. Thenderin Echo of Spice.

Portia's second litter was sired by Ch. End O'Maine Luckalone and that produced the great Ch. Thenderin Brian Tristan, sire of 30 champions. Her third litter, by Ch. Caldene Mickey Mischief, who Joyce acquired from Dr. Jay Calhoon, produced Ch. Thenderin Deeper than Gayety and Thenderin Design by Fire.

Ch. Seaforth Dark Rex (Ch. Tyrone Farm Malone ex Ch. Seaforth Red Velvet) was bred by George and Barbara Brodie and whelped in 1947. Rex sired 20 champions, and much of the quality of the West Coast dogs can be traced directly to him. He is behind Innisfail, Webline, Varagon, Coppercountry, Whiskey Hill and others, as well as Thenderin. Joyce bought him from the Brodies about 1952.

Rex was bred to important Thenderin bitches: Thenderin Gossip of Del Rey, bred to Rex, produced Ch. Thenderin Nor'Wester and Ch. Thenderin Nomad. Ch. Memory of Devon (Ch. Charles River Color Sergeant ex Shawnee of Devon), bred to Rex, produced Ch. Thenderin Kismet (dog), Ch. Thenderin Keepsake (bitch), and Ch. Thenderin Kiss (bitch).

Joyce considers Kiss among the finest bitches she has bred. There is no doubt her bloodlines nicked marvelously with the Thenderin line already started. When bred to Rex's son, Ch. Thenderin Nomad, she produced Thenderin Sunswift, who when bred to Benedictine produced the three prepotent sires, Wind Warrior, Whistler and Endorsement. However, it was when Kiss was bred to her grandson, Wind Warrior, that she proved her worth as a brood bitch. From the first Wind Warrior-Kiss litter came Ch. Thenderin Drum Hills, whelped 1958. He, when bred to Ch. Thenderin Mi-Spice, produced the "O" litter of seven champions: Odyssey (bitch), Odin Emperor (dog), O'Toole (dog), O'By Jingo (dog), Orion (bitch), Oralie Overture (bitch) and Ocean Lorelie (bitch). The second litter produced Jarah Meg, who, bred to O'By Jingo, was the dam of Ch. Thenderin Xtra Margin, and Ch. Thenderin Jacynth, foundation of Whiskey Hills. Jacynth was bred to Ch. Webline Very Coppercountry (Ch. Thenderin Endorsement ex Ch. Weblyn Madrigal) to produce Ch. Thenderin Expectation, Ch. Thenderin Etching, Thenderin Emberglo, Thenderin Electra, and Ever Merrily (dam of Ch. Thenderin the Heir Apparent, an important producer for Thenderin on the East Coast).

Thenderin Wind Warrior was never shown but was a prepotent sire. His most important offspring was Ch. Thenderin Chaparal Cayenne, from his breeding to Thenderin Red Maeve (Ch. Seaforth Dark Rex ex Ch. Thenderin Echo of Spice).

Ch. Thenderin Chaparal Cayenne was the sire of Ch. Webline Golden Jubilee. But it was the breeding of Cayenne to Ch. Thenderin Odyssey that produced Ch. Thenderin Wind Ruler, in 1963. Wind Ruler truly set the Thenderin type as we know it best. He finished with three 5-pt. Specialty majors and became a dominant sire for Thenderin.

Ch. Thenderin Odyssey, in addition to her son, Wind Ruler, produced an important bitch for Thenderin, when bred to Ch. Thenderin Endorsement. This was Thenderin Omen O'Mulholland, who when bred to Wind Ruler, produced Ch. T. Leif O'Mulholland, Ch. T. Loyal O'Mulholland, and Ch. T. Legacy.

Wind Ruler was used predominantly on Thenderin bitches and only those of great quality. In 1968, he was bred to Ch. Treasure Trove's Xmas Holly and from this litter came Ch. Thenderin Winter Wind (Winners' Bitch at the First National Specialty) and Am. & Can. Ch. Thenderin Woods of Autumn, CD. Woods of Autumn had a splendid show record, but it is as the dam of Ch. Thenderin William Muldoon that she will be best remembered.

Ch. Thenderin William Muldoon (Ch. Thenderin Spellbinder ex Ch. Thenderin Woods of Autumn, CD) is a multi-Best in Show, Group, and Specialty winner. Joyce considers him to be the best Irish she has ever bred. He has sired a number of champions, among them Ch. Kilgary Dungannon and Ch. Kimberlin O'Killea of Top O.

In recent years Joyce has cut back considerably in showing and breeding, but the Thenderin lines are still being produced—in the East by Ann Savin Dunn with Ch. Thenderin the Heir Apparent and Ch. Thenderin Xclusive Edition, and in Florida with the Gilberts. Lisa Schrank is helping Joyce carry on in California.

Following are some of the important Thenderin dogs and their records as producers:

Ch. Kinvarra Portia—Dam of 12 champions. Best Brood Matron in 1948, 1949 and 1950. Best of Breed, Irish Setter Club of the Pacific in 1947.

Ch. Seaforth's Dark Rex—Sire of 20 champions. Best in Show winner; Best of Breed, Irish Setter Club of So. Calif. in 1953 and 1954. Some of his champion get are the following:
Ch. Thenderin Nomad (in the East)
Ch. Thenderin Nor'Wester (in the West)—Several times BOB and Group placer; twice BOB at Golden Gate KC. I know he was the sire of the following champions, at least:
Ch. McGowan's Delaney, Ch. McGowan's Michael, Ch. McGowan's Miss Mahoney—bred by Ruth and Curtis Davis. Also *Am. & Mex. Ch. Bel Air Barbara, CD,* owned by Dr. Maurice Fergesen and Gladys Burt.
Ch. Coppercountry Brian O'Boy, bred and owned by Leone Wixson; BOB from the classes over an entry of 93, including 10 Specials, at Irish Setter Club of So. Cal. in 1957, which finished him.
Ch. Margevan Madcap of Innisfail, owned by Roy Jerome and Orrin Evans, BOB at the Irish Setter Club of the Pacific Specialty in 1957.
Ch. Thenderin Kismet—BOB at the Irish Setter Club of the Pacific in 1958 and 1959. Sire of champs, including *Ch. Thenderin Paddy's Hero,* multi-Group winner, owned by Sam and Barbara Topliss.
Paddy's Hero was the sire of several champs, including *Ch. Thenderin Xerxes Shannon, Ch. Thenderin Top 'O Xound* and *Fury, Ch. Thenderin Top 'O Xron Leader,* and *Ch. Thenderin Hallucination* (owned by Esther Dickson).

Ch. Dorkim Typhoon, ex the bitch Thenderin Margevan Music.
Ch. Kalarama Pagan—an Eastern dog that sired a few Thenderin champions.
Ch. Thenderin Keepsake, sister to Kismet and Kiss.
Ch. Thenderin Kiss, ex Ch. Memory of Devon. An important Thenderin dam of *Ch. Thenderin Drum Hills* and *Ch. Thenderin Jacynth.*
Ch. Innisfail Color Scheme, bred by the Jeromes, ex Thenderin Champagne. BIS and Specialty winner. Sire of Champs, including *Ch. Flashback of Varagon* (owned by Selma Stoll), *Ch. Legend of Varagon* (owned by Ron and Renee Taylor), and the bitch, *Ch. Enchantment of Varagon*—bred by Ray and Valerie Gonsor, ex Ch. Innisfail Best Regards. Color Scheme also was the sire of *Ch. Weblyn Mystic Mark, Ch. Weblyn Madrigal, Ch. Webline Mi-Golden Flame, CD, Ch. Weblyn Masterpiece;* the Webline "Z" litter of champions: Zamara, Zeason Ticket, Zingaro and Zephyr; Bob and Jean Donovan's Shiralee champions; and more.
Ch. Innisfail Encore, brother to Color Scheme, owned by Charlie Jones in Ohio.
Ch. Innisfail Mona Lisa, sister to Color Scheme.

Ch. Memory of Devon—Dam of Kismet, Keepsake and Kiss.

Ch. Thenderin Barbary Jean—BOB, Irish Setter Club of the Pacific in 1960.

Thenderin Wind Ruler (Ch. nderin Chaparal Cayenne ex Thenderin Odyssey).

Ch. Thenderin Endeavor, CD (Ch. Thenderin Mist O'Mulholland ex Thenderin Maureen).

Ch. Thenderin William Muldoon Ch. Thenderin Spellbinder ex m. & Can. Ch. Thenderin Woods f Autumn, CD).

Ch. Thenderin Maximillian (C
Thenderin Wind Ruler ex Dor
Cloud).

Ch. Kilgary Dungannon (Ch.
Thenderin William Muldoon ex
Ch. Charlton's Auburn Tresses).

Thenderin Wind Warrior—One of Joyce's great studs. A Thenderin prototype. Sire of innumerable champions, including *Ch. Thenderin Chaparal Gossip, Ch. Thenderin Chaparal Wind, Ch. Thenderin Chaparal Cardinal, Ch. Thenderin Chaparal Cayenne, Ch. Thenderin Maximillian, Ch. Thenderin Drum Hills,* and *Thenderin Jacynth.*

Ch. Thenderin Kiss—Dam of *Ch. Thenderin Drum Hills* and *Ch. Thenderin Jacynth.*

Ch. Thenderin Maximilliam—Several times a Breed and Group winner. Sire of champions. A lovely dog with a marvelous headpiece. Owned by Ellen Hammon.

Ch. Thenderin Excise Tax—BOB, Irish Setter Club of So. Cal. in 1959.

Ch. Thenderin Endorsement—Full brother to Wind Warrior. Winners Dog, Westminster in 1963 to finish him. BOB Irish Setter Club of So. Calif., 1963. Owned by Leone Wixson (Coppercountry). Sire several important champions:

> *Ch. Thenderin Accent O'Banner* and *Ch. Thenderin Adam O'Banner,* bred by Linda Schreiner (O'Banner) ex her foundation bitch, Ch. Thenderin Titian O'Banner.
> *Ch. Thenderin Olympian Beauty* and *Ch. Thenderin O'Dunn's Glory.*
> *Ch. Webline Very Coppercountry,* owned by Leone Wixson, and *Ch. Webline Venus,* the lovely bitch owned by Warren Ellis. These two were ex Ch. Weblyn Madrigal.
> *Ch. Tirvelda Laird O'Limerick,* ex Ch. Tirvelda Nutbrown Sherry and owned by Joe and Irish Smith (Limerick Lane).

Ch. Thenderin Chaparal Cayenne—All-breed BIS and specialty sinner, Irish Setter Club of So. Cal. in 1962. Sire of the following, that I know of:

> *Ch. Webline Golden Jubilee, CD, Ch. Webline Golden Lyric, CD, Ch. Webline Golden Symphony, CD,* ex Loretta and Bill Golden's Ch. Weblyn Mi-Golden Flame.
> *Ch. Thenderin Wind Ruler,* Joyce's important stud.
> *Ch. Thenderin Demon of Shanderin.*

Ch. Thenderin Drum Hills—Sire of the famous "O" litter of seven champions, ex Ch. Thenderin Mi-Spice, whelped in 1961. Son of Wind Warrior and Kiss.

Ch. Thenderin Mi-Spice—Dam of the famous "O" litter whelped in 1961. Best Brood Matron in 1963. The "O" litter included the following;

> *Ch. Thenderin Odyssey, Ch. Thenderin O' By Jingo, Ch. Thenderin Odin Emperor, Ch. Thenderin O'Toole, Ch. Thenderin Ocean Lorelie, Ch. Thenderin Oralie Overture* and *Ch. Thenderin Orion.*

Ch. Thenderin Orion—Group winner. Bitch. Owned by Glen Mahoney.

Ch. Thenderin Odyssey—Dam of *Ch. Thenderin Olympian Beauty, Ch. Thenderin O'Dunn's Glory,* the important *Thenderin Omen O'Mulholland* (major points but never finished), and *Ch. Thenderin Wind Ruler.*

Ch. Thenderin O' By Jingo—Sire of *Ch. Thenderin Blarney O'Dunn, Ch. Thenderin Xina Cinnamon; Ch. Thenderin Xtra Margin* (dam of Ch. Thenderin Spellbinder); and others.

Am. Can. Ch. Thenderin Irish Clancy, CDX, PCE, Can. CDX, owned by Raleigh McKisson.

Ch. Thenderin Jacynth—Shown twice as a special, BOB and Group 1 and Group 2. Dam of the Thenderin "E"s, sired by Ch. Webline Very Coppercountry, that included *Ch. Thenderin Expectation, Ch. Thenderin Etching, Thenderin Emberglo* and *Thenderin Ever Merrily.* Also *Ch. Whiskey Hill's Drummer Boy,* sired by Ch. Thenderin Trailblazer, brother to Linda Schreiner's Ch. Thenderin Titian O'Banner. Jacynth was the foundation of Bill and Dilly Allen's Whiskey Hill line.

Ch. Thenderin Expectation—Sire of *Ch. Thenderin Foremost, UD, Ch. Thenderin Wind Wizard Sean, UD* (owned by the Ellithorpes), *Ch. Thenderin Future of Tara Hill, Ch. Whiskey Hill Irish Miss,* and *Ch. Thenderin Venture* (Winners Dog at Westminster in 1970 and BOW at the Irish Setter Club of So. Calif. in 1970), owned by Ellen Hammon.

Thenderin Emberglo—Leased to the Jeromes for a litter sired by Ch. Innisfail Flashback's Design. Dam of *Ch. Innisfail Gallant Guy,* owned by Dick Smith, and *Ch. Innisfail Gaelic Glory,* owned by Dilly Allen. Ember had two 5-pt. majors when we lost her. Owned by Bill and Dilly Allen.

Thenderin Ever Merrily—Never shown. Dam of *Ch. Thenderin Freestyle* and *Ch. Thenderin The Heir Apparent.*

Ch. Thenderin Endeavor—Breed winner and BOS at the Garden.

Ch. Thenderin Huckster's Gambit—BOB, BOW, WB for 5 pts. at Irish Setter Club of Colorado in 1970.

Ch. Thenderin Wind Ruler—Shown only 3 times and finished with three 5-point specialty majors under breeder judges. Among the champions he sired were:

Ch. Thenderin Just Taggart, owned by Ellen Hammon
Ch. Thenderin Huskster's Gambit
Ch. Thenderin Hestia of Tara Hill, CD, owned by Bruce and Caren Lea.
Ch. Thenderin Gaima of Gavilan, bred and owned by Carl and Joan Lagg (Gavilan)
Ch. Thenderin Signature—finished with 4 majors
Ch. Thenderin Parader—finished with 4 majors
Ch. Thenderin Leif O'Mulholland, brother to Loyal and Legacy
Ch. Thenderin Loyal O'Mulholland, owned by Leone Wixson (Coppercountry) and Dilly Allen; a dark, dark dog with an exquisite headpiece.
Ch. Thenderin Legacy, owned by Joyce
Ch. Thenderin Winter Wind
Am & Can. Ch. Thenderin Woods of Autumn, CD

Ch. Thenderin Legacy—Sire of *Ch. Thenderin Freestyle, Ch. Thenderin The Heir Apparent, Ch. Thenderin Spellbinder,* and others (Some of the Fuelling's Brynlaw champs.)

Ch. Thenderin The Heir Apparent—Owned by Ann Savin Dunn and Jane Zaderecki, the sire of several champions, ex Ch. Thenderin Xclusive Edition.

Ch. Thenderin Xclusive Edition—Owned by Ann Savin Dunn, Jane Zaderecki *and* Thenderin Kennels, the dam of several champions sired by The Heir Apparent.

Ch. Thenderin Spellbinder—Breed winner and Group placer. Best Stud Dog, ISCA National 1974). Sire of *Ch. Thenderin William Muldoon, Ch. Thenderin War and Peace,* and *Ch. Thenderin Wishing Star* (owned by Brynlaw Setters, Tom and Jeannette Fuelling, and dam of *several* of their champions). Also the sire of champions out of a litter bred by Lucille Harvey and Larry and Alberta Johnson in Colorado: *Ch. O'Hara Devon Card-in-al, Ch. O'Hara Delin Card-in-al, Ch. O'Hara Delilah Card-in-al.*

Ch. Thenderin Winter Wind—Winners bitch, First National Specialty in 1973. Sired by Wind Ruler ex Ch. Treasure Trove's Xmas Holly.

Am. & Can. Ch. Thenderin Woods of Autumn, CD—Sister to Winter Wind. Owned by Nancy Davison. Winners Bitch at both the Combined Specialties and Westminster in 1971; several times all-breed BOB and specialty BOB. Dam of *Ch. Thenderin William Muldoon, Ch. Thenderin War and Peace,* and *Ch. Thenderin Wishing Star,* sired by Spellbinder.

Ch. Thenderin War and Peace—Brother to Muldoon. Finished to almost all his points by his top Junior Handler and owner, Claudia Weniger.

Ch. Thenderin Wishing Star—Owned by Tom and Jeanette Fuelling (Brynlaw) and dam of several champions by Ch. Thenderin Legacy and their Thenderin Filibuster. Sister to Muldoon.

Ch. Thenderin William Muldoon—Best of Breed, Second National Specialty Show in 1974; multi Group and BIS winner; No. 1 Irish Setter in 1975, all systems. Owned by Thenderin. Sire of a number of champions, including:

Ch. Thenderin Joshua M, CD, VC, owned by Roger and Pat Riley.
Ch. Thenderin Ja Olin, Breed winner, owned by Esther Dickson.
Ch. Bangor V Traynor Muldoon and *Bangor Vaneicha Muldoon,* and other pointed, almost finished get from a litter bred by Jo Ann Berry, Colorado.
Ch. Kilgary Dungannon, owned by Joyce, ex Ch. Charlton's Auburn Tresses. Breed, Group and Specialty winner.
Ch. Kimberlin O'Killea of Top 'O—Bred by Claire Andrews, owned by Sam and Barbara Topliss. All-breed BIS, Group and Specialty BOB winner. BOB at Westminster in 1982.

Thenderin Spellbinder (Ch. Thenderin Legacy ex Thenderin Margin).

Ch. Thenderin Expectation (Ch. Webline Very Coppercountry ex Ch. Thenderin Jacynth).

Am. & Can. Ch. Erinova's Aristocrat (Can. Ch. King's Sean Beret Montague ex Can. Ch. Amaralinn's Bonni Erin).

Ch. Kilgary Dungannon—As noted above, a good record. Sire of several champions including:
> *Ch. Brookfield Frontier Drifter,* bred and owned by Mike and Kristy Hanes, ex their Ch. Shawnee Indian Sonnet.
> *Ch. Bonne Lass of Castle Kilgary,* owned by Virginia Bowie and Janet Ziech.

Ch. Thenderin Vintage of Brynlaw — Owned by Lisa Schrank. Siring champions, including:
> *Ch. Thenderin Vintage Gustav*—A lovely dog, recently finished. Owned and bred by Henning and Marion Behrens, ex Ch. Thenderin Vintage Crescendo. We may hear more of this one.

Thenderin Arista O'Dungannon—Sired by Muldoon, ex Thenderin Mystique, CD, and bred by the Gilberts in Florida. Owned by Charles Oldham. Needs 1 point to finish. (May be by now. I have not heard. DA.) Winners Bitch at back-to-back specialties in Oklahoma, April 1982, for 4-pts. each. Sweepstakes winner. A little beauty.

Ch. Thenderin Guarantee—BOB winner and Winners Bitch at the Third National Specialty in 1975. Owned by Dilly Allen and Pat Haynes.

Nowinski, Donna A. — San Jose, CA

Being in love with Irish Setters for years, Donna's first was purchased in 1974—Lady Samantha Jane Eyre, a field trial winner and excellent Obedience prospect. Firmly believing that show stock is also field material, Tirvelda Martial Rule was obtained in 1975, followed by Tirvelda Serenade in Scarlet in 1976. Rule was proving himself a field contender when tragedy took him in July, 1977. Scarlet shows potential in show, field and Obedience and has a litter by Ch. Tirvelda Lord Brian Boru.

Nunnally, Penny and Glyn — *Scarlly Setters* — Oak Ridge, NC

Ch. Scarlly's Sundance was whelped in 1972 and was the first Irish to bear the Scarlly name and the first dog Penny ever showed. He became their first champion and his record certainly encouraged this beginning: One all-breed Best in Show, 8 Group Firsts and 8 Specialty BOBs.

The Nunnallys' main breeding program centered around their two foundation bitches, Ch. Rendition Irish Inspiration and Ch. Rendition Razzle Dazzle, and their second male, Ch. Meadowlark's Masterpiece. They are a strong combination of Ch. Shannon's Erin and Ch. Tirvelda Michaelson. Inspiration finished with five majors and has six champions to her credit to date. Razzle Dazzle finished with a Specialty BOB from the classes and has three major pointed get from her first litter.

Ch. Meadowlark's Masterpiece was owner-handled to 12 Group Firsts and 12 Specialty BOBs. He has been test-bred clear and has proven himself to be an outstanding sire.

The first breeding of Masterpiece and Inspiration produced three champions: Ch. Scarlly's Showboat, Sassafras, and Dreamboat Annie. Showboat's record stands at two all-breed Bests in Show, 12 Group Firsts and 4 Specialty BOBs; Dreamboat Annie was a Group winner from the classes and Winners Bitch at the Ohio Specialty over 96 bitches; Sassafras was twice Winners Bitch at the Georgia Specialty (her brother, Showboat, was Winners Dog both times also) and scored Group placements as a Special.

Inspiration was then bred to Sundance Rowdy and produced two champions. One was Ch. Scarlly's Rowdy Revenge, who finished at 19 months of age with 4 BOBs from the classes and two Group placements. He was a Group winner and a Specialty BOB winner before the age of two.

As of 1982 there were nine Scarlly champions, of which 7 are Group and Specialty winners, and these were produced from three litters since 1977. Penny

Meadowlark's Masterpiece
adowlark's Honor Guard ex
Tirvelda Meadowlark Ebb-
).

Scarlly's Sweet Success (Ch.
adowlark's Masterpiece ex
Rendition Irish Inspiration).

Scarlly's Showboat (Ch.
adowlark's Masterpiece ex
Rendition Irish Inspiration).

aims to limit their breeding program to one litter a year. In 1982 she bred Showboat to his sister, Ch. Scarlly's Sweet Success, who was herself a Specialty and breed winning bitch from the classes. Herein lies their future.

Oldfield, Barbara and David — *Connemara* — Oklahoma City, OK

A flashy, stylish Group-winning bitch, Ch. Connemara's Crimson Keepsake, is the pride of Connemara. Her sire, Innisfail Irish Design (Ch. Innisfail Flashback's Design ex Ch. Rad's Rondelet of Innisfail) was their first Irish Setter and the inspiration to continue active interest in the breed. Flashback's Lass of Connemara, daughter of Ch. Willowdale Crimson Count, also makes her home with the Oldfields.

Olich, Mary — *Glenavan* — Aptos, CA

Mary's kennel prefix is derived from Navan County in Ireland, her great-grandfather having come from that County.

In 1965, when she was thirteen, Mary went to her first dog show and saw her first Irish Setter. It was love at first sight! The following year, after saving all her baby-sitting money, she bought her first Irish puppy, a predominantly Thenderin bitch, who she later finished: Ch. Mistyglades Miss Magnificent, CDX. "Maggie" was bred to Ch. Draherin County Leitrim which produced four puppies: the BIS winning brothers Ch. Glenavan Hallelulia, CD, and Ch. Glenavan Sensation, and the bitches Glenavan Magnificent Edition (Brynlaw) and Glenavan Taste O'Honey (Ash-Ling). "Maggie" was then bred to Ch. Webline Wizard of Macapa. None from this litter were ever shown but several of their offspring are Group winners. One from that litter, Glenavan Beloved Shenandoah, bred to Ch. Thenderin William Muldoon produced Am. & Can. Ch. Glenavan Shenandoah's Gaiety, a Group winner from the classes and #2 Irish bitch for 1976. "Maggie" was bred for her last litter to her son Sensation. The bitch from this litter, Ch. Glenavan Inspiration, was a breed winner from the classes.

Some great moments for Mary have included finishing Hallelulia from the Am. Bred class with a BOB over more than 100 Irish; taking BOS with Maggie at the Far West Specialty from the Veteran Bitch class when she was 10 years old; winning BOB the next year at the Far West Specialty with Hallelulia; and finishing "Maggie's" grandson, Celebration, the same way she finished her son, with a BOB and Group 3rd at Santa Barbara in 1977.

In 1978, Celebration's sister, Ch. Lapointe's Lady Kate Ash-Ling, was bred to Ch. Tirvelda Hunter's Moon, and produced an outstanding litter of 8 bitches and 1 dog. That one dog was Ch. Glenavan Harvest Moon. "Harvey" won Best Puppy at the ISCA National 1979, went BOW from the BBE class at the ISCA National 1980, won an all-breeds Best in Show "from the classes" at Santa Clara Valley KC 1981, and finished the next weekend with BOW at the ISC San Diego Specialty, thereby finishing with three 5-pt. majors. He has since gone on to win numerous Groups, as well as another all-breeds BIS, all of this breeder/owner/handled. Harvey is co-owned with Joe and Vicki Wisher.

Oney, Cherie L. — *Kingscourt* — Dade City, FL

Cherie, who is one of the founding members of the Bay Area ISC of Tampa, owns Group and Specialty winner, Ch. Tirvelda Corrigan of Dunholm (Ch. Tirvelda Michaelson ex Am. & Can. Ch. Tirvelda Bridget Susie Ann). Tirvelda Emma of Dunholm (Ch. Tirvelda Mistral of Dunholm ex Ch. Tirvelda Tirana) was acquired from John and Anne Savory as a foundation brood bitch. She was bred to

Ch. Tirvelda Red Baron of Dunholm (BOB and Group III at Westminster 1974) resulting in the "Red" litter. Cherie's son, Wade, combined showing his Kingscourt Red Regent in conformation (wins include a Group placement) and in Junior Showmanship, and qualified and showed at Westminster twice in the JS competition.

Pace, Roy C. and Jean R. — *Pacesetter Irish* — Newport News, VA

The Paces founded their kennel in 1973 with the purchase of the puppy, Tirvelda Call to Fame, a son of Ch. Tirvelda Distant Drummer ex Ch. Tirvelda Sarabande. Fame began his show career by taking his first points from the puppy class. Later on the way to his championship he went from the Open class to Best in Show at two years of age. The Paces' have bred two of their bitches to him.

Pahy, Marion — *Faith Farm* — San Antonio, TX

Marion and Dan Pahy were active for many years in field activities in the East. Their dogs are mentioned in the chapter on field dogs. They originally operated with the kennel name McGovern, then O'Red and eventually Faith Farm. For years they chaired the field program of the Eastern Irish Setter Association and Dan was Treasurer of the famous Jockey Hollow Field Trial Club for over 20 years and Secretary-Treasurer of the Associated Field Trial Clubs of New Jersey for 10 years. After his passing, Marion moved to San Antonio, Texas where she remains active in field work.

Pickett, Charles H. — *Somerset* — Staunton, VA

Somerset Irish Setters was established in 1969. The foundation was formed around its first two champions, Ch. Tirvelda Prince, CD, and Ch. Tirvelda Red Angel, both of whom were Michaelson offspring. Red Angel produced several multi-BOB, Specialty and Group-placing champions including Ch. Sunny of Somerset, Ch. Somerset's Gaelic Traveler and Am. & Can. Ch. Dierling Patrick O'Somerset. Charles later received a bitch from Tirvelda Farms named Tirvelda Red Dawn of Sharilyn, who produced Am. & Can. Ch. Somerset Colonial Spirit, Ch. Somerset's Freedom Express, Ch. Autumn's Dawn of Somerset and Can. Ch. Somerset Autumn's Melody, Can. UD, Am. CD. Charles' third-generation homebred, friend and housepet is Somerset Royal Woodsman, a show-pointed multi Best in Sweepstakes Specialty winner.

Pomeroy, Mrs. Betty — *Myhill* — Cincinnati, OH

Betty started in Irish Setters by baby-sitting for a puppy belonging to her son in 1968. Later, the puppy , which became Ch. Innisfail Kismet of Gala Glen, was acquired. He came to Betty after a very bad early experience, a frightened little fellow who hid under the bed at any sign of smoke. It took a lot of love and patience to bring out his basically excellent temperament. It was well worth the effort, for Kismet eventually was a multi Specialty and Group winner and although only shown within 150 miles of his home, Kismet became the No. 8 Irish Setter in 1976. Betty also owns Myhill's Traces of Gala Glen, Gala Glen's Happy Holiday, and Meadowlark's Headliner (Meadowlark's Honor Guard ex Ch. Tirvelda Meadowlark Ebbtide).

Prescott, Leona and Derby, Lucille — *Tirnanog* — Sheridan, OR

In addition to several Tirnanog champions and Obedience titlists, these kennels had Ch. Ri Daragh Gorgeous Georgaine, CD, Ch. Muckamoor's Merry

Malarky, CD, and the well known field trial winner Tir Na N Og Merrymike Larkey.

Pybus, Harold and Susan — *Erinova* — Surrey, B.C. CANADA

The Pybus's obtained their foundation bitch, Ch. Tammarlinn's Bonnie Erin, as a youngster in 1972. Two years later she whelped a litter sired by Can. Ch. King's Sean Beret of Montague, a son of Am. Ch. Taradell's Synbad. This litter contained four Canadian champions, an American champion and two Canadian Obedience titleholders. Retained from the litter was Can. Ch. Erinova's Renaissance Layde, CD. The litter brother, Am. & Can. Ch. Erinova's Aristocrat, is a Canadian Group and Best in Show winner.

Quace, Richard — Greeley, CO

Started in 1967, Dick's interest is breeding and handling. His first home-bred champion was Ch. Livingston's Heidi.

Ramon, J. A. and Linda — *Saraval* — Danville, CA

The Ramons began in 1970 with the purchase of three foundation puppies. All three became champions at maturity, ably piloted by Jose Ramon. These puppies were: Tirvelda Staffa of Dunholm (Ch. Tirvelda Michaelson ex Ch. Tirvelda Bridget Susieann); Summit Rise Sonnet of Saraval (Ch. Tirvelda Michaelson ex Summit Rise Sendai Doll); and Dunholm Saraval Sue Eireann (Ch. Shannon's Erin ex Ch. Tirvelda Bridget Susieann).

After this auspicious start and a sound breeding program that produced such notable West Coast winners as Ch. Saraval Kerrick, Ch. Saraval Justesse and Dual Ch. Saraval Jadestarr, there was a halt. Jose departed to live in Spain and Linda continues on a limited scale.

Jadestarr, a son of Ch. Tirvelda Rustic Duke ex Ch. Dunholm Saraval Sue Eireann, was handled by Bill Eichenberger and his owner Vince Mangis. He completed his field championship in just five weeks.

Ratkovich, George and Linda — *Cloverleaf* — Crete, IL

Cloverleaf's foundation bitch, Ch. Kilgary Castle Carra (Ch. Dunholm's Finn McCool ex Ch. Draherin Tamara) was finished owner-handled. Her daughter, Ch. Cloverleaf's Stone Fox (by Ch. Marverbrook Camelot) finished by going BOS (5 pts.) at the 1977 Kentuckiana Irish Setter Specialty. George and Linda also formerly owned Ch. Kilgary Dungannon (Ch. Thenderin William Muldoon ex Ch. Charlton's Auburn Treasure), a Specialty and many times Best of Breed winner. Their fine young dog, Ch. Cloverleaf's Ascendant, by Dungannon out of Stone Fox, was one of the top winning Irish Setters in the country in 1981 and 1982.

Reed, Flora M. — *Portrait* — Phoenix, AZ

As of this writing, Portrait has produced three litters, a total of 21 puppies, in four years. They have accounted for two American champions, one Canadian champion, one Group winner, four Best of Breed winners, and have won over 76 championship points. Ch. Bryfield Portrait O'Eve, CD, along with two daughters and her promising son, Portrait O'Copper Commander, are permanent residents here.

Reese, Sally — *Candia* —

Sally Reese owned Tyronne Farm Flame, Ch. Draherin Echo's Guy, and Ch. Draherin Echo's Hope. Later she owned Ch. Candia Big Red, Ch. Candia Pride,

. Shangrila Scarlet O'Hara
rvelda Eamon of Gabhantyr ex
. Shannon's Scarlet Urchin).

Am. & Can. Ch. Santera Tristan Troubadour (Ch. Ballycroy's Northern Sunset ex Wilson Farm Scarlet Tirvelda, CD).

. & Can. Ch. Santera Tamber-
k, CD (Ch. Ballycroy's Northern
nset ex Wilson Farm Scarlet Tir-
da, CD).

and Ch. Candia Fatima, who when bred to Ch. Bayberry Kinkaide produced Ch. Candia Indeed.

Reilly, Miss Ellen L. — *Derrinraw* — Ho-Ho-Kus, NJ

The Reillys bought their first Irish Setter in 1943. In the early 60's they started registering under the Derrinraw prefix. They purchased Red Barn Symphony, CD, as a puppy and later bred her to Ch. Titian Intrepid. The present Derrinraw Irish all go back to this breeding with the use of famous studs, Ch. Tirvelda Beau James and Ch. Barrewyne Highland Lancer. For years bitches dominated their showing including Ch. Derrinraw's Shannon, CD, and Ch. Derrinraw's Antrim, CD.

In recent years, the littermates, Am. & Can. Ch. Derrinraw's Royal Erin, and Am. & Can. Ch. Derrinraw's Sir Michael, who were both finished from the Bred by Exhibitor Class, have gone on to win the breed and place in the Group. On one three day weekend in Canada, both dogs finished Canadian titles going Winners and/or Best of Breed each day, Group I each day, and Erin went on to Best in Show.

Ellen and her mother, the late Mrs. Ellen Reilly, shared a strong interest in dogs. Ellen has served as president of the Eastern Irish Setter Association and as an officer in many other clubs, and is an AKC judge of Irish Setters and American cocker spaniels.

Remaley, Carol — *Dunravin* — Orange Village, OH

Carol and Louis Smith established the Dunravin Kennels on a strong Knockcross' foundation. They are now divorced and Carol continues with the dogs.

All the Dunravin dogs are descended from Knockcross' O'Boy and all but two are from Ch. Knockcross' Molly, CD. They owned Ch. Dunravin's Claret, CD, Ch. Knockcross' Russet and his sister Ch. Knockcross' Branbevin, CD. The latest to finish for them was Ch. Knockcross' Irish Muffin who is a great-granddaughter of Russet and Molly. One additional granddaughter of Russet and Molly should be mentioned here—Ch. Gala Glen September Dawn, the noted bitch owned by Pat Gallagher and Geri Cuthbert.

A great believer in Obedience work, almost all the Dunravin dogs have at least a CD degree.

Louis is now a judge of Irish Setters.

Reynolds, Wayne and Barnes, Thomas — *Barrewynne* — Sellersville, PA

Notable Barrewynne dogs include Ch. Knightscroft Rene, Ch. Barrewyne Brian Redmond and Ch. Barrewyne Highland Lancer, who is behind much of the current breeding of Ellen Reilly's Derrinraw Kennels.

Roberts, Gerry and Shirlee — *Robalee* — Mountain View, CA

The Roberts started their kennel with a combination of Varagon-Innisfail and Merry-Dell breeding. One of their favorite matings was their Robalee Tara of Saratoga (Varagon and Merry Dell) to Ch. Innisfail Gallant Guy (Innisfail and Thenderin), which produced Ch. Robalee Echo of Taru, Robalee Endeavor (14 pts., both majors), Ch. Robalee Flirtation and Can. Ch. Robalee Encore of Innisfail.

When an Australian gentleman came to this country and visited the specialties and most of the top breeders in the nation, the Roberts became intrigued with his mission to acquire American stock to take to Australia. He kept returning to the Roberts and a deep friendship developed, and when he proposed using Tara to breed to Ch. Glendee's Bourbon on the Rocks, CD, to "manufacture" the type he

Ch. Innisfail Gallant Guy (Ch. Innisfail Flashback's Design ex Thenderin Afterglow).

balee Endeavor (Ch. Innisfail llant Guy ex Robalee Tara of ratoga).

Summit Rise Sonnet of Sara- (Ch. Tirvelda Michaelson ex nmit Rise Sendai Doll).

was seeking, the Roberts complied. A year later the Australian returned to select the dog and bitch, who were to become Robalee Yank and Ch. Robalee Velvet. Two years later other Australians came to visit and acquire American stock. They bought Robalee Goldspinner (who became the first American import to finish her Australian championship, going Best in Show from the classes) and Robalee Kandu, a young dog the Roberts were saving for themselves and who is now an Australian champion.

When P.R.A. became a problem for setters Gerry and Shirlee were able to locate a blind bitch to use for test-breeding Endeavor. He became one of the first clear Irish Setter males in the country with a test litter of 13.

Other dogs the Roberts have bred include Argentinian Champion Robalee Royal Destiny, Robalee Christopher, CDX, Robalee Ironside, UD, and Robalee Gus Again (lacking a major for his Field Championship).

Rodman, Richard and Jeannine — *Rich-Lee* — Dayton, OH

In Irish Setters since 1967, the Rodmans obtained their first show dog, Jonna's Red Mountain Flame, from a western kennel. Their foundation bitch, Wilson Farm Nuttoma Miss, was obtained from Wilson Farm Kennels. She produced their first homebred champions, Am. and Can. Ch. Rich-Lee Wilson Farm Brandy and his sister, Ch. Rich-Lee Wilson Farm Sherry. Brandy was shown by Tom Glassford, and became the No. 4 Irish Setter of 1976 with 10 Group Firsts and many placements.

Ronald, Betty — *Holly Berry* — Wayzata, MN

This small kennel houses some big winners. Foremost is the much titled Am. & Can. Ch. Holly Berry Red IV, UD and Can. CD. This daughter of Ch. Muckamoor's Marty McCuhl and Ch. Draherin Echo's Hope was Betty's foundation bitch, and there are four descending generations from her in the kennel. Her daughter is Can. Ch. Holly's Merry Malarky, CDX, and both mother and daughter have received the Dog World award in Obedience. Also in the kennel is Ch. Holly's Dunbrook Barnaby, the Merry Malarky son by Dunbrook Express.

Ross, Rose Marie and F. Allen — *Meadowlark* — Midland, VA

Rose tells the Meadowlark story:

"Not new in dogs, we acquired our first show Irish from Ted Eldredge in 1970. Unfortunately, she had to be spayed at a year of age. We went back to Ted for another foundation bitch, and this time came away with two Irish in the back seat of our station wagon (we didn't even have crates); they were Tirvelda Samaria and Tirvelda Fortune Teller.

"Our next acquisition, from the Dave Wilsons, was future Ch. Wilson Farm Royal Count. The Treutels provided Sportmirth Pageantry ('Dawn'), a full sister to Ch. Tirvelda Valentine. Dawn produced three champions: Am. & Can. Ch. Meadowlark Drury Lane, Am., Can. & Bda. CD; Lance Corporal; and O'Brian.

"From the single mating of Ch. Draherin King's Ransom to Tirvelda Samaria came not only Chs. Tirvelda Meadowlark Ebbtide, T.M. Elysian, T.M. Embrace, Tirvelda Ensign of Meadowlark and Am., Can. & Bda. Ch. T.M. Encore, but also the incidental acquisition of Glen Cree Merriment. Merrie contributed Chs. M. Katy of Misty Morn, M. Interlude, M. Impossible Dream, M. Inherit the Wind, M. Indian Summer—the I-litter by Am. & Can. Ch. Rendition Erin of Sunny Hills, of which Impossible Dream and Indian Summer both won ISCA's coveted Golden Leash award. Sister Interlude was tied and runner-up with Impossible Dream, but

Meadowlark's Impossible Dream (Ch. Rendition Erin of Sunny Hills ex Glen Cree Merriment).

Meadowlark's Interlude (Ch. Rendition Erin of Sunny Hills ex Glen Cree Merriment).

Tirvelda Meadowlark's Ebbtide (Ch. Draherin Kings Ransom ex Tirvelda Samaria).

has asserted herself by producing two more Golden Leash winners for us—Ch. M. Centurion by Am. & Can. Ch. McCamon Marquis and M. Glorianna by Ch. M. Anticipation. Interlude's daughters, Ch. M. Chances Are and Ch. M. Glorianna have both been Winners Bitch at National Specialties. Glorianna finished with four Specialty majors.

"The very special pride of our household has been Ch. Tirvelda Meadowlark Ebbtide, who produced three champions by Meadowlark's Honor Guard (Chs. M. Masterpiece, M. Madrigal and M. Moonlight Magic), and three champions by Ch. Candia Indeed (Best in Show-winning Ch. M. Anticipation, M. Argosy and M. Royal Nobleman). These six get won a total of 9 Specialty majors en route to championship.

"A Christmas present from Fee Phillips became Ch. Mos'n Acre Patrician who, bred to Ch. Tirvelda Michaelson, produced four champions: M. High 'N Mighty, M. High Society, M. Nike and M. Nuance.

The Patti-Mike son, Meadowlark's Honor Guard ('Gunner') has so far produced six champions for Meadowlark: Masterpiece, Madrigal, Moonlight Magic, O'Brian, and M. Bouquet and M. Firey Rebellion. Am. & Can. Ch. Rendition Erin of Sunny Hills came to us from Pat Haigler and produced 19 champions before his death in 1982, including three Golden Leash award winners (Ch. Rendition Santana, Ch. Meadowlark's Impossible Dream and Ch. Meadowlark's Indian Summer), two National Specialty winners (Ch. Liafail Lovely Light and Ch. Rendition Santana). Erin was grandsire of two-time National breed winner, Ch. Shawnee Pipedream O'Charlton.

"A more recent addition, Tirvelda Magic Moment, produced Ch. Tirvelda Meadowlark Heiress and Am. & Can. Ch. T.M. Galicia, CD. To round out our 32 homebred champions are Chs. Meadowlark Epilogue and Aria O'Deargain, finished with a combination of seven majors. Our major-winning dogs have enabled us to win the coveted ISCA Breeders Trophy for five consecutive years."

Royston, John F. and Muriel — *Killane* — Meadowvale, Ont., CAN
Am. & Can. Ch. Argo Lane's Rising Star, Am. & Can. Ch. Killane Rogue, Ch. Killane Duffy, Can. Ch. Ellair Velvet Token and six or more Killane Canadian champions were owned by the Roystons.

Rumbaugh, Hugh and Virginia — *Fleetwood Farms* — Akron, OH
The first Fleetwood champion was a son of Ch. Kleiglight's Red Tuxedo, Am. & Can. Ch. Fleetwood Farms Emperor. Their next Irish was O'Shannon's Sally, daughter of Ch. Tyronne Farms Shamus. Sally, bred to Red Tuxedo, produced Fleetwood Farms Peg O'My Heart, Fleetwood Farms Sheila and Fleetwood Farms Miracle Boy—all champions. Peg O'My Heart, a Best in Show winner, was Top Bitch of the Year in 1951, '52 and '53.

Next to come to Fleetwood Farms, from Jack Cooper's Aragon Kennels, was the youngster Gay Guy of Aragon. A son of Ch. Knightscroft Danny O'Boy ex a Kleiglight of Aragon daughter, he quickly finished and was bred to Peg O'My Heart. The resultant litter contained the great producer, Ch. Fleetwood Farms Noreen. Noreen later bred to Ch. Thenderin Brian Tristan produced the "car" litter—actually whelped in a car. It contained Champions Fleetwood Farms Sixty Special, Coupe de Ville and Sedan de Ville. Sixty Special was retained and the bitches went to the Van Hobbs. Coupe de Ville when bred to Ch. Draherin Irish Chieftain, produced for the Hobbs that lovely Best in Show bitch, Ch. Merry-Dells Autumn Glory.

Am. & Can. Ch. Rhu Rory, Am. Can. Mex. Ch. Legend of Varagon, Am. Can. & Mex. Ch. Enilen High Flyer.

Ch. Meadowlark's Anticipation
(Ch. Candia Indeed ex Ch. Tirvelda Meadowlark's Ebbtide).

A granddaughter of Peg O'My Heart, Ch. Fleetwood Farms Flaming Glo was bred to Sixty Special and produced Ch. Fleetwood Farms Brougham. Brougham sired five champions—two Best in Show winners. Bred to the Weicks' Ch. Shannon Susie Starlet, he produced the top winning Irish Setter in the breed's history. Ch. Starheir's Aaron Ardee was whelped at the Weicks and grown to adulthood at their kennel. Shown to his championship by the Weicks, he was then acquired by the Rumbaughs, Under the Fleetwood Farm banner, piloted by Dick Cooper, Aaron Ardee defeated over 70,000 dogs during his record-setting show career. Perhaps his greatest win was Best in Show at the Chicago International, but many prestigious victories fell to him including a Group second at Westminster.

Extensively used as a sire Aaron Ardee produced Ch. Herihunda's Jennifer O'Shannon who, piloted by her young owner Maggie Schneider, was Best of Breed at the third National Specialty of the Irish Setter Club of America.

The litter containing Aaron Ardee had only four puppies. A sister, Ch. Starheir's Audacious Miss, in her first win as a Special went clear through to Best in Show.

The Weicks repeated the breeding that produced these two and Ch. Fleetwood Farms Grand Marshall, who went Winners Dog at the first ISCA National Specialty, and Ch. Starheir's Quest for Glory resulted from the second combination.

Ch. Shannon's Gypsy was leased for a breeding to Grand Marshall. This gave the Rumbaughs Ch. Fleetwood Farms Kerry Rose.

Not showing as consistently as a few years back, the Rumbaughs with a heavy advertising program built around Aaron Ardee are concentrating on a breeding program involving the two full brothers and the blood of these two grand dogs is being widely disseminated.

Salt, Patricia and Stephen — *Pauncefoot* — Ontario, CANADA

Pauncefoot Setters started in 1965, in the small village of Bentley Pauncefoot in the English Midlands. The first acquisition of Wendover breeding inoculated the owners with the show bug, and two years later the initial purchase was joined by her daughter and an excellent puppy of related Wendover-Marrona bloodlines.

The Salts' English show career was cut short in 1969 when work took the family and a nucleus of 3 bitches to Jamaica. However, they succeeded in leaving a mark on the Jamaican dog scene by making one of their bitches the first Irish Setter Jamaican champion—and a male they bred became the second.

In 1974, work again moved the family, this time to Ontario, Canada. But by this time their dogs were past their prime for the show ring. In 1976 the Salts imported Marrona Mystic Star, acquired from a friend—Mrs. Margaret Stokes of southern England, whose breeding was Marrona strain. The new puppy bitch, called "Petra," made a quick impact, taking a Best Puppy in Group at 10 months, and numerous Best Puppy in Breed awards. In 1978, she became a Canadian champion, winning her title with 3 majors. As a bonus, "Petra" proved to have considerable bird-sense and field training work was begun, resulting in her obtaining the Canadian title of Field Dog, the first Irish Setter to ever do so.

Savory, Dr. John and Anne D. — *Dunholm* — Wake Forest, NC

The Savorys bought their first show bitch from Tirvelda in 1963. She became Am. & Can. Ch. Tirvelda Bridget Susie Ann, a Best in Show and multi-Group winner and a top producer, with 11 champions to her credit. She was the only bitch to place in the Top Ten Irish Setters (Phillips System) for 1967 and 1968, and was

Ch. Starheir's Aaron Ardee
(Ch. Fleetwood Farms Brougham ex Am. & Can. Ch. Shannon's Susie Starlet).

Ch. Fleetwood Farms Sixty Special
(Ch. Thenderin Brian Tristan ex Ch. Fleetwood Farms Noreen).

the recipient of ISCA's Matron of the Year award in 1972. She was bred to Ch. Tirvelda Michaelson and Am. Can. & Bda. Ch. Shannon's Erin—to each twice— with excellent results. Each combination produced Best in Show and Specialty winning dogs, notably: Ch. Tirvelda Red Baron of Dunholm, a multi-Best in Show dog, BOB and GR4 at Westminster in 1974; Am. & Can. Ch. Dunholm's Finn McCool, another multi-Best in Show and Specialty winner and the top Sporting Dog in Canada for 1975 and 1976; and Ch. Dunholm Katrina, a Specialty Breed winner from the classes. Katrina, in turn, was bred twice to Ch. Tirvelda Michaelson and there are three finished offspring from the first combination.

John and Anne have now established separate kennels—John is near Charlottesville, Virginia and Anne is in Wake Forest, NC. The dogs have been divided and both have excellent foundation animals for future breeding programs. Anne is a professional handler and has finished numerous Irish Setters to championship.

Schaar, Mrs. Pamela and Vayda, Ronald — *Majestic* — Howell, MI

In 1969, Pam purchased the foundation bitch, Kilkenny's Gay Tribute (BIS Ch. Harmony Lane Northern Light ex Am. & Can. Ch. Argo Lane Gay Victoria, CD) from which came Gay Star of Erin, CD, winner of the Irish Setter Club of Michigan most blues award. She finished her CD at the 1974 Irish Setter Club of America National with a score of 197. Another bitch owned by Pam is Ch. Kirk's Kelly Lynn.

Ron's first Irish became Am. & Can. Ch. Aaragon's Regal Duke of Earl.

Also co-owned are the brace winning the Merry-Dell trophy; Can. Ch. Aaragon's Lovely Lady Lynet and Aaragon's Captain Lightfoot. Their ownership of Ch. Briarwood's Blazing Sunset (Ch. Shannon Shawn of Erin ex Ch. Briarwood's Meadowlark) and Tara Hill Harvest Moon (Ch. Tirvelda Telstar ex Ch. Rockerin Rebecca) has proven rewarding for Majestic, as both have produced well bred to various bitches. Both have been test-bred clear of P.R.A.

Scherrer, Dr. Robert and Kristin — *Riversong* — Moseley, VA

Their foundation bitch is Ch. Tapnar Even Song (Ch. Tirvelda Distant Drummer ex Tapnar Adventuress, CD) whelped October 2, 1975. Her first litter whelped February 5, 1981 by Ch. Tirvelda Royal Coachman produced River Song Grand Summit, Kassandra, and Kari-Ann.

Schneider, James A. and Margaret K. — *Herihunda* — McKinney, TX

From Maggie and Jim Charnel's Herihunda Mollee, retired with 12 points, bred to Ch. Starheir's Aaron Ardee, came Ch. Herihunda's Jenifer O'Shannon, Ch. Charnel's Reuben Rex, and Ch. Nickol Bunch of Hollee.

Ch. Herihunda's Jenifer O'Shannon took Best of Breed honors at the ISCA Third National Specialty in Atlanta, Georgia at the age of two. On the way home she was bred to Ch. Tirvelda Distant Drummer, and produced Ch. Herihunda's Cherokee Drummer, who took a 4-point Specialty major at 12 months and won the Bred-By-Exhibitor class at the ISCA National Specialty in Washington, D.C. Also in this litter are Ch. Herihunda's Carolina of Kenora (Penwell), and Ch. Herihunda's Jenifer O'Kerrizan. When bred to Am. & Can. Ch. McCamon Marquis, she produced Ch. Herihunda's Joint Venture and Ch. Herihunda's Chase Manhattan.

Schwartz, Harris A. and Patricia B. — *Gaelsong* — Maywood, NJ

Pat and Harris own Ch. Redwhiskey's Merlyn and Ch. Ronita Gaelsong, both

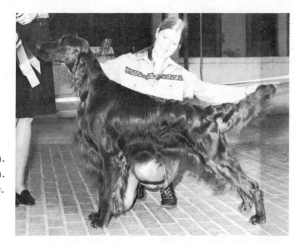

Glenavan Hallelulia, CD (Ch.
herin County Leitrim ex Ch.
yglades Miss Magnificent, CDX).

Glenavan Harvest Moon
. Tirvelda Hunter's Moon
Ch. La Pointe's Lady Kate
-Ling).

& Can. Ch. Rendition Erin of
ny Hills (Ch. Shannon's Erin ex
Michael's Patti O'Shea).

amateur-owned-handled to their titles with three Specialty majors between them. Merlyn, a son of Ch. Tirvelda Court Jester, was purchased from Doug and Carol Brown in 1972 and Gaelsong is one of the litter of several champions by Ch. Candia Indeed ex Ch. Redwhiskey's Royal Victory bred by Robert and Anita Dunn. The Schwartzes also owned Gaelsong's brother, Ch. Ronita Royal Burgundy, now dead. A brother-sister breeding carries on the line.

Both Pat and Harris have been very active in the affairs of the Eastern Irish Setter Association, Harris having served as its president, and Pat on the Board of Directors.

Schweitzer, Miss Emily — *Verbu* — Dundee, IL

Miss Schweitzer acquired her first Irish Setter in 1923, when she was a schoolgirl with braids down her back—and the braids, in harmony, were titian, too. The dog was Glencho Ruddy Oogh, out of Ch. Glencho Annabelle Oogh. (Oogh is pronounced as in rouge.) Ruddy came as a 3-months-old puppy from Mrs. E. Alban Sturdee's famous Glencho Kennels in Albany, New York. Although purchased as a family pet, Ruddy was shown by Emily a few times—placing Reserve Winners two years in a row at the Specialty shows of the Western Pointer and Setter Club, and scoring Best Sporting Dog at the Illinois State Fair in 1928. Ruddy was not used at stud until 7 years of age, but sired Am. & Can. Ch. Verbu Killeen Oogh, CDX, and Ch. Shan of Innisfree, as well as several others with points.

His kennelmate, Verbu Red Mollie (Ch. Bergneil Red Helmet ex Palmerston Mollie Bawn), bred in Missouri by Mrs. Lee Kneedler, wife of the field trial handler, was used as a gun dog. Because she was good afield, the handler trained his young stock with her. Miss Schweitzer purchased Mollie in 1930 at 5 years of age and showed her to championship. As I remember Mollie, she was a great bitch with a lovely Irish expression, nicely chiseled head that never grew coarse, and a beautiful coat.

Miss Schweitzer is one of the great pioneers of Obedience in America. Her Am. & Can. Ch. Verbu Killeen Oogh was the first Irish Setter in the United States to win the CD (Companion Dog) title, and her Am. & Can. Ch. Verbu Norna Oogh was the first to earn the UD (Utility Dog) title. Norna won all the titles available, including UDT (Utility Dog Tracker). One so often hears the remark that Obedience work spoils a dog for the show ring. That this is not so is proven by Am. & Can. Ch. Verbu Killeen Oogh, CDX, Am. & Can. Ch. Verbu Peter Oogh, CDX, and Am. & Can. Ch. Verbu Norna Oogh, UDT—all won their titles competing in the breed and Obedience rings at the same shows.

In the early 1950s, Verbu Irish Setters moved to the rolling hills of Dundee, Illinois. This gave the opportunity to add field work to shows and Obedience. In 1953, Verbu Maura took first place in the Pointer and Setter Exhibition stake at the International KC of Chicago dog show.

During the next few years, the following Verbu dogs all acquired field championship points: Am. & Can. Ch. Verbu Shawn Oogh, CD; Ch. Verbu Missy Oogh, CD; Ch. Caldene Maura, CD; Verbu Midgie Oogh, CD; and Verbu Shuna Oogh, CD, VC.

In the show ring, the 1960s saw the litter sisters Ch. Verbu Erin and Ch. Verbu Maureen, CD (a field trial winner) star. The lovely Maureen is the only Irish Setter bitch to date to win Best of Breed at both the Combined Setter Specialty and Westminster. Ch. Erin had 17 Best of Breed wins, including 7 Specialty shows. They were daughters of Ch. Caldene Maura, CD.

Ch. Bayberry Happy Time, CD (Ch. Bayberry Sommerset ex Ch. Tirvelda Bayberry Sundown).

Am. & Can. Ch. Tirvelda Bridget Susie Ann (Ch. End O'Maine Jack High ex Ch. Hartsbourne Sally-ann of Tirvelda).

Ch. Dunholm Red Ribbons (Ch. Tirvelda Michaelson ex Ch. Dunholm Katrina).

A dream came true for Verbu in 1972—a dual champion! Under the expert care and training of Jake and Sally Huizenga of Salinas, California, Ch. Duffin Miss Duffy, CD, VC, made her field championship. "Pup-Pup" was out of Verbu Miss Duffy, who was a daughter of Ch. Caldene Maura, CD.

Then came the magnificent Ch. Verbu Caragh, ably handled in the show ring by Jack Funk. Shown only 10 times in completing her championship, she was Winners or better 8 times. During the next several years, she was shown as a Special 19 times, and was BOB or BOS in 17 of them. Her last show was at 8½ years of age, when she took Best of Opposite Sex at the Western Irish Setter Club Specialty over many outstanding bitches.

In 1978, some 55 years after the arrival of Glencho Ruddy Oogh in the Schweitzer home, there was a new triple winner—Ch. Verbu Katie Oogh, CD, VC, and with 8 field trial awards.

In 1978, too, the Irish Setter Club of America inaugurated its Versatility Certificate. Naturally, some of the Verbu dogs were qualified. They are: Verbu Shuna Oogh, CD, VC; Ch. Verbu Katie Oogh, CD, VC and Dual Champion Duffin Miss Duffy, CD, VC.

During these many years there have been numerous other titleholders—among them, Ch. Verbu Oona Oogh, WB at Westminster in 1949, and Ch. Verbu Shamrock, "Rocky" to his legion of admirers. Every dog at Verbu with the Oogh suffix is a descendant of Ruddy—the others are all progeny of Ch. Caldene Maura, CD. There are never more than a dozen Irish at the kennel—including all the old-timers who are always kept and loved. The breeding program has also been very limited—only one litter approximately every three years.

Emily has done much for the breed in all phases of the sport. Unfortunately for us all, she does not allow anyone to breed to her studs, nor does she sell any puppies. This effectively stops her valuable bloodlines from contributing to breed progress. There is a reason for Miss Schweitzer's position. She feels very strongly that breeders are far too careless as to whom they sell their dogs, and that many animals suffer as a result. No Verbu dog has ever been put in a position where a change of circumstance could endanger it. There is great food for thought in her position.

Shaver, Don and Marilyn — *Summit Rise* — Bainbridge Island, WA

The Shavers obtained their first Irish Setter, a pet, Shaver's Bonny Red Queen, in 1963, but Summit Rise began, officially, on February 21, 1965, when Killane Kate of Harmony Lane, a bitch obtained from and co-owned with Anne Smith of the Harmony Lane Kennels in Georgia, whelped a litter by young Ch. Blayneywood Country Squire. From that litter of three, one lived to maturity, to become the foundation of the kennel, Summit Rise Sendai Doll. "Dolly" was bred four times, producing three champions and several others with points.

This is a small kennel of eight grown Irish. There are no kennel runs at Summit Rise, and because of this freedom, the dogs must be of good temperament and get along with each other at all times. One litter is whelped about every two years. The bloodline primarily is a cross back and forth between the old lines of Ch. Tyronne Farm Malone II and Ch. Thenderin Brian Tristan, through Ch. Blayneywood Country Squire and Ch. Michael Bryan Duke of Sussex.

Champions have included Ch. Summit Riser of Harmony Lane, CD, Ch. Flicka of Summit Rise, Ch. Summit Rise Sonnet of Saraval, Can. Ch. Summit Rise Cheyenne Autumn (Sporting Group winner in Canada), Ch. Summit Rise Sensation, Ch. Summit Rise Flare O'Legerwood, and Ch. Summit Rise Rampart.

Ch. Verbu Erin (Knockross O'Boy ex Ch. Caldene Maura).

Ch. Fieldstone Trace of Burgundy (Ch. McCamon Marquis ex Glen Cree Merriment).

Am. Can. & Bda. Ch. Bare Cove Brannigan (Dual Ch. Donnington Crackerjack ex Clancool Cardyn of Bare Cove).

Others include Summit Rise Medallion, Summit Rise Noele, Summit Rise Maura O'Legerwood and Summit Rise Forever Amber, who accumulated seven points owned and shown by the Shavers' young daughter, Laura.

Shelor, Linda — *Lochinvar* — Jeffersonville, KY

Linda started her Irish Setter activities with the puppy who later became Ch. Tullamore Bull Abadden (Ch. Bayberry Sommerset ex Wilson Farm Heart Flush). He finished with three majors which included BOW at the New Orleans Specialty and WD at the ISC of Tampa Specialty. She also owns the littermates, Ch. Lochinvar Ace in the Hole and Lochinvar's Penny Ante (by Ch. Tullamore Desperado ex Bayberry Rohirrim Star Trek).

Smith, Joe and Irish — *Limerick Lane* — Waller, TX

Irish Smith (Mary Margaret O'Harra), having wise parents, shared her life from infancy with ponies and Irish Setters. Joe and Irish started "Limerick Lane" on its way in 1965 with the future Ch. Cherry Point Limerick Melody. Joe placed Melody under their Christmas tree. "Melody" (Ch. Cherry Point Ambush ex Ch. Hartmann's Tyronne Queenie) finished at 16 months. Melody was bred to their young male from Tirvelda, "Terry", Ch. Tirvelda Laird O'Limerick (Ch. Thenderin Endorsement ex Ch. Tirvelda Nutbrown Sherry.) Terry received his O.F.A. certification as a young dog and was re-radiographed normal at age 11½ years. To date, from limited breeding, he has produced seven AKC champions and two Canadian champions plus numerous Obedience titleholders. Melody and Terry produced Ch. Limerick Lane Liffey, dam of Ch. Kerrizan's Meg O'Limerick Lane.

Limerick Lane's next acquisition was the puppy, now Ch. Sleepy Hollow's Dardenella. This bitch (from Warren Ellis), by Ch. Draherin County Leitrim ex Ch. Webline Venus, was bred one time to "Terry", producing Ch. Tullamore Lear O'Limerick, CD (Fortune) and Am. and Can. Ch. Limerick Lane's North Star, Can. CD (Dunn), winner one year of Canada's award for Highest Scoring Irish Setter. The latter's one litter by Ch. Limerick Lane Terryson O'Kate has to date produced several Canadian champions plus Obedience titleholders.

After climbing into their car at Tirvelda with four-months-old "Kate", later to become Ch. Tirvelda Kathleen O'Limerick (Ch. Tirvelda Tambourlane ex Ch. Tirvelda Bayberry Sundown), the Smiths started this young bitch's Texas career by winning her first major at 11 months. She finished with two more majors, all under age two. Kate's first litter was by Terry and together they produced: Ch. Limerick Lane Terryson O'Kate, Ch. Candere Arcturus, Ch. Limerick Lane's Red, Red Rose, and Ch. That Deirdre O'Limerick. Kate was then bred to Ch. Padre Island Sea Storm, the Ch. Tirvelda Earl of Harewood son, and from this came Ch. Limerick Lane Merry Maker. Kate was mated to Terry twice more, and several of these dogs are pointed. She has whelped five AKC champions and one Canadian champion to date.

Next to finish was their homebred Ch. Limerick Lane Kerry Sue Pat (Ch. Limerick Lane Terryson O'Kate ex Shannon's Special—a granddaughter of Ch. Headliner The Flaming Beauty. Pat was bred and whelped a litter in 1975 by Ch. Padre Island Sea Storm, CD, producing several winners.

Ch. Limerick Lane Morgan (Ch. Tirvelda Hunter's Moon ex Ch. Limerick Lane Merry Maker) finished at two and a half by goint BOW for a major at Houston, and the very next day went BOB from the classes at the Specialty of the ISC of Houston. He earned his CD soon thereafter, but one week later, a virus caused his untimely death.

Other Limerick Lane hopefuls include: Santera Limerick Lane Sally (Am. & Can. Ch. Santera Tamberluck, CD, ex Wilson Farm Santera Hope); Limerick Lane Cindy Lou; Ch. Limerick Lane Tipperary, a daughter of Ch. Padre Island Sea Storm, CD, and Ch. L. L. Kelly Sue Pat.

Joe is a former member of the Board of the Irish Setter Club of America. He also was president of the ISC of Texas and president of the ISC of Houston. Irish has been secretary and president of the ISC of Texas and is an approved judge of Irish Setters.

Smith, Linda — *Tioga* — Camino, CA

Tioga started with the acquisition of Tirvelda Redwood Eire, UD, a daughter of Ch. Webline Wizard of Macapa and Ch. Tirvelda Nutbrown Sherry. In her only litter of two puppies, sired by Ch. Innisfail Flashback's Design, Kelly produced Ch. Tirvelda Tioga, CD, who finished with back-to-back Specialty majors. "Yogi" died shortly after finishing his championship, but he left behind a litter out of his half-sister, Ch. Enniscorthy Crimson N' Clover. Two of the puppies came to live at Tioga. One is the lovely Ch. Enniscorthy Tioga Aspenglo, and the other is Enniscorthy Tioga, CD, who started in his Dad's footsteps by taking his first points at the 1980 Far West Setter Specialty.

Smith, Richard E. and Anne — *Harmony Lane* — Woodstock, GA

Anne is the daughter of Dr. Arthur W. Erkfitz, one of the founders of the Irish Setter Club of Michigan, and has had Irish Setters since 1943. Dick is a professional handler, and the Harmony Lane prefix started in 1960 with his Ch. Argo Lane's Fancy Dancer, CD, and her Am. & Can. Ch. Erin of Ellair, CD. These dogs came from Joe Frydrych's Argo Lane and Hayden Martin's Sunny Acre Kennels. There have been 33 champions and 10 Obedience titleholders to date, including Specialty breed winners, Ch. Beauhart Bets On Harmony Lane and Ch. Harmony Lane's Pipe Dream, BIS winner Ch. Harmony Lane's Northern Light, and Ch. Harmony Lane's Red Oak, sire of a dual champion.

Much more could be written about Harmony Lane. Anne is modest and very busy and this is all the information I received.

Sporre, Dennis J. and Cynthia — *Blueprint* — Wilmington, NC

In 1967 the Sporres acquired their first show Irish, Can. Ch. Bryn Sean Fiona, a daughter of Ch. End O'Maine Reddy-go and Ch. Valmar's Cherokee Maid. Their first American champion was Ch. Tirvelda Ambition of Dunholm, a Specialty Best of Breed winner. He was followed by Ch. Dunholm's Danielle of Erin and Ch. Dunholm Kachina Doll, the Irish Setter Club of America's Winner's Bitch of the Year for 1975. All of the Sporres' champions have been owner-handled. Two Blueprint litters whelped in 1974 and 1977 have produced Ch. Dunholm Blueprint Americana, Ch. Dunholm Blueprint Liberty, and Ch. Dunholm Colonial Blueprint, Ch. Blueprint Kachina Kewpi Doll, Ch. Blueprint Kachina Doll, and Ch. Blueprint Kachina Doughboy, all Specialty winners. Americana was bred to Ch. Tirvelda Royal Coachman (Ch. Ash-Ling Celebration ex Ch. Tirvelda Sarabande) carrying on the Sporres' limited breeding program.

Dennis is a past president of the Plattsburgh (NY) Kennel Club and Irish Setter Club of Greater Tucson, a former board member of the Tucson Kennel Club, and was First Vice President of the Irish Setter Club of America. Cynde is a past treasurer of the Tucson Kennel Club. In 1980 the Sporres moved to Wilmington, North Carolina where Dennis is Chairman of the Department of Creative Arts at the University of North Carolina at Wilmington.

Stead, Harlan and Dawn — *Woodland* — Woodland Hills, CA

Harlan and Dawn N. Stead purchased their first Irish, a pet, in 1962. This "pet", Fantasy's Scarlet Lady grew to become a 5-pt. Specialty Show winner the first time shown, thus starting the Steads on a fascinating hobby. She was the dam of Am., Can. & Mex. Ch. Scarlet Flash of Varagon and Ch. Varagon Spring Storm. These two dogs are in the background of many of today's great Irish. The Steads assumed the kennel name "Woodland" in 1970 with a stud puppy from A., Can. & Mex. Ch. Scarlet Flash of Varagon and Moira Shonee of Shannon. This dog is Am., Mex., (F.C.I.), Venezuelan and Colombian Ch. Varagon Woodland Duke. A triple Best in Show winner (one a large Specialty show), "Woody" was retired from the show ring at age five to be field trained. He has earned many placements at field trials. The Steads also own Am. & Mex. Ch. Flashback Woodland Storm, who has been test-bred clear of P.R.A. Both Harlan and Dawn have been active in the Irish Setter Club of Southern California.

Steele, Jim and Darlene — *Rossans* — Woodridge, IL

Rossans actually began with Darlene receiving her first Irish Setter, Colleen of Belfast, CDX, as a birthday present in September 1969. The bitch became Rossans foundation and a major factor in the success of their breeding program.

Colleen was bred to Ch. Kilgary Aman in 1975. This produced their first homebred champion, Rossans Charlie, an all-breed and Specialty Best in Show winner. Colleen was then bred to Ch. Kilgary Dungannon in 1976, which produced Ch. Rossans Oliver Twist.

Ch. Rossans Charlie, bred to Beaverbrook Rya of Rossan, sired Ch. Rossans Afternoon Delight, Ch. Rossans Charlie's Angel and Rossans Maggie Mae. Bred to Ch. Cloverleaf's Stone Fox, Charlie sired Rossans Good Time Charlie.

Stewart, Doug and Robin — *Wilangi* — King Island, Tasmania, Australia

A 2000-acre sheep farming ranch on King Island, situated between Tasmania and Australia, is the setting for the Wilangi Irish Setters.

Pride of place goes to Aust. Ch. Wilangi Red Alice, shown from March 1979 to April 1980 by Greg Browne for the Stewarts. Alice became the top winning Irish in Australia for 1979, winning three Royal Show Bests of Breed, the big ones "down under": the Melbourne Royal under judge Lee Huggins, U.S.A.; the Royal Brisbane, under judge Mikks Maljanen; Sweden; and the Sydney Royal, under judge C. Sutton, England. At the latter show her son, Ch. Wilangi King Quail, won the Dog Challenge Certificate, making it a unique mother-son combination.

In 1980, Alice was Best of Breed under Roy Jerome at the Irish Setter Club Championship show. In addition, she has three Best in Show all-breeds and four Best of Opposite Sex to Best in Show.

Stoll, Dr. Selma — *Flashback* — Canoga Park, CA

Flashback Farms had its beginning when Dr. Selma Stoll acquired her first Irish Setter in October of 1957. Prior to this, her Setter interest had been with the English.

In 1964 Dr. Stoll realized the dream of all Irish owners and breeders when her Ch. Flashback of Varagon was awarded Best in Show at prestigious and beautiful Santa Barbara. This was to be the first of three generations of Best in Show winning Irish to be owned during the next ten years. Conceived less than eighteen hours before his sire's death, Ch. Innisfail Flashback's Design followed his father's footsteps to become a multi-Best in Show winner, as well as producer of several

Am. & Can. Ch. Tirvelda Best Regards, CD (Ch. Charles River Streamliner ex Ch. Tirvelda Nutbrown Sherry).

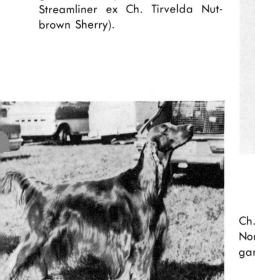

Ch. Tirvelda Valentine (Ch. Tirvelda Nor'Wester ex Ch. Tirvelda Best Regards, CD).

Ch. Tirvelda Sportin' Life, CD (Ch. Tirvelda Nor'Wester ex Ch. Tirvelda Best Regards, CD).

Best in Show winning sons and daughters. A son, Ch. Willowdale Crimson Count, became Dr. Stoll's third generation Best in Show winner.

It is hoped that fourth generation Flashback Killary Design will further prove that quality—rather than quantity—litters can successfully result in generation after generation of Breed, Group and Best in Show winning Irish.

Swanson, Mr. and Mrs. Thomas — *Tramore* — Boulder, CO

The Swansons' first bitch was purchased in 1971 as a pet. Their second bitch, this time of show quality, was obtained in 1972. She was Bo-Cham's Whisper of Tramore, a linebred Shannon's Erin granddaughter. Although pointed, she did not finish, but as a brood bitch proved her real value. Her first litter by the double-Erin grandson, Ch. Kilgary Aman, produced their first champion, Tramore Flannery, who finished at 25 months with four majors, and is a multi-breed winner, including the ISC of Colorado Specialty.

Their second owner-handled champion is Ch. Tapnar Emerald Eran (Ch. Tirvelda Distant Drummer ex Tapnar Adventuress, CD), who finished with back-to-back 4-pt. majors, and a BOB over Specials.

Their younger generation includes Tramore Couldn't Resist (Ch. Candia Indeed ex Bo-Cham's Whisper of Tramore) and their D litter, sired by Carra-J's Echo of Tirvelda ex Flannery.

Taylor, Renee — *Kamron* — Reseda, CA

As a child of ten, Renee received her first Irish Setter, Manorvue Magnificent, bought from A. C. Foster. He was never shown, but lived to 12 years of age, a devoted house dog. After marrying Ron, Renee bought another Irish, Rhu Rory of Haleridge. He also never made it to the show ring, but earned his CD in the States, Canada and Mexico.

Determined to own an Irish to show, Renee became very interested when Lauretta Golden mentioned an upcoming Varagon litter out of Ch. Innisfail Best Regards, CDX, by her half-brother, the Webb's Ch. Innisfail Color Scheme, CD. Reserving the second choice male from the Gonsors, Legend of Varagon started the Taylors in the world of dog shows, Obedience and breeding.

Legend ("Trofi") won a total of 13 titles to become: Am., Mex., & Can. Ch. Legend of Varagon, UDT, PR, PU, Can. CDX—the most titled Irish in breed history.

Renee's biggest weekend with Trofi was in Mexico in 1965. Together they earned a Tracking degree on Friday, Gr. I on Saturday, and his UD degree and Gr. II on Sunday—proving that an Irish *can* compete in both rings successfully.

Trofi sired 12 American and 17 Canadian champions, including two BIS sons; Ch. Danalee Bright Legend, bred by Leigh McGinnis, and Can. Ch. Julerin Image of Trofi, bred by Julia Currie. Bright Legend and Am. & Can. Ch. Callaway's Kamron Casey are also Specialty BOB winners.

The Taylors leased one of the first bitches bred to Trofi, this breeding producing Can. & Am. Ch. Kamron Crest of the Meadows. One of the closest breedings was a Trofi daughter, Kamron Connemara, Am., Can. & Mex. CD, (owned by Carol Burgasser), back to Trofi, producing three Canadian champion brothers, Kamron Aristocrat, Kamron Avant-Garde, and Kamron Aurora, Can. CD.

Renee's first bitch was Enilen High Flyer, from the Bayless's Enilen Kennels. It was Madeline Bayless who taught Renee so much about advanced Obedience and Tracking. High Flyer became Am., Can. & Mex. Ch. Enilen High Flyer, CDX, PC,

Am. & Can. Ch. Holly Berry Red VI, UD, Can. CD (Ch. Muckamoor's Marty McCuhl ex Ch. Draherin Echo's Hope).

Ch. Mistyglades Miss Magnificent, CDX (Thenderin Bright as Blazes ex Mistyglades Miss Cindy Lee).

Ash-Ling Celebration (Am. Can. Mex. Ch. Draherin Kings Ransom Glenavan Taste O'Honey).

252

Can. CD. Bred to Legend, she produced two Canadian champions, Kamron Legend's Conquest and Kamron Confetti, the latter owned in Canada by Shirley Shires. Confetti was an excellent bitch, but an early injury prevented her from being campaigned in the States. Conquest was a big dog, just under 30″. In very limited Canadian showing, he earned 7 Group Firsts, owner-handled, but his size and lack of coat for that height stopped him in the States. Two Canadian champions, Kamron Initiator of Shaunell and Kamron Inlander of Robi Lee resulted from the breeding of Jubilee Farms Love of Kamron to Conquest.

Flyer was next bred to BIS Ch. Webline Wizard of Macapa. The top bitch was bought by Carol Burgasser, who campaigned her to Am., Mex. Can., Ber. & Int'l. Ch. Kamron Dominique, a Group and BIS winner.

The repeat breeding of Ch. Sanderson's Holly High Hopes to Trofi gave Renee Am. & Can. Ch. Julerin Curri of Kamron.

Trefrey, Mrs. Cindy — Avon, CT
Mrs. Trefrey's first show Irish Setter was Am. & Can. Ch. Barrewyne Crimson Courier—a full-brother to Ch. Barrewyne Highland Lancer. Courier finished his championship by going Best of Winners at Philadelphia over an entry of 100.

Cindy then acquired Ch. Kincora Blazing Banner, and added his Canadian and Bermuda titles. He was to become her first Specialty winner, which included the Combined in New York City over 292 Irish. This son of Ch. Tirvelda Earl of Harewood and Wilson Farm Country Belle, finished with four majors, including Best of Breed at the Ohio Specialty, handled by his young owner, Joyce Diamond. Handled by Tommy Glassford for his new owners, Banner won 7 all-breed Bests in Show, 3 Specialty Bests, and 25 Group firsts. In the one year he was extensively campaigned—1974—he was the No. 1 Irish Setter in the country.

Later, Banner was returned to his breeder, Miss Joyce Diamond, who had originally handled him to his American championship. Along the way Minnie Keifer came in as a co-owner, and he is officially listed as being owned by all three ladies.

Banner's most outstanding offspring was Ch. Rockerin Bandilane Bridget. Acquired by Cindy Trefrey at 13 months, Bridget has also had several co-owners but all her points, including back-to-back majors, were won with Trefrey-Diamond as co-owners. Her wins include a Best in Show all-breeds. Bridget was bred to Ch. McCamon Marquis and produced Ch. Rockerin Follow the Sun and Ch. Rockerin Raffin.

In 1981, Cindy acquired Ch. Meadowlark's Anticipation, who she co-owns with Judy Boston-Payne.

Treutel, Edward and Helen — *Sportmirth* — Leonia, NJ
Helen and Ed Treutel bought a five-month-old bitch from Tirvelda in 1965, and began an all-consuming hobby. Am. & Can. Ch. Tirvelda Best Regards, CD (Ch. Charles River Streamliner ex Ch. Tirvelda Nutbrown Sherry) owner-handled, won the ISCA Best Bitch Award twice, 1967 and 1969. Bred only twice, to Ch. Tirvelda Nor'Wester, who lived with the Treutels until his death at 13½ years, Best Regards produced four champions and several other pointed offspring.

The Treutels kept three from the first litter: Ch. Tirvelda Valentine, who died in September 1981, a record-winning bitch in Irish Setter history (ISCA Best Bitch 1970 and 1971); Ch. Tirvelda Sportin' Life, CD, sire of the ISCA Best Bitch in 1973, Ch. Kimberlin Kyrie; and Tirvelda Taralee, CDX. From the second litter by Nor'Wester came Ch. Sportmirth Starbright.

Tirvelda Royal Coachman
Ash-Ling Celebration ex Ch.
elda Sarabande).

Tapnar Even Song (Ch. Tir-
a Distant Drummer ex Tap-
Adventuress, CD).

Marverbrook Camelot (Am.
. & Bda. Ch. Shannon's Erin
h. Candia Ambrosia).

Valentine, in turn, when bred to Ch. Danalee Bright Legend, produced Ch. Sportmirth Blazing Legend and Bda. Ch. Sportmirth Bright Promise. Bred to Ch. Ballycroy's Northern Sunset, she produced one puppy, Sportmirth Evergreen Brian, CD, VC.

Ch. T. Sportin' Life was bred late in life to Honeyrock Galadriel. A stud puppy from that breeding, Sportmirth Caro Mio Ben, carries on the line at the Treutels.

Ed, a licensed judge for all Setters and German Shorthairs, is a past president of the ISCA, as well as of the Eastern Irish Setter Club, the Palisades Kennel Club and the New Jersey Dog Federation. He was chairman of the first three ISCA National Specialty shows, and originated the EISA's independent Specialty. Helen is active in Obedience. She also was president of the Eastern Irish Setter Assn., and was the ISCA's Recording Secretary for three years.

Vallier, W. Eugene and Susie — *Reverie* — San Antonio, TX

Ch. Reverie Essence of Bayberry, CD, and other pointed youngsters with Mary McKim of San Antonio, were bred by the Valliers.

Vanacore, Fred and Connie — *Ballycroy* — Mendham, NJ

Ballycroy started in 1956 with the purchase of Phantom Brook's Ballycroy from the kennels of J. Brooks and Dodie Emory. This dog, who was the littermate of Ch. Phantom Brook's Brian Boru, a big winner of the day, was bred to Knockross Seana. That mating produced Ch. Dureen O'Tara, who was owned by the late Walter Nickerson.

Tara, bred to Ch. Tirvelda Rick O'Shea, litter brother of Michaelson, Nor'Wester and Earl, produced Ch. Tirvelda Beau James. At the same time the Vanacores purchsed Banshee Irish Mist, a daughter of Knockross O'Boy, from Ivan and Leonore Klapper. She was bred to Beau James, producing Ch. Ballycroy's Buccaneer and Ballycroy's Rua Catlin (5 points, including a major). Catlin was bred to Ch. Tirvelda Nor'Wester. The outcome of that union was Ch. Ballycroy's Northern Pride, Ballycroy's Northern Robin (9 points) and Best in Show Ch. Ballycroy's Northern Sunset. The latter sired two Best in Show sons by Wilson Farm Scarlet Tirvelda, litter brothers Ch. Santera Tristan Troubadour and Ch. Santera Tamberluck. These two brothers are the ninth generation of Best in Show winners in direct male line going back to Ch. Higgins Red Coat in 1927. Their get have made Northern Sunset a second generation top producer.

Connie co-owns, with Mary Ann Alston, Ch. Fieldstone Trace of Burgundy (Ch. McCamon Marquis ex Glen Cree Merriment). This young bitch was Best in Sweeps and Best of Breed from the classes while garnering points towards her championship.

Connie has held offices in ISCA and in the Eastern Irish Setter Association. She is a Contributing Editor to the American Kennel Club *Gazette,* a frequent contributor to *Kennel Review,* and a newspaper columnist. Her column won awards for eleven consecutive years from the Dog Writers Association of America.

Vance, Jerry and Helen — *Mount Forest* — Lincoln, NB

The Vances started their kennel in the early 1960s. Today they have nine Irish Setters and a thriving kennel, handling and training business.

Housed at Mount Forest are three generations of champions: Ch. Mount Forest Jackson, Best of Breed at the 1970 Regional Specialty; his daughter, Ch. Mount Forest Bee-Bee; and her Ch. Courtwood Summer Forecast son, Ch. Mount Forest Special Mascot.

. Kimberlin O'Killea of Top 'O
. Thenderin William Muldoon
Ch. Kimberlin Kyrie).

. Ballycroy's Northern Sunset
. Tirvelda Nor'Wester ex
lycroy's Rua Catlin).

. Rockerin Bandilane Bridget
n. Can. & Bda. Ch. Kincora
zing Banner ex Ch. Rockerin
ce).

Bee-Bee had a litter by Ch. Tirvelda Telstar and the first to be shown, Mount Forest Hi Noon, was Best in Sweepstakes at the Tulsa Oklahoma Specialty in November 1978.

Viola, Ernest and Joan — *Kinvale* — Huntington, LI, NY

Ernie's first Irish Setter was purchased from Kelly Fox (Kilkara) in 1964. "Bran" obtained his CD in 4 shows; his three qualifying scores were all over 190. "Bran" became Ch. Kilkara Firebrand, CD, amateur owner-handled completely by Ernie. In 1966, Ernie went back and bought a puppy bitch from Kelly. She became Ch. Kilkara Fireflame, CD—obtaining her CD in 3 consecutive shows and amateur owner-handled to her championship. "Flame" became Kinvale's foundation bitch. She has had three litters (1969, 1972 and 1973) and is the dam of their male, Kinvale Robin Hood (sire Ch. Tirvelda Michaelson). In 1971 Kinvale Tara (Ch. Tirvelda Nor'Wester ex Ch. Kilkara Fireflame, CD) had a litter of 9 sired by Ch. Tirvelda Middle Brother. Out of this breeding came their Specials bitch, Ch. Kinvale Majorette of Kendel, CD, co-owned with Mrs. Dana Haskell. "Sandy" finished completely from the Bred by bitch class, Ernie handling. She had several BOBs, and many BOS's (including Westminster 1975 and the ISCA 1977 National Specialty). The Violas also owned Mundy, CD (Joan's first Irish), Kinvale Kelly, Kinvale Andrew (co-owned with Suellen Williams) and Dariabar Kinvale Keepsake (co-owned with Harriet T. Burkart). Two of the Viola daughters, Megan and Heather, did well in Junior Showmanship.

Ernie and Joan are past presidents of the Irish Setter Club of Long Island, and Joan was a Recording Secretary of the Irish Setter Club of America.

Wagoner, Marsha S. — *Rockmoor* — Austin, TX

Owner of Tirvelda Bright Legend, Tirvelda Free Spirit, Donmaura Indian Emerald.

Watters, Mary Therese — *TippeCork* — Spring Lake, MI

The foundation dam of TippeCork was Lady Patrick O'Donohoe T.C., of Argo Lane and Sunnymoor breeding. From this foundation they have produced Am. & Can. Ch. Lady Tress O'Donohoe T.C., winner of the ISCA Glendee BOS award for 1973. Tress' notable children and grandchildren are: Am. & Can. Ch. Autumn Storm T.C. (son); Ch. Runwild Brian O'Donohoe (son); Am. & Can. Ch. Apacheacre T.C. Shirli, Am. & Can. CD (granddaughter); Apacheacre T.C. Luci, UD (pointed) (granddaughter); Apacheacre T.C. Jumpin Ginni, CD (granddaughter); Apacheacre T.C. Andrea, Am. & Can. CDX (pointed) (granddaughter); Apacheacre T.C. Betti, (pointed) (granddaughter).

Tress, Brian, Lady Mary Ellen Murphy, T.C.—a Tress daughter and dam of the Apacheacre litter, have field placements as do O'Donohoe T.C. (Tress' litter brother) and their first field trial dog, Mistress Molly Monahan T.C., a Lady Patrick granddaughter.

TippeCork are also the breeders of Am. & Can. Ch. SandPiper of Erin, TippeCork's Shiela Ne Gara (pointed) and Argo Lane's High King (pointed) from Am. & Can. Ch. Argo Lane Gay Victoria, CD, a Tress half-sister.

Weick, Paul and Lorraine — *Starheir* — Ohio

Although there is no longer a Starheir Kennels and Lorraine is the wife of Louis D. Smith, an Irish Setter breeder and judge, it is important to give the Starheir background for the sake of Irish Setter history.

After several unfortunate starts, Paul and Lorraine purchased Ch. Shannon's Susie Starlet (as a baby puppy) and Merry Dell's Darlin' Debutante. The latter was a full-sister of the renowned Ch. Merry Dell's Autumn Glory. Debutante had to be put down at two with an esophageal problem, and Von and Dorothy Hobbs gave the Weicks Ch. Merry Dell's Heiress as a replacement—incidentally hence the kennel name, Starlet + Heiress = Starheir.

Susie Starlet produced six champions for Starheir in three litters. The first litter by Ch. Fleetwood Farm Brougham produced two Best in Show winners; the famous Ch. Starheir's Aaron Ardee and Ch. Starheir's Audacious Miss.

The second litter, sired by Ch. Bronze Blaze of Tamarisk, produced Ch. Starheir's Donovan O'Briarwood and Ch. Starheir's Dianthus.

The third litter, again sired by Brougham, contained Ch. Fleetwood Farms Grand Marshall, who won the points at the first Irish Setter National Specialty and Ch. Starheir's Quest For Glory.

The Weicks also bred four other champions, and purchased as a puppy, finished and specialed, Ch. Bronze Blaze of Tamarisk.

Pride of place, of course, and of interest to breed historians is the renowned Aaron Ardee. His Best in Shows and Group wins piloted by Dick Cooper are legendary, and according to his stud ads he has defeated more Irish Setters than any other dog in history. (Repeated attempts to elicit information on the Fleetwood Farms Kennels, who owned Aaron Ardee, have met with failure.)

Paul and Lorraine sold Aaron Ardee ("Chance") as a show prospect to a couple who wanted to show but never got started, in spite of the Weicks' encouragement. Finally the Weicks gave up. One day, out of the blue, when "Chance" was almost three, this couple called to ask if the Weicks wanted to repurchase their "pet." Paul rushed over before they could change their minds, acquired "Chance" and turned him over to Tommy Glassford who quickly finished him—they thought. Brought out as a Special for the first time at Sewickley, I had the pleasure of giving him a Group 3, but then came a letter from the AKC saying that "Chance" still needed one point to complete his title. Since Tommy was then tied up with another class dog, Dick Becker finished him at his first show a couple of months later.

Somewhere at one of the shows Dick Cooper had seen "Chance" and been much impressed. He felt that the Rumbaughs would be interested in this dog as they owned his sire. Dick asked Dr. Helferty to make the initial contact for him and the rest is history. The Rumbaughs purchased the new champion and "Chance," so aptly named, was on his way to breed immortality.

Paul, a former director of the ISCA, is presently completely involved with Papillons, but now that Lou is judging Lorraine comes to many Irish events.

Weizenegger, Col. and Mrs. J. A. — Jacksonville, FL

Audiences enjoy watching the Weizenegger dogs perform in the Obedience rings. The dogs love their work so much they are apt to clown, which brings the house down with laughter. That the Colonel and his lady know how to train with a light but firm hand is demonstrated by their three title-holders: McGeehan's Mahogany Shandon, UD; Tirvelda Ulster King, UD, and Princess Mavourneen, UD.

Wells, Jacquie — *Encore* — Van Nuys, CA

Jackie has shown Irish since the early 1970s. She owns Flashback Celebration, a winning daughter of Ch. Padre Island Sea Storm, bred by Dr. Selma Stoll.

Westra, Kenneth G. and Katja — *Krisfield* — Brookeville, MD

Their first Irish Setter, Krisfield Rivendell Redstone, CD, a Ch. Tirvelda Earl of Harewood grandson, was the winner of the ISCA Companion Dog Trophy, Dog World Award of Canine Distinction and three Highest scoring dog in trials, with scores of 197½, 197½, 199½, 196½, 197 and 197 for six consecutive shows. They presently own Wenvarra Krisfield Drumbeat, purchased from the Bermans. Ken has been a president of the Potomac Irish Setter Club.

Wheatley, Frank and Katherine — *Rockerin* — South Rockwood, MI

The Wheatleys purchased their first Irish Setter from Maple Ridge Kennels in 1953, Ch. Red Rogue of Maple Ridge, a Thenderin Brian Tristan son out of Crosshaven Lea of Maple Ridge who provided them with many unforgettable moments on the way to his title. Before his untimely death, at six years, Red Rogue sired ten champions, two Best in Show Dogs.

One of these was Ch. Conifer's Lance. In 1961, Lance was the top winning Irish Setter in the nation. His Best in Show at Chicago International was a brilliant victory for the breed. Lance won the ISCA Best Sire award in 1963. Again fate seemed to take a hand, for Lance died suddenly at the age of 6½, but not before he had sired 15 champions.

It was while showing Lance that the Wheatleys acquired Ch. Caldene Ailene through the late Dr. Jay W. Calhoon. This magnificent bitch highlighted her rather brief show career with BOW and BOS from the classes at the New York specialty in 1961. She was the first bitch to win Best of Breed at the Irish Setter Club of Michigan Specialty and was BOS at the Garden in 1962.

Ailene, bred to Rockherin Flynn—a Lance grandson, produced one of their finest litters, which included Ch. Rockherin Race and Ch. Rockherin Rebecca. Race finished undefeated in five straight shows. Rebecca topped an exciting show career with Best of Breed at the Combined Specialties in 1971. The latter is now proving a great producer, being the dam of Ch. Tirvelda Hunter's Moon, winner of many Group firsts, Ch. Tirvelda Vanity Fair, Ch. Rebecca's Irish Lace, Am. & Can. Ch. McCamon's Royal Burgundy, a Canadian Best in Show winner and Best of Winners at the 1974 National Specialty of the Irish Setter Club of America.

The Wheatleys co-own (with Cindy Trefrey) Ch. Rockerin Bandilane Bridget. When bred to Ch. McCamon Marquis, Bridget produced Ch. Rockerin Raffin (Wheatley) and Ch. Rockerin Follow the Sun (Dale Hood and Cindy Trefrey). Bred to Ch. Meadowlark's Anticipation, she produced Ch. Rockerin Royale Guardsman (Latimer) and Ch. Rockerin Royal Ragen (Wheatley).

Frank is a popular judge of Irish Setters.

Wilson, Cary A. and Karen C. — *Karengary* — Manassas, VA

In 1967 the Wilsons obtained their first Irish Setter. Ch. Killagay's Cinnamon Charlin, CD. She was owner-handled to her championship in top West and East Coast competition. Cinnamon was the foundation bitch of Karengary; to combine East and West Coast lines, she was bred to Ch. Bayberry Tobago, and produced Group winner Ch. Karengary's Klassic, and his stylish sisters Karengary's Keepsake and Karengary's Exquisite. The Wilsons also have bred a number of well-known Airedales.

Windhorn, Lorelei — *Sallynoggin* — Seattle, WA

Lorelei is one of the lucky ones who started in Irish as a child. Her first Irish was acquired when she was 11 in 1964. Her first champion came along in 1970, Am.

Ch. Rockerin Race (Rockerin Flynn ex Ch. Caldene Ailene).

Ch. Mount Forest Bee Bee (Ch. Mount Forest Jackson ex Jo-Ett's Hazel Nut O'Bonner).

Ch. Tirvelda Earl of Harewood (Ch. Michael Bryan Duke of Sussex ex Ch. Tirvelda Nutbrown Sherry).

& Can. Ch. Tarywood's Boomerang, CDX. Boomerang is the dam of Can. Ch. Sallynoggin Camelar Flik O'Sun and the field trial winner Sallynoggin Accent on Autumn, CD. In 1975, the lovely bitch Ch. Bayberry Happy Time, CD, was acquired and was bred to Ch. Candia Indeed. One of this litter is now Am. & Can. Ch. Sallynoggin Happy Ending, CD, owned by Lorelei, Scott Thomson and Susan Van Dyke. Happy Ending finished her championship by winning the breed from the classes and then going on to Group 1 at the Sammamish KC in August 1978, and has since won a second Group at the Dog Fanciers Association of Oregon. Also from Indeed and Happy Time is Ch. Charlton's Indeed I Do, owned by Mrs. Thomas Arland.

Another at Sallynoggin is Am. & Can. Ch. Afterglo Happy Talk, CD (Ch. Tirvelda Earl of Harewood ex Ch. Bayberry Happy Time) who had a 1978 litter by Ch. McCamon Marquis.

Associated with Lorelei in the ownership of most of the dogs is Scott Thomson, whose kennel name is Camelar. In 1971, he acquired a puppy by Ch. Bayberry Tobago ex Ch. Bayberry Sonnet who was to become Ch. Bayberry Free Spirit. She had a 1977 litter by Ch. Candia Indeed, and one of these had a Canadian Specialty win at a year of age. Scott is an excellent handler and has handled his and all the co-owned dogs to their championships.

Wilson, Dave and Ruth — *Wilson Farms* — Volant, PA
In the early 1940s the Wilsons obtained daughters of Ch. Milson Topnotcher, Ch. Tirvelda Storm Lark and Ch. Kleiglight of Aragon. From only a few litters they concentrated primarily on field dogs for themselves.

In 1965, they decided to take a much more active position in the breed and with Dave giving up dairying, they had the space and more time to devote to the Setters. They purchased Cherry Point Grouse, a daughter of Ch. Yorkhill Achilles ex Ch. End O'Maine Morning Bird, and Tirvelda Toma Maid, by Ch. Wautoma ex Ch. Hartsbourne Sallyann of Tirvelda. Toma Maid finished her championship, but Grouse died unexpectedly with seven points to her name. Both produced winners for Wilson Farms, and the latter produced the great brood bitch, Ch. Wilson Farm Partridge.

They then purchased Tirvelda Earl of Harewood from Tirvelda. Earl acquired his points rapidly. He was sold to the Wilsons needing only his last major, and he obtained this two weeks after his purchase by going from the classes to Best of Breed at the Potomac Irish Setter Specialty. Earl is the sire of thirty champions. More is written of him and his littermates in the story of Tirvelda.

One of the highlights of the Wilsons' many noted successes in the breed was the honor of having produced Ch. Mos'n Acre Wilson Farm Harmony. This lovely daughter of Earl and Ch. Wilson Farm Country Charm placed Best of Breed at the first National Specialty of the Irish Setter Club of America.

Dave and Ruth, having had problems with P.R.A., decided to test-mate all their breeding stock. This has been done and now all their dogs are test-mated clear. In so doing they acquired Am. & Can. Ch. Rich-Lee Wilson Farm Brandy. Brandy, a double grandson of Earl, is the winner of 11 Sporting groups. He has also been successfully test-mated.

Although now primarily concerned with the bench, Wilson Farms is yet another kennel closely identified with the field. Dave's original interest was with Irish Setters as shooting dogs, and he has made sure the dogs he raises can hunt.

Wilson Farm Partridge (Ch. erry Point Brask II ex Cherry nt Grouse).

Wilson Farm Touch of Class . Santera Tristan Troubadour Ch. Wilson Farm Tiffany).

Kinvale Majorette of Kendel . Tirvelda Middle Brother ex vale Tara).

Ch. Tirvelda Red Baron of Dun-
holm (Ch. Tirvelda Michaelson ex
Am. & Can. Ch. Tirvelda Bridget
Susie Ann).

Witherington, Larry and Cheryl — *Cherwyn* — Pinellas Park, FL

Cheryl has been around show dogs all her life, as both parents are professional handlers. Her parents raised Miniature Schnauzers and Pomeranians, and at the age of twelve Cheryl acquired her first Irish Setter from the Savorys in 1968. She showed her in Junior Showmanship and later put a CD on her. Then in November of 1969, Cheryl acquired her most noted dog, Ch. Tirvelda Red Baron of Dunholm, at the age of three months. He was entirely owner-handled and finished with four majors, one of which was obtained by going Best of Winners at Westminster in 1972. In May of 1972 Baron got his first of six Bests in Show, and in 1973 Cheryl and Baron placed second in the Junior Showmanship finals at Westminster. In 1974 Baron went Best of Breed and Group third at Westminster. Baron was in the top ten Irish Setters for three years and retired with the very impressive show record of 6 Bests in Show, 27 Group 1st, 28 other placements and 74 Bests of Breed, all owner-handled.

Cherwyn is a small kennel; since 1968 only five litters have been whelped for a total of 35 puppies. Two winners are Am. & Can. Ch. Cherwyns Trojan Warrior, who was BOS Sweepstakes at the 1st National Irish Setter Specialty, and finished (all but one point) from the Bred by Exhibitor class, and Cherwyns Erin go Bragh o'Han, a Group winner from the classes.

Wright, Dr. Roy and Chesta — *Callaway* — Tacoma, WA

Roy, a veterinarian with a very active practice, and Chesta started in Irish in 1967.

Their first was Can. Ch. Rivercrest Pride of Shannon, who they bred to Am., Can. & Mex. Ch. Legend of Varagon, UDT, producing Am. & Can. Ch. Callaway's Legacy of Sheila, CD; Am. & Can. Ch. Callaway's Kamron Casey, CD; Can. Ch. Callaway's Kamron Muldoon, CD, and Callaway's Shamrock Shamus who had points in Canada and the U.S. before his untimely death. Callaway's Tara of Clover Park, bred to Am. & Can. Ch. Varagon's After Glow produced the Specialty winning Am. & Can. Ch. Callaway's Classic Afterglo.

In 1973, the Wrights purchased a young bitch from Carol Burgasser and Renee Taylor. She became Ch. Shalimar Kai of Callaway, and was the top winning bitch in the country the year she was shown. In 1978 she was bred to Afterglo, and from this breeding Callaway hopes to produce its future champions.

Roy and Chesta are active in local and national Irish Setter Clubs and Roy serves on the Board of the American Irish Setter Foundation.

Yates, William and Grace Ann — *Wmgay* — Beale AFB, CA

The Yates' got their first Setter in 1964. Among those they have bred or owned are Ch. Tirvelda Celt Legend of Wmgay, Can. Ch. Wmgay Ain't Misbehavin, Can. Ch. Wmgay Patrick Henry and Can. Ch. Tirvelda Vanessa.

The nomad life in the U.S.A.F. hasn't prevented Grace Ann and Bill from keeping Irish Setters. Grace Ann was an Iowa farm girl. Bill was a son of a noted goose and duck hunter who served as guide to many noted sportsmen including Adlai E. Stevenson and Governors Steele and Craige. Much of this rubbed off on Bill and he learned to hunt with dogs at an early age.

The Yates' first Irish Setters were mostly field breeding and one, Wildfire Meridell, left his mark on many of the Texas pedigrees when Bill was stationed in that state.

Moving to Plattsburgh, New York, they bred their original bitch to Ch. Tirvelda Jim O'Shea, a dog little used and almost lost from view because of his location. Jim was a full brother of Chs. Nutbrown Sherry and Sybil, and in a short but successful show career enjoyed a brief moment of special glory when he came from the classes to defeat Rio Hondo, when the latter was all but invincible. From this breeding the Yates kept Ch. Wmgay Ain't Misbehavin.

Then, from Tirvelda they purchased Ch. Tirvelda Kensington Red. He had just finished his American title in seven weeks with three majors, including a 5-pt. win in his first show. He was the eleventh and last to finish in the litter by Ch. Michael Bryan Duke of Sussex ex Ch. Tirvelda Nutbrown Sherry. The Yates took Red to his Canadian title and, then until he was ten, and the Yates were transferred to Texas, Red remained unused and forgotten in the remoteness of Plattsburgh.

After Texas came California, and after winning the Veterans class at the Far West Specialty, Red sired a few litters just before his death at thirteen.

Fine dogs from many kennels end up in remote areas, and are never heard from again. It is interesting to speculate—how many potentially valuable studs and brood bitches have been lost to the breed in this way?

Zirkle, Jay and Kellie — *Dunbrook* — Eugene, OR

Jay and Kellie started with their first Irish Setter in 1966, Ch. Tirnanog Charleen O'Duibhin, CD (Ch. Muckamoor's Marty McCuhl ex Glen Erin's Satin Sheen), and their first litter in 1968 from Varagon Crimson Classic, CD (Ch. Crimson Satan of Varagon, CD ex Burgundy Belle of Varagon). They have bred the following champions from their occasional litters: Dunbrook Debonaire, Dunbrook Dream, CD, Dunbrook Escapade, Dunbrook Enchantment, Dunbrook Glamour Girl, and Dunbrook Love Is Blue.

All were amateur-handled to their respective titles. Glamour Girl won two Sporting Groups in 1976 from the Open Bitch Class to become the first Irish Setter bitch to win the Sporting Group in over ten years in the Pacific Northwest. Five of the champions are at home with the Zirkles. Jay is a past Treasurer of the Irish Setter Club of America, and has served on its Board of Directors.

Fld. Ch. Ike Jack Kendrick
(Ike Kendrick-Fld. Ch. Askew's Carolina Lady).

Willow Winds Hobo
(Rusty's Jinx-Willow Winds Eve).

9

The Irish Setter
In The Field

THE first Irish Setter to win a scheduled field trial according to available literature was Queen owned by Charles V. Kaeding, a San Francisco sporting goods dealer. It was a match race with four starters at $50 per entry, held in Marin County, California, in 1870.

Another purely local event was run October 8, 1874, a few miles from Memphis by the Tennessee State Sportsmen's Association. In the Free-For-All Stake with an entry of ten gundogs, H. C. Pritchett's black setter, Knight, placed first and J. H. Drew's red and white setter placed fourth.

The second Memphis trial the following year was a battle between the native bird dogs and the blue-blooded imports from Europe. Imported English Setters won all three places in the Puppy Stake; but the native red and white setter Tom (Joe - Buck Sr.), owned by George W. Campbell, Spring Hill, Tennessee, won the Free-For-All Champion Stake (5 starters).

Tom was a rugged dog with plenty of pace, range and class. Campbell, who handled him, was a big fellow with a voice to fit his size. As he walked through a cornfield he would fill his pockets with ears of corn. When Tom came tearing by, George would yell and fire an ear at him. Then Tom, a hard-headed rascal, would turn on more speed and get as far away as possible. This was the first Irish Setter to win a Championship Stake. He was said to be an excellent shooting dog and bevy finder. Colonel Hughes of Texas paid $300 for him, a good price in those days.

At the fourth annual Tennessee trials held on General Harding's Belle Meade Estate near Nashville, the famous English Setter Gladstone won the Puppy Stake and the native red setter, Joe Jr., owned by M. C. Campbell, won the Champion Stake (20 starters).

Fld. Ch. Oxton's Shosaph (Oxton's Irish Perfection ex Oxton's Imp O'Erin) and owner Sally Huizenga in 1952.

Fld. Ch. Countess Shamrock Rose, CDX (Donnington Cadence Count ex Siobhan Bridget Kendrick), receiving award at ISCA National Field Trial, 1974. Trained and handled by J.D. Huizenga.

The battle between the blue bloods and the natives was reopened in 1878, at the fifth and last Tennessee Association trials when Joe Jr. and Adam's Drake tied for first place in the Champion Stake.

Probably the culmination of the feud was the two-day match race on quail at Florence, Alabama, in December 1879, when the native red setter, Joe Jr., defeated the renowned English Setter Gladstone by a score of 61 to 52 points. Joe was a fast dog with a wonderful nose and great bird sense. Bigger than average, he traveled with a long-stretching, wolf-like gait. He was red with a little white and was registered as an Irish Setter. His sire was the noted Irish Setter Ch. Elcho and his dam was the native cross-bred Buck Jr., (old Joe - Buck Sr.) of the Campbell strain.

During the next decade Ch. Elcho's progeny (Berkley, Raleigh, Jessie, Leigh Doane, Yoube and Bruce) were prominent in the trials of the Fishers Island, Eastern and Philadelphia Clubs. Raleigh, probably the best of them, placed second in the All-Age Stake at Robins Island in 1879. Since the trials were infrequent and open to all breeds, they evidently were highly competitive. The significant thing about this period was that the Irish Setter owners ran their bench dogs in the field trials and also used them as shooting dogs.

Max Wenzel, one of the founders of the Fishers Island Club and active in promoting the red setter afield, owned Ch. Tim, Ch. Yoube and Jersey Beauty. His Ch. Chief, a field trial winner, sired six field trial dogs of about average merit. J. S. McIntosh's Biz placed in two major circuit trials in the Midwest; Victoria and imported Desmond II won several All-Age Stakes in the vicinity of Philadelphia.

But field trials were not going too well for the Irish Setter. Like other breeds he had his ups and downs. In spite of an occasional win by an exceptional red dog, the trend for him was not bright. Until about 1890, he had competed with other breeds on even terms. As the number and popularity of field trials increased, Llewellin Setters and Pointers flourished. Imported in overwhelming numbers, they were bred solely for field trial use. "100% Llewellin" was all the rage; Rip Rap and Jingo were magic names! No longer was the all-purpose shooting dog in vogue. Field trials had changed, had become a specialized activity. With dogs worked from horseback, more emphasis was placed on speed and range. An early maturing dog, fast in getaway, wide going to locate many coveys and stylish on point was required. A dog had to be bred for all these qualities, and it was not sufficient that he just possess the instinct to hunt.

Because Irish Setters had not been bred to meet these new specifications, they lost out in major circuit competition. Hoping to improve the situation the breeders imported field stock like Finglas (Fingal III - Aveline) and his litter sister, Coleraine. The former was the Absolute Winner All-Age Stake, American Field Trial Club, 1892 (21 starters). Seven of his progeny placed in trials: Fingaln, Loo, Currer Maud, Donoway, Flyaway, Nugget II and Lady Finglas.

The inaugural trials of the Irish Setter Club were held at High Point,

Fld. Ch. Faith Farm Lehigh Little Bit (Buddwing ex Kopper Key Ginger).

Dual Ch. Tyrone Mahogany Mike CDX (Lord Tyrone Trent ex McIvor's Kathleen, CD).

Fld. Ch. Ivor Glen Duffy O'Mi (Loo's Mike-O-Shane ex Jocely D'Guibhas Lech'Uisg).

North Carolina, on November 23, 1891. There were four annual Carolina trials at which the dogs of George E. Gray, Dr. Gwilym G. Davis and E. B. Bishop predominated. Gray was a professional trainer of field dogs, Davis was long the President of the Irish Setter Club and Bishop was proprietor of the Glenmore Kennels in Kansas.

In general, the picture for the first 20 years of the twentieth century was not encouraging, for according to the records there were only 18 Irish Setter field trial placements in open stakes during that period. Five of these wins were obtained by the Law strain dogs of F. A. Johnson of Detroit, who made a sincere effort to further the cause of the red setter afield.

It was during this era that the Fremont, Nebraska, fancier, Otto Pohl assembled his Donegal Kennels of Irish Setters with a similar purpose in mind. He was making good progress toward that goal when his death occurred in 1919. He had acquired the native hunting stock of the Midwest in Ch. Drug Law, Ch. Pat-A-Belle and McKerry. From the West Coast came Ch. St. Lambert's Caltra M and Donegal's Noreen, representing the old California hunting strains. In addition there were his English imports Ch. Rheola Clanderrick, Rheola Judy, Rheola Pedro and Morty Oge. The small, dark mahogany Pedro was reputedly the best field dog among them.

A prefix to gain considerable notoriety about this time was "Smada," which spelled backwards referred to Dr. L. C. Adams, one of the early presidents of the Dayton Pointer Club. This sportsman, who had owned Irish Setters for thirty years, obtained the Donegal dogs after Pohl died; and he raised a few litters from them, in one of which was Donegal Morty Oge II (Donegal's Morty Oge - Donegal's Noreen). Morty II sired two champions, but his real claim to fame lay in being the sire of that famous little field trial winner, Smada Byrd.

Dr. Adams was the breeder of the litter whelped in 1921, from Killarney Babe of utility stock. J. Horace Lytle of Dayton, dog writer and field trial judge, obtained Byrd as a puppy, trained her, handled her in trials and cherished her unil her death in 1935. Much of her success afield might be attributed to the bond of affection and mutual understanding which existed between the little setter and her master. The pride, joy, tribulations and triumphs of a field trial man are described by Lytle in his fascinating biography of Smada Byrd, *Breaking A Bird Dog* (1924). In her busy field trial career, Byrd placed in strong open competition at eight Class B Midwestern trials, which had a total of 139 starters. She had two litters sired by King, in the first of which was Smada Byrd's King, which was advertised at stud by Lytle for a number of years.

Some excellent field trial stock has come from Ireland. A popular import was Tipperary Eamon, brought to America by G. O. Smith in 1920. Everyone had a good word to say about this dog. In a short three-year period he sired 47 litters, which included four field trial winners: Tipperary Eamon's Ghost, Tipperary's Bell, Tipperary June and Queen Alizon.

Every part of the country had its field trial advocates. In California Irish Setters were represented for a number of years by the Valley View prefix of Dr. J. C. Negley of Los Angeles. His initial stock came from Dr. R. H. Washburn of Colorado, who raised ten litters from one pair of setters, his own Major Clanderrick and Patsy Jane Law. Negley obtained Valley View Peggy from one of these matings and bred her to Duke Clanderrick, thereby making a double cross to imported Ch. Rheola Clanderrick. Thus came to be Valley View Jiggs, the prolific sire of more than 200 registered dogs from 46 bitches. The fact that one third of his puppies bore the name of "Jiggs" is an excellent example that advertising pays, for this setter was widely publicized as a producer of field dogs. Perhaps the greatest of his offspring was Ch. Valley View Pat, a bench champion as well as a field trial winner. Other progeny of note were Valley View Ruddy, Valley View Butterfly, Valley View Hogan and Valley View Dinty.

About 1932, the new field trial rules of the American Kennel Club became effective. To acquire the title of field champion, a setter had to obtain a total of ten points by winning first place at approved field trials, the number of points per stake being based on the number of starters in the stake. Under the *American Field* rules, the winner of a designated championship stake was referred to as a field trial champion, but if the dog's performance was not considered of championship calibre, the title was withheld by the judges.

The turn of events at this period more or less classified the Irish Setter field trial dogs into those that placed in restricted breed trials and those that won in open competition against Pointers, English Setters and other breeds. Very few Irish Setters competed in the major circuit trials, but there was a marked increase in the number of entries in Irish Setter Stakes at the all-breed trials and the specialty club events. About this time the Western Pointer and Setter Club, Jersey Irish Setter Club, Irish Setter Club of Southern California, Irish Setter Club of New England and others held field trials.

The Irish Setter Club of America, which renewed its field trial program in 1927, had an impressive list of first place winners in the All-Age Stakes of the pre-war years.

Fld. Ch. Elcova McTybe (Ch. Elcova's Terence McSwiney - Modoc Bedelia), the first Irish Setter field champion under the new American Kennel Club rules, sired seven field trial winners.

A consistent winner at a score of Eastern trials in open competition over a ten-year period was J. H. Graham's Duke IX of Canadian breeding. Among the noted Hibernian color-bearers from Massachusetts was Sally of Kildare, owned by Patrick W. Hehir, who also had Polly of Kildare, Lassie of Kildare and Bright Eyes O'Kildare.

H.A. Simms' Fld. Ch. Tipperary McKerry (Skyline Valley's Red - Betsy McKerry) had more than a dozen field trial wins, most of which were in open competition with other breeds. Another field Irish Setter of similar bloodlines was Skyline Ephraim (Skyline Tex - Princess McKerry's Pat), owned by the noted Pennsylvania judge, Thomas M. Marshall. Charles M.

ial Ch. Duffin Miss Duffy, CD
Merry Dell's Gay Gremlin ex
rbu Miss Duffy).

n. Ivor Glen Gorgeous George
Ch. Carcey's Kim-O-Mike ex Ivor
len Red Colleen).

annon's Irish Mike (Fld. Ch. Ivor
len's Duffy' O'Mike ex Kunkel's
rimson Brooke).

Coale's Lehigh Pat, a grandson of Rheola Pedro and Donegal's Morty Oge II, was a favorite of Pennsylvania sportsmen. Then there was Fld. Ch. Uncle Ned R (Chamois R - R. Belle), owned by Alvin R. Bush. Among his contemporaries were Padriag Reddleman, Wheeler's Rusty, Niall of Aileach, Paul's Andy and Judge Red Pal of Oakdene. Jack Spear's Tyronne Farm Lady placed in several Open All-Age Stakes at Missouri Valley trials. Other winners from his kennels included Tyronne Farm Collette, Malone, O'Flare, Red Robin and Monahan. On the West Coast, Mason's Bridget O'Flynn was a well-known field trial Irish Setter.

The Sulhamstead Kennels of Mrs. Florence Nagle of England, which bred so many splendid field trial setters from 1925 to 1965, were represented in American trials of the pre-war period by Sulhamstead Beppo D'Or and Sulhamstead Trace D'Or, both imported by Ernest D. Levering.

In 1976 Mrs. Nagle moved to Maryland. Unfortunately, no dogs came with her, but her valuable, extensive collection of paintings, show catalogues, pictures and records reside permanently in the Baltimore County S.P.C.A. Exhibition Hall.

S. L. Taylor, Mount Sterling, Kentucky, owned a prepotent sire of good field stock called Joffre Rookwood (Appreciation Joffre - Walters' Fay), an honest-to-goodness bird dog, big going, with brains and bird sense. He would rapidly cover a 40-acre field and snap decisively into a stylish point on locating quail. His owner posted "a $1000 wager against any Irishman his age as a shooting dog in the field"—and no one ever challenged it. Joffre was solid red, compact in build and about 24 inches at the shoulder. Although he himself was never entered in field trials, he was the sire of eight field trial winners. His progeny must have numbered several hundred, for most American-bred shooting dogs of the Fifties had him as an ancestor. In fact later on, Taylor sold numerous puppies sired by Joffre's great grandson Rookwood's Field Master and out of Trace D'Or's Belle, a daughter of Sulhamstead Trace D'Or.

There were certain breeders in various parts of the country who bred and sold Irish Setters shooting dogs without much regard to their bench qualifications. These persons, recognizing the fundamental importance of intensity, style and staunchness on point in a gun dog, used only certain hunting strains. The blood of McKerry, Morty Oge, Rheola Clanderrick, Tipperary Eamon, Raneagown, Smada Byrd, Rufus McTybe O'Cloisters, Chieftain Law, Joffre Rookwood and many others seemed to carry the instinct to point and to retrieve naturally from land and water; also Jordan Farm Abe was considered a good dog to have in any pedigree.

Among those breeders of field stock were W.J. Thayer, Bergen, N.Y. with Skyline Tobias; Mrs. Beatrice Everett, Atkinson, Neb. with Everett's Irish Skipper; Les Blackwell, Sacramento, Calif. with Sulhamstead Major D'Or; E. A. Smith, Clover, S.C. with Tipperary Smada King; Bill Duncan, Weston, Mo. with Boyne's Carolina Pat; J. E. Hill, Ward, Ark. with Hill's Rambling Red; Earl Bond, Albert Lea, Minn. with Kentucky Bill.

& Amateur Fld. Ch. Sunny of
Glen (Alley Oop ex Lar's
antha Dawn O'Ouf).

& Amateur Fld. Ch. Devilera
or Glen (Cannon's Irish Duke
d. & Amateur Fld. Ch. Sunny
or Glen).

Glen Spud (Cannon's Irish
e ex Fld. & Amateur Fld. Ch.
y of Ivor Glen).

In the early Fifties a group of sportsmen was organized under the banner of the National Red Setter Field Trial Club for the purpose of promoting the Irish Setter afield. Among the members were A. E. Church, A. E. Bortz, R. C. Baynard, Herm David, W. E. LeGrande, J. G. Cassidy, J. T. Clifton, John Van Alst, Charles Winter, T. P. Ward, Robert and James Finn, D. Martin and others. They held semi-annual field trials for the red dog alternately in Delaware and Ohio, the first event being on April 13, 1952.

The first National Red Setter Open Shooting Dog Championship Stake, run on October 17, 1953, was won by Askew's Carolina Lady (Kentucky Bill - Poker Faced Alice), although the title was withheld. In spite of the fact that Lady failed to obtain the championship crown on this occasion, she gave many fine performances in her long career, and later was awarded the title of AKC field champion. She won at least 28 stakes, most of them in open competition, defeating more than 300 dogs.

Her forte was not only in winning at trials—she did that in between litters—but it was as the great producing dam of 15 field trial winners and the granddam of many more. She had six litters by Ike Kendrick, Ike Jack Kendrick, Willow Winds Duke and Willow Winds Hobo.

Lady, a key bitch in the Willow Winds breeding program of Ned LeGrande, was bred by Earl Bond, Albert Lea, Minnesota, from a mating that was repeated six times. Her sire was from the Rookwood Kennels of S. L. Taylor in Kentucky and her dam represented Minnesota and Western Illinois hunting stock. She had the ability to convey to her offspring that quality of exceptional style on point for which she was famous. It is said that she even stamped her progeny with a few white hairs on the chin as though they were her trademark.

In 1972, AKC Fld. Ch. Askew's Carolina Lady was elected to the Field Trial Hall of Fame, sponsored by the American Field. She was the first Irish Setter, and the only one to date, to be so honored.

The most noted of her sons was Fld. Ch. Ike Jack Kendrick, the winningest Irish Setter in field trials, having placed in 66 stakes. He never was started in the Puppy and Derby Stakes; most of his wins were obtained in Open Shooting Dog Stakes.

"Happy Jack," as he was called, was a plucky, little, perfectly trained shooting dog that possessed great heart and a most appealing personality. Afield he was conscientious and thorough, exhibiting unusual endurance and stamina. Like his dam, he pointed and backed with high style. Appearancewise, he was a small, compact, dark red setter, strong in loin and hard as nails.

At least 30 bitches were mated to Jack, some of which had several litters sired by him. The records of his 40 or more field trial winning get are evidence of his great worth to the breed. Among these get are such well-known ones as Fld. Ch. Windyridge Tammy, Shooting Dog Ch. Lady's Queen, Shadycrest Shawn, Taylor's Whirlaway Pat, Moffat's Apache Bill, Thorleen and others with impressive field trial wins. The progeny by Jack

ual Ch. Mahogany Titian Duke,
D (Mahogany Tim II ex King Size
arlet Lady).

ual Ch. Mahogany Titian Jingo
ual Ch. Mahogany Titian Duke,
D ex Mahogany's Miss Fire Ball).

d. Ch. O'Lannon's Titian Boyd
ual Ch. Mahogany Titian Jingo
x O'Lannon's Lucky Lady).

out of F. Ch. Askew's Carolina Lady, Lady's Colleen and Willow Winds Kate, seemed to be especially successful at the trials. It is fortunate that several of Jack's sons have carried on as producing sires, including in addition to those named previously, Bruns Red Ike, Draherin Lord Kendrick, Phil's Red Ike, Mike's Jack Dandy, Cherry Point Nickjack, Lady's Last Son.

Besides Lady and Jack, LeGrande owned Willow Winds Smada and Citation Lass of Ardee as foundation stock in his Willow Winds Kennels at Douglassville, Pennsylvania. Then with the infusion of early American hunting strains, represented by Royal Red Patrick of Erin and that old campaigner Rusty's Jinx, he began his breeding program. About 1955, he imported for outcross purposes Sulhamstead Norse D'Or (Shane) from Mrs. Florence Nagle of England; and found afterward that some of the same Sulhamstead blood occurred in the background of his Fld. Ch. Askew's Carolina Lady.

With the cooperation of the National Red Setter Club and other sportsmen in various sections of the country, the LeGrande setters and their progeny became popular field trial dogs. In the thirteen years following 1952, these dogs placed in more than 500 recognized field trials by actual count.

What a far reaching accomplishment this is! The Irish Setter is indeed a worthy competitor to be reckoned with in the field trial game. Such prefixes are prominent as Tweedhall, Byrdfield, Highpoint, Davant, Springwillow, Gaythorn, Windyhill, Windyridge, Kopper Key, Murcrest, Barton Creek, Magnolis Run, Schnets, Shady Crest, Autumn Hills, Coopers, Turkey Talk, Erin, Valli Hi, Marflow, County Clare, Verbu, Runwild, and many more.

While space does not permit an account of every dog, mention should be made of some of them. Particularly impressive are the numerous wins of Shooting Dog Champion Willow Winds Hobo and Willow Winds Cathy in Puppy and Derby Stakes at open competition trials. The fact that Hobo lost the sight of one eye due to spear grass while training on the Canadian prairies did not seem to handicap his performance afield.

The Dude (Willow Winds Duke - Fld. Ch. Askew's Carolina Lady), owned by Herm David, sired seven field trial winners, including Fld. Ch. Fyn. Others of note include Mr. Mack Triplett, Mr. Finnigan, Mr. O'Malley and Mr. Mulligan. Mr. O'Leary (Willow Winds Hobo - Fld. Ch. Askew's Carolina Lady), a Shooting Dog Champion owned by F. C. Bean, Athens, Ohio, turned in many a consistent field trial performance over a ten-year period. As a sire he stamps his progeny not only with field ability but also with short coupled loin and high tail placement.

Another Shooting Dog Champion, Autumn Hills Duke (Mr. O'Leary - Redfield Ginger), owned by the late Frederick A. Kremer of Minneapolis, has a long list of field trial wins, mostly in open competition. He received the *Sports Afield* All American Award three times. Fred, who owned Irish Setters since 1936, was dedicated to the progress of the red setter afield.

d. Ch. O'Lannon Copper Penny,
D (Fld. Ch. Mahogany Friction II
x Ch. Shanty Kate III).

d. & Amateur Fld. Ch. Norab's
uke (Dual Ch. Mahogany's
tian Jingo ex Red San of
harles).

ld. & Amateur Fld. Ch. Blue
ngel's Cherry Pie (Fld. Ch.
Mahogany's Red Baron of Erin ex
ed San of Charles).

After his death in 1964, his wife Ruth continued the Autumn Hills Kennels.

Ralph C. (Rusty) Baynard's Double Jay (Rusty's Jinx - Willow Winds Eve) won the Shooting Dog Championship twice, in 1955 and again in 1957. This fast, wide-going dog was trained in open country on native quail. He was the prepotent sire of at least a dozen field trial winners, including Son of Double Jay, Valli Hi Jay and several of the G. Wood Smith Windyhill dogs. Baynard also owned Rusty's Jinx, which placed in ten stakes.

The Valli Hi setters of David and Jane Hasinger of Philadelphia have been prominent in trials for many years. Their Fld. Ch. Valli Hi Lacey well deserved her title, having at least 20 field trial placements. Valli Hi Jay also assembled a good record. When these two dogs were mated, two field trial winners resulted, Rhapsody owned by Paul Whiteman and Tax Free by Thomas McCahill. Then when the Hasingers bred their Ike's Lady Pride (Fld. Ch. Ike Jack Kendrick - Fld. Ch. Askew's Carolina Lady) to Fld. Ch. Sulhamstead Norse D'Or, four Valli Hi field trial setters of great merit were produced: Counselor, Country, Esquire and Town.

The Faith Farm setters of Dan and Marion Pahy began with bench dogs of the McGovern line with Ch. McGovern's Rusty O'Rourke, McGovern's Kerry O'Red, Kathleen's Kerry O'Red and others. Dan acquired Faith Farm Lehigh Little Bit, and after his death, Marion continued and gained her Field Championship. Marion is still active in field and Irish Setter club activities.

Fld. Ch. Sulhamstead Norse D'Or, descended from Mrs. Nagle's stock, was a top contender and also a potent stud. He sired as many as 21 field trial winners, including four from Valli Hi, two from Fld. Ch. Miller's Bonnie Loo, four from McGovern's Kerry O'Red, three from Betty Schneider's Rustic Lady III and two from John Lane's The Babe. His get inherited his good looks and his strong running style afield.

One of Shane's sons is the field trial winner, Schnet's Little Red, owned by Retired Marine Lt./Col. Edward L. Schnettler, St. Cloud, Minnesota. Ed has had Irish Setters since the 1930's; and the Schnet prefix appears in the names of many well known dogs, such as Schnet's Hellfire, S. Rufus of Havelock, S. Timuquana Jackie, S. Beau, S. Joe C, S. Tara, S. Darky and others. More than a score of field trial winners have come from his kennels, representing the bloodlines of Rufus McTybe O'Cloisters, Wheeler's Red Boy, Willow Winds Hobo, Ike Jack Kendrick and Mr. O'Leary.

About 1960, James R. and Lil Lewis, Georgetown, Kentucky, acquired The Golden Doll (Schnet's Hellfire - Bridey Murphy) and her half-brother, Mighty Red Man, from B. C. Cotton. They also obtained Erin's Sally (Mr. O'Leary - Fld. Ch. Pride of Millis) from J. G. Cassidy. From this stock a number of field trial winners have been produced, including Mighty Fawn, Diamond, Golden Hoss Colt, Mighty Gale and others.

Mighty Fawn, purchased by Ernest J. Lewis of Los Angeles in 1962, won the Midwestern Red Setter Open Shooting Dog Championship title in

Fld. Ch. Killagay's Duke Rust-of-Fur, CDX (Killagay's St. Duke of Harlan ex Killagay's Bridget Donoho), left, and Fld. Ch. Jubilee Farms Kismet (Ch. Webline Ranger, CD, ex Webline Golden Serenade).

Fld. Ch. O'Lannon's Titian Boyd (l) and Fld. Ch. Norab's Duke.

October 1964, under the guidance of the noted West Coast professional trainer, Stanley Head. He has trained and handled other E.J. Lewis setters, including Fld. Ch. Oxton's Shosaphine, County Clare's McCool and County Clare's Shandy (Mr. O'Leary - Fld. Ch. Windyridge Tammy). Shandy won the Midwestern Red Setter Open Championship title in October 1965.

Shooting Dog Champion Mr. O'Leary with over 40 field trial placements and Fld. Ch. Windyridge Tammy with more than 45 were owned by Fred C. Bean, who also had Moffat's Apache Bill and Windyridge Vixen.

The first dual champion made under American Kennel Club rules was Bench and Field Champion Tyrone's Mahogany Mike, CDX, bred and owned by "Mr. Field Trial" Edgar W. McIvor of Blanchard, Michigan. Ed McIvor's association with the field spans 35 years and he is still winning Field championships on his Ivor Glen dogs. Ed started with some bench stock, in addition to Mahogany Mike but decided early on to try to develop a dog with high style and class, breeding from the original bloodline descended from Mike. His interpretation of "style" is a dog who hunts with a happy, eager spirit, covering ground with a minimum of handling, locking up on birds with a high head and tail on point. One of the first to finish, combining all the attributes Ed sought was Fld. Ch. Ivor Glen Duffy O'Mike, a grandson of the original dog. He then purchased Ivor Glen Jim Dandy from Canada. His greatest contribution to the line was intensity and high style on point. He also purchased Cannon's Irish Duke, a great grandson of Mahogany Mike, a powerful, big running dog.

In the early 1970s Rod and Kelly Martin became associated with Ed and have co-owned and co-bred several top winning field dogs with him. The first and one of the most influential is Fld. and Amateur Fld. Ch. Sunny of Ivor Glen, whom the Martins purchased from Ed as a puppy. She was a bitch of such promise that the Martins offered her back to Ed on a co-ownership, and she proved to be an outstanding winner. Sunny was bred to Cannon's Irish Duke four times. Among the important products of those breedings were: Fld. and Amateur Fld. Ch. Devilera of Ivor Glen, owned by Ed; Fld. Ch. Ivor Glen Dinah, owned by Mike Jones; Fld. Ch. Ivor Glen Ruben, owned by Ken Ruff and Ivor Glen Duke Too, owned by Curtis Martin. Several other field winners resulted from those matings, with some just starting out.

Kelly also owns Fld. Ch. Ivor Glen Delphinium with Ed. The most recent Ivor Glen field champion is Ivor Glen Rowdy, owned by Ken Culver. Ed is now in the seventh generation breeding quality field dogs from the original stock.

To return for a moment to Mahogany Mike, during the period from 1952 to 1960, Mike placed in two dozen stakes from New England to Michigan. He sired four bench champions and at least 23 field trial winners, including Fld. Ch. Miller's Bonnie Loo, Ivor Glen's Red Hellion, Ch. Red Arrow Smooth Sailing and others.

. & Amateur Fld. Ch. Kaymar
gar O' The Plains (Fld. Ch.
awn of Kaymar ex Fair Isolde).

Dual Ch. Donnington Crackerjack (Ch. Red Arrow Gold
Feathers ex Ch. Webline Kavala
of Donnington, CD).

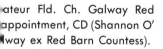

ateur Fld. Ch. Galway Red
appointment, CD (Shannon O'
way ex Red Barn Countess).

Dual Ch. Cynthia of Woodland
(Ch. Harmony Lane's Red Oa
Camp's Penelope of Pace).

Fld. & Amateur Fld. Ch. Lord Mike of
Ardee (Fld. Ch. Red Ace of Ardee III
ex Fld. Ch. Dresden Coppertone
Kelly).

Dual Ch. County Cork's Red Knigh
(Greenhill's County Cork Coun
Greenhill's Countess Colleen).

Another famous dual champion died in 1965, B. & F. Ch. Red Arrow Show Girl, UDT, who won the top titles in field, obedience and bench, plus a Mexican PC degree (comparable to CD). Owned by Lawrence and Eleanor Heist, Fontana, California, she was whelped in 1953. Although she placed in twenty field trial stakes, she was best known as being the dam of eight bench champions, all obedience trial winners. Two of them were sired by Dual Ch. Tyrone's Mahogany Mike and the other six were in a litter by Am. & Can. Ch. Esquire of Maple Ridge. Four of the latter litter also won Canadian championships: Red Arrow Solid Gold, Smart Guy, Sportsman's Guide and Son of a Gun.

O'Lannon, one of the breed's most famous field kennels, was started in 1942 as a boarding kennel. Boarding was quickly dropped. In 1948, a bitch, Small Change, out of Jahud, and a linebred Denhaven, was bred to Ch. Charles River Color Sergeant. Out of that mating came Mahogany Tim II, whelped 8-20-49, who Mrs. Walker believes was the first Irish Setter to win points on the bench and in the field. Tim, bred to a Ch. King Size bitch, came up with Field Ch. Mahogany Friction, CDX, in 1955 and in 1956 with Dual Ch. Titian Duke, CD. Tim bred to Shanty Kate produced Ch. Shanty Kate II, CD, in 1952.

Friction produced Field champions Lady Bronze, O'Lannon's Copper Penny, CD, and Rubin Dearg. Dual Ch. Titian Duke produced show Ch. Dorwayne's Kandi Shannon, Dual Ch. Mahogany's Titian Jingo and Field Ch. Mahogany's C. J. Duchess.

Dual Ch. Mahogany's Titian Jingo produced seven field champions, a record undisputed and a first in AKC annals. Jingo started in the field in May of 1965 and finished his field championship in May of 1966. He was just over three. He was entered in 27 stakes and placed in 23. In that year he garnered 21 points defeating 241 dogs. He was entered in 14 bench shows and won a total of 36 points!

Many other famous dogs have been produced by the O'Lannon Kennels, finishing on the bench and in the field. To bring their history full circle, the son of Jingo, Field Ch. Mahogany's Red Baron of Erin, has produced Field Ch. Blue Angel's Cherry Pie, who in 1975 won 23 field points defeating 289 dogs. It is Cherry Pie who will carry the banner for Irene Walker, and at Tony Baron's this famous bitch is taking time out to raise the next generation of O'Lannons and Norabs.

But back to the sire of Cherry Pie, Field Ch. Mahogany's Red Baron of Erin. Erin was sold to a doctor in Homewood, Illinois when he was twelve months old. He won his first points in Derby at fourteen months, trained and handled by the Walkers. While owned by the doctor, he made life a little hectic for the whole family—he was always alert to open doors. The good doctor soon decided a new chain-link fence was in order; he hadn't seen the children at the table all at one time since they got the dog! When the new fence had been installed, Erin was turned out in the yard, with everyone standing at the windows to watch a frustrated dog check the fence for his usual spots to escape. Just about that time one of the youngest children came along and heard the laughter, and opened the gate to see what the attraction was. Erin saw the opening he had been looking for—FREE again! To make a long story short, Erin found his way to the Washington Park Race Track. Having been raised on a farm, horses were of great interest to him. What more could he ask for, a big cheering audience, horses and all those many people trying to catch him. Needless to say, he had a ride home in the police car, with his owner receiving a notice to never let them see that red dog loose again or else! The very next day Erin was back at the Walkers. He died in June of 1971, their first case of heartworm.

Irene makes an interesting comment. "The only way Wisconsin came into the field trial scene was through the wonderful cooperation of many fine people. Many novice people want instant success, but to remain in the game there must be patience. The modest people we don't hear about but who we must thank for their splendid, unselfish efforts over the years are the Eberhardts, Dansins, Clarks, Krausses, Pollichs, Norcrosses and Ramages. These are the people we must thank for our success."

This chapter would not be complete without a word about Harry Dean (Ardee Kennels), Saskatoon, who has done so much since 1934 to support the cause of the Irish Setter in field trials. He has owned or bred more than 25 Canadian Irish Setter champions, including the five dual champions of the breed in Canada:

Ardee's Irish Ace 450130
    (Dual Ch. Moanruad Ambassador - Ch. Bird Dixie of Ardee)
Elmcroft Mahogany Sue 182455
    (Ch. Sugaun of Shaunavon - Ch. Elmcroft Molly)
Glenderry's Amber Prince 420234
    (Ch. Monarch of the Vale - Ch. Ardee's Shooting Star)
Lady Amber of Ardee 248428
    (Ch. Red Echo of Ardee - Kenogami Queen of Ardee)
Moanruad Ambassador 396714
    (Fld. Ch. Admiral of Rye - Fld. Ch. New Square Red Lassie)

Some of his other well-known dogs were: Ch. Bird Dixie of Ardee, Ch. Elmcroft Red Ace, Ch. Lady Gadeland of Ardee, Ch. Red Ace of Ardee III and Ch. Red Echo of Ardee. He imported Ch. End O'Maine Billboard from the United States and Dual Ch. Moanruad Ambassador from Ireland. The latter, of select hunting stock with 8 field trial champions in his immediate pedigree, is the prepotent sire of 7 Canadian champions and several field trial winners. In the United States he is represented by Fld. Ch. Bird Comet of Ardee, Willowview Gamester, Lady Claire of Ardee and others.

In 1967, after training on the Canadian prairies with Harry Dean for two years, Ron Surdam of Laramie, Wyoming, brought the Ardee Kennels south of the border. Some of the recent outstanding dogs bred or owned by

al Ch. Saraval Jadestarr (Ch.
velda Rustic Duke ex Ch. Dun-
lm Saraval Sue Eireann).

d. Ch. Dubhagan O'Shillelagh
ounty Clare's Hogan ex Ciar-
d O'Shillelagh).

l. Ch. Rust-of-Fur Maid of Dia-
nds (Fld. Ch. Killagay's Duke
st-of-Fur, CDX, ex Eric's Lady of
isfail).

the Ardee Kennels include Fld. Ch. and Am. Fld. Ch. Lord Mike of Ardee and Fld. Ch. Lady Claire of Ardee II.

The most outstanding Ardee dog in the last decade has to be Lord Mike of Ardee, who has 40 field trial wins. This dog's greatness is measured not only by his field trial achievements, but by his ability to transmit outstanding qualities to his progeny. In this respect, Mike has produced two field champions and numerous field trial winners. The objective of the Ardee Kennels has been and is to develop a moderate-sized, well balanced, dark mahogany Setter with high intelligence, ample pointing intensity, keen bird sense and a friendly disposition.

Among current field trial participants are Faunt and Helen Ekey of Spencerport, New York. They have owned eight field trial winners at their Kopper Key Kennels. Faunt also frequently judges at trials.

Frank and Polly Glynn own Of the Lodge Kennels in Waukesha, Wisconsin. Their field trial winner, Lady of the Lodge, earned her UD title in three trials in 9 days. Shela, Darby and Sugar are also winners in the field.

Georgia and Dennis Brown of Brownhaven Kennels, Canyon Lake, Texas, are enthusiastic trialers. In 1981 their Fld. Ch. Kopper Key Boni of Brownhaven won the Amateur National Championship. Jim Fike of High Country Kennels owns Fld. Ch. Sage of Johnny Red, who won the 1980 Amateur National Championship. Ken and Linda Ruff own Fld. Ch. Ivor Glen Ruben, who won the 1981 Open National Championship.

Richard and Jane Scurlock, Ricane Kennels, Lubbock, Texas, were given their first Irish Setter, Fair Isolde, when they became interested in bird hunting. Isolde was bred to Fld. Ch. Shawn of Kaymar, and produced Fld. & Amateur Fld. Ch. Kaymar Sugar of the Plains. Sugar was the winner of several ISCA annual field awards in 1979. The Scurlocks are also interested in the show ring, and have obtained Tapnar Sign of the Times (Tapnar Ballagbadarreen ex Ch. Tapnar Erineen).

Alex Soutar, who died suddenly in 1981, was instrumental in training many of the Eastern field trialers at his Orion Farm in Gardiner, New York. He was a highly respected judge and also trialed dogs himself. His most famous dog was Fld. and Amateur Fld. Ch. Orion's Moppet. He also bred and trained Fld. & Amateur Fld. Ch. Orion's Chearta Sun, owned by Dick Butterer.

Jill Ross of O'Shillelagh Kennels in Littleton, Colorado, owns Fld. & Amateur Fld. Ch. Ardee's Maeve O'Shillelagh, and Fld. & Amateur Fld. Ch. Dubhagen O'Shillelagh.

Patty and Don Harris, both trial and show their Rust-of-Fur Setters in California. Patty was a member of the ISCA Board of Directors.

Maypine Kennels of Dr. R. Watkins of Crete, Illinois, is based on the Norab stock of Tony Baron. His most notable dog is Fld. Ch. Norab's Algernon. Also from Illinois are Hugo and Judy Kosmel, O'Shannon Kennels. The Kosmels are active both in bench and field. They own Fld. &

Amateur Fld. Ch. Shamrock Sue O'Shannon, Ch. Jo-Ett's John Francis, Ch. Sir Duke O'Shannon, and Fld. and Amateur Field Ch. O'Shannon's Wild Knight, co-owned with A. Marco.

George and Georgia Clark of Highland, Michigan own the Cider Mills Kennels. They own Fld. Ch. Cider Mill's Gonna Fly Now.

Ron Pollock of Menomenee Falls, Wisconsin, owns the Dearg Kennels. He owns Fld. Ch. Ruben Dearg, Fld. Ch. O'Lannon's Titian Tim and O'Lannon's Titian Kellwind.

Others active in the field are Robert Peterson of Kaymar Kennels, Bill and Karen Eichenberger, Ray Dohse of Eshod Kennels, and Jim Haupt's Basham Kennels. Charlotte and Bud Ballard own Balloral Kennels, and were active in both conformation and field. Herb and Smokey Hiles of Pasadena, Maryland, use the Lu-Chorpan prefix for their field trialers. Leon Mudgett campaigned Fld. Ch. Leprechaun Riley O'Donnel in the West. Jim Kirby trialed Fld. Ch. Superposed Whiskey and garnered many placements.

Anne Marie and Randy Kubacz of Freehold, New Jersey, are extremely active in both bench and field with their Ramblin' Red Irish. Their most famous field dog is Fld. & Amateur Fld. Ch. Ramblin' Red Banshee, who has been twice winner of the ISCA Open National Championship. (See Chapter 8 for the Kubacz's conformation achievements.)

Tony and Sue Baron of Wadsworth, Illinois began in Irish in 1965 with a bitch puppy given to them because her owners could not keep her because of her housewrecking abilities. The Barons took Red-San of Charles and Norab Kennels were born.

Red-San was a strongly linebred Charles River bitch, whose sire was owned by Dorothy Cory, a lady who brought Charles River to the Midwest with Ch. Charles River Color Sergeant. Red-San was bred to Dual Ch. Mahogany's Titian Jingo, owned by Irene and Dale Walker. From that litter came three Field Champions: Norab Duke, Kahlua's Red Baron and Shamrock Sue O'Shannon. Another in the litter, Brandie Sniffer, earned a UDT.

Sandy was then bred to a Jingo son, Fld. Ch. Mahogany's Red Baron of Erin and produced Fld. & Amateur Fld. Ch. Blue Angel Cherry Pie. A student of Tony's, Ray Dohse, bought her, and later she returned to Norab, where Tony finished her Field Championship in 1973. Cherry Pie is presently the top winning AKC Field Irish Setter in history. She accumulated over 69 AKC points and defeated 696 dogs by the age of 5-1/2.

On one of their trips to the South, the Barons saw a bitch with great potential, owned and bred by Diane Camp of Atlanta, Georgia. Tony bought a co-ownership on Cynthia of Woodland Brook, and in November 1975 Cindy finished as the breed's tenth Dual Champion. Cynthia is also an American Field Champion.

Tony has finished five Field Champions. Dogs bred by Norab have earned 175 AKC points in the field since 1970 and dogs either bred or sired by Norab stock have earned 247 AKC points in the field in that time. Tony is now professionally training Irish Setters for the field.

Irish Setter participation in Field Trials has remained fairly constant in recent years. The National Field Trial, including the National Championship stake, draws a dedicated following each year. Irish are consistently represented in AKC all-pointing-breeds-trials throughout the country. Interest in a "dual dog," one that can win in both bench and field competition, has dedicated devotees in Don and Patty Harris and their Rust-of-Fur Kennels, Virginia Hardin of Runwild Kennels, Emily Schweitzer of Verbu, Dr. and Mrs. Glenn Christie and others who are just beginning.

With the introduction of the Versatility program by ISCA, more conformation-minded owners are beginning to test their dogs in the field and are finding that their innate bird-sense is still present. It is hoped that more "show Irish" will be given their chance to prove themselves capable of being the pointing dogs for which they were bred.

Ch. Padre Island Sea Storm and his son, Flashback Celebration.

10

The Irish Setter Club of America

Written by Edward F. Treutel

EVERYTHING must have a beginning, and it is the task of the historian to discover origins as accurately as possible. Writing a dog club history nearly requires delving into the drawings in caves, deciphering hieroglyphics, and searching for lost scrolls containing dates, places and events.

A short study of the background of the sport of dogs, and of the transition of the Irish Setter in particular during the period of the cultivation of his dual heritage, will help in understanding the directives and guidelines of the Irish Setter Club of America (ISCA).

On June 28, 1859 the first benched dog show was held in the town hall at Newcastle-On-Tyne, England, in conjunction with a poultry show. It was limited to Pointers and Setters and drew 60 entries. Fifteen years would pass before the exhibition of dogs could take hold in America, primarily because we were recuperating from the Civil War.

The first Westminster Kennel Club show was held at the New York Hippodrome on May 8-10, 1877. Sporting dogs predominated. During the next decade the number of pedigreed dogs and dog shows increased, prompting a group of fanciers to join together to form the American Kennel Club on September 17, 1884.

On October 12, 1894, the Tennessee Sportsman's Association organized America's first field trial in Memphis, Tennessee.

William H. Child, first president of the Irish Setter Club of America.

In February, 1891, 21 dedicated Irish Setter fanciers, benched together at the fifteenth annual Westminster Kennel Club show (Max Wenzel judged Irish), banded together to form a club. William Dunphy called the meeting to order, and the Irish Setter Club of America was born. The Constitution was formally filed with AKC on May 30, 1891. ISCA has been the only recognized Irish Setter club and, therefore, is the Parent Club of all local Irish Setter Associations. ISCA is the spirit, guiding light, and fulcrum of the breed under whose aegis all local Irish Setter clubs function.

Special Bronze Medal, Irish Setter Club of America. Designed by Warren Delano, 1918.

The 21 charter members at the meeting at Westminster in 1891:

H.B. Anderson - Glen View, NJ
E.M. Beale - Lewisburg, PA
E.B. Bishop - Coffeyville, KA
J.B. Blossom - Morrisania, NY
William H. Child - Phila., PA
B.L. Clements - New York, NY
Louis Contoit - West Farms, NY
Dr. G.G. Davis - Phila., PA
William Dunphy - Peekskill, NY
Michael Flynn, Jr. - Bristol, RI

Dr. William Jarvis - Claremont, NH
George T. Leach - High Point, NC
J.J. Mannioers - Pittsburgh, PA
Frank H. Perry - Des Moines, IA
Dr. N. Rowe - Chicago, IL
Boyd D. Rothrock - Williamsport, PA
John J. Scanlon - Fall River, MA
Charles T. Thompson - Phila., PA
W.L. Washington - Pittsburgh, PA
Max Wenzel - Hoboken, NJ

William H. Child was chosen as the first president of ISCA. He later became the third president of AKC. Dr. N. Rowe, editor of *American Field,* was elected vice-president, and later became ISCA's second president. Dr. Gwilym G. Davis was secretary-treasurer and later served for 23 years as president of ISCA. An ardent supporter of Irish Setter affairs for three decades, Dr. Davis owned the Currer Kennels.

The Executive Committee members were Max Wenzel (a judge and founder of Fisher's Island Field Trial Club), Charles T. Thompson, (Rockwood Kennels), and F. L. Cheney (Nota Kennels), from the East. The West, which extended only to Kansas, was represented by E. B. Bishop and Frank Perry. The majority of the original members were from the East, a few reaching to North Carolina and west to Kansas and Iowa.

At this time the Irish Setter in both Great Britain and America was used primarily as a hunting dog. One of the first ventures of ISCA was to hold a field trial at High Point, North Carolina on November 23, 1891. There were 24 starters in two stakes. Cash prizes of $350. were donated by the club. With its success, additional trials were run in 1892, '93 and '95. Interest in field trials waned until they were revived by ISCA in 1907-1908, when they were held at Barber Junction, N.C. This was largely due to the influence of Dr. Davis, who was a strong supporter of field dogs and field trials.

One of the first official acts of ISCA was to adopt a "standard of points of judging the Irish Setter" which had been in effect since 1886. This standard was patterned after one used by the Red Irish Setter Club of Dublin, Ireland. Preservation of certain bloodlines, prolonged purity of strains, types that were successful in field and show, popularity and sales value were the elements for a standard, or blueprint, of type for a particular breed, especially at a time when breeds were undergoing great changes.

This early standard emphasized breed characteristics such as a long, lean head, well defined occipital protruberance, deep chest, etc. It was quite satisfactory over a long period, undergoing only slight revisions in 1895, 1908 and 1919.

The early "standard of points" established arbitrary ratings for eleven parts of the ideal Irish Setter:

Head	10	Hind Legs	10
Eyes	5	Tail	8
Ears	5	Coat & Feathering	8
Neck	5	Color	8
Body	15	Size, Style &	
Shoulders, Feet, & Forelegs	12	General Appearance	14
		TOTAL	**100**

During the Twenties, ISCA conducted a campaign to promote the breed and encourage breeders to improve their stock by offering generous prizes at bench shows and field trials. By 1926, ISCA was flourishing with more than 200 members and was the most active and progressive specialty organization in the dog fancy. At that time dog shows attracted between 450 and 600 total entries.

The decade of the Twenties prior to The Great Depression was a productive growth period for the dog world. In January, 1926, AKC made a constructive attempt at better communication among the breeds by offering member clubs a column in the *Gazette* for their news items. ISCA's first breed correspondent was William Cary Duncan, a professional writer, who worked in this capacity until 1945. Mr. Duncan was a director of AKC, 9th president of ISCA, its delegate, and a well-known judge. He also edited the *Irish Setter Club's News*, the forerunner of the present *Memo To Members*, which was begun in 1945 by the 14th president, John C. Neff. The *News* was a four to eight page newsletter, prepared after each executive meeting to inform members of the club's activities. It contained items about show events and dog accomplishments. In 1981, under editor Shirley Boyer, the *Memo* won three first place awards in the Dog Writers' Association of America Annual Writing Competition.

ISCA conducted its first Combined Specialty and Field Day in Albany, New York on August 26, 1927. The second event was held at the Milson Kennels in Harrison, New York on October 6, 1928. At this show a prize cup was offered for each exhibitor who had not previously shown an Irish Setter. The third and fourth Specialty Shows followed in succession on the estate of Miss Elizabeth Stillman, Cornwall, New York and the fifth was held in conjunction with the Storm King Kennel Club all-breed show. Then came six specialties associated with the spectacular Morris and Essex shows in Madison, New Jersey (1932-1937), followed by eight specialties held in conjunction with the Westchester Kennel Club (1938-1946).

The first four organized local clubs showed an early wide distribution and national interest in Irish Setters. The honor of being the first local Irish Setter Club belongs to the Irish Setter Club of New England. On November 14, 1928, a group of twelve New Englanders gathered at the home of Mr. and Mrs. Roderic M. Blood in Newton Center, Massachusetts, and organized the ISC of Massachusetts (which it was called for a short while) and designated John Cuneo, a judge and the 11th president of ISCA, as the club's first president. Frank Addyman judged their first specialty show, held in conjunction with the 1930 Worcester County Kennel Club. Their first field trial was held in May, 1938. Their publication, *The Green Sheet,* is the oldest continuing local club bulletin.

William Williamson was elected as the first president of the Irish Setter Club of Southern California, the second oldest Irish Setter Club. They conducted their first specialty show in conjunction with the California Association of Canine Specialty Clubs in Los Angeles on August 6-7, 1932. Nancy Nannetti of Oakland, judged the Irish.

The third oldest club is Western Irish Setter Club. James Menhall judged their first specialty show which was held in the Chicago Coliseum on November 23, 1935. H. Jack Cooper was the first president. This club was formed after the AKC required a split of the Western Pointer and Setter Club, founded in 1925 by Dr. J. M. Kaiser, who was the first president. As a combined Pointer and Setter group, they conducted shows in the Chicago Armory. This policy was not acceptable to the AKC and thus the division into individual breed clubs resulted.

Fourth in age is the Eastern Irish Setter Association. A group headed by Lee Schoen, judge and 16th president of ISCA, Harry Hartnett, famous handler of Ch. Milson O'Boy, and William L. Lubben, board member of ISCA, and EISA's first president, formed the Talmadge Hill Club, which was the Schoen address. The name was changed, first to the Irish Setter Breeders' Association, and later to Eastern Irish Setter Association. The club participated in a sponsored show on August 15, 1936, at the Ox Ridge Hunt Club in Darien, Connecticut and was judged by Edward V. Ireland with an entry of 82 Irish Setters. They did not have their first specialty show until June 11, 1938, held in conjunction with the Kennel Club of North Westchester, home of the Sherman Hoyts in Katonah, NY. F. W. Wolfenden judged the specialty show.

When, in 1931, AKC revised its field trial regulations, ISCA, cognizant of the hunting potential of the Irish Setter, offered attractive prizes to stimulate interest in the field trials. The first championship points under the new rules were awarded to Ch. Elcova's Admiration, and the first Irish Setter to win the newly created AKC Field Championship title was Fld. Ch. Elcova McTybe. In 1938, to perpetuate this great start, the club offered the Elcho prize of $500, to be awarded to the first Irish Setter winning ten points in field competition with Pointers and Setters. In order to emphasize dual purpose, the dog also must have won at least five regular classes at dog shows with at least four competitors in each class.

In 1940, Michael J. Flynn, the last living charter member, was elected an honorary life member of ISCA.

An eminent name in ISCA history is that of John C. Neff, who served as Secretary (1937-'39), President (1940-'46), Delegate (1946-'64) and was

AKC Executive Secretary from 1947 to '51 and Executive Vice-President from 1951 to '64. He received the Gaines "Fido" award as "Dog Man of the Year" in 1951. His dedication and contribution to the Irish Setter and the ISCA continued unflinchingly through 27 years of faithful service.

The importance of Sweepstakes and Futurity programs is noted in the ISCA booklet of 1946: "To encourage the production of excellent stock." The first Irish Setter Futurity was held by the Eastern Irish Setter Association, whose president at the time was Harry Hartnett, on June 11, 1938.

ISCA Secretary Ralph H. Mathiessen advocated holding a Futurity Day. This took eighteen months to formulate and was held at the Westchester Country Club, Rye, New York on September 7, 1946. A purse of almost $500 was offered. Edward Dana Knight, a foremost authority on dog anatomy, was the judge.

By 1947, Irish Setter Club membership had increased in all parts of the country and in that year ISCA divided the United States into four "regions". A system of regional events, hosted by local clubs, was organized. The first ISCA regional specialty was hosted by the Irish Setter Club of New England, and was held with the Ladies Dog Club show on June 7, 1947. A well documented, widely acclaimed show, which was considered almost national in scope, was the ISCA Region One Specialty, held as part of the Combined Setter Specialty in New York City the day before the Westminster show. ISCA board member, Dr. Wolfgang Casper, was the innovator, perpetuator, and chairman of this prestigious event. The first show, February 7, 1960, was judged by Joseph P. Knight, who was ISCA's 15th president. This regional show was conducted on the same weekend as the ISCA annual meeting and annual awards dinner until 1973, when a change in the by-laws scheduled the meeting and dinner to be held in conjunction with the new National Specialty.

The first regional field trial, hosted jointly by the Western Irish Setter Club and the Irish Setter Club of Milwaukee, did not take place until October 24, 1965—18 years after the first regional specialty—during the presidency of Ivan Klapper. Nevertheless, enthusiasm ran high with great competition, 21 Irish Setters in the Open Gun Dog Stake. The spirit of duality was present, for three of the starters were field champions, four were show champions, and there was one dual champion and several Obedience titlists. One of the judges, Wolfram C. Stumpf, remarked, "Now most Irish Setter breeders are proud of their dogs looks as well as of their hunting ability." The next year, the ISCA Region One Field Trial was hosted by the Eastern Irish Setter Association on October 16, 1966. Five field champions were among the 21 Irish Setters in the Open Gun Dog Stake.

In 1957, James Bayless, ISCA publicity chairman, created an annual file of newspaper and advertising clippings pertaining to the Irish Setter.

This annual file developed into a big, green scrap book of some historical importance. Jim Bayless was also instrumental in publishing the attractive brochure, "The Irish Setter," to help promote the breed in the field, Obedience, bench, and as a companion. The text was written by five authors, all well known in the breed: Lee Schoen, W. C. Thompson, Emily Schweitzer, Edgar McIvor, and Bart Lanier Stafford III.

During the administration of Lester Gatchell, 17th president, the ISCA Board undertook a study of the standard. The new standard, which abandoned the scale of points, was the result of more than four years of intensive study by the Board, which canvassed all the Irish Setter clubs for their recommendations. The standard as it now reads was unanimously approved by the ISCA membership and became effective on June 14, 1960.

During the '60s, the responsibility for publication of the *Memo* was handed from its originator, John Neff, to Ivan Klapper, the 18th president, who with the engaging rhetoric and fluid literary style of a professional writer, wrote and published it entirely alone. This expanded, bi-monthly publication sometimes reached over 50 pages. In 1968, ISCA published *The Irish Setter Champions and Obedience Title-Holders* by W. C. Thompson, the first international record of Irish Setter titlists, consisting of more than 3,000 listings. In 1967, ISCA distributed hundreds of copies of *"The Fight Against Bloat,"* a compendium of reports on acute gastric dilatation, compiled by president Ivan Klapper and issued as a supplement to the *Memo.*

When the population of a breed proliferates it is usually sparked by some impetus. In the case of the Irish, it was a motion picture, "Big Red," adapted from a novel by James Kjelgaard. At a preview to the first showing in Chicago in 1962, members of the Western Irish Setter Club gathered in front of the movie house and gave a demonstration of Obedience work starring Emily Schweitzer with Ch. Verbu Missy Oogh, CDX, and others showing their dogs in conformation. The Irish Setter in the movie, "Big Red," was Ch. Red Aye Scraps, UD. His stand-in was his kennelmate, Ch. Red Arrow Smooth Sailing, UDT. Both dogs were owned by Lawrence and Eleanor Heist. The part of Molly in the whelping scene was played by Princess Cenna, owned by James and Evelyn Hale.

Louis Iacobucci, the 19th President, took over the reins in 1970, and found the club with a depleted treasury. He was a vigorous promoter, an innovator with many new ideas who traveled to most of the local clubs in order to make ISCA more national in scope. Working through his committees, he instituted the "Pictorial," a once-in-five-years publication of pictures and pedigrees which helped greatly to make ISCA solvent once again. The Pictorial Editors were Ron and Renee Taylor in 1970, Bernard and Wilma Baron in 1975, and Shirley Boyer and Barbara Lyons in 1981.

On March 9, 1971, W. L. "Slim" Newhall, vice president of ISCA, offered a proposal to the Board that had long been a dream of his—a research project for Irish Setters. This project, approved as the ISCA Foundation and later changed to The American Irish Setter Foundation with Slim Newhall as its first president, was founded for the purposes of educational and scientific projects of benefit to Irish Setters.

Throughout the years the parent club had collected various literary items and in 1974 an Irish Setter library was established. Presiding over this repository of Irish Setter history and reference material is Edell Peters. Mr. Iacobucci also instituted a booklet, *"A Guide to Grooming Your Irish Setter."* Written and illustrated by Board member, Dennis Sporre, it was published in 1975.

Because ISCA is constantly aware of the Irish Setter standard as the pillar of the breed, Mr. E. Irving Eldredge suggested a graphic illustration of the wording. Thus, in 1975, Board member Harriet T. Burkart and AKC delegate Eldredge persuaded a former member of the Board, renowned animal artist and veterinarian, Dr. Robert F. Way, to produce "An Illustrated Study of the Irish Setter Standard."

In an effort to promote communication and to keep accurate records, Ed. Treutel, ISCA's 20th President, persuaded the Board to establish a *"Yearbook."* This was to be a record of the accomplishments for the previous year. It was first published in 1977 and 1978, but was reduced in 1979 and incorporated as part of the *Memo* for financial reasons.

The by-laws of the club were amended in 1972 to provide for at least one meeting of the Board in each of the four ISCA regions. Where possible, general membership meetings are also held at these "regional meetings."

ISCA, enjoying the wisdom of age, encompassing a large membership, and occupying a prestigious reputation, was selected for the first AKC breed film. Consultations between AKC and ISCA resulted. The purpose of the film was to benefit and guide breeders and to act as an aid for judges by presenting the standard in motion. Work began in 1974 under the guidance of Ted Eldredge. Some of the footage was taken at the National Specialty in Atlanta in 1975; some at the National Field Trial; and some at other appropriate locations. Called *"The Irish Setter, A Breed Study,"* this beautiful, instructive film was released to the dog fancy in 1976.

The first National Specialty Show, Sweepstakes, and Obedience Trial was held at the Valley Forge Military Academy, Wayne, Pennsylvania, on August 10-11, 1973. No expense was spared to make the show a memorable occasion. The record-breaking catalog contained 280 pages, 206 of advertising and recorded 511 dogs with 767 entries. Judges for the First National were: Dogs, Ward Gardiner; Bitches, Irene Castle Khatoonian; Intersex, English judge J. W. Rasbridge; Obedience, Emily Schweitzer; Sweepstakes, Ann Buck. Chairman for the first three National Specialty Shows was Ed. Treutel. Bernard Baron was show secretary for the fifth to ninth specialties.

The National Specialty rotates each year, covering each of the four ISCA regions. Events in conjunction with the Specialty are an educational symposium, the annual membership meeting, and the gala awards dinner. Following is the location of the National Specialties through 1982:

1973	Wayne, PA		1978	Elyria, OH
1974	Pontiac, MI		1979	San Antonio, TX
1975	Atlanta, GA		1980	Costa Mesa, CA
1976	Tucson, AZ		1981	Danvers, MA
1977	Washington, DC		1982	Louisville, KY

The forerunner to the National Field Trials was held in Lenexa, Kansas in 1973. Virginia Hardin, who became ISCA's 21st President, chaired and Tony Baron was secretary of the event. The first ISCA National Field Trial was held the following year, November 15-17, 1974, with Robert Oram as chairman and Marjorie Dillard as secretary. This new phase of major significance in Irish Setter history was held at Fort Ord, California. Judges were: L. Deane Baker, Faunt Ekey, Virginia Hardin, and James Ferguson. There were 15 Open Puppies, 37 Open Gun Dogs, 26 Open Derbies, 31 Open All Age, 17 Limited All Age, 21 Open Limited Gun Dogs, and 33 Amateur Gun Dogs.

The sites of the National Field Trials have been:

1974	Fort Ord, CA		1978	Commerce City, CO
1975	Medford, NJ		1979	Rend Lake, IL
1976	Kenosha, WI		1980	Ardmore, OK
1977	Edmond, OK		1981	Rend Lake, IL
			1982	Rend Lake, IL

In 1975 and '76, Ron Surdam chaired the ISCA Field Futurity and Gun Dog Classic, which was held in conjunction with the National Field Trial in Joliet, Illinois. The Gun Dog Classic's first secretary was Bob Fitch. Tony Baron was secretary of the 1976 event. At the conclusion of the second Gun Dog Classic, upon recommendation of the Classic Committee and with approval of the ISCA Board, it was decided that ISCA was ready to hold National Championship Trials and The Gun Dog Classic became the ISCA National Derby Classic.

Just as the Lenexa event had been a forerunner to the National Field Trial, so the National Field Trials were forerunners to the National and Amateur National Championship Trials, the first of which was held at Rend Lake, Illinois, October 30 through November 2, 1979. For this history-making trial, Marion Pahy was chairman, and Georgia Brown was secretary. There were 9 Open puppies, 14 in the ISCA Derby Classic, 21 in the National Amateur Championship Stake. Judges were: Jim Wortman, Leon Sienkowski, Jack Cooper, and Dorothy McDonald.

The second ISCA National Championship Trial was held in 1980 in Ardmore, Oklahoma. The ISCA Field Trial Advisory Board then strongly recommended that the Rend Lake, Illinois grounds be the site for the next three Nationals. It was felt necessary to make such a commitment due to the increasing difficulty of reserving National caliber field trial grounds at affordable cost.

For many years ISCA was concerned about the continuing disparity

ISCA National Specialties draw large entries each year. Here Judge Elsworth Howell awards Best of Breed (R) to Ch. McCamon Marquis, handled by George Alston, and Best of Opposite Sex to Ch. McCamon Anastasia, handled by owner Malinda Bischoff, at the

in the breeding of Irish Setters and Irish "Red" Setters. In October, 1975, ISCA received, upon request, an announcement from AKC that its policy of reciprocal registration of Irish Setters from the American Field Stud Book would be rescinded. It was also felt that something should be done about the prejudices and myths which had beset the Irish Setter in the field for over fifty years—that something should be done about having one type of Setter for the field and another for the bench. Early in 1975 Edell Peters, ISCA librarian, submitted a working certificate program to ISCA. This single field exposure idea was designed after the programs of several Sporting breeds. The suggestion was put into action in 1976 when Ed. Treutel formed, with Board approval, a Working Certificate committee with Edell Peters as Chairman. He felt there was a real need for practical and immediate action to bring the field and bench people into close communication. He developed many drafts of a working program which the Board reviewed and studied. On August 20, 1978, after two years of work on the program, the Board adopted a versatility program encompassing field, obedience and breed. Its success can be demonstrated by the fact that in the first three years of operation nearly 100 tests were conducted, and ISCA has issued 50 Versatility Certificates. The certificate program and its operation is seen as being a step forward in narrowing the gap between field and bench.

At the beginning of 1982 ISCA is on the doorstep of supplementing the VC program by formulating a VC-Excellent program which will further the primary objects of the Versatility Tests: to demonstrate the Irish Setter's hunting ability and reasonable obedience to the handler's commands, and to determine whether the overall breeding program adheres to the Irish Setter standard.

Among the first of the ISCA delegates to AKC was G. H. Thomson, who held that post for several years. Throughout its existence the club has been fortunate in having dedicated delegates, some of whom had long tenures in office: R. Walter Creuzbaur (1910-1922), William Cary Duncan (1925-1945), John C. Neff (1945-1965), Joseph P. Knight (1965-1968) and E. Irving Eldredge (1968 to the present).

Following is a list of the presidents of ISCA:

1891-1892	William H. Child	1938	Walter C. Ellis
1893-1894	W. L. Washington	1939	Dr. G. S. Currier
1895-1918	Dr. G. G. Davis	1940-1946	John C. Neff
1919-1920	Joseph S. Wall	1947-1949	Joseph P. Knight, Jr.
1921-1922	Dr. C. A. Gale	1950-1952	Lee M. Schoen
1923-1927	Dr. J. D. DeRonde	1953-1960	Lester O. Gatchell
1928-1929	Walter Arnold	1961-1969	Ivan Klapper
1930	Mrs. E. A. Sturdee	1970-1975	Louis Iacobucci
1931-1933	William Cary Duncan	1976-1978	Edward F. Truetel
1934-1935	Walter C. Ellis	1979-1981	Miss Virginia Hardin
1936-1937	John A. Cuneo	1982-	Bernard Baron

Throughout 91 years, ISCA has been the guiding spirit for Irish Setter affairs. The objects of the parent club are pronounced in the constitution:

"To encourage and promote the breeding of pure-bred Irish Setters and to do all possible to bring their natural qualities to perfection; to encourage the organization of independent Irish Setter Specialty Clubs; to promote, amend, and define a standard of the breed, to do all in its power to protect and advance the interest of the breed, and to encourage sportsmanlike competition at all events; to conduct Sanctioned Matches and Specialty Shows, Field Trials and Obedience Trials under the rules of the AKC."

APPENDIX

Selected Pedigrees

On the pages that follow are the pedigrees of 53 Irish Setters who, as winners or producers (or both), have made a strong impact on the breed over the last fifty years.

Parents, grandparents and great-grandparents of each dog are shown in regular pedigree form. The sire and dam of each great-grandparent are listed (in the same descending order) at the right. An asterisk preceding the name identifies the dog as an import. The number in parentheses following a name indicates the number of AKC champion offspring.

More on these dogs will be found in the stories of their producing kennels, in Chapters 7 and 8. Many of them are pictured there, and location of the picture is noted with the pedigree.

A historic trio of the 1930s. From left to right: Ch. Milson O'Boy, Ch. Milson Top-Notcher and Ch. Higgins' Red Pat.

CH. HIGGINS' RED COAT (dog) — 634787 — 9/30/27 — (Photo, P. 96)

	Benmore
Eng. Ch. Brian of Boyne (1)	Dolly of Boyne
Eng. Ch. Terry of Boyne (1)	Daniel of Boyne
Young Norah of Boyne (1)	Noreen of Boyne
Sire: **Higgins Paddy of Boyne** (7)	Eng. Ch. Brian of Boyne (1)
Eamon of Boyne	Noreenogue of Boyne
Dora of Boyne	Young Paddy of Boyne
Lady Joan	Judieth

	Ch. Ben Law (7)
Ch. Conn Law (3)	Elcho Bess (3)
Ch. Lissmore Freedom (6)	Woodmere Brian (3)
Ch. Lissmore Colleen (4)	Ch. Midwood Ruby (3)
Dam: **Craigie Lea Mona** (6)	Mager's Elcho (1)
Ch. St. Cloud's Fermanagh (2)	Peggy Finglass (1)
Clare II (1)	Riversdale Red Star (1)
Ch. Bob White Red Storm (1)	Eng. Ch. Riversdale Red Light (1)

CH. MILSON O'BOY (dog) — 850620 — 3/8/32 — (Photo, P. 103)

	Brian of Boyne
Terry of Boyne	Young Norah of Boyne
Higgins' Paddy of Boyne	Eamon of Boyne
Dora of Boyne	Lady Joan
Sire: **Ch. Higgins' Red Coat**	Ch. Conn Law
Ch. Lismore Freedom	Ch. Lismore Colleen
Craigie Lea Mona	Ch. St. Cloud's Fermanagh
Clare II	Ch. Bob White Red Storm

	Ch. St. Joe Kenmore's Boy of Kelt
Ch. Elcova's Terence McSwiney	Glencho
Ch. Terence of the Cloisters	Kenmard
Milson Colleen	Lismore Norma
Dam: **Milson Miss Sonny**	St. Cloud VII
Ch. St. Cloud's Fermanagh III	St. Cloud's Colleen
Milson Goldie	Ch. Lismore Freedom
Ch. Milson Peggy	Ch. Swifty Holden

CH. MILSON O'BOY II (dog) — A94054 — 2/10/36

	*Eng. Ch. Terry of Boyne (1)
*Higgins' Paddy of Boyne (7)	Dora of Boyne
Ch. Higgins' Red Coat (30)	Ch. Lismore Freedom (6)
Craigie Lea Mona (6)	Clare II (1)
Sire: **Ch. Milson O'Boy** (17)	Ch. Elcova's Terence McSwiney (4/1 Fι
Ch. Terence of the Cloisters (2)	Milson Colleen (3)
Milson Miss Sonny (2)	Ch. St. Cloud's Fermanagh III (3)
Milson Goldie (0)	Ch. Milson Peggy (3)

	Barney
Red Brea (1)	Acetylene
*Ch. Flornell Squire of Milson (1)	Shaftoe Ranger (0)
Lady Bessie (1)	Nora Crafty (0)
Dam: **Milson Vanda** (2)	Ch. Londonderry's Legion (6)
Ch. Londonderry's Legion II (8)	Mollie Mahone (1)
Orchid Lady (0)	Am. & Can. Ch. Higgins' Red Pat (6)
Milson Pat's Girlie (2)	Ch. Patsy VI

CH. KINVARRA KERMIT (dog) — A217049 — 3/31/37 — (Photo, P. 113)

	Ch. Higgins' Red Coat (30)		*Higgins' Paddy of Boyne (7)
	Ch. Kinvarra Son of Red Coat (7)		Craigie Lea Mona (6)
	Ch. Queen Maive (3)		Ch. Terence O'Brien Law (1)
re: Ch. Kinvarra Craig (8)			Ch. Kenridge Kinlass (1)
	Rheola Boniface		Eng. Show Ch. Rheola Bryn (1)
	*Borrowdale Yseult of Kinvarra (4)		Rheola Mallie
	Eng. Ch. Norna (0)		Loc Garmain Barney
			Eng. Show Ch. Rheola Didona

	*Ch. Golden Dawn of Gadeland		Eng. Show Ch. Rheola Bryn (1)
	O'Aragon (8)		Lassie O'Murrell (1)
	Eng. Ch. Brigand of Usan (1)		
	Garnet O'Murrell of Usan		Brendan O'Murrell
m: *Ch. Kinvarra Mollie of Gadeland (5)			Colleen of Wendover
	Eng. Ch. Son of a Gun of Gadeland (1)		Eng. Show Ch. Shamus of Ballyshannon
	Monica of Gadeland (1)		Eng. Ch. Gadeland Neula of Boyne
	Eng. Ch. Rebel Maid of Gadeland		Rheola Boniface
			Eng. Show Ch. Biddy of Gadeland

CH. KLEIGLIGHT OF ARAGON (dog) — A380784 — 2/27/39 — (Photo, P. 119)

	*Higgins' Paddy of Boyne (7)		*Eng. Ch. Terry of Boyne (1)
	Ch. Higgins' Red Coat (30)		Dora of Boyne
	Craigie Lea Mona (6)		Ch. Lismore Freedom (6)
re: Ch. Redwood Russet of Harvale (16)			Clare II (1)
	Redwood Ranger (1)		Ch. Londonderry's Ambition (5)
	Ch. Redwood Rita (5)		Ch. Lady Betty of Kelt (4)
	Redwood Ruby (1)		Ch. Londonderry's Ambition (5)
			Ch. Chancery Joan O'Shagstone (2)

	Ch. Higgins' Red Coat (30)		*Higgins' Paddy of Boyne (7)
	Redwood Rocket (14)		Craigie Lea Mona (6)
	Am. & Can. Ch. Redwood Rhoda		*Beorcham Barney (1)
m: Ch. Stardust of Crosshaven (2)			*Peggy of Newrie (1)
	Ch. Higgins' Red Coat (30)		*Higgins' Paddy of Boyne (7)
	Ch. Ruxton's Shannon of Boyne (7)		Craigie Lea Mona (6)
	*Sally of Ballybay (1)		Eng. & Ir. Ch. Barney of Boyne
			Ravenhill Florrie (0)

AM. & CAN. CH. RED STAR OF HOLLYWOOD HILLS, CDX — A932359 — 4/27/45

	Ch. Higgins' Red Coat (30)		*Higgins' Paddy of Boyne (7)
	Ch. Redwood Russet of Harvale (16)		Craigie Lea Mona (6)
	Ch. Redwood Rita (5)		Redwood Ranger (1)
re: Ch. Rufus of Hollywood Hills (6)			Redwood Ruby (1)
	The Bronze Baron of Wamsutta (0)		Ch. St. Cloud's Fermanagh III (3)
	Penny Tax of Hollywood Hills (2)		Ch. Emma of Shanagolden (4)
	Royal Irish Radiance (0)		Ch. Royal Irish Dawn (0)
			Royal Irish Prim (0)

	Ch. Higgins' Red Coat (30)		*Higgins' Paddy of Boyne (7)
	Ch. Redwood Russet of Harvale (16)		Craigie Lea Mona (6)
	Ch. Redwood Rita (5)		Redwood Ranger (1)
m: Ch. Faig-a-Baile of Crosshaven (4)			Redwood Ruby (1)
	Redwood Rocket (14)		Ch. Higgins' Red Coat (30)
	Ch. Sally O'Bryan of Crosshaven (2)		Am. & Can. Ch. Redwood Rhoda
	Ch. Ruxton's Shannon of Boyne (7)		Ch. Higgins' Red Coat (30)
			*Sally of Ballybay (1)

CH. TYRONNE FARM MALONE II (dog) — S45636 — 5/6/46

	Ch. Kinvarra Craig (8)
	Ch. Kinvarra Kermit (29)
	*Ch. Kinvarra Mollie of Gadeland (5)
Sire: **Ch. Tyronne Farm Malone (9)**	
	Ch. Higgins' Red Coat (30)
	Ch. Ruxton's Mollie O'Day (14)
	Ruxton's Tadg (7)

Ch. Kinvarra Son of Red Coat (7)
*Borrowdale Yseult of Kinvarra (●
Eng. Ch. Brigand of Usan (1)
Monica of Gadeland (1)
*Higgins' Paddy of Boyne (7)
Craigie Lea Mona (6)
*Eng. Show & Am. Ch. Tadg (1)
*Ch. Mairgread Dileas (1)

	*Ch. Knock A Voe
	Jordan Farm Abe (9)
	Lady Pamela Redfeather (1)
Dam: **Ch. Tyronne Farm O'Flare (1)**	
	Ch. Higgins' Red Coat (30)
	Ch. Ruxton's Mollie O'Day (14)
	Ruxton's Tadg (7)

Achcha (1)
Lady Lustre (1)
Ch. Admiration (2)
Ch. Lady Betty of Kelt (4)
*Higgins' Paddy of Boyne (7)
Craigie Lea Mona (6)
*Eng. Show & Am. Ch. Tadg (1)
*Ch. Mairgread Dileas (1)

CH. SEAFORTH'S DARK REX (dog) — S158260 — 8/18/47 — (Photo, P. 13

	Ch. Kinvarra Craig (8)
	Ch. Kinvarra Kermit (29)
	*Ch. Kinvarra Mollie of Gadeland
Sire: **Ch. Tyronne Farm Malone (9)**	
	Ch. Higgins' Red Coat (30)
	Ch. Ruxton's Mollie O'Day (14)
	Ruxton's Tadg (7)

Ch. Kinvarra Son of Red Coat (7)
*Borrowdale Yseult of Kinvarra (●
Eng. Ch. Brigand of Usan (1)
Monica of Gadeland (1)
*Higgins' Paddy of Boyne (7)
Craigie Lea Mona (6)
*Eng. Show & Am. Ch. Tadg (1)
*Ch. Mairgread Dileas

	Ch. Wamsutta Jack High (0)
	Charles River Red Don (1)
	Ch. Charles River All Afire (2)
Dam: **Ch. Seaforth's Red Velvet (4)**	
	Ch. Charles River Color Sergeant (17)
	Charles River Juanita (1)
	Tyronne Farm Honey O'Day (2)

Saint Cloud's Ballinhoe (3)
Queen of Wamsutta (1)
*Ch. Red Sails of Salmagundi (7)
Wamsutta Susie Q (3)
*Ch. Red Sails of Salmagundi (7)
Wamsutta Susie Q (3)
Ch. Tyronne Farm Tipperary (5)
Ch. Ruxton's Mollie O'Day (14)

CH. THENDERIN BRIAN TRISTAN (dog) — S226483 — 3/17/48 — (Photo, P.

	Ch. Milson O'Boy II (20)
	Ch. Rosecroft Premier (4)
	Rosecroft Fern (1)
Sire: **Ch. End O'Maine Luckalone (8)**	
	Ch. Kinvarra Kermit (29)
	Ch. End O'Maine Best Wishes (5)
	Beg Pardon Rury Limerick (4)

Ch. Milson O'Boy (17)
Milson Vanda (2)
Ch. Milson O'Boy (17)
Ch. Loudon Aroon (0)
Ch. Kinvarra Craig (8)
*Ch. Kinvarra Mollie of Gadeland
Ch. Milson Top-Notcher (6)
Ch. End O'Maine Burnie Burn (2)●

	Ch. Kinvarra Craig (8)
	Ch. Kinvarra Kermit (29)
	*Ch. Kinvarra Mollie of Gadeland (5)
Dam: **Ch. Kinvarra Portia (12)**	
	Ch. Milson Top-Notcher (6)
	Beg Pardon Rury Limerick (4)
	Ch. End O'Maine Burnie Burn (2)

Ch. Kinvarra Son of Red Coat (7)
*Borrowdale Yseult of Kinvarra (4
Eng. Ch. Brigand of Usan (1)
Monica of Gadeland (1)
Ch. Milson O'Boy (17)
Milson Squire's Janice (1)
Ch. Higgins' Red Coat (30)
Ch. End O'Maine Beg Pardon (2)

H. INNISFAIL COLOR SCHEME, CD (dog) — S557130 — 8/1/52 — (Photo, P. 126)

Ch. Kinvarra Kermit (29)
Ch. Tyronne Farm Malone (9)
Ch. Ruxton's Mollie O'Day (14)
ire: **Ch. Seaforth's Dark Rex** (20)
Charles River Red Don (1)
Ch. Seaforth's Red Velvet (4)
Charles River Juanita (1)

Ch. Kinvarra Craig (8)
*Ch. Kinvarra Mollie of Gadeland (5)
Ch. Higgins' Red Coat (30)
Ruxton's Tadg (7)
Ch. Wamsutta Jack High
Ch. Charles River All Afire (2)
Ch. Charles River Color Sergeant (17)
Tyronne Farm Honey O'Day (2)

Ch. Kendare Stout Fellow (1)
Ch. Kendare Red Duke (1)
Ch. Kendare Ardri (1)
)am: **Thenderin Champagne** (4)
Ch. Red Ranger Pat (9)
Thenderin April Anthem (1)
Ch. Kinvarra Portia (12)

Ch. Kinvarra Kermit (29)
Kinvarra Marguerite (1)
Am. & Can. Ch. Tyronne Farm Tyrone (2)
Ch. Molly of Crosshaven (1)
Schreiber's Captain (1)
Ravenhill's Geraldine (1)
Ch. Kinvarra Kermit (29)
Beg Pardon Rury Limerick (4)

AM. & CAN. CH. ESQUIRE OF MAPLE RIDGE (dog) — S589256 — 12/19/52

Ch. Rosecroft Premier (4)
Ch. End O'Maine Luckalone (8)
Ch. Kinvarra Portia (12)
ire: **Ch. Thenderin Brian Tristan** (30)
Ch. Kinvarra Kermit (29)
Ch. Kinvarra Portia (12)
Beg Pardon Rury Limerick (4)

Ch. Milson O'Boy II (20)
Rosecroft Fern (1)
Ch. Kinvarra Kermit (29)
Beg Pardon Rury Limerick (4)
Ch. Kinvarra Craig (8)
*Ch. Kinvarra Mollie of Gadeland (5)
Ch. Milson Top-Notcher (6)
Ch. End O'Maine Burnie Burn (2)

Ch. Charles River Color Sergeant (17)
Am. & Can. Ch. Red Sails Michael of
Oak Grove (11)
Ch. O'Shaungabragh's Lady (6)
)am: **Crosshaven Lea of Maple Ridge** (5)
Redwood Rory of Crosshaven (3)
Crosshaven Molly O'Bryan
Ch. Faig-a-Baile of Crosshaven (4)

*Ch. Red Sails of Salmagundi (7)
Wamsutta Susie Q (3)

Ch. Hinman's Duke of Denver (3)
Ch. O'Shaungabragh's Red Star (2)
Redwood's Baron of Crosshaven (0)
Ch. Sally O'Bryan of Crosshaven (2)
Ch. Redwood Russet of Harvale (16)
Ch. Sally O'Bryan of Crosshaven (2)

KNOCKROSS' O'BOY (dog) — S786189 — 4/9/55 — (Photo, P. 106)

Ch. Caldene Judson (5)

Ch. Caldene Picardy (4)
Ch. Caldene Pixie (3)
ire: **Ch. Caldene Mick O'Boy** (9)
Ch. Caldene Mickey Mischief (6)
Ch. Molly of Terry-Tom (1)
Ch. Caldene Pixie (3)

Ch. Harvale Hero (7)
Am. & Can. Ch. Judy Legore
Colquohoun (2)
Ch. Milson O'Boy (17)
Ch. Caldene Patricia (1)
Ch. Milson O'Boy II (20)
Jordan Farm Molly (2)
Ch. Milson O'Boy (17)
Ch. Caldene Patricia (1)

Ch. Rufus of Hollywood Hills (6)
Am. & Can. Ch. Red Star of Hollywood Hills,
CDX (23/1FC)
Ch. Faig-a-Baile of Crosshaven (4)
)am: **Ch. Sharoc Coquette** (1)
*Ch. Red Sails of Salmagundi (7)
Charles River Destiny (4)
Ch. End O'Maine Best Wishes (5)

Ch. Redwood Russet of Harvale (16)
Penny Tax of Hollywood Hills (2)

Ch. Redwood Russet of Harvale (16)
Ch. Sally O'Bryan of Crosshaven (2)
Beorcham Blazes (2)
Beorcham Radiant (2)
Ch. Kinvarra Kermit (29)
Beg Pardon Rury Limerick (4)

AM. & CAN. CH. MICHAEL BRYAN DUKE OF SUSSEX (dog) —
S778836 — 11/8/55 — (*Photo,* P. 167)

Ch. Rosecroft Premier (4)	Ch. Milson O'Boy II (20)
Ch. End O'Maine Luckalone (8)	Rosecroft Fern (1)
Ch. End O'Maine Best Wishes (5)	Ch. Kinvarra Kermit (29)
Sire: **Ch. Thenderin Brian Tristan** (30)	Beg Pardon Rury Limerick (4)
Ch. Kinvarra Kermit (29)	Ch. Kinvarra Craig (8)
Ch. Kinvarra Portia (12)	*Ch. Kinvarra Mollie of Gadeland (5)
Beg Pardon Rury Limerick (4)	Ch. Milson Top-Notcher (6)
	Ch. End O'Maine Burnie Burn (2)
Ch. Redwood Russet of Harvale (16)	Ch. Higgins' Red Coat (30)
Ch. Kleiglight of Aragon (30)	Ch. Redwood Rita (5)
Ch. Stardust of Crosshaven (2)	Redwood Rocket (14)
Dam: **Am. & Can. Ch. Merrilynn of Glenfield** (2)	Ch. Ruxton's Shannon of Boyne (7)
Killeshandra's Beacon Light	Ch. Kleiglight of Aragon (30)
Celestina of Glenfield (1)	Kermit's Redleen of Boyne
Theodora of Kinvarra	Ch. Kinvarra Kermit (29)
	Kinvarra Marguerite (1)

CH. DRAHERIN IRISH REGARDLESS (dog) — S861186 — 4/6/57

Ch. Kinvarra Kermit (29)	Ch. Kinvarra Craig (8)
Ch. Tyronne Farm Malone (9)	*Ch. Kinvarra Mollie of Gadeland (5)
Ch. Ruxton's Mollie O'Day (14)	Ch. Higgins' Red Coat (30)
Sire: **Ch. Tyronne Farm Malone II** (25)	Ruxton's Tadg (7)
Jordan Farm Abe (9)	*Ch. Knock A Voe (0)
Ch. Tyronne Farm O'Flare (1)	Lady Pamela Redfeather (1)
Ch. Ruxton's Mollie O'Day (14)	Ch. Higgins' Red Coat (30)
	Ruxton's Tadg (7)
Broughshane Ekim (1)	Robinhood of Kenstra (0)
Ch. Rheola Shaun of Bail-lo (3)	Broughshane Miguelita
Ch. Rheola Sharon of Bal-Lo (1)	*Shaun Grellan of Wendover (1)
Dam: **Am. & Can. Ch. Thenderin Elixir, CD** (8)	Wamsutta Jacynth (1)
Ch. Red Ranger Pat (9)	Schreiber's Captain (1)
Ch. Thenderin All Spice (3)	Ravenhill's Geraldine (1)
Ch. Kinvarra Portia (12)	Ch. Kinvarra Kermit (29)
	Beg Pardon Rury Limerick (4)

CH. WEBLYN MYSTIC MARK (dog) — S845913 — 8/29/58 — (*Photo,* P. 129)
CH. WEBLYN MADRIGAL (bitch)

Ch. Tyronne Farm Malone (9)	Ch. Kinvarra Kermit (29)
Ch. Seaforth's Dark Rex (20)	Ch. Ruxton's Mollie O'Day (14)
Ch. Seaforth's Red Velvet (4)	Charles River Red Don (1)
Sire: **Ch. Innisfail Color Scheme, CD** (29)	Charles River Juanita (1)
Ch. Kendare Red Duke (1)	Ch. Kendare Stout Fellow (1)
Thenderin Champagne (4)	Ch. Kendare Ardri (1)
Thenderin April Anthem (1)	Ch. Red Ranger Pat (9)
	Ch. Kinvarra Portia (12)
Ch. Knightscroft Fermanagh (7)	Ch. Milson O'Boy II (20)
O'Shay's Gaylord (1)	Jordan Farm Scarlett O'Hara (4)
Ch. Linn's Lady O'Shay	Brendomino (2)
Dam: **Ch. Knightscroft Erin McCuhl** (4)	Linn's Queen (1)
Ch. Knightscroft Fermanagh (7)	Ch. Milson O'Boy II (20)
Knightscroft Dee Dorn (1)	Jordan Farm Scarlett O'Hara (4)
Knightscroft Babette	Knightscroft Chris Robin
	Ch. Knightscroft Dreamer (1)

CH. BLAYNEYWOOD COUNTRY SQUIRE (dog)
SA61424 — 8/12/60 — (Photo, P. 122)

	Ch. Tyronne Farm Malone (9)	Ch. Kinvarra Kermit (29)
Ch. Tyronne Farm Malone II (25)		Ch. Ruxton's Mollie O'Day (14)
	Ch. Tyronne Farm O'Flare (1)	Jordan Farm Abe (9)
Ch. Draherin Irish Chieftain (7)		Ch. Ruxton's Mollie O'Day (14)
	Ch. Rheola Shaun of Bail-Lo (3)	Broughshane Ekim (1)
Am. & Can. Ch. Thenderin Elixir, CD (8)		Ch. Rheola Sharon of Bal-Lo (1)
	Ch. Thenderin All Spice (3)	Ch. Red Ranger Pat (9)
		Ch. Kinvarra Portia (12)

	Ch. Tyronne Farm Malone (9)	Ch. Kinvarra Kermit (29)
Ch. Tyronne Farm Malone II (25)		Ch. Ruxton's Mollie O'Day (14)
	Ch. Tyronne Farm O'Flare (1)	Jordan Farm Abe (9)
Ch. Kinvarra Shiela (1)		Ch. Ruxton's Mollie O'Day (14)
	Mike O'Toole II (0)	Shanty O'Neal
Peggy Primrose (2)		Patty O'Rourke
		Am. & Can. Ch. Field Master of Maple Ridge (2)
	Pennie Shelia	Kendare Norin Darnoc

M., CAN. & MEX. CH. LEGEND OF VARAGON, UDT, PR, PU, CAN. CDX (dog)
SA67238 — 1960 — (Photo, P. 192)
CH. FLASHBACK OF VARAGON (dog) — (Photo, P. 182)

	Ch. Tyronne Farm Malone (9)	Ch. Kinvarra Kermit (29)
Ch. Seaforth's Dark Rex (20)		Ch. Ruxton's Molly O'Day (14)
	Ch. Seaforth's Red Velvet (4)	Charles River Red Don (1)
Ch. Innisfail Color Scheme, CD (20)		Charles River Juanita (1)
	Ch. Kendare Red Duke (1)	Ch. Kendare Stoutfellow (1)
Thenderin Champagne (4)		Ch. Kendare Ardri (1)
	Thenderin April Anthem (1)	Ch. Red Ranger Pat (9)
		Ch. Kinvarra Portia (12)

	Ch. Tyronne Farm Shamus	Ch. Kinvarra Kermit (29)
Ch. Thenderin Checkmate (2)		Beg Pardon Rury Limerick
	Ch. Charles River Blazing Beauty	Ch. Red Sails of Salmagundi (7)
Ch. Innisfail Best Regards, CDX		Wamsutta Susie Q (3)
	Ch. Kendare Red Duke (1)	Ch. Kendare Stoutfellow (1)
Thenderin Champagne (4)		Ch. Kendare Ardri (1)
	Thenderin April Anthem (1)	Ch. Red Ranger Pat (9)
		Ch. Kinvarra Portia (12)

H. RUNWILD FINNAGAIN (dog) — SA78670 — 11/19/60 — (Photo, P. 187)

	Ch. Charles River Color Sergeant (17)	*Ch. Red Sails of Salmagundi (7)
Ch. Carrvale's Sergeant Terrence (5)		Wamsutta Susie Q (3)
	Shawnee of Devon (3)	Ch. Kleiglight of Aragon (30)
Ch. Carrvale's Terry Terhune (14)		Wamsutta Dream Girl (0)
	Ch. Tyronne Farm Malone (9)	Ch. Kinvarra Kermit (29)
Tyronne Farm Sherry (4)		Ch. Ruxton's Mollie O'Day (14)
	Ch. Tyronne Farm Merriwynne (3)	Ch. Tyronne Farm Tipperary (5)
		Ch. Tyronne Farm Debutante (2)

	Ch. Charles River Blazes (2)	*Ch. Red Sails of Salmagundi (7)
Ch. Sergeant Red Sails of Devon (14*)		Molly o' Ballyclough (1)
	Ch. Red Mollie of Devon (1)	Ch. Charles River Color Sergeant (17)
Ch. Runwild Fiona (5)		Shawnee of Devon (3)
	Runwild Sergeant Shawn (2)	Ch. Charles River Color Sergeant (17)
Ch. Tara's Theme (6)		Ch. Runwild Alannah, CD (1)
	Peggy of Aragon II (1)	Ch. Kleiglight of Aragon (30)
		Sarah of Aragon (4)

CH. TIRVELDA EARL OF HAREWOOD (dog) — SA170811 — 9/3/62 — (Photo, P
Also: CH. TIRVELDA MICHAELSON (dog), P. 167; CH. TIRVELDA NOR'WESTER
CH. TIRVELDA CATHY O'RINN (bitch), P. 144

Ch. End O'Maine Luckalone (8)	Ch. Rosecroft Premier (4)
Ch. Thenderin Brian Tristan (30)	Ch. End O'Maine Best Wishes (!
Ch. Kinvarra Portia (12)	Ch. Kinvarra Kermit (29)
Sire: Am. & Can. Ch. Michael Bryan Duke of Sussex (32)	Beg Pardon Rury Limerick (4)
Ch. Kleiglight of Aragon (30)	Ch. Redwood Russet of Harvale
Am. & Can. Ch. Merrilynn of Glenfield (2)	Ch. Stardust of Crosshaven (2)
Celestina of Glenfield (1)	Killeshandra's Beacon Light
	Theodora of Kinvarra
Ch. Tyronne Farm Malone II (25)	Ch. Tyronne Farm Malone (9)
Ch. Kinvarra Malone (12)	Ch. Tyronne Farm O'Flare (1)
Peggy Primrose (2)	Mike O'Toole II
Dam: Ch. Tirvelda Nutbrown Sherry (23)	Pennie Shelia
Hartsbourne Clovis (1)	Eamon of Casamia
*Ch. Hartsbourne Sallyann of Tirvelda (12)	Hartsbourne Clover
Hartsbourne Sabrina Fair (1)	Eng. Show Ch. Hartsbourne O'H
	Hartsbourne Flush (1)

CH. DONAMAR BOLD ECHO OF VARAGON (dog) — SA192360 — 4/5/63

Ch. End O'Maine Luckalone (8)	Ch. Rosecroft Premier (4)
Ch. Thenderin Brian Tristan (30)	Ch. End O'Maine Best Wishes (!
Ch. Kinvarra Portia (12)	Ch. Kinvarra Kermit (29)
Sire: Am. & Can. Ch. Michael Bryan Duke of Sussex (32)	Beg Pardon Rury Limerick (4)
Ch. Kleiglight of Aragon (30)	Ch. Redwood Russet of Harvale
Am. & Can. Ch. Merrilynn of Glenfield (2)	Ch. Stardust of Crosshaven (2)
Celestina of Glenfield (1)	Killeshandra's Beacon Light
	Theodora of Kinvarra
Ch. Seaforth's Dark Rex (20)	Ch. Tyronne Farm Malone (9)
Ch. Innisfail Color Scheme, CD (29)	Ch. Seaforth's Red Velvet (4)
Thenderin Champagne (4)	Ch. Kendare Red Duke (1)
Dam: Ch. Enchantment of Varagon (1)	Thenderin April Anthem (1)
Ch. Thenderin Checkmate (2)	Ch. Tyronne Farm Shamus (2)
Ch. Innisfail Best Regards, CDX (5)	Ch. Charles River Blazing Beaut
Thenderin Champagne (4)	Ch. Kendare Red Duke (1)
	Thenderin April Anthem (1)

CH. THENDERIN WIND RULER (dog) — SA524031 — 1963 — (Photo, P. 221

Thenderin Sunswift	Ch. Thenderin Nomad
Thenderin Wind Warrior	Ch. Thenderin Kiss
Ch. Thenderin Benedictine	Ch. Brynmount Maydorwill Brar
Sire: Ch. Thenderin Chaparral Cayenne	Ch. Thenderin Amaranth
Ch. Seaforth's Dark Rex	Ch. Tyronne Farms Malone
Thenderin Red Maeve	Ch. Seaforth's Red Velvet
Ch. Thenderin Echo of Spice	Ch. Rheola Shaun of Bail-Lo
	Ch. Thenderin All-Spice
Thenderin Wind Warrior	Thenderin Sunswift
Ch. Thenderin Drum Hills	Ch. Thenderin Benedictine
Ch. Thenderin Kiss	Ch. Seaforth's Dark Rex
Dam: Ch. Thenderin Odyssey	Ch. Memory of Devon
Ch. Thenderin High 'N' Handsome	Ch. Margevan's Real McCoy
Ch. Thenderin Mi-Spice	Ch. Thenderin Deeper Than Gay
Ch. Innisfail Mona Lisa	Ch. Seaforth's Dark Rex
	Thenderin Champagne

AHERIN COUNTY LEITRIM (dog) — SA199784 — 5/20/63 — (Photo, P. 215)

Ch. Innisfail Color Scheme, CD (29)
    Ch. Seaforth's Dark Rex (20)
    Thenderin Champagne (4)
Am. & Can. Ch. Draherin Auburn Artistry (14)
Ch. Draherin Echo of Elixir (7)
    Patrick Redjacket (1)
    Am. & Can. Ch. Thenderin Elixir, CD (8)

- Ch. Tyronne Farm Malone (9)
- Ch. Seaforth's Red Velvet (4)
- Ch. Kendare Red Duke (1)
- Thenderin April Anthem (1)
- Rusty of Modra Rhu's Red Dust**
- Gypsy Redjacket
- Ch. Rheola Shaun of Bail-Io (3)
- Ch. Thenderin All Spice (3)

Am. & Can. Ch. Yorkhill's County Kerry II, CD (2)
End O'Maine Guest Star (1)
    Ch. Carrvale's Terry Terhune (14)
    End O'Maine Claret (11)
Ch. Yorkhill's Achilles (3)
The Pretty Peggy (1)
    Hedgewood Rose of Sharon

- Ch. Carrvale's Sergeant Terrence (5)
- Tyronne Farm Sherry (4)
- Am. & Can. Ch. Laurel Ridge Star Rocket
- Ch. Mid-Oak Rose of Sharon (4)
- Ch. Tyronne Farm Shanahan (5)
- Ch. Yorkhill's Red Rhapsody, CDX (2)
- Timothy O'Shea
- Ch. Hedgewood Regret

CAN. CH. RED ARROW GOLD FEATHERS (dog) — SA316387 — 10/22/64

Dual Ch. Tyrone's Mahogany Mike, CDX (4/2FC)
    Can. Ch. Lord Tyrone Trent, CD (1DC)
    McIvor's Kathleen, CD (1DC)
Ch. Red Arrow Smooth Sailing, UDT (1)
Dual Ch. Red Arrow Show Girl, UDT, Mex. PC (8)
    Ch. Hollywood Hills O'Shaughnesy, CDX (1DC)
    Marted Annie Rooney, CDX (1DC)

- Am. & Can. Ch. Tyronne Farm Tyrone (2)
- Lady Trent (1)
- Red King of Farmdale
- McKay's Linda
- Ch. Rufus of Hollywood Hills (6)
- Ch. Faig-a-Baile of Crosshaven (4)
- Ch. Marted Red Pepper
- Redwood Rhoda's Reward

Am. & Can. Ch. Esquire of Maple Ridge (32)
    Ch. Thenderin Brian Tristan (30)
    Crosshaven Lea of Maple Ridge (5)
Am. & Can. Ch. Red Arrow Solid Gold, CDX (1)
Dual Ch. Red Arrow Show Girl, UDT, Mex. PC (8)
    Ch. Hollywood Hills O'Shaughnesy, CDX (1DC)
    Marted Annie Rooney, CDX (1DC)

- Ch. End O'Maine Luckalone (8)
- Ch. Kinvarra Portia (12)
- Am. & Can. Ch. Red Sails Michael of Oak Grove (11)
- Crosshaven Molly O'Bryan
- Ch. Rufus of Hollywood Hills (6)
- Ch. Faig-a-Baile of Crosshaven (4)
- Ch. Marted Red Pepper
- Redwood Rhoda's Reward

EMERALD ISLE ANGEL'S LAD (dog) — SA472735 — 2/5/66

Moffat's Apache Bill
    Fld. Ch. Ike Jack Kendrick (1FC)
    Lady's Colleen
Miller's Lad O'Lil (1FC)
Fld. Ch. Miller's Tiger Lily
    *Fld. Ch. Sulhamstead Norse D'Or (3FC)
    Fld. Ch. Miller's Bonny Loo (1FC)

- Ike Kendrick (1FC)
- Fld. Ch. Askew's Carolina Lady (1FC)
- Willow Winds Duke
- Fld. Ch. Askew's Carolina Lady (1FC)
- Sulhamstead Montebellos Norseman (1FC)
- Sulhamstead Banco D'Or (1FC)
- Dual Ch. Tyrone's Mahogany Mike, CDX (4/2FC)
- Ch. Lady La Rouge (1/1FC)

*Fld. Ch. Sulhamstead Norse D'Or (3FC)
    Sulhamstead Montebellos Norseman (1FC)
    Sulhamstead Banco D'Or (1FC)
Fld. Ch. Emerald Isle Angel (1FC)
The Babe (1FC)
    Dual Ch. Tyrone's Mahogany Mike, CDX (4/2FC)
    Gay Lady of Wildwood (2)

- Gronsjoens Ripper
- Nor. Ch. Montebellos Jappy
- Sulhamstead Blast D'Or
- Sulhamstead Bantam D'Or
- Can. Ch. Lord Tyrone Trent, CD (1DC)
- McIvor's Kathleen, CD (1DC)
- Red Pat of Jilda
- Lady Amber IV

DUAL CH. MAHOGANY'S TITIAN JINGO (dog)
SA203715 — 7/1/62 — (Photo, P. 275)

Ch. Charles River Color Sergeant (17)	*Ch. Red Sails of Salmagundi (7
Mahogany Tim II (1/1DC/1FC)	Wamsutta Susie Q (3)
Small Change (0)	Jahudi (0)
Sire: Dual Ch. Titian Duke, CD (1/1DC/1FC)	Judy to Bea (0)
Ch. King Size (2)	Major Red Flag (1)
King Size Scarlet Lady (1DC/1FC)	Lady Red Velvet (1)
Ch. Love Creek Farm Memory (1)	Ch. End O'Maine Luckalone (8)
	Macha Mong Ruad (2)
Am. & Can. Ch. Esquire of Maple Ridge (32)	Ch. Thenderin Brian Tristan (30
Ch. Jim O'Reilly of Oakshire	Crosshaven Lea of Maple Ridge
Pat's Kathryne of Oakshire (1)	Ringleader of Glen Ryan (1)
Dam: Mahogany's Miss Fire-Ball (1DC)	Argyle's Upland Christina (0)
Mahogany Tim II (1/1DC/1FC)	Ch. Charles River Color Sergean
Ch. Shanty Kate III, CD (1/2FC)	Small Change
Shanty Kate (1)	End O'Maine Roger's Squire (0)
	Lady Left Over

CH. BAYBERRY SOMMERSET (dog) — SA275785 — 1964 — (Photo, P. 14

Ch. Tyronne Farm Malone	Ch. Kinvarra Kermit
Ch. Tyronne Farm Malone II	Ch. Ruxton's Molly O'Day
Ch. Tyronne Farm O'Flare	Jordan Farm Abe
Sire: Ch. Kinvarra Malone	Ch. Ruxton's Molly O'Day
Mike O'Toole	Shanty O'Neal
Peggy Primrose	Patty O'Rourke
Pennie Sheilah	Ch. Fieldmaster of Maple Ridge
	Kendare Norin Darnoe
Ch. Thenderin Brian Tristan	Ch. End O'Maine Luckalone
Am. & Can. Ch. Michael Bryan Duke of Sussex	Ch. Kinvarra Portia
Ch. Merrilynn of Glenfield	Ch. Kleiglight of Aragon
Dam: Ch. Tirvelda Cathy O'Rinn	Celestina of Glenfield
Ch. Kinvarra Malone	Ch. Tyronne Farm Malone II
Ch. Tirvelda Nutbrown Sherry	Peggy Primrose
Ch. Hartsbourne Sallyann of Tirvelda	Hartsbourne Clovis
	Hartsbourne Sabrinafair

AM. & CAN. CH. BAYBERRY KINCAIDE (dog) — SA421704 — 5/1/66

Kinvarra Hartsbourne Kim	Eng. Sh. Ch. Hartsbourne Tobia
Ch. Kinvarra Kimson	Ch. Hartsbourne Popsy
Kinvarra Dragon Club II	Kinvarra Michaelmas
Sire: Ch. Kinvarra Flicker	Ch. Kinvarra Bootsie
Ch. Kinvarra Hartsbourne Flurry	Ch. Hartsbourne Brilliant
Kinvarra Derrydown Sally	Hartsbourne Flush
Kinvarra Sally Lunn	Ch. Kinvarra Ensign
	Ch. Seaforth's Red Velvet
Ch. Thenderin Brian Tristan	Ch. End O'Maine Luckalone
Am. & Can. Ch. Michael Bryan Duke of Sussex	Ch. Kinvarra Portia
Ch. Merrilynn of Glenfield	Ch. Kleiglight of Aragon
Dam: Ch. Tirvelda Cathy O'Rinn	Celestine of Glenfield
Ch. Kinvarra Malone	Ch. Tyronne Farm Malone II
Ch. Tirvelda Nutbrown Sherry	Peggy Primrose
Ch. Hartsbourne Sallyann of Tirvelda	Hartsbourne Clovis
	Hartsbourne Sabrinafair

AM., CAN. & BDA. CH. SHANNON'S ERIN (dog)
SA256351 — 3/25/64 — (Photo, P. 213)

Ch. Tyronne Farm Malone (9)	Ch. Kinvarra Kermit (29)
Ch. Tyronne Farm Malone II (25)	Ch. Ruxton's Mollie O'Day (14)
Ch. Tyronne Farm O'Flare (1)	Jordan Farm Abe (9)
re: **Ch. Draherin Irish Regardless** (24)	Ch. Ruxton's Mollie O'Day (14)
Ch. Rheola Shaun of Bail-lo (3)	Broughshane Ekim (1)
Am. & Can. Ch. Thenderin Elixir, CD (8)	Ch. Rheola Sharon of Bal-Lo (1)
Ch. Thenderin All Spice (3)	Ch. Red Ranger Pat (9)
	Ch. Kinvarra Portia (12)
Ch. Caldene Mick O'Boy (9)	Ch. Caldene Picardy (4)
Knockross' O'Boy (36)	Ch. Molly of Terry-Tom (1)
	Am. & Can. Ch. Red Star of Hollywood Hills, CDX (23/1FC)
Ch. Sharoc Coquette (1)	Charles River Destiny (4)
am: **Ch. Knockross' Ruby** (21)	Ch. Caldene Picardy (4)
Ch. Caldene Mick O'Boy (9)	Ch. Molly of Terry-Tom (1)
Ch. Knockross' Milo (2)	Ch. Milson Christopher Robin (4)
Knockross' Glad Rags (1)	Ch. Caldene Pollyanna

STARHEIR'S AARON ARDEE (dog) — SA434199 — 11/13/66 — (Photo, P. 239)

Ch. Thenderin Brian Tristan (30)	Ch. End O'Maine Luckalone (8)
Ch. Fleetwood Farm Sixty Special (1)	Ch. Kinvarra Portia (12)
Ch. Fleetwood Farm's Noreen (2)	Ch. Gay Guy of Aragon (1)
ire: **Ch. Fleetwood Farm's Brougham** (5)	Ch. Fleetwood Farm's Peg O'My Heart (1)
Tall-Y-Ellyn's Fleetwood	Ch. Gay Guy of Aragon (1)
Fleetwood Farm's Flaming Glo (1)	Ch. Fleetwood Farm's Peg O'My Heart (1)
Gay Guy's Flame	Ch. Gay Guy of Aragon (1)
	Heintzman's Lady Ginger
Ch. Tyronne Farm Malone II (25)	Ch. Tyronne Farm Malone (9)
Ch. Draherin Irish Regardless (24)	Ch. Tyronne Farm O'Flare (1)
Am. & Can. Ch. Thenderin Elixir, CD (8)	Ch. Rheola Shaun of Bail-lo (3)
am: **Am. & Can. Ch. Shannon's Susie Starlet, CD** (6)	Ch. Thenderin All Spice (3)
Knockross' O'Boy (36)	Ch. Caldene Mick O'Boy (9)
Ch. Knockross' Ruby (21)	Ch. Sharoc Coquette (1)
Ch. Knockross' Milo (2)	Ch. Caldene Mick O'Boy (9)
	Knockross' Glad Rags (1)

CH. THENDERIN LEGACY (dog) — SA658416 — 4/27/68

Thenderin Wind-Warrior (7)	Thenderin Sun Swift (2)
Ch. Thenderin Chaparal Cayenne (5)	Ch. Thenderin Benedictine (1)
Thenderin Red Maeve (4)	Ch. Seaforth's Dark Rex (20)
ire: **Ch. Thenderin Wind Ruler** (12)	Ch. Thenderin Echo of Spice (2)
Ch. Thenderin Drum Hills (8)	Thenderin Wind-Warrior (7)
Ch. Thenderin Odyssey (2)	Ch. Thenderin Kiss (2)
Ch. Thenderin Mispice (8)	Ch. Thenderin High N' Handsome (1)
	Ch. Innisfail Mona Lisa (1)
Thenderin Sun Swift (2)	Ch. Thenderin Nomad (3)
Ch. Thenderin Endorsement (9)	Ch. Thenderin Kiss (2)
Ch. Thenderin Benedictine (1)	*Ch. Brynmount Maydorwill Brandyson (8)
am: **Thenderin Omen O'Mulholland** (3)	Ch. Thenderin Amaranth (4)
Ch. Thenderin Drum Hills (8)	Thenderin Wind-Warrior (7)
Ch. Thenderin Odyssey (2)	Ch. Thenderin Kiss (2)
Ch. Thenderin Mispice (8)	Ch. Thenderin High N' Handsome (1)
	Ch. Innisfail Mona Lisa (1)

AM. & CAN. CH. DRAHERIN KING'S RANSOM (dog) — SA776119 — 12/24/

	Ch. Tyronne Farm Malone (9)
Ch. Tyronne Farm Malone II (25)	Ch. Tyronne Farm O'Flare (1)
Ch. Draherin Irish Regardless (24)	Ch. Rheola Shaun of Bail-lo (3)
Am. & Can. Ch. Thenderin Elixir, CD (8)	Ch. Thenderin All Spice (9)
Sire: Am., Can. & Bda. Ch. Shannon's Erin (46)	Ch. Caldene Mick O'Boy (9)
Knockross' O'Boy (36)	Ch. Sharoc Coquette (1)
Ch. Knockross' Ruby (21)	Ch. Caldene Mick O'Boy (9)
Ch. Knockross' Milo (2)	Knockross' Glad Rags (1)
Am. & Can. Ch. Draherin Auburn	Ch. Innisfail Color Scheme, CD (:
Artistry (14)	
Ch. Draherin County Leitrim (22)	Ch. Draherin Echo of Elixir (7)
Am. & Can. Ch. Yorkhill's County	End O'Maine Guest Star (1)
Kerry II, CD (2)	
Dam: Ch. Draherin Merry Kerry (5)	The Pretty Peggy (1)
Am. & Can. Ch. Draherin Auburn	Ch. Innisfail Color Scheme, CD (:
Artistry (14)	
Glen Cree High Time (2)	Ch. Draherin Echo of Elixir (7)
Draherin Coronet	Ch. Thenderin Brian Tristan (30)
	Am. & Can. Ch. Thenderin Elixir,

FLD. CH. SHAWN OF KAYMAR (dog) — SA756422 — 3/13/69

	Rufus McTybe O'Cloisters (1FC)
Schnet's Hellfire of Havelock	Schnet's Irish Rose
Schnet's Joe C.	Am. & Can. Ch. Red Star of
	Hollywood Hills, CDX (23/1FC
Boxley Starlet (0)	Boxley Patria
Sire: King Flame of Kaymar (2FC)	Rufus McTybe O'Cloisters (1FC)
Schnet's Hellfire of Havelock	Schnet's Irish Rose
Missie B.	Fld. Ch. Sulhamstead Norse D'Or
Shu Fly C.	Bridey Murphy
Mr. O'Leary	Willow Winds Hobo
Autumn Hills Duke (1FC)	Fld. Ch. Askew's Carolina Lady (1
Redfield Ginger	Patrick of Stanton
Dam: Fld. Ch. Miss Colleen of Kaymar (2FC)	Staunton's Lady
Mr. Morgan	Autumn Hills Duke (1FC)
Blarney Rock's Flame (1FC)	Wilson's Red Doll
Miss Molly O'Leary	Autumn Hills Duke (1FC)
	Cherry Hills Duchess

CH. TIRVELDA DISTANT DRUMMER (dog) — SB234662 — 1/2/72 — (Photo, P

	Ch. Tyronne Farm Malone
Ch. Tyronne Farm Malone II	Ch. Tyronne Farm O'Flare
Ch. Kinvarra Malone	Mike O'Toole
Peggy Primrose	Pennie Sheilah
Sire: Ch. Bayberry Sommerset	Ch. Thenderin Brian Tristan
Am. & Can. Ch. Michael Bryan	
Duke of Sussex	Am. & Can. Ch. Merrilynn of Gler
Ch. Tirvelda Cathy O'Rinn	Ch. Kinvarra Malone
Ch. Tirvelda Nutbrown Sherry	Ch. Hartsbourne Sallyann of Tirve
Ch. Draherin Irish Chieftain	Ch. Tyronne Farm Malone II
Ch. Blayneywood Country Squire	Ch. Thenderin Elixir, CD
Ch. Kinvarra Shiela	Ch. Tyronne Farm Malone II
Dam: Ch. Tirvelda Red Heather	Peggy Primrose
Ch. Kinvarra Flicker	Ch. Kinvarra Kimson
Ch. Tirvelda Divine Sarah	Kinvarra Derrydown Sally
Ch. Hartsbourne Sallyann of Tirvelda	Hartsbourne Clovis
	Hartsbourne Sabrinafair

CH. CANDIA INDEED (dog) — SB94222 — 3/6/72 — (*Photo,* P. 141)

Ch. Kinvarra Kimson (6)
Ch. Kinvarra Flicker (12)
Kinvarra Derrydown Sally (2)
e: **Am. & Can. Ch. Bayberry Kincaide** (3)
Am. & Can. Ch. Michael Bryan Duke
of Sussex (32)
Ch. Tirvelda Cathy O'Rinn (8)
Ch. Tirvelda Nutbrown Sherry (23)

*Kinvarra Hartsbourne Kim (1)
Kinvarra Dragon Cub II (1)
*Ch. Kinvarra Hartsbourne Flurry (2)
Kinvarra Sally Lunn (2)
Ch. Thenderin Brian Tristan (30)

Am. & Can. Ch. Merrilynn of Glenfield (2)
Ch. Kinvarra Malone (12)
*Ch. Hartsbourne Sallyann of Tirvelda (12)

Ch. Weblyn Mystic Mark (24)
Am. & Can. Ch. Draherin Echo's Guy (2)
Ch. Draherin Echo of Elixir (7)
m: **Ch. Candia Fatima** (1)
Am. & Can. Ch. Draherin Auburn
Artistry (14)
Ch. Candia Camille (2)
Ch. Candia Pride (5)

Ch. Innisfail Color Scheme, CD (29)
Ch. Knightscroft Erin McCuhl (4)
Patrick Redjacket (1)
Am. & Can. Ch. Thenderin Elixir, CD (8)
Ch. Innisfail Color Scheme, CD (29)

Ch. Draherin Echo of Elixir (7)
Ch. Muckamoor's Marty McCuhl (14)
Ch. Draherin Echo's Hope (11)

AM. & CAN. CH. McCAMON MARQUIS (dog)
SC040451 — 1/1/75 — (*Photo,* P. 196)

Ch. Michael Bryan Duke of Sussex
Ch. Tirvelda Michaelson
Ch. Tirvelda Nutbrown Sherry
e: **Ch. Tirvelda Telstar**
Ch. Tirvelda Rustic Duke
Ch. Tirvelda Queen Mab
Ch. Tirvelda Maidavale

Ch. Thenderin Brian Tristan
Am. & Can. Ch. Merrilynn of Glenfield
Ch. Kinvarra Malone
Ch. Hartsbourne Sallyann of Tirvelda
Ch. Kinvarra Malone
Ch. Hartsbourne Sallyann of Tirvelda
Am. Can. & Mex. Ch. Legend of
Varagon, UDT
Ch. Tirvelda Sabrina

Ch. Michael Bryan Duke of Sussex
Ch. Tirvelda Michaelson
Ch. Tirvelda Nutbrown Sherry
n: **Can. & Am. Ch. McCamon's Royal Burgundy**
Rockherin Flynn
Ch. Rockherin Rebecca
Ch. Caldene Ailene

Ch. Thenderin Brian Tristan
Am. & Can. Ch. Merrilynn of Glenfield
Ch. Kinvarra Malone
Ch. Hartsbourne Sallyann of Tirvelda
End O'Maine Jack High
Ch. Rogue Molly O'Malley
Knockross O'Boy
Katy-Did of Maple Ridge

CH. RUXTON'S MOLLIE O'DAY (bitch) — 911477 — 9/4/32

	*Eng. Ch. Terry of Boyne (1)	Eng. Ch. Brian of Boyne (1)
*Higgins' Paddy of Boyne (7)		Young Norah of Boyne (1)
Dora of Boyne		Eamon of Boyne
Sire: **Ch. Higgins' Red Coat** (30)		Lady Joan
Ch. Lismore Freedom (6)		Ch. Conn Law (3)
Craigie Lea Mona (6)		Ch. Lismore Colleen (4)
Chare II (1)		Ch. St. Cloud's Fermanagh (2)
		Ch. Bob White Red Storm (1)

	Eng. Ch. Gruagach (3)	Come Up Tipp
*Eng. Show & Am. Ch. Tadg (1)		Beltane
Oona of Derrynane (3)		Peter the Pride
Dam: **Ruxton's Tadg** (7)		Una
Southdown Larry (1)		
*Ch. Mairgread Dileas		
Glanduff Peggy the Rebel (1)		

CH. KINVARRA PORTIA (bitch) — A580097 — 12/7/41 — (*Photo,* P. 114)

	Ch. Kinvarra Son of Red Coat (7)	Ch. Higgins' Red Coat (30)
Ch. Kinvarra Craig (8)		Ch. Queen Maive (3)
*Borrowdale Yseult of Kinvarra (4)		Rheola Boniface
Sire: **Ch. Kinvarra Kermit** (29)		Eng. Ch. Norna
Eng. Ch. Brigand of Usan (1)		*Ch. Golden Dawn of Gadeland O'Ar.
*Ch. Kinvarra Mollie of Gadeland (5)		Garnet O'Murrell of Usan
Monica of Gadeland (1)		Eng. Ch. Son of a Gun of Gadeland (1
		Eng. Ch. Rebel Maid of Gadeland (1)

	Ch. Milson O'Boy (17)	Ch. Higgins' Red Coat (30)
Ch. Milson Top-Notcher (6)		Milson Miss Sonny (2)
Milson Squire's Janice (1)		*Ch. Flornell Squire of Milson (1)
Dam: **Beg Pardon Rury Limerick** (4)		Orchid Lady (0)
Ch. Higgins' Red Coat (30)		*Higgins' Paddy of Boyne (7)
Ch. End O'Maine Burnie Burn (2)		Craigie Lea Mona (6)
Ch. End O'Maine Beg Pardon (2)		*Ch. Beg-Zit of Bodicgo (1)
		End O'Maine Autumn Leaf (1)

AM. & CAN. CH. THENDERIN ELIXIR, CD (bitch) — S363040 — 12/5/49

	Robinhood of Kenstra	*Shaun Grellan of Wendover (1)
Broughshane Ekim (1)		Wamsutta Jacynth (1)
Broughshane Miguelita (0)		Ch. Broughshane Michael
Sire: **Ch. Rheola Shaun of Bail-lo** (3)		Tipperary Sadie
*Shaun Grellan of Wendover (1)		Eng. Ch. Grellan of Matsonhouse
Ch. Rheola Sharon of Bal-Lo (1)		Dawn of Wendover
Wamsutta Jacynth (1)		Ch. Paddy of Shanagolden (5)
		Ch. Hana of Shanagolden

	Schreiber's Captain (1)	Jordan Farm Abe (9)
Ch. Red Ranger Pat (9)		Clar's Nancy Baby (2)
Ravenhill's Geraldine (1)		Ch. Michael of Ravenhill
Dam: **Ch. Thenderin All Spice** (3)		Red Blaze Pegga of Farhill
Ch. Kinvarra Kermit (29)		Ch. Kinvarra Craig (8)
Ch. Kinvarra Portia (12)		*Ch. Kinvarra Mollie of Gadeland (5)
Beg Pardon Rury Limerick (4)		Ch. Milson Top-Notcher (6)
		Ch. End O'Maine Burnie Burn (2)

315

END O'MAINE CLARET (bitch) — S751758 — 6/9/55

Ch. Rufus of Hollywood Hills (6)
Am. & Can. Ch. Red Star of Hollywood Hills,
CDX (23/1FC)
Ch. Faig-a-Baile of Crosshaven (4)
re: **Am. & Can. Ch. Laurel Ridge Star Rocket** (4)
Ch. Red Ranger Pat (9)
Ch. Honors Even Rakish Jane (2)
Ch. Kinvarra Portia (12)

Ch. Redwood Russet of Harvale (16)
Penny Tax of Hollywood Hills (2)

Ch. Redwood Russet of Harvale (16)
Ch. Sally O'Bryan of Crosshaven (2)
Schreiber's Captain (1)
Ravenhill's Geraldine (1)
Ch. Kinvarra Kermit (29)
Beg Pardon Rury Limerick (4)

Ch. Highlight of Denhaven (4)
Ch. Red Dawn of Sunny Acre (12)
Debutante Daughter (3)
am: **Ch. Mid-Oak Rose of Sharon** (4)
Ch. Kleiglight of Aragon (30)
Ch. Mid-Oak Aragon Flash (2)
Ch. Charles River All Afire (2)

Ch. Kleiglight of Aragon (30)
Ruxton's Peggy the Rebel (2)
Ch. Kleiglight of Aragon (30)
Lady Envy of Aragon
Ch. Redwood Russet of Harvale (16)
Ch. Stardust of Crosshaven (2)
*Ch. Red Sails of Salmagundi (7)
Wamsutta Susie Q (3)

H. HARTSBOURNE SALLYANN OF TIRVELDA (bitch) — S986504 — 7/12/57

Eng. Ch. Gaelge Copperplate of Ide
Eamon of Casamia
Eng. Show Ch. Gail of Casamia
re: **Hartsbourne Clovis** (1)
Eng. Show Ch. Hartsbourne Tobias
Hartsbourne Clover
Eng. Show Ch. Hartsbourne
Meadowsweet

Branscombe Robyn
Eng. Show Ch. Ronor Rena of Ide
Beau of Wendover
Lady Casamia
Hartsbourne Masterstroke
Hartsbourne Flame
Hartsbourne Masterstroke

Hartsbourne Sweetness

Eng. Show Ch. Hartsbourne Tobias
Eng. Show Ch. Hartsbourne O'Hara
Eng. Ch. Hartsbourne Popsy
am: **Hartsbourne Sabrina Fair** (1)
Brynmount Redgaynes Mars (1)
Hartsbourne Flush (1)
Hartsbourne Flame

Hartsbourne Masterstroke
Hartsbourne Flame
Hartsbourne Senor of Shadowood
Hartsbourne Poppet
Rheola Bendickson
Brynmount Shailamhor
Ir. Ch. Brilliant Bob
Derrybrien Sally

CH. KNOCKROSS' RUBY (bitch) — SA16021 — 3/7/58

Ch. Caldene Picardy (4)
Ch. Caldene Mick O'Boy (9)
Ch. Molly of Terry-Tom (1)
ire: **Knockross' O'Boy** (36)
Am. & Can. Ch. Red Star of
Hollywood Hills, CDX (23/1FC)
Ch. Sharoc Coquette (1)
Charles River Destiny (4)

Ch. Caldene Judson (5)
Ch. Caldene Pixie (3)
Ch. Caldene Mickey Mischief (6)
Ch. Caldene Pixie (3)
Ch. Rufus of Hollywood Hills (6)

Ch. Faig-a-Baile of Crosshaven (4)
*Ch. Red Sails of Salmagundi (7)
Ch. End O'Maine Best Wishes (5)

Ch. Caldene Picardy (4)
Ch. Caldene Mick O'Boy (9)
Ch. Molly of Terry-Tom (1)
am: **Ch. Knockross' Milo** (1)
Ch. Milson Christopher Robin (4)
Knockross' Glad Rags (1)
Ch. Caldene Pollyanna

Ch. Caldene Judson (5)
Ch. Caldene Pixie (3)
Ch. Caldene Mickey Mischief (6)
Ch. Caldene Pixie (3)
Ch. Rosecroft Premier (4)
Milson Acushla of Annally (2)
Ch. Seekonk Patty O'Byrne (1)
Caldene Polly (2)

CH. TIRVELDA NUTBROWN SHERRY (bitch) — SA91894 — 12/9/60

Ch. Tyronne Farm Malone (9)	Ch. Kinvarra Kermit (29)
Ch. Tyronne Farm Malone II (25)	Ch. Ruxton's Mollie O'Day (14)
Ch. Tyronne Farm O'Flare	Jordan Farm Abe (9)
Sire: **Ch. Kinvarra Malone** (12)	Ch. Ruxton's Mollie O'Day (14)
Mike O'Toole II	Shanty O'Neal
Peggy Primrose (2)	Patty O'Rourke
	Am. & Can. Ch. Field Master of Ma
	Ridge (2)
Pennie Shelia	Kendare Norin Darnoc
Eamon of Casamia	Eng. Ch. Gaelge Copperplate of Ide
Hartsbourne Clovis (1)	Eng. Show Ch. Gail of Casamia
Hartsbourne Clover	Eng. Show Ch. Hartsbourne Tobias
Dam: ***Ch. Hartsbourne Sallyann of Tirvelda** (12)	Eng. Show Ch. Hartsbourne Meade
Eng. Show Ch. Hartsbourne O'Hara	Eng. Show Ch. Hartsbourne Tobias
Hartsbourne Sabrina Fair (1)	Eng. Ch. Hartsbourne Popsy
Hartsbourne Flush (1)	Brynmount Redgaynes Mars (1)
	Hartsbourne Flame

DUAL CH. RED ARROW SHOW GIRL, UDT, MEX. PC (bitch) — S595678

Ch. Redwood Russet of Harvale (16)	Ch. Higgins' Red Coat (30)
Ch. Rufus of Hollywood Hills (6)	Ch. Redwood Rita (5)
Penny Tax of Hollywood Hills (2)	The Bronze Baron of Wamsutta
Sire: **Ch. Hollywood Hills O'Shaughnesy, CDX** (DC)	Royal Irish Radiance
Ch. Redwood Russet of Harvale (16)	Ch. Higgins' Red Coat (30)
Ch. Faig-a-Baile of Crosshaven (4)	Ch. Redwood Rita (5)
Ch. Sally O'Bryan of Crosshaven (2)	Redwood Rocket (14)
	Ch. Ruxton's Shannon of Boyne (7)
Ch. Waterford Bronze Monarch (1)	Ch. Bronzed Apollo (3)
Ch. Marted Red Pepper	Ch. Rocket's Red Radiance (3)
Waterford Maggie Star (1)	Waterford Busy Britches
Dam: **Marted Annie Rooney, CDX** (1DC)	Waterford Gamble
Redwood Rory of Crosshaven (3)	Redwood's Baron of Crosshaven
Redwood Rhoda's Reward	Ch. Sally O'Bryan of Crosshaven (2
Ch. Waterford Shanty Irish II	Ch. Redwood Russet of Harvale (16
	Ch. Katie O'Shea (1)

CH. TYRONNE FARM GLORIBEE (bitch) — SA123208 — 2/5/61

Ch. Carrvale's Sergeant Terrence (5)	Ch. Charles River Color Sergeant (1
Ch. Carrvale's Terry Terhune (14)	Shawnee of Devon (3)
Tyronne Farm Sherry (4)	Ch. Tyronne Farm Malone (9)
Sire: **Ch. End O'Maine Red Cloud** (5)	Ch. Tyronne Farm Merriwynne (3)
Am. & Can. Ch. Laurel Ridge Star	Am. & Can. Ch. Red Star of Hollyw
Rocket (4)	Hills, CDX (23/1FC)
End O'Maine Claret (11)	Ch. Honors Even Rakish Jane (2)
Ch. Mid-Oak Rose of Sharon (4)	Ch. Red Dawn of Sunny Acre (12)
	Ch. Mid-Oak Aragon Flash (2)
End O'Maine Covert (1)	Ch. Tyronne Farm Shanahan (5)
Ch. End O'Maine Lord Bourbon (3)	End O'Maine Sarah Jane (2)
Darling's Shamrock Queen, CDX (1)	Ch. Charles River Color Sergeant (1
Dam: **Tyronne Farm Victoria** (1)	Darling's Light O'Day, CD
Timothy O'Shea	Ch. Pinebrook's Hi-Hat (2)
Hedgewood Lady Victoria	Ch. End O'Maine Refrain (2)
Ch. Hedgewood Regret	Ch. Charles River Color Sergeant (1
	Hedgewood Highland Maid (2)

CH. DRAHERIN ANNIE LAURIE (bitch) — SA146977 — 2/28/62

	Ch. Tyronne Farm Malone (9)	Ch. Kinvarra Kermit (29)
	Ch. Seaforth's Dark Rex (20)	Ch. Ruxton's Mollie O'Day (14)
	Ch. Seaforth's Red Velvet (4)	Charles River Red Don (1)
e: **Ch. Innisfail Color Scheme, CD** (29)		Charles River Juanita (1)
	Ch. Kendare Red Duke (1)	Ch. Kendare Stout Fellow (1)
	Thenderin Champagne (4)	Ch. Kendare Ardri (1)
	Thenderin April Anthem (1)	Ch. Red Ranger Pat (9)
		Ch. Kinvarra Portia (12)

	Rusty of Modra Rhu's Red Dust	Ch. Modra Rhu's Red Dust
	Patrick Redjacket (1)	Jahudi's Elm Grove Gypsy (1)
	Gypsy Redjacket	Radar
m: **Ch. Draherin Echo of Elixir** (7)		Dawn's Patricia McKerry
	Ch. Rheola Shaun of Bail-lo (3)	Broughshane Ekim (1)
	Am. & Can. Ch. Thenderin Elixir, CD (8)	Ch. Rheola Sharon of Bal-Lo (1)
	Ch. Thenderin All Spice (3)	Ch. Red Ranger Pat (9)
		Ch. Kinvarra Portia (12)

TYRONNE CLEMENTINE KELLY (bitch) — SA163983 — 7/12/62

	Ch. Tyronne Farm Malone (9)	Ch. Kinvarra Kermit (29)
	Ch. Tyronne Farm Jeffrey, CD (1)	Ch. Ruxton's Mollie O'Day (14)
	Tyronne Farm Katherine (2)	Ch. Tyronne Farm Tipperary (5)
e: **Ch. Tyronne Jeffery's Tipperary**		Ch. Tyronne Farm Kay (4)
	Fld. Ch. Oxton's Shosaph (1/1FC)	Ch. Oxton's Irish Perfection, CDX (1FC)
	Country Girl Scarlet (1)	Oxton's Imp O'Erin (1FC)
	Oxton's Mallyree (1)	Terry O'Quinn
		Caldene Sheila

	Ch. McGowan's Senator	Ch. McGowan's Dugan (4)
	McGowan's Casey (1)	Ch. Tyronne Farm Charleen (3)
	Ch. Tyronne Farm Charleen (3)	Ch. Tyronne Farm Malone (9)
m: **Kerry's Kelly**		Ch. Tyronne Farm Merriwynne (3)
	Casey Red Coat	Sean of Court MacSherry
	Shammy De Vegas (1)	Patrician Lady Mischief
	Milson Maggie Mischief	Sean of Court MacSherry
		Patrician Lady Mischief

CH. DRAHERIN ECHO'S HOPE (bitch) — SA213285 — 6/13/63

	Ch. Seaforth's Dark Rex (20)	Ch. Tyronne Farm Malone (9)
	Ch. Innisfail Color Scheme, CD (29)	Ch. Seaforth's Red Velvet (4)
	Thenderin Champagne (4)	Ch. Kendare Red Duke (1)
e: **Ch. Weblyn Mystic Mark** (24)		Thenderin April Anthem (1)
	O'Shay's Gaylord (1)	Ch. Knightscroft Fermanagh (7)
	Ch. Knightscroft Erin McCuhl (4)	Ch. Linn's Lady O'Shay
	Knightscroft Dee Dorn (1)	Ch. Knightscroft Fermanagh (7)
		Knightscroft Babette

	Rusty of Modra Rhu's Red Dust (0)	Ch. Modra Rhu's Red Dust
	Patrick Redjacket (1)	Jahudi's Elm Grove Gypsy
	Gypsy Redjacket (0)	Radar
m: **Ch. Draherin Echo of Elixir** (7)		Dawn's Patricia McKerry
	Ch. Rheola Shaun of Bail-lo (3)	Broughshane Ekim (1)
	Am. & Can. Ch. Thenderin Elixir, CD (8)	Ch. Rheola Sharon of Bal-Lo (1)
	Ch. Thenderin All Spice (3)	Ch. Red Ranger Pat (9)
		Ch. Kinvarra Portia (12)

AM. & CAN. CH. TIRVELDA BRIDGET SUSIE ANN (bitch) — SA233289 — 8/29/

Sire: **Ch. End O'Maine Jack High** (2)	Ch. Conifer's Lance (15)	Ch. Red Rogue of Maple Ridge (10)
		Can. Ch. Conifer's Princess Ace (2)
	Ch. End O'Maine Flyaway (4)	Ch. Yorkhill's Achilles (3)
		Ch. End O'Maine Morning Bird (3)

- Ch. Red Rogue of Maple Ridge (10)
  - Ch. Thenderin Brian Tristan (30)
  - Crosshaven Lea of Maple Ridge (5)
- Can. Ch. Conifer's Princess Ace (2)
  - Can. Ch. Ace Flyer of Aragon
  - Coronation Princess
- Ch. Yorkhill's Achilles (3)
  - Ch. Tyronne Farm Shanahan (5)
  - Ch. Yorkhill's Red Rhapsody, CDX (2)
- Ch. End O'Maine Morning Bird (3)
  - Ch. Carrvale's Terry Terhune (14)
  - End O'Maine Claret (11)

Dam: ***Ch. Hartsbourne Sallyann of Tirvelda** (12)

- Hartsbourne Clovis (1)
  - Eamon of Casamia
  - Hartsbourne Clover
- Eng. Show Ch. Hartsbourne O'Hara
  - Eng. Ch. Gaelge Copperplate of Ide (0)
  - Eng. Show Ch. Gail of Casamia
- Hartsbourne Sabrina Fair (1)
  - Eng. Show Ch. Hartsbourne Tobias
  - Eng. Show Ch. Hartsbourne Meadows
- Hartsbourne Flush (1)
  - Eng. Show Ch. Hartsbourne Tobias
  - Eng. Ch. Hartsbourne Popsy
  - Brynmount Redgaynes Mars (1)
  - Hartsbourne Flame

RED-SAN OF CHARLES (bitch) — SA326103 — 4/23/65

Sire: **Ch. Abbeyleix Cavanaugh** (1)

- Ch. Sergeant Red Sails of Devon (14)
  - Ch. Charles River Blazes (2)
  - Ch. Red Mollie of Devon (1)
- Abbeyleix 'Shee An Gannon (2)
  - Ch. Sergeant Red Sails of Devon (14)
  - Charles River Dream Girl (1)

- Ch. Charles River Blazes (2)
  - *Ch. Red Sails of Salmagundi (7)
  - Molly o' Ballyclough (1)
- Ch. Red Mollie of Devon (1)
  - Ch. Charles River Color Sergeant (17)
  - Shawnee of Devon (3)
- Ch. Sergeant Red Sails of Devon (14)
  - Ch. Charles River Blazes (2)
  - Ch. Red Mollie of Devon (1)
- Charles River Dream Girl (1)
  - Ch. Tirvelda Aran (1)
  - Ch. Charles River Red Blanket (2)

Dam: **Tam-O-Ric**

- Ch. Sergeant Red Sails of Devon (14)
  - Ch. Charles River Blazes (2)
  - Ch. Red Mollie of Devon (1)
- Janneth of Aragon
  - Ch. Even Direct of Aragon (4)
  - Ch. End O'Maine Pigeon (4)

- Ch. Charles River Blazes (2)
  - *Ch. Red Sails of Salmagundi (7)
  - Molly o' Ballyclough (1)
- Ch. Red Mollie of Devon (1)
  - Ch. Charles River Color Sergeant (17)
  - Shawnee of Devon (3)
- Ch. Even Direct of Aragon (4)
  - Ch. Knightscroft Danny O'Boy (2)
  - Ch. Noreen of Aragon (2)
- Ch. End O'Maine Pigeon (4)
  - *Ch. Red Sails of Salmagundi (7)
  - Ch. End O'Maine Best Wishes (5)

FLD. CH. CYNTHIA DUSTIN KERR (bitch) — SA536417 — 4/12/67

Sire: **Dual Ch. Mahogany's Titian Jingo** (1/7FC)

- Dual Ch. Titian Duke, CD (1/1DC/1FC)
  - Mahogany Tim II (1/1DC/1FC)
  - King Size Scarlet Lady (1DC/1FC)
- Mahogany's Miss Fire-Ball (1DC)
  - Ch. Jim O'Reilly of Oakshire (0)
  - Ch. Shanty Kate III, CD (1/2FC)

- Mahogany Tim II (1/1DC/1FC)
  - Ch. Charles River Color Sergeant (17)
  - Small Change
- King Size Scarlet Lady (1DC/1FC)
  - Ch. King Size (2)
  - Ch. Love Creek Farm's Memory (1)
- Ch. Jim O'Reilly of Oakshire (0)
  - Am. & Can. Ch. Esquire of Maple Ridg
  - Pat's Kathryne of Oakshire (1)
- Ch. Shanty Kate III, CD (1/2FC)
  - Mahogany Tim II (1/1DC/1FC)
  - Shanty Kate (1)

Dam: **Fld. Ch. Astra of the Lodge** (1FC)

- Moffat's Apache Bill (1FC)
  - Fld. Ch. Ike Jack Kendrick (1FC)
  - Lady's Colleen
- *Fld. Ch. Sulhamstead Norse D'Or (3FC)
  - Fld. Ch. Emerald Isle Angel (1FC)
  - The Babe (1FC)

- Fld. Ch. Ike Jack Kendrick (1FC)
  - Ike Kendrick (1FC)
  - Fld. Ch. Askew's Carolina Lady (1FC)
- Lady's Colleen
  - Willow Winds Duke (0)
  - Fld. Ch. Askew's Carolina Lady (1FC)
- *Fld. Ch. Sulhamstead Norse D'Or (3FC)
  - Sulhamstead Montebellos Norseman (
  - Sulhamstead Banco D'Or (1FC)
- Fld. Ch. Emerald Isle Angel (1FC)
  - Dual Ch. Tyrone's Mahogany Mike, CDX (4/2FC)
  - Gay Lady of Wildwood (2)

& CAN. CH. SHANNON KELLY O'GREEN (bitch) — SA812456 — 3/1/70

Ch. Marflow Red Defender (2)
Ch. Jo-Ett's Marflow Esquire (8)
Tuxedo's Copper Mist (1)
ir Patrick of Alpine Meadows (1)
Ch. Shamrock Flamingo, CD (12)
Ch. Jo-Ett's Mon Cheri (4)
Danolyn's Meggin O'Fallon (1)

Am. & Can. Ch. Esquire of Maple Ridge (32)
Marflow Red Russet (2)
Ch. Draherin Irish Regardless (24)
Ch. Tuxedo's Sugar and Spice (1)
Ch. Draherin Coronado (2)
Shamrock April Anthem (2)
Ch. Sir Jeffrey of Sunny Acre (1)
Laurie of Sunny Acre

Ch. End O'Maine Red Cloud (5)
Ch. Tyronne Farm Shenandoah, CDX (1)
Ch. Tyronne Farm Sharon (2)
Citadel Daybreak O'Tipperary (1)
Knockross' O'Boy (36)
Bangor Barberry, CD
Ch. Seekays Berry Gay Rhu, CD (8)

Ch. Carrvale's Terry Terhune (14)
End O'Maine Claret (11)
Ch. Tyronne Farm Shanahan (5)
Tyronne Farm Thana (1)
Ch. Caldene Mick O'Boy (9)
Ch. Sharoc Coquette (1)
Red Barn Owen (4)
Neerb's Colleen Rue (4)

& CAN. CH. RENDITION'S INDIAN SUMMER (bitch) — SA952516 — 1/29/71

Ch. Draherin Irish Regardless (24)
Am., Can. & Bda. Ch. Shannon's Erin (46)
Ch. Knockross' Ruby (21)
h. Rendition Erin of Sunny Hills (14)
Ch. Sir Michael Galway of
Glendee (5)
Ch. Michael's Patti O'Shea (5)
Lady Kerrybrooke (3)

Ch. Tyronne Farm Malone II (25)
Am. & Can. Ch. Thenderin Elixir, CD (8)
Knockross' O'Boy (36)
Ch. Knockross' Milo (2)
Ch. Tyronne Farm Midnight Flash, CD (2)

Ch. Tyronne Farm Midday Flame, CD (7)
Red Rock Thundercloud
Generills' King's Favorite (1)

Ch. Draherin Irish Regardless (24)

Am., Can. & Bda. Ch. Shannon's
Erin (46)
Ch. Draherin Legendary (3)
Ch. Draherin Echo of Elixir (7)
ayde Red of the Rio Grande (2)
Still's Colonel Mike
Princess of Summit Rise
Shaver's Bonny Red Queen

Ch. Knockross' Ruby (21)
Patrick Redjacket (1)
Am. & Can. Ch. Thenderin Elixir, CD (8)
Marclair's Colonel O'Keefe
Hedges' Gill
Marclair's Colonel O'Keefe
Mollie O'Gay

CH. REDWHISKEY'S ROYAL VICTORY (bitch) — SA937466 — 5/19/71

Am., Can. & Bda. Ch. Shannon's
Erin (45)
Am. & Can. Ch. Draherin Questionnaire (6)
Draherin Irish Caprice (2)
elmora Sabre Dance (3)
Ch. Kinvarra Flicker (12)
Draherin Anastasia (5)
Am. & Can. Ch. Draherin
Fantasia (1)

Ch. Draherin Irish Regardless (24)

Ch. Knockross' Ruby (21)
Am. & Can. Ch. Draherin Auburn Artistry (14)
Draherin Field Caprice (2)
Ch. Kinvarra Kimson (6)
Kinvarra Derrydown Sally (2)
Am. & Can. Ch. Draherin Auburn Artistry (14)

Draherin Field Caprice (2)

Ch. Draherin Irish Regardless (24)
Am., Can. & Bda. Ch. Shannon's Erin (45)
Ch. Knockross' Ruby (21)
Ch. Victory's Royal Sensation, CD (6)
Ch. Draherin County Leitrim (22)
Glen Cree Kerrion (1)
Draherin Dark Memory (3)

Ch. Tyronne Farm Malone II (25)
Am. & Can. Ch. Thenderin Elixir, CD (8)
Knockross' O'Boy (36)
Ch. Knockross' Milo (2)
Am. & Can. Ch. Draherin Auburn Artistry (14)
Am. & Can. Ch. Yorkhill's County Kerry II, CD (2)
Patrick Redjacket (1)
Draherin Coronation

BIBLIOGRAPHY

ALL OWNERS of pure-bred dogs will benefit themselves and their dogs by enrichin
knowledge of breeds and of canine care, training, breeding, psychology and other important
of dog management. The following list of books covers further reading recommended by
veterinarians, breeders, trainers and other authorities. Books may be obtained at the fine
stores and pet shops, or through Howell Book House Inc., publishers, New York.

Breed Books

AFGHAN HOUND, Complete	Miller & Gilbert
AIREDALE, New Complete	Edwards
AKITA, Complete	Linderman & Funk
ALASKAN MALAMUTE, Complete	Riddle & Seeley
BASSET HOUND, Complete	Braun
BEAGLE, New Complete	Noted Authorities
BLOODHOUND, Complete	Brey & Reed
BORZOI, Complete	Groshans
BOXER, Complete	Denlinger
BRITTANY SPANIEL, Complete	Riddle
BULLDOG, New Complete	Hanes
BULL TERRIER, New Complete	Eberhard
CAIRN TERRIER, Complete	Marvin
CHESAPEAKE BAY RETRIEVER, Complete	Cherry
CHIHUAHUA, Complete	Noted Authorities
COCKER SPANIEL, New	Kraeuchi
COLLIE, New	Official Publication of the Collie Club of America
DACHSHUND, The New	Meistrell
DALMATIAN, The	Treen
DOBERMAN PINSCHER, New	Walker
ENGLISH SETTER, New Complete	Tuck, Howell & Graef
ENGLISH SPRINGER SPANIEL, New	Goodall & Gasow
FOX TERRIER, New Complete	Silvernail
GERMAN SHEPHERD DOG, New Complete	Bennett
GERMAN SHORTHAIRED POINTER, New	Maxwell
GOLDEN RETRIEVER, Complete	Fischer
GREAT DANE, New Complete	Noted Authorities
GREAT DANE, The—Dogdom's Apollo	Draper
GREAT PYRENEES, Complete	Strang & Giffin
IRISH SETTER, New	Thompson
IRISH WOLFHOUND, Complete	Starbuck
KEESHOND, Complete	Peterson
LABRADOR RETRIEVER, Complete	Warwick
LHASA APSO, Complete	Herbel
MINIATURE SCHNAUZER, Complete	Eskrigge
NEWFOUNDLAND, New Complete	Chern
NORWEGIAN ELKHOUND, New Complete	Wallo
OLD ENGLISH SHEEPDOG, Complete	Mandeville
PEKINGESE, Quigley Book of	Quigley
PEMBROKE WELSH CORGI, Complete	Sargent & Harper
POODLE, New Complete	Hopkins & Irick
POODLE CLIPPING AND GROOMING BOOK, Complete	Kalstone
PULI, Complete	Owen
SAMOYED, Complete	Ward
SCHIPPERKE, Official Book of	Root, Martin, Kent
SCOTTISH TERRIER, New Complete	Marvin
SHETLAND SHEEPDOG, The New	Riddle
SHIH TZU, Joy of Owning	Seranne
SHIH TZU, The (English)	Dadds
SIBERIAN HUSKY, Complete	Demidoff
TERRIERS, The Book of All	Marvin
WEST HIGHLAND WHITE TERRIER, Complete	Marvin
WHIPPET, Complete	Pegram
YORKSHIRE TERRIER, Complete	Gordon & Bennett

Breeding

ART OF BREEDING BETTER DOGS, New
BREEDING YOUR OWN SHOW DOG
HOW TO BREED DOGS
HOW PUPPIES ARE BORN
INHERITANCE OF COAT COLOR IN DOGS

Care and Training

DOG OBEDIENCE, Complete Book of	S
NOVICE, OPEN AND UTILITY COURSES	S
DOG CARE AND TRAINING FOR BOYS AND GIRLS	S
DOG NUTRITION, Collins Guide to	
DOG TRAINING FOR KIDS	E
DOG TRAINING, Koehler Method of	
DOG TRAINING, Step by Step Manual	Volhard
GO FIND! Training Your Dog to Track	
GUARD DOG TRAINING, Koehler Method of	
OPEN OBEDIENCE FOR RING, HOME AND FIELD, Koehler Method of	
STONE GUIDE TO DOG GROOMING FOR ALL BREEDS	
SUCCESSFUL DOG TRAINING, The Pearsall Guide to	
TOY DOGS, Kalstone Guide to Grooming All	
TRAINING THE RETRIEVER	
TRAINING YOUR DOG TO WIN OBEDIENCE TITLES	
TRAIN YOUR OWN GUN DOG, How to	
UTILITY DOG TRAINING, Koehler Method of	
VETERINARY HANDBOOK, Dog Owner's Home	Carlson

General

CANINE TERMINOLOGY	
COMPLETE DOG BOOK, The	Official Public American Ken
DOG IN ACTION, The	
DOG BEHAVIOR, New Knowledge of	Pfaffe
DOG JUDGE'S HANDBOOK	
DOG JUDGING, Nicholas Guide to	
DOG PEOPLE ARE CRAZY	
DOG PSYCHOLOGY	
DOGSTEPS, Illustrated Gait at a Glance	
DOG TRICKS	Haggerty & E
ENCYCLOPEDIA OF DOGS, International	Dangerfield, Howell
FROM RICHES TO BITCHES	S
IN STITCHES OVER BITCHES	S
JUNIOR SHOWMANSHIP HANDBOOK	Brown &
MY TIMES WITH DOGS	
OUR PUPPY'S BABY BOOK (blue or pink)	
SUCCESSFUL DOG SHOWING, Forsyth Guide to	
TRIM, GROOM AND SHOW YOUR DOG, How to	S
WHY DOES YOUR DOG DO THAT?	E
WILD DOGS in Life and Legend	
WORLD OF SLED DOGS, From Siberia to Sport F	Cc